PRELUDE TO PROTECTORATE IN MOROCCO

Studies in Imperialism
Robin W. Winks, Editor

Edmund Burke, III

PRELUDE TO PROTECTORATE IN MOROCCO

Precolonial Protest and Resistance, 1860–1912

THE UNIVERSITY
OF CHICAGO PRESS
Chicago and London

EDMUND BURKE, III, is associate professor of history at the University of California at Santa Cruz. He has written several articles on Morocco and spent five years doing research in that country.

THE UNIVERSITY OF CHICAGO PRESS, CHICAGO 60637
THE UNIVERSITY OF CHICAGO PRESS, LTD., LONDON

81 80 79 78 77 76 987654321

Library of Congress Cataloging in Publication Data

Burke, Edmund, 1940–
Prelude to protectorate in Morocco.

(Studies in imperialism)
A rev. version of the author's thesis, Princeton University, 1970.
Bibliography: p.
Includes index.
1. Morocco—History—19th century. 2. Morocco—History—20th century. 1. Title.
DT324.B844 1976 964'.03 75-43228
ISBN 0-226-08075-7

For My Mother and Father

CONTENTS

MAPS

SERIES EDITOR'S PREFACE

At last we are beginning to learn as much about the French empire as the British, so that generalizations about imperialism need not continue to be skewed, as they have been in the past, by drawing too many of our data from the British experience. The present study makes a major contribution in this direction, providing as it does the first nearly definitive account of a central series of episodes in the French, African, and Islamic experiences with imperialism.

Edmund Burke's book is a particularly good example of a truth historians have long understood, although polemicists who want immediate answers will resist that truth: by a careful scrutiny of a series of connected events about which we had supposed ourselves to know virtually all that needed to be known, the historian can alter substantially our angle of vision and lead us to conclusions that differ from the easy ones of the conventional wisdom. Further, by traversing again an extent of history that to many has had almost romantic connotations, Professor Burke shows us how the elements of popular romanticizing about empire (at the time, favorably; since, unfavorably) can have grown out of the facts both as they were and as they were perceived to be. This volume, political and economic at first glance, again serves to support the contention that imperial history is, at heart, a branch of intellectual history.

ROBIN W. WINKS

PREFACE

Know too that during these years the power of these Europeans has advanced to a shocking degree and has manifested itself in an unparalleled manner. The progress and improvement in their condition of life have accelerated at an ever growing pace—like the [proverbial] doubling of the grains of wheat in the geometrical squares of the chess board. Indeed, we are on the brink of a time of [complete] corruption.

Knowledge of the consequences and limits of [all] this belongs to God, may He be exalted, who is alone in [knowing] the hidden.

"I know well today and the yesterday before it.
But as for knowing what tomorrow holds, I am blind."

Kitāb al-Istiqsā, IX, 208

With these plaintive words the great nineteenth-century Moroccan historian Aḥmad ibn Khālid al-Nāṣirī concludes his chronicle of the ʿAlawī dynasty. The incorporation of Morocco into the modern world-system produced unprecedented strains upon the society and resulted in widespread movements of protest and resistance. This book is a study of the ways in which Moroccans coped with a time of rapid change and social disruption. In a sense, it might be said that the book is about the Moroccan side of the Moroccan Question—that tangled question in the diplomatic history of Europe (1900–1912) which forms part of the causes of World War I. International great-power rivalries certainly help to define my subject and give it substance. But my aim is ultimately more far-reaching than this.

In studying the climactic period during which Morocco stumbled over the threshhold into the modern world, I seek to shed light on the broader process of change of which the Moroccan case is only one example. The precolonial period in Middle Eastern history is now beginning to get the attention which it merits, after a great concern with the rise of nationalism and the onset of the process of modernization. Insofar as Morocco partakes in the same rich cultural tradition of Arab Islam, my findings will perhaps be useful to students of Middle Eastern history. Unlike previous studies, however, which have sought to trace out the process of modernization in North Africa and the Middle East, this one intends to depict a broad environment of change, in which the power of Europe constitutes the most fundamental datum. From our present postcolonial vantage point, it is difficult to believe in modernization as a unilinear process of change which is experienced by all societies in similar fashion. The facts of dependency and the existence of enclave economies make such a view no longer justifiable.

Morocco is one of a small number of Islamic countries having a well established local dynasty and a tradition of independence which managed to survive into the modern age. Others include Iran, Afghanistan, and Yemen. These countries, all of which combined tribalism and some semblance of centralized bureaucratic rule, owed their survival to the vagaries of topography (all are mountainous) and the rivalries of the great powers. In the case of Morocco, only the diplomatic support of Great Britain during the nineteenth century prevented it from sharing the fate of Algeria, occupied by France in 1830. As a result Morocco was able to retain its old system intact until well into the century. Not until 1860 (when my study commences) did Morocco begin to show the effects of European penetration. Not until 1900, however, did the threat of European takeover pose itself in an acute fashion.

During the period from 1860 to 1912 Morocco experienced three distinct but interrelated sets of change. The first was the massive penetration of European goods and capital into local markets. This had a cumulatively devastating effect on the existing social and economic structures. The second was an internally generated modernization effort which resulted in the dismantling of the old administrative structures and the launching of a program of reforms. It largely failed to accomplish its objectives and generated serious internal opposition. The third broad axis of change was that set in motion by the French colonial offensive after 1900. The intersection of these three processes of change was to lead to the collapse of the old Morocco and the birth of the new. Their collision was to produce a variety of political responses: reforms, resistance, popular revolt, the overthrow of a sultan, and the eventual disaffection of most of the elite. It is the aim of this book to examine each of these complex patterns of change and in the process to shed new light on the crisis of the old order in Morocco.

Morocco is a good country in which to observe the effects of incorporation into the modern world-system. It is relatively small, and because the phases of European encroachment were delayed and foreshortened, the changes that occurred can be observed with special clarity. One can get a good sense of the conflicts of interest, culture, and purpose which divided the Moroccan elite and resulted in their defection by 1912. Morocco experienced the same general phases of modernization and imperialism as the countries of the Middle East, but these phases were telescoped over a briefer period. Comparisons between Morocco and the Middle East can therefore be productive of important insights.

This book is based primarily upon the very ample published and unpublished materials which exist in Western languages. Published Arabic materials were also consulted. (For a fuller discussion of the nature of this material, see the Selected Bibliography.) In an effort to capture something of the spirit of the times and the fierce pride of the men who took part in the events recounted here, I have also interviewed many former French *officiers des affaires indigènes* and Moroccan *mujāhidīn* (patriots—literally, fighters in the holy war). Neither group, I sincerely hope, will feel betrayed by my treatment of them, although both will certainly disagree with some of my interpretations.

When I first took up this subject, I was interested in tracing the precolonial roots of Moroccan nationalism. I was convinced that Moroccan reformism had its origins in the resistance efforts of the late nineteenth and early twentieth centuries. I still believe that this is so. But in the course of much additional thought and research I have become aware of the vitality of rural traditions of protest and resistance in the precolonial period, and of the existence of a non-elite patriotism grounded in Islam. At the same time, I have come to see the real ambiguity which cloaks the actions of all of the actors in the Moroccan drama, including leading resistance figures. A complex web of emotion and material interest tugged men now this way and now that. As a result of these discoveries I began to grope for a way of dealing with the full range of political responses which I had observed. This book is the result. It is revisionist in its intentions and methods. While seeking to be respectful of Moroccan culture and the dilemma in which Moroccans found themselves in the wake of the changes of the nineteenth century, it refuses to take either Moroccan bureaucrats or French bankers and diplomats at face value. In the end, a new generation of Moroccan historians will write the definitive history of these years. For the moment, however, there is much which we can learn from the Moroccan experience.

In the course of ten years' research in a previously little studied field, one accumulates many personal debts, both large and small. I am happy to acknowledge some of the more important ones here. An earlier version of this work saw service as a doctoral dissertation at Princeton University. The original research was conducted in France and Morocco in 1965–67 under the auspices of an NDEA-related Fulbright-Hays grant, and I should like to record my gratitude to the fellowship program. Needless to say the opinions expressed herein and the conclusions are my own and in no way implicate the granting agency. In Paris my research was greatly facilitated by M. le Colonel Jouin, then director of the Section d'Afrique of the Ministry of War archives at Chateau Vincennes, and General Pierre Rondot, director of the Centre des Hautes Etudes sur l'Afrique et l'Asie moderne. Thanks are also due the director and staff of the Archives Nationales and the Bibliothèque Nationale and the conservator of the archives of the Ministry of Foreign Affairs. I am also indebted to the keeper of the Public Record Office in London and the director of the German Foreign Ministry archives in Bonn for permission to consult documents in their possession. In Morocco I am above all grateful to Abdullah Regragui, former curator of the Bibliothèque Générale in Rabat, for his kind interest and advice, and to M. Jacques Cagne, head of the Section Historique of the University Research Center in Rabat.

There are, in addition, the many persons whose influence has been significant in the maturing of my thoughts about Morocco. First is the late Professor Roger LeTourneau, who introduced me to North African history and provided me with the essential groundwork within this discipline. David M. Hart and Professors L. C. Brown and Ernest Gellner have provided me with encouragement and advice along the way. At a crucial juncture, thanks to the interest of Clifford Geertz, I was given a chance to rethink my approach as a research associate of the Committee on the Comparative Study of New Nations at the University of Chicago (1969–70). The participants in the Comparative History Seminar at the University of California at Santa Cruz, by plaguing me with questions for which it seemed at first there were no answers, furthered this process of deprovincialization. Finally there are my friends and colleagues in matters Moroccan, Ross E. Dunn, Lawrence Rosen, Kenneth Brown, and Raymond Jamous, from whose influence I have benefited greatly, both personally and intellectually. To all of the above, and to the many Moroccans and Frenchmen whose names I have not been able to mention, I am grateful.

The manuscript was typed by Carolyn Brown, Susan Beach, Virginia Moore, and Carmela von Bawey. A debt of thanks is owed to them all. Research for the maps was done by Louise Quenneville.

This research was supported by faculty research funds granted by the University of California, Santa Cruz.

A NOTE ON TRANSLITERATION

The system of transliteration which has been adopted makes some effort to satisfy both the general convenience of the nonspecialist and the curiosity of the purist. Inevitably there will be places where neither is wholly satisfied, and for these I beg the reader's indulgence: the difficulties of transliterating Moroccan Arabic and Berber, often through faulty French initial transliterations, present constant problems to any English-speaking student of North Africa.

Arabic geographical and tribal names will be cited commonly in the standard modern Moroccan transliteration, but for the purist the classical Arabic transliteration will be given in parenthesis in the first occurrence. All other nouns will be cited in a transliteration of the classical Arabic, with the most common French version given in parenthesis in the first occurrence. The system of transliteration of Arabic consonants followed is the Princeton system, as exemplified in R. B. Winder and F. J. Ziadeh, *Introduction to Modern Arabic*. The one exception to this practice is that the letter *hamza* is omitted in the system followed here. The purist will know where to insert it, and the nonspecialist will not be unnecessarily confused.

In the absence of a commonly agreed-upon method of transliterating the various Berber dialects spoken in Morocco into English, the French system used by Emile Laoust will be followed. An approximate English transliteration will be given in the first occurrence, where possible.

All translations are my own, unless it is specified otherwise.

CHRONOLOGY

1830 French intervene militarily in Algeria.

1844 Battle of Isly. Moroccan forces acting in support of Algerian resistance leader, Amir ʿAbd al-Qādir, are defeated by the French near the Moulouya River.

1856 Anglo-Moroccan commercial treaty. Moroccan market opened to British manufactured goods; European commercial penetration begins in earnest.

1859–60 Tetouan War between Spain and Morocco. Morocco loses, must pay large indemnity.

1859–73. Reign of Sultan Muḥammad IV. Adoption of program of military reforms and internal improvements.

1873–94. Reign of Sultan Ḥasan I. Continuation of reform program, other efforts of governmental centralization. Social disruptions gradually become intense as reforms, commercial penetration erode old structures.

1894–1908. Reign of Sultan ʿAbd al-ʿAzīz. Until 1900, Aḥmad Ibn Mūsā is regent, continues policies of Ḥasan I, court in residence at Marrakech. Thereafter ʿAbd al-ʿAzīz rules in his own right.

Further efforts at reform and weakness in the face of French imperial threat progressively alienate much of elite, provoke protests throughout the country.

1892 Hispano-Moroccan war fought near Mellila. Again Morocco loses, must pay large indemnity.

1900 French seize ʿIn Salah and Touat oasis complex. First loss of Moroccan territory. Beginning of reform program under British sponsorship.

1901 Court moves from Marrakech to Fez. Rebellion of Abū Ḥimāra threatens regime, involves tribes north of Fez, leads to end of program of reforms under British sponsorship.

First foreign loan.

Franco-Moroccan conflicts along Algerian border end in accord.

1902 Kidnappings of prominent British and American citizens by Raysūnī create international difficulties for regime.

Second foreign loan.

1903 Establishment of Compagnie marocaine.

Comité du Maroc created by French colonial interests.

1904 Anglo-French entente makes possible French colonial offensive.

Major foreign loan taken up by French banking consortium headed by Banque de Paris et des Pays-Bas.

Moroccan government decides to resist French reform program, fires all European advisors in its employ.

1905 French obtain reversal of firings, present reform program to sultan at Fez.

Landing of German Kaiser at Tangier.

Moroccan opposition to French reforms

stiffens, resulting in downfall of French foreign minister Delcassé, convoking of international conference at Algeciras.

1906	Algeciras conference decides upon internationalization of Moroccan question, pursuit of reforms under French auspices.
1907	Serious economic difficulties throughout Morocco.
	Killing of Dr. Mauchamps, French medical missionary, at Marrakech. This provokes French military occupation of Oudjda and surrounding region.
	Attacks on Europeans at Casablanca in July lead to dispatch of Franco-Spanish expeditionary force to restore order.
	Popular resistance to French forces soon evolves into jihad, lasts for six months.
	ʿAbd al-Ḥafīẓ is proclaimed sultan at Marrakech, opposes his brother ʿAbd al-ʿAzīz in a civil war which lasts a year.
1908	ʿAbd al-Ḥafīẓ proclaimed sultan by ʿulama of Fez, after popular insurrection calls for deposition of ʿAbd al-ʿAzīz.
	In August, ʿAzīz is defeated in battle, and the civil war comes to an end.
	French troops continue to occupy Oudjda and Chaouia provinces.
	1908–1912. Reign of Sultan ʿAbd al-Ḥafīẓ. Initially identified with a program of jihad, ʿAbd al-Ḥafīẓ is compelled to accept the Algeciras convention and eventually French financial and military aid. By 1911 he acquiesces in French occupation of Fez. The protectorate follows in 1912.
1909	France and Great Britain recognize ʿAbd al-Ḥafīẓ, after latter agrees to renounce

program of jihad, take out another major loan.

Rebellions of al-Kattānī and Abū Ḥimāra are crushed by troops of government.

Outbreak of fighting between Spanish forces and tribesmen near Mellila.

1910 Military reform program under Turkish instructors squelched by French protest.

French reform schemes approved; major new loan agreement signed.

1911 Rebellion of tribes around Fez leads to French military intervention, occupation of Fez and the interior.

Agadir incident. German opposition to French policies results in Franco-German treaty resolving major differences.

Spanish intervention at Larache.

1912 Treaty of Fez leads to French protectorate over Morocco.

Spanish assert authority in northern zone.

Mutiny and rebellion at Fez severely shakes French control in April.

General Lyautey is named resident general of French protectorate.

Rebellion of tribes around Fez in May put down only with difficulty.

ʿAbd al-Hafiz abdicates in favor of his brother Yusuf.

Marrakech is captured by El Hiba, leader of a jihad with major backing in southern Morocco.

French recapture Marrakech, as El Hiba flees. French authority is quickly established in the south.

1

STATE AND SOCIETY IN PRECOLONIAL MOROCCO

An Ecology of Uncertainty

Precolonial Moroccan society was distinguished by a number of features which mark it off as part of the North African subcultural area of the Islamic world.[1] Like the other states of the Arab Maghrib, Morocco exhibited a curious blend of Ottoman-style bureaucratic government and the kind of tribalism and popular Islam which one associates with Iran and Afghanistan. This not quite centralized but no longer wholly tribal society provided the framework around which some of the fundamental Moroccan social and political institutions were to develop.

The shape of politics and the kind of social life which was possible in precolonial Morocco were greatly influenced by the geography and ecology of the country. The inability of the government to master its environment had a great deal to do with its perennial weaknesses in the face of unruly tribal pastoralists and would-be insurgents. An examination of Moroccan society and politics should appropriately begin with a brief look at the central geographic features of the country.

"Jazirat al-Maghrib" the classical Arab geographers called North Africa, "the island of the West," and if the phrase fits North West Africa in the broader sense, an island surrounded by the Mediterranean and the Sahara, it can with equal appropriateness be applied to the Moroccan segment of the Maghrib. Separated from the rest of North Africa by the Atlas Mountains and the pre-Saharan steppe on the east and south, Morocco was bounded on the west by the Atlantic Ocean. The coast was renowned for its treacherous tides, sand bars, and the absence of good natural harbors. To the north, access from the Mediterranean was blocked by the imposing Rif Mountains. This combination of geographical factors helped to cushion Morocco from outside influences, giving it more time to respond and permitting it to accept or reject such influences on more nearly its own terms. (This is not the same as saying, it is important to insist here, that Morocco was isolated from the rest of the world. Moroccan connections with Europe, Africa, and the Middle East were well established and of considerable importance.)

The predominant ecological influence on Morocco has undeniably been its mountains, especially the Atlas chain.[2] These mountains have served not only to isolate Morocco on its landward side, they also intrude at various points into central Morocco, arresting the rain clouds borne in on the prevailing winds from the Atlantic and creating, in effect, a series of microecologies within the larger Moroccan one. Because of them, the region between Algeria and Morocco has become a vast semiarid steppe, and the steep valleys of the Middle and High Atlas are well-watered and capable of supporting considerable populations. Indeed, the mountains have been described by some French scholars, impressed with the density of settled life which crowds the Western High Atlas, as "reservoirs of men." Since Morocco's mountains divide the country into more than a dozen major ecological zones, the need to adapt to the exigencies of a variety of different environments has led to the evolution of a series of partially autonomous units within the Moroccan empire, often marked by differences in speech, dress, traditions, and way of life.

The possibilities of political development in Morocco were similarly influenced by the topography. Because of the mountains, the problems of internal communications and security were that much greater for any would-be centralized government. Regions could (and periodically did) seek more autonomy in relation to the central authorities. Ultimately, however, all regions were condemned by ecology, religion, and the trade routes to membership in a greater Moroccan entity. Also because of the mountain ranges, tribalism could remain a pronounced characteristic of Morocco into the twentieth century. In addition to sheltering large populations, the mountains provided a refuge to inhabitants of the nearby plains whenever the central government became too insistent in its demands. The history of Morocco has therefore been described as an unending tug-of-war between the forces of regionalism and the central power. Despite the development of a more modern Moroccan army toward the end of the nineteenth century, the government was still unable to subdue the fierce tribesmen who inhabited the mountains. In the end, rural dissidence did much to bring about the downfall of the government during the period from 1900 to 1912, and this dissidence was made possible at least in part by mountainous terrain. Largely because of the topography, there was rarely a powerful central government, and most of the country most of the time was free from direct governmental control.

In comparison with most of the countries of the Arab East the population of Morocco was remarkably homogeneous. There were but two main linguistic groups, Berbers and Arabs, and only two religious communities, Sunni Muslims of the Maliki legal rite, and Jews. The distinction between Arab and Berber was not always clear, for bilingualism was common, especially in the fringe areas between mountain and plain. Customs and ways of life were also broadly shared between the two groups. For the most part the Arabs inhabited the broad central plain between the Atlantic and the mountains, while the Berbers inhabited the mountains. Approximately 60 percent of the population was Berber in 1900. Three different Berber dialect groups have been distinguished: Rifians, Middle/Central Atlas speakers, and Sousis. They inhabited territorially discontinuous regions. The Jewish minority was both rural and urban and shared many customs with Muslims. They were also Arabic speakers. Finally, the absence of a Christian minority should be noted. The political significance of these facts is clear: an emerging sense of Moroccan nationalism would encounter little competition from other foci of group pride and identity.

The size of the Moroccan population in 1900 is not known with any precision and is still the occasion of serious dispute among scholars. Scattered travelers' reports and the impressionistic accounts of European diplomats and merchants constitute our chief sources prior to the protectorate. Eventually it may be possible to make more accurate estimates, using official tax records. A partial French census estimated a population of around three million people in 1913, but since the populations of the Atlas and Rif mountains were largely excluded, a total of around five million seems more likely.[3] The urban population is easier to estimate. In 1905 it was around 230,000 people.[4] As for other agrarian societies, both the birth and death rates were high, and the population trend was essentially stable over time, with periodic famines and epidemics erasing the gains.

The Urban World: Trade and Politics

When the systematic study of Moroccan society started around the beginning of the present century, it was the cities of Morocco which first captivated the interest of European travelers and ethnologists.

The instinct of these scholars, the majority of whom were French, was sound. Moroccan cities were the centers of government, trade, and religion (in short, of civilization) and held an importance which was out of proportion to their small size. (The largest city in Morocco in 1900 was Fez, and its population was less than 100,000.)[5] In many respects these cities recalled medieval European cities, surrounded by high walls and divided into numerous semiautonomous quarters with narrow, twisting streets in which two loaded donkeys could scarcely pass abreast, with a bustling network of workshops and bazaars where artisans and merchants were still organized into guilds.

The existence of a proud and cultivated elite of scholars and merchants set the tone of the cities and served to distinguish them from the smaller towns. An important segment of this elite was composed of descendants of families who had been expelled from Spain in the fifteenth and sixteenth centuries. These families, known as Andalusians, tended to form a caste apart which disdained intermingling with the local elite. By virtue of their talents and education they tended to dominate the ranks of the religious classes, the *ʿulamā*, and to excel in business. They were concentrated in four cities, Tangier, Tetouan, Salé, and Fez. Trade and commerce provided the chief occupation of an important group of merchants, including local dealings with the rural populations and the more lucrative but risky trade with foreign countries. The workshops of the cities produced a broad array of cloth goods, household furnishings, and luxury items and gave employment to a numerous and skilled artisanry. Leather-working and the production of cotton and woolen goods were among the most prominent industries. Irrigated gardens just beyond the walls of a city occupied the labor of an indeterminate, although considerable, portion of the city's inhabitants. Apart from these gardens, which gave a city the appearance of an oasis, the uncultivated tribal areas came up virtually to the walls. Unlike the lands of the Arab East, however, Morocco lacked a wide-spread village life, a sedentary and docile peasantry, or a class of absentee landowners. As a result a key link between urban and rural areas was missing, and the task of administering and maintaining order was made that much more difficult. Despite their undoubted importance in the cultural and economic life of the country, therefore, the cities of Morocco were overbalanced by the largely tribal populations of the countryside.

From a contemporary vantage point, it is difficult to imagine the extent of the weakness of urban civilization in precolonial Morocco. Yet it was not until after the coming of the French that Moroccan cities became powerful radiating centers of Arabism, high Islam, and modern values. Once beyond their walls, the nineteenth-century traveler found himself in a country inhabited by tribes who were not definitively fixed to the soil and who could and often did move from place to place with a disquieting disrespect for the property rights of others. Cities like Fez, Meknes, Rabat, and Marrakech were, to be sure, the centers of high Islamic culture in Morocco, and the word of the religious scholars (the ʿulamā) carried great weight in the countryside, especially the word of the ʿulamā of Fez. But the merchants lived in perpetual fear of a tribal insurrection and dared not invest their surplus capital in land, as their Near Eastern cousins were doing with regularity by the nineteenth century.

Despite the danger of tribal revolt, the cities were not isolated from their hinterlands but were instead closely tied to them by religion, trade, and political patronage. The main religious institutions of Islam were urban-based and exerted a pervasive influence over the countryside. The Moroccan style of Islam will be discussed further below. Of special note here is the importance of the ʿulamā of Fez: their collective opinion on weighty matters (Ar. *fatwā*) carried much prestige in the countryside. While less is known about the economic interpenetration of city and country, it is already clear that existing colonial stereotypes of rural autarchy are in need of revision. Urban merchants often provided the capital for the raising of livestock by transhumant Berber tribes, as well as by the Arab tribes of the plains, and sold the animals in Algeria or at Mellila or Tangier. Tribesmen had need of the city markets for purchases of arms and ammunition, tea and sugar, cloth, and luxury items. Although itinerant peddlers (many of them Jewish) made regular rounds of the countryside markets from the cities, rural men went up to the city for important dealings. Many of the more wealthy tribal leaders came in this way to acquire houses in the cities, and eventually some moved permanently into the city. The industry of the cities depended in its turn on the rural areas for the raw materials from which leather, cloth, and metal goods were manufactured. In short, there were considerable economic ties between the cities and the tribes.[6]

The Rural Areas: A Society in Movement

Unlike the more complex societies of the Middle East, with their deeply rooted agrarian structures, Moroccan rural society was always much more flexible, not to say volatile. Instead of entrenched

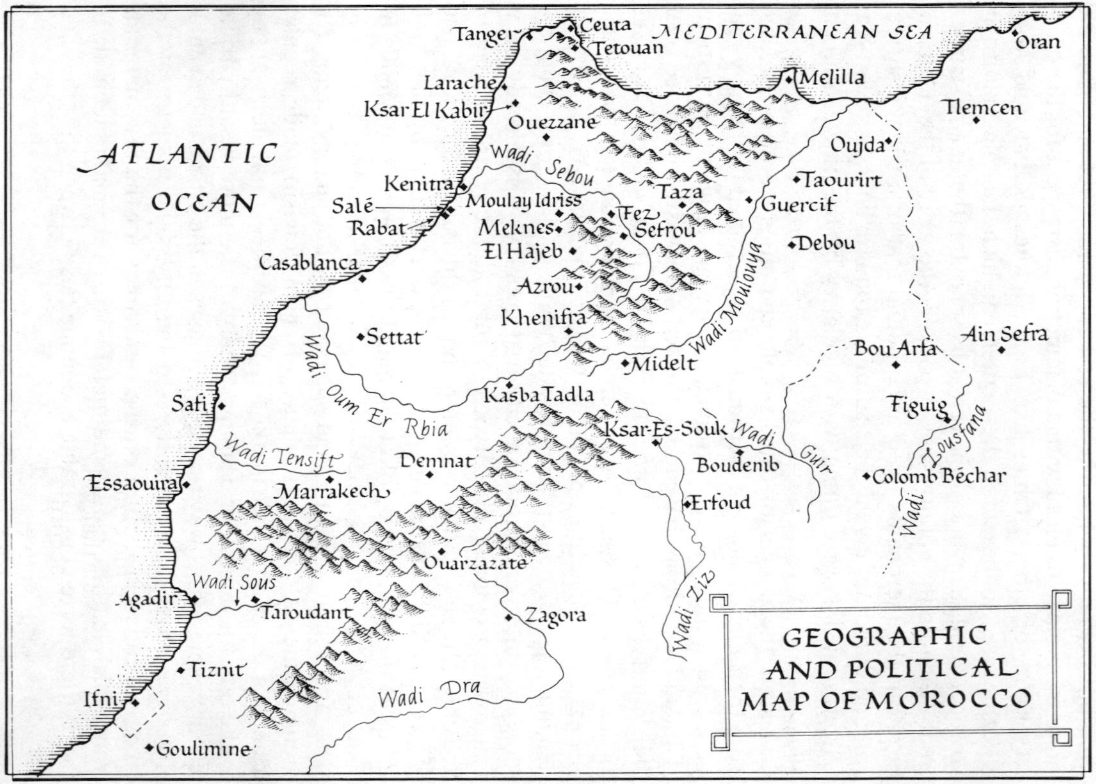

GEOGRAPHIC
AND POLITICAL
MAP OF MOROCCO
ATLANTIC
OCEAN
MEDITERRANEAN SEA
Tanger
Ceuta
Tetouan
Oran
Melilla
Larache
Ksar El Kabir
Ouezzane
Tlemcen
Oujda
Wadi Sebou
Kenitra
Salé
Rabat
Moulay Idriss
Meknes
El Hajeb
Fez
Sefrou
Taza
Taourirt
Guercif
Debou
Casablanca
Azrou
Khenifra
Wadi Moulouya
Settat
Midelt
Bou Arfa
Ain Sefra
Wadi Oum Er Rbia
Kasba Tadla
Safi
Figuig
Ksar-Es-Souk
Wadi Guir
Boudenib
Wadi Zousfana
Colomb Béchar
Wadi Tensift
Demnat
Essaouira
Marrakech
Erfoud
Ouarzazate
Wadi Sous
Agadir
Taroudant
Zagora
Wadi Ziz
Tiznit
Ifni
Wadi Dra
Goulimine

classes of peasants and landlords, Moroccan rural society was organized in tribes, based on descent from a common ancestor. To speak of the role of tribes in Moroccan history is to enter an area of controversy among scholars. What was a Moroccan tribe? It is well to beware of the misplaced concreteness conveyed by the term *tribe*.[7] A great variety of groups living quite different ways of life and having widely differing political, social, and economic structures can be included under the label.

One model which has been put forward to explain the organization and functioning of Moroccan tribes is the British social anthropological theory of lineage segmentation.[8] Such societies are organized around the principle of genealogical descent, and levels of segmentation (lineage, clan, tribe) correspond to major divisions in the genealogical chart of the group. Characteristically, segmentary societies are acephalous (lack an overall chief) and have power more or less equally distributed among the segments; feuding between subgroups is common. Yet in the face of a common enemy, such tribes will coalesce in a united front. In this way segmentary tribes could often generate astonishing power. A concomitant of this form of social organization is a deep suspicion of strangers, of those unrelated by blood and by bonds of common nurture. In theory at least, segmentary tribes are in a state of equilibrium between segments, and it is supposed to be possible to predict the lines along which internal fission will occur by use of the principle: "I against my brother; my brother and I against my cousins; my cousins and I against the outsider."

Some Moroccan tribes are clearly well described by classical segmentary theory, and others are not. Among those who are can be found some of the most militarily important groups in Morocco: the Ait Atta of the desert fringe, the Ait Waryagher of the eastern Rif Mountains, and the Ait Yafelman of the central Atlas. In general, the Berber tribes of the Rif, Central and Middle Atlas, and the pre-Saharan steppe zone tend to conform to the theory better than the Arab tribes of the central plains. A source of potential misunderstanding is the fact that virtually all Moroccan tribes claimed to be grouped together according to the fiction of genealogical descent. Kinship, real or fictive, provided access to the resources controlled by the group. In fact, the social organization of particular tribes, especially at lower levels of segmentation, often reflected the residence patterns of the component groups, rather than the genealogical model itself. The structural completeness of a given tribe in segmentary terms tended to be a function of its ecological situation, the strength and disposition of its neighbors, and the extent to which segmentation had become intertwined with landholding patterns. An easier ecological situation and more peaceful neighbors generally led to the gradual atrophy of higher levels of segmentation due to the lack of compelling need for a broader solidarity.

For still other reasons the concept of tribe is a weak reed upon which to lean. Despite the fiction of genealogical descent from a common ancestor, many tribes turn out upon examination to be composed of a high percentage of families who have originated elsewhere. Segmentation is therefore a model, not a description, of reality. Many tribes in the central plains regions were literally the creations of the central government. The Ait Ndhir in the Middle Atlas was assembled from the remnants of the old Ait Idrassen confederation, and the small tribes which inhabited the Sais plain near Fez were installed there during the nineteenth century. The best example of such artificial groups are *jaysh* (Fr. *guich*) tribes, which were implanted along the route between Fez and Tangier, and around Meknes, Rabat, and Marrakech. They were granted the usufruct of crown lands and exemption from taxes, in return for which they were required to provide the government with its troops. Jaysh forces formed the backbone of the Moroccan army until well into the nineteenth century. They seem to have been quite heterogeneous in origin. Among the better known jaysh tribes were the Oudaia, Cherarda, and the Cheraga.

Finally, it should be borne in mind that far from consisting of small quasi-autarchic republics, each fiercely jealous of its own prerogatives and individuality, Moroccan tribes existed within the context of a complex society with a central bureaucratic government and a richly elaborated cultural tradition. Morocco itself formed part of the wider world of Arab-Islamic civilization. While Moroccan tribes retained their own customs and sense of identity, they also submitted to the influence of the broader society of which they were a part. There is but a limited truth to the myth of tribal autarchy. The rural world of Morocco was a richly variegated one in other ways as well. Tribes followed many different ways of life. Some, like the Berbers of the Rif and Western High Atlas were sedentary agriculturists, who raised tree crops for the market. Those of the Middle Atlas and pre-Saharan steppes were pastoral transhumants, making two annual migrations with their sheep and goats. The Arab tribes of the central plains practiced a mixture of agriculture (particularly cereal grains) and pastoralism. By the late nineteenth century commercial agriculture had penetrated deeply among them. In fact all of these distinctions tended to blur, since the uncertain ecology favored a diversification of efforts.

An important key to the understanding of the dynamics of the relations between the central government and the tribes is that the central plains region (the breadbasket of Morocco) was distinctly underpopulated. There was always far more arable land than there were people to farm it. With weak agrarian structures and a thinly settled population, rich regions like the Gharb and the Chaouia produced well under their potential. Due to the dangers of marauding pastoralists on the one hand and government tax collectors on the other, there was little capital investment in these lands, and land titles remained uncertain. Instead, the Arab tribes of the plains tended to remain mobile. This weakness in the very heart of the Moroccan state was to prove of fundamental importance.

Even in the central plains area, however, there were some clusters of power and the beginnings of a ruling class.[9] The rural notability, such as it was, consisted of wealthy tribal notables, important religious figures, and major government officials. Religious figures of great prestige and power locally, like the sharifs of Wazzan, possessed entire villages, which they had been granted by the sultans. These appanages, known as *ʿazīb*-s (Ar. pl. *ʿazzabā*), were analogous to the jaysh lands. Lesser sharifs and other religious figures held smaller allotments of land. The inequities of this inchoate class system were made bearable by a number of factors. These included the obligation of wealthy patrons to defend even their humblest servants, the traditional rivalries between notables, and the periodic redivision of land among the adult males of the clan that was practiced in many tribes.

Only in a few places in the rural landscape do we encounter anything resembling the overmighty subjects, the great dukes and barons, who so bedeviled the life of would-be modernizing monarchs the world over. These were the so-called "great *qāid*-s" of the Western High Atlas. The most important of them include Madani al-Glawi, ʿAbd al-Malik al-Mtouggui, and Tayyib al-Gundafi. Each owed his rise to power to his control over a major pass through the Atlas, privileged ties with the central government, and a remarkable ability to maneuver in the faction-ridden world of tribal politics. Others who should be mentioned were Siʿ Aissa ibn ʿUmar, head of the militarily powerful Abda near the city of Safi, and Moha ou Hamou, head of the equally important Zaian of the district surrounding Khenifra. Powerful allies of the crown when they wished, they could be no less potent enemies when it suited their purpose.

All possessed large private armies and at the end of the nineteenth century were extending their influence to other tribes.

Islam in the Making of Morocco

It was Islam which gave a semblance of unity to this heterogeneous collection of tribes and rural groups. The prevalence of feuding and mutual jealousies and suspicions between tribes made social intercourse beyond the limits of the kin bond difficult even in the best of times. Normal trade and communications were made possible only through the existence of a number of religiously sanctioned methods of forming crosscutting alliances with individuals in other tribes. Most of these were based on some form of *ʿar* (literally, "shame") sacrifice.[10] Intertribal alliances against a common foe were in this fashion guaranteed by a religious sanction. Disputes between groups were often mediated by popularly acclaimed saints, known as *murābitūn,* or marabouts, who arranged for the payment of blood money (Ar. *diya*) in the event of homicide and intervened in various other ways to ease transactions and trade between tribes. Thanks to his spiritual prestige, known as *baraka* (literally, "blessing" or "charisma"), the marabout was able to provide a buffer between groups which might otherwise have been constantly at war.[11]

Sufi brotherhoods, known as *ṭarīqa*-s, provided another important link between individuals of different clans. They existed in great number throughout Morocco and often played important political roles.[12] The most important was the Wazzānīya, which had members throughout the country, with particular strength in the region between Fez and the coast. Other politically significant orders included the Tijānīya (favored by the urban bourgeoisie), the Darqāwa (particularly strong in southeastern Morocco), and the ʿAynaynīya. Ṭarīqa-s were mystical "paths" or "ways" with distinctive litanies and esoteric beliefs. They were organized in *zawīya*-s, each headed by a *muqaddim,* with the ensemble under the shaykh of the order. Like marabouts, these were often involved in the arbitration of quarrels and the provision of food and shelter for needy travelers. In return they received the regular offerings of the faithful (known as *ziyāra*), and a degree of obedience which fluctuated with their personal influence. The more important ṭarīqa-s were kept in line by the grant of special favors from the sultan, tax exemption, the usufruct of government lands, or gifts of money and goods.[13]

Moroccan popular Islam shaped and molded the fabric of society in other ways as well. Sharifian descent from the family of the Prophet or his companions represented a kind of nobility of blood, and there was a great proliferation of sharifism in Morocco. The most important were the three groups that traced their descent from Hasan ibn ʿAlī—the Idrīsīs, the ʿAlawīs, and the Qadarīs.[14] Among them the Idrīsīs were the most numerous and deeply rooted, particularly at Fez, where the shrine of Mawlāy Idrīs provided them with a powerful focus of popular devotion.[15] Since the rise of the Saʿadian dynasty (1515–1659) the sharifian principle had been reemphasized as a means of legitimating the rule of the sultans. The dynasty which followed, the ʿAlawīs (1659–present), was strongly attached to its sharifian heritage. Many of the members of the ʿulamā (Ar. sing., *ʿalim*) of Fez and the other major cities of Morocco claimed sharifian descent, as did other prominent rural and urban families. Being a sharif entitled one to tax immunities, justice by one's peers, and, in the case of certain prominent sharifian families, made one eligible for pensions and grants of agricultural properties or urban buildings by the government. Idrīsī sharifs also received an annual share in the offerings made at the shrine of Mawlāy Idrīs located in the Jabal Zarhūn, near the city of Meknes.[16] Yet there were also beggar sharifs, and sharifism was thus no guarantee to wealth, power, or high status.

Although there were a great many sharifs in Morocco, and by no means all of them were politically significant, one dominated them all. This was the sultan, who as paramount sharif was the ruler of Morocco. In circumstances where the tribes were dominant and the government lacked either the will or the capacity to intervene effectively, the role of the sultan was less that of a chief executive and more that of an interest broker between the major factions of the realm. His power derived from his ability to use the political leverage inherent in his position. While the sultan's sharifian descent greatly enhanced his position in the eyes of his subjects and made him an object of veneration, if he lacked a strong personality or the requisite political skills descent alone could not make him an effective ruler.

Order in Disorder: The State

If rural Moroccan society was internally structured and subdivided along tribal lines, this tribal mass existed within the framework of a bureaucratic Muslim state, organized along lines roughly akin to the great Islamic empires of the Middle East. Herein lies one of the paradoxes of the Moroccan system. At the head of the Moroccan state was the sultan, whose power derived chiefly from his personal and religious prestige as a descendant of the Prophet. The sultan presided over a bureaucracy known as the makhzan. The government apparatus was tenuous at best, being based upon an extension of the royal court and army. The army and the rural administration (if these misleadingly concrete terms can be used to describe such a meager reality) sought to impose a modicum of order over their perennially fractious charges and to raise sufficient tax revenues to make the effort worthwhile. When the sultan was strong, he could impose his will over most of the plains tribes and some of the mountain tribes and freely extract taxes. But when there was a weak sultan, the tribes would refuse to pay the least amount.

The Moroccan state has been pictured as divided into two zones: one, known as *bilād al-makhzan*, where the central government was supreme, taxes were collected, governors governed, and laws were respected; the other, known as *bilād al-siba,* where the central government was impotent and unruly tribes devoted themselves to feuding and banditry.[17] Depending upon the power and authority of the particular sultan, the area which comprised *bilād al-makhzan* increased or decreased in size. Some observers have added an intermediary zone, which at times would accept makhzan rule and at other times would reject it. In the hands of French apologists of colonial domination the division of Moroccan society into *makhzan* and *siba* tended to become an article of faith. When the French government went on to erect a policy founded upon this supposed difference, the stage was set for the perpetuation of a stereotype. By thus seizing upon a few aspects of the nature of the Moroccan polity while ignoring others of equal importance, French policy-makers disguised what they sought most to explain.

The realities of the structure of the Moroccan state are more complex. In the first place, one must come to grips with the nature of the authority of the sultan. The legitimacy of the sultan lay in the fact of his ability to perform the chief duties incumbent upon all Muslim rulers: to defend the lands of Islam against external aggression and to govern justly, that is, according to the precepts of the Holy Law, the *sharīʿa.* In other words, his authority derived from his suitability as a leader of the just community, the *ummah muḥammadīya.* Given the indivisibility of the political and religious in Islam, it is therefore misleading to claim as some have done that the sultan possessed only religious authority over the populations who lived in *bilād al-siba,* and to insist on the impotence of the government and the independence of the tribes. The European notion of territorial empire, with its abstract lines on maps and criteria of effective governance as the test of a state is an inappropriate measure of an Islamic polity, where more personal standards, like submission to Islam and allegiance to the *amīr,* held sway. For a Muslim the fundamental fact was membership in the *Dār al-Islām,* the Abode of Islam, and participation in the ongoing life of the community of the faithful.[18]

There is a second objection which may be raised against the makhzan/siba stereotype. To stress the willingness of a tribe to pay taxes and accept makhzan-appointed governors, is to risk caricature of a situation of much greater subtlety. There were in fact a wide variety of kinds of relations which tribes could have with the makhzan, from full-fledged acceptance of government rule, to the exchange of letters, the periodic sending of embassies to court, the supply of troops at moments of external threat, and the occasional contribution of gifts at the principal Muslim festivals. According to a particularly keen observer of Morocco, "even in the most distant parts of *bled es-siba* there is no tribe which is not in relations with the *makhzan.*" These relations continue even while the battle between the tribes and the makhzan rages.[19] For this reason it is folly to attempt to draw a map of Morocco which seeks to delimit the extent of makhzan and siba territories. In addition, depending upon circumstances, the relationship of a particular tribe with the central power varied over time with the differential power of the makhzan and the changing fortunes of its leaders. The particular degree of interaction depended a great deal upon the individuals and circumstances involved.

A Ramshackle Bureaucracy in Search of Itself

The division of functions in the makhzan was along the same archaic lines commonly found in medieval regimes—"master of the stables," "master of the bedchamber," and the like.[20] There was a council of viziers, but it was functionally rudimentary and lacked a clear separation of tasks, established procedures, or impersonal criteria of operation. The sultans tended to draw their officials from the influential hereditary families of the jaysh tribes who had been accorded privileged positions in earlier times. Other lesser jaysh tribes provided occasional service to the makhzan in the north, and elsewhere in Morocco. The jaysh bureaucrats were qualified for positions in the makhzan primarily by virtue of a well-developed talent for political intrigue. By the end of the nineteenth century, their military importance had diminished greatly. Increasingly, the makhzan began to turn to the Andalusian families of Fez, Tetouan, Tangier, and Salé whose education, talent, and skills best suited them for the task of seeking to transform and modernize the state.[21]

On the level of the rural administration the rudimentary and inadequate character of the system was even more apparent. Tribal governors (Ar. *qāid*) were most often selected by their tribes, whether ultimately they were in fact directly appointed by the sultan, or merely proposed for nomination to the office by a tribal council. In either case, the governors had to have sufficient personal authority to be able to impose their will, or their gestures of command remained merely symbolic. Since the makhzan had little control over its local officials, those qāid-s who possessed some personal authority were more likely to employ it on their own behalf than on that of the government. Tax revenues were rarely forwarded to the capital in their entirety, and the local governor pocketed a suitable percentage.[22]

Rural security depended largely upon the collective personal authorities of the qāid-s and on their continuing acceptability to their tribes. It was the qāid-s who called out the local *ḥaraka,* or militia, which was composed of those men in a tribe with sufficient wealth to afford a horse and a mounted retainer. It was the *ḥaraka* which put down local disorders. If a qāid offended the local notables, he might find himself deserted by them in a time of crisis.[23] Cities would generally have a small garrison of imperial troops which were drawn from the jaysh contingents and placed under the local pasha. In the event of widespread disorders, government troops could be sent to punish the offending tribes, but such expeditions included a large element of risk since royal forces were often no better armed, trained, and led than the tribes. The sultan had to avoid alienating the local governors, or chance the loss of his throne. Lacking a cadre of bureaucrats endowed with sufficient coercive powers, local administration in Morocco prior to 1912 was bound to be vulnerable to the effects of the inevitable local quarrels. The attempted modernization of the army and the administration under Sīdī Muḥammad IV and Mawlāy al-Ḥasan could make but little headway in such circumstances.

If to this portrait of government in nineteenth-century Morocco is added a further weakness, namely, that there was no distinction made on the local level between tax collectors and tax assessors, the difficulty of instituting reforms becomes even more apparent. The local qāid tended to exact as much in taxes and extraordinary levies as the population under his control would put up with. The principal check against abuses of this system lay in the revolt of the people, or in the alienation of the local notables. Tribal administration thus often consisted of the familiar cycle of "squeeze," "revolt," and "repress" with all of the tremendous waste and inefficiency which it implied. To speak of the modernization of the system of local administration is thus, in a sense, tantamount to calling for its creation, as the nineteenth-century reforming sultans discovered.

During the nineteenth century, as a result of makhzan patronage, a number of major rural political figures began to emerge, while other great families, whose fortunes had once been large experienced a decline as the makhzan withdrew its favor. The creation of the great qāid-s, as they were called, is but the most dramatic example of the way in which the political composition of the rural areas could be affected in important ways by government action. On a lower level, a very similar process can be discovered. These complex connections lie at the roots of any explanation of the peculiar patterns of Moroccan resistance and collaboration during the period prior to the protectorate. They also go a long way toward explaining many of the French errors of policy under the protectorate and provide a vantage point from which to view contemporary Morocco.

The Politics of Uncertainty

In discussing the nature of politics in Morocco, the relative instability of power looms large in any analysis which would deal with the dynamic, and not merely the static, aspects of the society. It is a fact of precolonial Moroccan society that few families or groups enjoyed substantial power for more than three generations. The few exceptions consist principally of saintly lineages, descendants of the Prophet, and families possessing strong ties to the government. Nothing in Morocco is really equivalent to the dynasties of Turkish mamluks or makhzan families in Ottoman Algeria or the Arab East. The rural areas, in particular, were marked by a continual precariousness in the political fortunes of individuals. The economy of uncertainty, the prevalence of feuding, and the usual enemies of aspirant aristocratic families everywhere—stupidity and impotence—brought down rural family dynasties with regularity. The inquiries of the French ethnologist Edouard Michaux-Bellaire in the Gharb province (which he had known for thirty years) failed to turn up any families in positions of authority in the 1920s who had held them in the 1890s.[24] In the cities, there were possibilities of hedging one's bets in such a way as to retain power, but those not enjoying connections at court or with European businessmen also tended to follow the same rhythm of rise and decline.

It is here that the absence of intermediary structures in the Moroccan polity that could intervene between the government and the people seems relevant. Precolonial society can usefully be described as a form of patrimonialism, in which an inchoate governmental bureaucracy ruled (at least in theory) over the people, and where the sultan (again in theory) owned most of the land in the kingdom and granted the usufruct of the land as prebends to loyal servants of the state.[25] Nineteenth-century Moroccan history has numerous examples of sultans seeking to retain their control of the monopoly over exports of wool and grain, for example, on the principle that it was the obligation of the makhzan to intervene in such cases. Ottoman society was organized according to similar principles. In Morocco, as in the Ottoman empire, the government sought at every opportunity to break down intermediary jurisdictions of all kinds, be they the right of sanctuary possessed by saintly lineages or the tax immunities and privileges of sharifian lineages. Even though few Moroccan sultans were able to implement fully a program of "pure" patrimonialism, the theory of Islamic sovereignty tended in that direction, and governments sought to carry out as much of the program as they could at every opportunity.

The consequences of this observation are not far to seek. Since Morocco never succeeded in generating free cities or an independent bourgeoisie (or any other quasi-independent group for that matter), as did Western Europe, politics became essentially a series of variations upon the patron-client network. Albert Hourani has spoken of the two major alternatives in the nineteenth-century Middle East: when the sultan was strong, the predominant mode of politics was court politics; when he was weak, the politics of notables dominated, as important mediators emerged between the government and the rest of the society.[26] Much the same thing can be said for the situation in Morocco, with the additional proviso that, because of the greater weight of rural and tribal interests in that society, the politics of notables tended to dominate most of the time. In Morocco many of the rural notables continued to live in their country domains, rather than moving to the cities like their Middle Eastern cousins.

One of the implications of a system of politics where the patron-client network in one or another of its forms—sufi ṭarīqa, economic partnership, political alliance—is the dominant style of politics, is that leadership and public opinion about the capabilities of specific patrons assume proportions that they do not have in countries where a range of intermediary bodies muffle the changes resulting from the rise and fall of individual leaders. Where there are few strong political institutions—be they medieval *parlements,* guild privileges, or urban liberties—political changes tend to be of greater intensity and rapidity. Political fortunes rise and fall according to the fate of particular patrons. Evidently, if a man put all of his trust into the hands of only one patron, given the overall instability of political power he would be sharply circumscribing his possibilities of success. If his patron suffered a turn in his fortunes, the man himself would be vitally affected as well. Such risks were built into the patron-client system. The greatest patron of all was of course the sultan, and alliances with him were especially valued. But the royal favor was generally fickle, and thus even here an anchor or two to windward was to be desired. Individuals, accordingly, tended to multiply their relationships with patrons and would-be patrons in an effort to avoid the harsh consequences attendant upon the failure of any one of them. Bet-hedging as a political device was characteristic of Moroccan and Middle Eastern society, but its importance was much greater than in our own (for bet-hedging exists in all societies) due to the particular precariousness of political fortunes and the absence of intermediary bodies.

The picture of the Moroccan state which emerges from the preceding considerations is broadly similar to the situation which existed in the eighteenth- and early nineteenth-century Middle East. Like most Middle Eastern governments of the period, the makhzan had to confront the tasks of creating a reliable army and administration and of subduing its rebellious provincial aristocracy. Since initially the makhzan possessed a monopoly of firearms, especially artillery, the outcome looked favorable. But the spread of arms smuggling, and the arming of some of the tribes by Mawlāy al-Ḥasan, in the end all but extinguished this advantage. Considered within the context of the rapid changes of the nineteenth century, Morocco possessed serious disadvantages when it came to adopting a program of defensive modernization. The relative weakness of the urban centers deprived the state of an important weapon in combatting rural values. Without a developed bureaucratic tradition or an effective provincial administration, government centralization could only be achieved by devising the necessary institutions virtually from scratch. Not having a docile peasantry or anything much resembling village life on the model of the Arab East, the makhzan was faced with the task of directly confronting a rural citizenry that was especially jealous of its traditional liberties. The effort to expand the power of the government would inevitably collide head-on with a rebellious tribal notability. Deeply entrenched popular religious beliefs tended to give much greater strength to conservative arguments against secular and religious innovation. Even the guardians of the high Islamic tradition among the ʿulamā were powerfully influenced by this popular religiosity, to the detriment of more far-sighted attempts at resistance. Although there was considerable dynamism in the rural areas, and no lack of ability among the urban elites, there was no clear method of harnessing any of this energy. The portrait of Morocco which I have drawn in the preceding pages, it will have been noted by now, is that of a stalemated society. Only time would tell whether Morocco would succeed in breaking out of its stalemate before succumbing to European domination.

2

MOROCCO AND THE WEST, 1860–1900

Economic and Social Changes, 1860–1900

It is difficult to understand the spectacular disintegration of the Moroccan economy and administration after 1900, or the efforts made to resist French encroachment, without some systematic attempt to relate these events to the changes which Morocco experienced during the latter half of the nineteenth century. The popular European image of Morocco in 1900 was that of an unchanging medieval Muslim state, assumed to be very much like the governments which ruled in North Africa ever since the coming of Islam.[1] Yet, as the researches of Jean-Louis Miège have convincingly established, Morocco in the nineteenth century was undergoing very great social, economic, and political transformations and was in fact very far from the immutable country it was often romantically pictured to be.[2] Most of the existing historical accounts of the "Moroccan crisis" that occurred after 1900 neglect entirely the heritage of the nineteenth century and base their explanation instead upon the weakness and incompetence of the young sultan, Mawlày ʿAbd al-ʿAzīz. This approach, because it leaves many significant questions about the origins of the crisis unasked, is unsatisfactory.

Prior to 1860 Morocco was but little affected by European influences. Economic relations with the West were relatively unimportant and subject not to the demands of the market but to the willingness of the sultans to permit trade in specific commodities. The Moroccan economy was in any event not oriented toward commercial dealings with the West but toward satisfying the modest needs of a quasi-traditional agricultural population and a small but industrious urban bourgeoisie and artisanry. While the presence of small colonies of Moroccan merchants in European and Near Eastern ports (Manchester, Marseilles, and Alexandria being the principal ones) testifies to a certain vigor in foreign trade, the margin of profitability on such operations was already being seriously undercut by changes in the European textiles industry. Diplomatic contacts between Morocco and the powers remained sharply limited, and the small resident European community in Morocco was subject to a variety of discriminatory regulations which dealt with where they could live, whether they could own land, and under what conditions they could conduct business.

The French invasion of Algeria in 1830 had set in motion a series of events that would by the end of the century lead to the undermining of the traditional system and the emergence of a new, precolonial Morocco. But the implications of the French presence in Algeria were for a long time not grasped by the Moroccan elite. Even the French victory at the battle of Isly in 1844 over a Moroccan army commanded by Muḥammad IV produced few echos in makhzan circles. Since the defeat occurred on the eastern frontier of the empire and France refrained from following up its victory, Moroccans were not compelled to recognize the full extent of their military inferiority. Following the battle of Isly, European commercial penetration of Morocco began to increase, and the first traits of the precolonial economic system appeared. From this time on, European merchants and speculators became increasingly aggressive in asserting their rights, the trade balance started to shift away from Morocco, and the monetary and financial situation of the makhzan became increasingly precarious. By the eve of the Hispano-Moroccan War of 1859–60, the economic stability of the country was already in jeopardy, and the first signs of the decay of the old structures were already visible to sharp-eyed European observers.

The war of 1859–60 between Spain and Morocco has been seen by historians of the period as one of the watersheds of nineteenth-century Moroccan history.[3] Where the French victory at Isly produced few lasting effects, the shock of defeat by a minor European power in 1860 forced the Moroccan elite to confront for the first time the evidence of growing Moroccan backwardness and to consider the need for reforms. From this point on, one can trace the development of an intense and multifaceted economic and political crisis of major dimensions, which by the end of the century had brought the traditional system to the point of collapse. One of the most important repercussions of the Tetouan War was the aggravation of an already precarious monetary and financial situation. By the terms of the peace treaty with Spain, the Moroccan government was required to pay an indemnity of 100 million pesetas, with payment to be made in specie and not in debased Moroccan coinage. As a result the Moroccan treasury was drained of its gold and silver reserves, and a large share of the customs receipts (the principal source of foreign exchange revenue) was earmarked for twenty-five years to pay the cost of the indemnity demanded by the Spanish.[4] The massive hemorrhage of specie from the Moroccan treasury soon led to the rapid depreciation of Moroccan currency and a sharp rise in domestic prices. The relative economic stability that Morocco had enjoyed up until then was destroyed in the monetary crisis which ensued.

The chief Moroccan money of account in 1860 was the silver *dirham*. By that date few dirham were still in circulation, however, and most of those remaining were used to pay the Spanish indemnity. Instead, European coin, especially the French *écu* (five-franc piece) and the Spanish *douro* (five-peseta piece) circulated as moneys of exchange and came to occupy the central position within the Moroccan economy. All transactions with foreign merchants were settled in French or Spanish coin.[5] Both the écu and the douro were inferior in weight to the supposedly equivalent-value dirham. After 1860, when European trade with Morocco picked up, speculators played upon this difference and succeeded in draining off the remaining good Moroccan silver.[6] In the 1890s, Spanish coin experienced a sharp inflation owing to the drop in the price of silver on the world market. The attempts of sultan Mawlāy al-Ḥasan to remedy the situation by creating a new dirham based on the traditional model collapsed under pressure from the douro.[7] Other makhzan attempts to deal with this grave and complex monetary crisis were equally unsuccessful. These included the proclamation of artificial rates of exchange (which the makhzan did not respect itself in its own dealings), the minting of more dirham to attempt to stabilize the runaway inflation, and the withdrawal from circulation of greatly depreciated issues of coin.[8]

Parallel to the monetary troubles which befell the dirham was the inflation which took place in Moroccan bronze coin, the *fils* (Ar. pl. *flūs*).[9] Peculiar to Morocco was a bimetallism of silver and bronze in which the bronze coin possessed an intrinsic value of its own and was the most commonly used medium of exchange in internal trade. The relationship between the dirham and fils shifted constantly to the disfavor of bronze throughout the nineteenth century. The efforts of speculators and counterfeiters and the wholesale dumping of debased bronze on the economy by the government further exacerbated the situation. The inflation of bronze, together with the depreciation and decline of silver, thus operated to reinforce the existing crisis.

One result, according to Ayache, was that the price of wheat quadrupled in the ten years after 1859 and continued to rise during the rest of the century. Most other consumer prices suffered a similar fate.[10] While taxes were raised, salaries tended to remain more stable. Those living on fixed revenues such as the rents from *ḥubus* (pious endowments), and those living in or near the port cities where the crisis was most intense, suffered accordingly.[11] Inflation also took its toll upon government tax revenues. The traditional Moroccan taxes, the *zakāh* and *ʿushr,* being taxes on agriculture (and thus generally payable in kind), were unable to produce sufficient revenue to help the treasury, although they were converted to money payment. To broaden the tax base, a new tax on merchandise entering the cities, the *maks*, was instituted, thereby attaining the urban populations, who were exempt from the agricultural tithe, or *ʿushr*.[12] Peasants who had formerly paid their taxes in kind found themselves in serious difficulties when payment was converted to money, and many lost their land to urban loan sharks during this period.[13]

The monetary crisis coincided with a second major economic disruption, the crisis in the Moroccan balance of trade. The Spanish indemnity was of course one aspect of this. There was in addition a persistent unfavorable movement in the Moroccan commercial balance, as depicted by Miège, in the transfer of specie from Morocco to Marseilles.[14] The terms of trade for Morocco's principal exports (wool, hides, wheat, and dates) were steadily eroded during the latter half of the nineteenth century by the opening of the Suez Canal, the introduction of steamships, and the inauguration of the transcontinental railroads, which made American and Russian wheat and Australian wool available to European markets at greatly reduced prices.[15] Sharply increased commercial competition between the powers, which found expression in German dumping of cheap goods on the Moroccan market after 1890, meant that Moroccan imports greatly increased at the same time that their chief European markets were declining.[16] The suddenness of these economic changes produced the usual complement of violent social disruptions, which affected first the coastal region and then, gradually, the interior of Morocco.

The monetary and financial crises in turn intersected with a series of disastrous agricultural years to further destroy whatever resilience might have remained in the traditional system. The first prolonged famine lasted from 1867 to 1869, with crop failures all over the country and the start of a rural exodus to the cities in search of relief.[17] After a good recovery, seven more years of severe and widespread famine wiped out whatever hope might have survived that Morocco could somehow regain its equilibrium. From 1878 to 1884, one of the most prolonged and intense famines ever to strike the country dominated the scene.[18] Smallpox and cholera epidemics raged out of control and decimated the already crippled rural populations. Families sought to gain a measure of relief by flooding into the port cities, but the overtaxed charitable efforts of the resident European communities there could do little to help. Contemporary estimates of the incidence of mortality placed the figure at one-fourth to one-third of the total rural population. While this seems excessive, Miège accepts a conservative estimate of 15 percent mortality in the coastal cities and a substantially higher rate in the interior.[19] As is usual in such circumstances, the rural folk and the poor were disproportionately hit. The demographic consequences of the crisis of 1878–84 make it one of the capital events in the social history of modern Morocco. Only those who already possessed a privileged economic position by virtue of protégé status or makhzan-granted patents and immunities emerged from the prolonged depression with their strength largely unimpaired.[20]

In 1856 the Moroccan government concluded a most-favored-nation treaty with England. This treaty served as the model for similar arrangements with France, Spain, and other European powers. The inevitable result of the lowering of customs duties on European imports was to open the Moroccan market to a flood of cheap manufactured goods and to hasten the decline of the Moroccan artisanry. For example, in 1830 the city of Salé was able to support hundreds of textile workshops making a variety of woolen and cotton items. By 1880, as a result of the importation of cheap Lancashire cottons, many artisans had been forced out of business.[21] A similar story could be told for the other cities of Morocco. While not all trades were uniformly affected, the last half of the nineteenth century sounded the end of the handicraft industry as a vital sector of the Moroccan economy.

The diffusion of new tastes for items of European manufacture is another important aspect of the changes of these years. By mid-century, cotton goods, candles, oil, and especially tea and sugar decreased markedly in price because of cheaper production and transportation costs. Moroccan imports of these items rose spectacularly, partly in function of their cheapness and availability, but also due to better market research by European firms. Miège has examined the impact of the diffusion of new tastes for European products on the budget of Moroccan families. The case of the spread of the consumption of tea and sugar (today a prominent feature of popular culture) is perhaps most dramatic. In order to support this newly acquired taste large numbers of Moroccans were led into debt.[22] Such changes helped to undermine the structures of rural society and to create a class of debt-ridden peasants near the main port cities.

An important by-product of the social and economic transformation of the old society was a rapid increase in urbanization. Attracted by new opportunities in the port cities and propelled by the prolonged agricultural slump of 1878–84, large numbers of peasants flocked to the towns. Initially the major share of the new urban growth took place in the coastal cities.[23] Their populations rose from 88,600 in 1856 to 176,000 in 1900. The growth of Tangier, which went from 10,000 to 45,000, and of Casablanca, which increased from 1,600 to 21,000, was especially notable. Tetouan alone remained outside this trend, and the five other port cities added between 4,000 and 8,500 during the same period.[24] The cities of the interior tended to languish. An export-oriented economy that was open to the world gradually replaced the old domestically oriented local economy.

Morocco, like the Ottoman empire, had early devised a means of dealing with the small group of European merchants and traders who lived in its ports whereby they would be granted tax and legal immunities and placed under the jurisdiction of their respective consuls. Known as "treaties of capitulation," these arrangements had originally been accorded as a gratuitous privilege by the sultans.[25] In Morocco, the capitulations had always been more strictly controlled by the makhzan, who restricted European settlement to the ports of Tangier and Essaouira (Fr. Mogador), and forbade foreigners to own land, to ride horses in town, and so on.[26] In the changed conditions of the later nineteenth century these treaties became subject to continual abuses and were regarded by arrogant Europeans as a minimum right owed to them by a decadent Muslim state. During the first half of the century, when the European population living in Morocco remained relatively stable, cases of friction with the makhzan were few. But in the latter half of the century the resident European population rose from 1,360 in 1864 to 9,000 in 1894, and incidents increased greatly.[27]

The European communities in Morocco possessed considerable leverage in domestic affairs due to the privileged position which they occupied on the fringes of that society and their connections with the major commercial houses of Europe. Their ability to call down diplomatic sanctions to enforce their will gave them a political influence at all levels of society out of all proportion to their numbers. As in the Ottoman empire, during the nineteenth century the European consuls tended to become powerful political patrons in their own right, no longer mere spectators of the local scene.[28] Muslim notables in the port cities learned to cultivate relations with Europeans in addition to elements within the makhzan. Inland, the old patterns of political relations continued unimpeded, but on the coast a new, precolonial style of politics was coming into existence. Economically the European merchants represented the tip of the vast European capitalist iceberg and were able to draw on the resources and techniques that modern enterprise had at its disposition. By dint of an aggressive business style they acquired extensive real estate in the ports and the nearby areas.[29] As a group the European merchants were largely oblivious to the corrosive effects which their often ruthless trading practices had upon age-old Moroccan economic and social patterns of action.

Another source of social dislocation was the practice of European merchants taking on Moroccan assistants, known as protégés, to facilitate commerce with the hinterland of the ports and the cities of the interior. The status of protégé in Morocco originated with the Franco-Moroccan commercial treaty of 1767. Until about 1857 the system appears to have functioned well enough, but the ensuing increase in the volume of commerce with Europe and in the size of the European resident community led to a rapid undermining of the system by all manner of abuses. There was an attempt at reform in the Tangier Convention of 1863, and the more inclusive Madrid Convention of 1880 restricted the number of commercial agents, or censals (Ar. *samsar*). Each commercial house was permitted two agents for each Moroccan port in which it did business. Conditions were also set for the employment of agricultural agents, or *mukhalaṭ*-s.[30] Not all of the powers were equally conscientious in adhering to the terms of these conventions.

Owing to their privileged position, Moroccan protégés soon developed into a bourgeoisie that differed from the indigenous one in important respects, most notably in the guaranteed durability of its fortune and its access to the European money market. By placing their flocks and herds under European protection and becoming *mukhalaṭ*-s, many rural notables managed to consolidate previously precarious fortunes. Some combined agriculture with commercial ventures and, by offering credit for the European products they sold, with land and crops accepted for security, tended to become absentee landowners on the Middle Eastern model as their customers defaulted in payment. The makhzan was deprived of the tax receipts of all protégés during a period when its revenue needs were sharply rising.[31] In addition to tax immunities, protégés enjoyed immunity from Moroccan laws and were placed under the legal jurisdiction of a European consul.[32] Some used their status as protégé to escape from fulfilling their obligations to supply men to the local *ḥaraka,* which had the effect of weakening rural security.[33] In practice protégé status tended to become hereditary and to be extended to all of a protégé's family, including his retainers. Many of the less scrupulous European merchants did not hesitate to sell patents of protection to the highest bidder.[34]

European Penetration and Moroccan Response, 1860–1900

The most visible manifestation of the changed balance of forces between Morocco and the West was the increasing aggressiveness of even minor European powers. The Tetouan War of 1859–1860 came as a great shock. This was further compounded by the French police action in the vicinity of the Moroccan city of Oudjda in 1860.[35] Although no serious military challenge arose for a decade thereafter, the Moroccan sultans experienced difficulties in resurrecting the old diplomatic position, which had been based on strong British support for the maintenance of Moroccan independence.[36] In the commercial expansion which came after 1860, the powers became more interested in increasing their position in Morocco and more aggressive in enforcing their demands for preferred treatment by the makhzan. At least three major causes of friction between the powers and the Moroccan government may be singled out for discussion: the status of protégés, commercial privileges, and frontier incidents between Moroccan tribesmen and French and Spanish troops.

Protection and commercial privileges can be considered together. Basically, they both related to the degree of autonomy which the Moroccan government was willing to grant resident foreign merchants. We have already observed some of the consequences which flowed from the privilege of extraterritoriality enjoyed by European merchants and from the extension of these privileges to Moroccan nationals under patents of protection: the development in the ports of an aggressive Moroccan bourgeoisie paying no taxes and immune from Moroccan legal jurisdiction; the flagrant sale of patents of protection by unscrupulous European diplomats and merchants; and the erosion of the authority of the makhzan around the ports, which tended to become autonomous European enclaves. The principal diplomatic issues pressed by the Europeans after 1860 included the following: the number of ports in which Europeans would be allowed to reside, the right of Europeans to own property, the right of Europeans to enforce sanitary regulations in the ports, the question of the free export of cereal grains, and the relative trading privileges of the powers. Later some of the powers also sought the right to introduce a broad spectrum of reforms in Morocco. Considering the wide range of privileges enjoyed or demanded by the European resident communities, and the corrosive effect which they had upon age-old Moroccan institutions, it is not surprising that the Moroccan sultans tended to view them as a threat to the sovereignty of the state.[37]

Protégés sought the support of their consuls at the least fancied affront, and the consuls on the whole proved perfectly willing to back them up. The right of protection was widely abused and was the subject of a series of diplomatic conferences, notably those at Tangier (1867) and Madrid (1880). The question was, however, never resolved, and Mawlāy al-Ḥasan was tempted to call another international conference to deal with the subject by 1887.[38] In general the British, with their minister at Tangier, Sir John Drummond Hay, tended to take the lead in the movement for the reform of protection, but by the time that Drummond Hay departed in 1886 little real progress had been made toward removing the major abuses. The chief result of the conferences on protection, especially of the Madrid Convention, was to confirm the status quo while at the same time beginning the internationalization of the Moroccan Question.[39]

The question of special trading rights and the introduction of a program of reforms was not seriously broached until after 1880, when first the French and then the British launched diplomatic offensives designed to win for themselves a favored position in Morocco, including the right to sponsor a comprehensive series of reforms and internal improvements. The first attempt came in 1884 when Ordega, the French minister at Tangier, deliberately provoked a crisis in his attempt to utilize the sharif of Wazzan (who had become a French protégé in 1883) to force reforms under French sponsorship. Coming as it did, soon after the establishment of the French protectorate over Tunisia (1880), this incident greatly alarmed Mawlāy al-Ḥasan. It also looked to many of the powers like a blatant imitation of the same aggressive French tactics which had been utilized in Tunisia. They accordingly protested and compelled the French government to abandon the project. Ordega was replaced by a less provocative French representative, and the French position in Morocco went into a temporary decline.[40] A little over a decade later the British produced an Ordega of their own in the person of Sir Charles Euan Smith, their minister at Tangier from March 1891 until January 1893. Earlier, Smith had played a leading role in the British acquisition of Zanzibar, and he sought to duplicate this earlier success of the hard line by presenting a stiff set of demands for reforms and privileges to the sultan during a diplomatic mission to Fez. When Mawlāy al-Ḥasan rejected his demands and received support from France, Smith was forced to retire in disgrace. The diplomatic edifice which Drummond Hay had painstakingly constructed for Great Britain was badly damaged in the process.[41] Both the Ordega and Euan Smith diplomatic offensives were suspected by Mawlāy al-Ḥasan as being aimed at the imposition of a quasi-protectorate on Morocco. Neither was successful, finally, because the sultan was able to rally sufficient diplomatic support in time; more important, in both cases the minister was proved to be acting largely on his own initiative, and was subsequently disavowed by his government and recalled. These efforts made it clear that: (1) the Moroccan Question was going to have no easy answer; (2) France possessed the better chance for a protectorate; and (3) a protracted and intense French diplomatic campaign would be necessary to secure the disengagement of all interested parties.

French and British intentions clearly, then, constituted a source of concern to the sultans. A more immediate danger was presented by the possibility that friction between Moroccan tribes and French or Spanish posts could serve as the pretext for a pacificatory expedition and the probable loss of Moroccan territory. The French victory over the Moroccan army at the battle of Isly (1844) earlier served as a pointed example of the danger of direct Moroccan government support for frontier tribes embroiled with the French. Only the diplomatic intervention of Great Britain and the absence of serious desire at Paris to add Morocco to France's possessions in North Africa prevented a worse outcome.[42]

Following the battle of Isly, periodic frontier incidents continued to occur. The Tetouan War and the French expedition of 1859 against the Beni Snassen (B. Ait Iznassen) were among the more serious. The former, in particular, revealed to the makhzan the shocking weakness of a Moroccan army based on jaysh contingents against even a very weak European power like Spain, and the need for far-reaching reforms. In 1864, the revolt of the Algerian tribe of Oulad Sidi Cheikh (Ar. Awlad Sīdī Shaykh) in Sud-Oranais drew into its orbit many of the Moroccan tribes along the southeastern frontier (Doui Menia, Oulad Jerir, and Beni Guil) and ultimately provoked a large French expedition to the Guir Valley in 1870 under General de Wimpffen. Only restrictive intructions from Paris and the outbreak of the Franco-Prussian War prevented French troops from reaching the Tafilalet oasis, royal necropolis of the reigning dynasty. For a time the sultan, Sīdī Muḥammad, was convinced that the French intended to annex Moroccan territory, and the tribes along the frontier formed a *ḥaraka* to resist further French encroachment. But the French, after their thorough defeat by the Germans, were in no mood for even minor military adventures, and for a decade thereafter disputes along the frontier were settled through diplomatic channels rather than by force.[43] Another important tribal revolt took place in the Sud-Oranais in 1881, led by the famous Abū ʿImāmah (Fr. Bou Amama), a marabout of Oulad Sīdī Cheikh origin. Once again the Moroccan tribes along the border were drawn into the conflict and eventually incited a French pacificatory expedition. A French post was created at Ain Sefra (Ar. ʿAyn Sifrā), and a military railroad was constructed to it in 1887 that by the end of the century became a magnet for much of the trade which had formerly gone from Tafilalet to Fez.[44] While the economic context of the southeastern Moroccan frontier was being transformed by steady French encroachment, the political situation was being no less drastically altered. A local Darqawa shaykh, Sī al-ʿArbī, who possessed considerable influence over the tribes in the frontier area became increasingly alarmed by the steady French advance. The apparent weakness of Mawlāy al-Ḥasan's response to this danger did nothing to reassure him. In the early 1880s Sī al-ʿArbi began calling for the tribes in the area to launch a *jihād* against the French in south Oran. Because of his considerable prestige, he soon acquired a substantial following. Soon his ambitions grew larger, and in 1888 he challenged the makhzan to take action against the French, failing which he would arm the tribes and himself send them against the infidel. For a number of years the situation in the frontier remained tense, and the makhzan itself seemed for a time threatened by the growing power of Sī al-ʿArbi, but the death of the marabout in 1892 and the subsequent visit of Mawlāy al-Ḥasan to Tafilalet restored a precarious order to the region.[45]

From 1893, as a way of asserting his sovereignty in the southeast frontier, Ḥasan I maintained a personal representative in the area. Since the extent of the sultan's authority in the frontier region was vague and no clear border had ever been traced, the situation continued to be productive of disputes.

Despite the looming importance of the French threat, the two most serious military conflicts during the latter half of the nineteenth century were with Spain. The first of these, already mentioned, was the Tetouan War of 1859–60, which had cost the makhzan 100 million pesetas in reparations payments. In 1893 hostilities again broke out with Spain. This time it was a conflict between the Spanish garrison at Melilla and the neighboring Rifian tribes. A Spanish attempt to encroach on Moroccan territory provoked a small-scale local holy war. Mawlāy al-Ḥasan wisely refrained from committing his newly modernized army to aid the Rifians and instead sought a diplomatic resolution to the crisis. The final peace terms were expensive; Morocco had to agree to pay 20 million pesetas in indemnities to win a perilous settlement.[46]

In general, the strategy of the Moroccan sultans in disputes along the border was to avoid direct makhzan military involvement, and to encourage the tribes to avoid precipitate action, while a diplomatic resolution could be sought. The example of Tunisia, where alleged violations of the Algerian border by Tunisian tribes had served as a pretext for the French "police action" that led to the creation of the protectorate, stood as an explicit warning of the dangers of a "hot" frontier. On the other hand, a sultan was obliged to show a willingness to defend Moroccan territory, or risk losing much of his domestic support. It was a very difficult position to be placed in, and even Ḥasan I never succeeded in finding a solution. His expedition to Tafilalet in 1893–94 had been designed to reassert makhzan authority in the area but was never followed up after his death in 1894. With the French taking an increasingly aggressive attitude along the frontier, and a new willingness to support a more active Moroccan policy developing in Paris and Algiers, the status quo became over more fragile in the area. The consequences of this new situation will be examined below, in chapter 4.

The latter part of the nineteenth century saw the rise of a new, more intolerant attitude among Muslims toward Europeans and a consequent stiffening of Muslim determination to resist imperial conquest. This phenomenon, which has been called the general crisis of Islam, was marked by the tendency of the countries of the Muslim world to strengthen relations with neighboring Muslim states.[47] In Morocco, the penetration of Near Eastern ideas of religious reformism during the nineteenth century is one indication of this rapprochement. The foreign policy of Ḥasan I is another and perhaps more substantial indication of the same trend. While striving to play off the powers against one another and maintain the status quo with Europe, Ḥasan I sought to safeguard his desert frontier by reasserting Moroccan claims over much of the central Sahara (including the Touat oasis complex), Mauretania, and parts of the Western Sudan (including the Muslim city of Timbuctu).[48] To this end the makhzan invested local chiefs in all these regions with Moroccan offices, maintained an active correspondence with them, received delegations from each of them to the Moroccan court, and supplied arms and ammunition to selected leaders. The local elites, for their part, were eager to buttress their own diplomatic positions, and actively sought Moroccan backing.

While Morocco's links with its Saharan outliers were being strengthened, its relations with the Ottoman empire and the Near East were undergoing a slower but no less important evolution. Moroccan sultans claimed by virtue of their sharifian descent to be the rightful heirs of the classical Islamic caliphs. The Moroccan claim thus posed a theoretical challenge to the legitimacy of the Ottoman hegemony over *Dār al-Islām,* since the Ottoman sultans could prove no such exalted origins. While the makhzan refrained from pressing its rights, it also avoided entering into direct relations with the Sublime Porte or from taking any action which might imply a renunciation of its claim.[49] Prior to 1900 the Ottomans made at least three attempts to enter into relations with the makhzan, each time with the aid of German intermediaries.[50] There were in addition reports of informal contacts, pan-Islamic agents circulating in the Moroccan countryside, and strong Moroccan sympathies for the rising of the Mahdī in the Sudan. In practical terms, indeed, the Moroccan refusal of formal relations meant that the only possible kind of contacts between the makhzan and the Ottomans were unofficial, quasi-secret ones. After 1900 and the intensification of European pressures on Morocco, reform-minded notables and makhzan officials began to urge the government to reinforce its connections with the Ottoman regime.

Currents of Reform

A recurrent theme of the years after 1860 was the attempt by succeeding sultans to modernize the Moroccan army. To this end they deemphasized the old system of jaysh tribes, which had been the backbone of previous Moroccan armies, and substituted new units: an elite infantry corps, (the *ʿaskar*); a sort of national guard drawn from all tax-paying tribes, (the *nuwāib*); a modern artillery section (*tobjia,* from the Turkish); and even a corps of engineers, or *muhandis.*[51] The old jaysh contingents gradually assumed the role of a rural constabulary and official urban police force, or ceased entirely to fulfill their functions. To train the new army, the sultans first tried using European renegades as instructors, then resorted to sending a few Moroccans to Gibraltar or to military schools in Europe, and finally invited some of the powers to supply military advisors.[52] The conscious policy of Mawlāy al-Ḥasan, who took a special interest in military reform, was to avoid relying exclusively on one or two European powers for either the furnishing of instructors or of arms and munitions. He recognized clearly the important diplomatic leverage which such arrangements conferred upon the European donor and was determined to avoid giving any one power too great an advantage. The variety of weapons acquired as a result of his policy introduced much duplication and lack of standardization into the state arsenals and greatly increased expenses. European training of Moroccan cadres tended to lose much of its raison d'être when officer candidates were parcelled out among three or four powers. Large government expenditures for cannon, rifles, ammunition, and uniforms, and the financing of costly makhzan military expeditions against recalcitrant tribes, helped further deplete the already weakened Moroccan treasury.[53]

The acquisition of modern weapons by the tribes, especially in the period after 1880 when there was an expansion in the sale of arms to the tribal populations of the interior, further undermined military reforms. Most modern weapons came into the hands of the tribes by smuggling, a lucrative business from which none of the great powers appears to have been able to refrain.[54] Even makhzan weapons had a way of disappearing from government arsenals and showing up in the hands of the tribes. Partly, this was brought about by corrupt makhzan officials intent upon feathering their own nests. Partly, also, this was the result of deliberate policy. Mawlāy al-Ḥasan adopted a policy of arming some of the great barons of the Western High Atlas with repeating rifles and Krupp cannon in order to secure their support—a fact which helps explain the rapid expansion of the fiefs of these great *qāid*-s in the years following 1890.[55] One gets the impression that between the efforts of the smugglers and those of the makhzan officials there was no shortage of modern arms among the tribes of central Morocco, although more isolated areas were less well equipped. The majority of the rifles acquired by the tribes were older weapons—French Chasspots and 1884-model Gras. But by 1900 the tribal leaders at least appear to have been well supplied with Remington and Winchester repeaters. While suitable ammunition for these weapons was not always in sufficient supply, empty shell casings could be recharged with gunpowder produced by the small domestic munitions industry.[56]

A number of consequences flowed from the ready availability of modern weapons. A reason why the successors of Ḥasan I failed to obtain the same military successes as the great sultan himself was that a much greater proportion of tribesmen possessed modern repeating rifles, which had previously been something of a makhzan monopoly. In this manner the sultans lost the one great advantage which they had hitherto enjoyed over the rural populations, namely, superior firepower. An additional consequence was an increased level of mortality from the feud in the countryside: it was much easier to hit a man with a Winchester repeater than it was with a bulky old muzzleloading Bouchfer. It seems likely that the availability of modern weapons had a considerable impact on the balance of power between tribal factions, if we posit (as seems likely) a differential rate of acquisition by tribesmen. The balance of power between the makhzan and the tribes began to tilt gradually toward the latter during the second half of the century. Within this altered political context must be situated the rural unrest and resistance movements of the period from 1900 to 1912.

In the Middle East, the army constituted an important force for change during the protonationalist period. From the modernizing segment of the army emerged the advocates of more radical political reforms—the Colonel ʿArabis, the Enver Pashas. In Morocco, by way of contrast, the attempted reform of the army never really got off the ground and, as a result, no proreform group of officers ever emerged. Lacking a modern army, the Moroccan government was unable to tame its potentially fractious provincial notability or push ahead on its program of centralization. Instead, the Moroccan equivalent of the Turkish *derebey*-s (valley lords) came to play a similar role to that played by the army elsewhere in the Middle East in the political reform of the state. It was the "lords of the Atlas," and not the army, which backed the Ḥafīẓīya revolution in Morocco, and it was their interests, rather than the army's, which were represented in the subsequent attempts to change the policies and political structure of the state.

Like the army, the Moroccan administration underwent a series of reforms during the nineteenth century due to the new need for a more reliable and efficient government. Rural administration, which had been confined to eighteen great qāid-s by Sīdī Muḥammad, was modernized under Mawlāy al-Ḥasan. In an effort to reduce the possibilities of several strong qāid-s grouping together to oppose him, this sultan created a fractionated rural administration of 330 tribal governorships.[57] Financial considerations may also have played a part in this arrangement, for taxes could be held back less easily by a single weak official and many more "gifts" could be extracted by the makhzan from those seeking appointment. This policy of dividing authority into a number of small, easily controllable units was contradicted by the simultaneous creation of a new group of great qāid-s in the Western High Atlas.[58] As long as Ḥasan lived, his matchless political skills kept the great qāid-s largely subservient and divided among themselves. The Grand Vizier Aḥmad ibn Mūsā, who ruled as regent for the young ʿAbd al-ʿAzīz after Ḥasan's death, lacked the necessary energy and ability to continue the same policy. The balance of power between the makhzan and the tribes began, as a consequence, to tilt increasingly in the direction of the tribes. The needs for tax revenues of the makhzan, which increased rapidly during the same period, caused the rural administration to become progressively harsher and more unjust in its collection of taxes. Movements of rural protest appeared with more frequency, and the security of country districts was steadily eroded. The attempt to reform the administration by Ḥasan I must be rated as a dubious achievement even during his own lifetime. Thereafter, the system rapidly began to come apart at the seams.

The financial administration was also reorganized during the nineteenth century, as increased dealings with European merchants called for more sophisticated accounting methods than the crude ones currently in force in the makhzan. The development of a special group of customs officials, the *umanā* (Ar. pl. of *amīn,* agent, administrator) to oversee the assessment and collection of duties took place under the sultan Mawlāy al-Sulaymān (1792–1822). Drawn from the principal merchants of the cities of Fez, Tetouan, Rabat, and Salé (and for the most part of Andalousian extraction), the umanā served as local bankers of the makhzan as well as financial agents of the government.[59] The customs officials were later paid a salary in an effort to keep down corruption, and to some extent this expedient appears to have worked. From among the families of umanā began to emerge by the close of the century a new bourgeoisie, privileged by its connections with the makhzan and European commercial interests and already beginning to acquire extensive urban and rural properties.[60] This group, bound by marriage and patron-client ties to the ʿulamā and the urban and rural notables, was politically of strategic importance in the years which followed. Having a stake in makhzan reforms and open to Middle Eastern reformist ideas, the umanā produced some of the leaders of the post-1900 protonationalist leaders. Yet, heavily compromised by close association with European business interests, they also provided many who eventually became ardent supporters of a protectorate.

As Morocco became drawn more deeply into the world economic system and its financial problems became more complex, a variety of other specialized administrative posts were created. When the *maks* (urban gate tax) was established after the Tetouan War, the position of *amīn al-mustafad* was developed to collect it and the other indirect taxes on the cities. The royal treasury developed a more complex and specialized administration during this period, and the position of *Wazīr al-māliya* (or, approximately, minister of finances) was created.[61] Because of their special financial and administrative talents the merchants and ʿulamā (especially those of Fez) came to fill a disproportionate number of these posts.[62] Officials were also appointed to oversee the collection of the taxes in rural areas, in an attempt to get away from the old, less efficient system under which the qāid collected the taxes and sent the makhzan more or less what he pleased from the proceeds. To control the qāid, the position of *amīn al-khirs* was devised. This official was to estimate the size of the harvest and assess the amount of tax to be paid by each family.[63] Lacking any effective power of sanction, the *amīn al-khirs* could do little to prevent the continuation of the old abuses, however. Thus this innovation, which might have gone far toward restoring order to the chaotic state of Morocco's finances by the end of the century, soon fell into desuetude. It was to be revived under ʿAbd al-ʿAzīz after 1900. As part of the supposed comprehensive solution of the protection issue at the Madrid Conference in 1880 a tax reform was agreed upon. The *tartīb,* as it was called, was to be a uniformly assessed tax on agriculture and livestock patterned supposedly on the British income tax—although its similarity to the eighteenth-century French *vingtième* was rather greater. There were to be no exemptions accorded to anyone, including hitherto privileged sharifs and protégés, but in return foreigners were to be allowed to own land in Morocco (clauses 12 and 13 of the Madrid

Convention). It was never put into practice.[64] Instead, abuses and systematic extortion by government officials at all levels came increasingly to characterize the system of taxation. Tax rebellions became more frequent in the countryside, especially after the death of Ḥasan I in 1894, and the protests of the powers and demands for compensation for alleged injustices to their protégés steadily mounted.

The field of education was one of the key sectors in the emergence of a reform-minded elite in the Ottoman empire during the nineteenth century. The introduction of secular education and the translation of Western books were of fundamental importance for the emergence of a modern army, staffed by a well-trained officer corps, and of an efficiency-oriented modern bureaucracy. In Morocco, by way of contrast, little of importance was done to change the education of the elite. In the absence of a supportive intellectual environment the few Moroccan cadets educated abroad languished and soon forgot what they had learned. There was no translation movement in Morocco. The education system in force continued to be the traditional Muslim religious training, based upon the rote learning of sacred texts. The Qarawīyīn mosque university at Fez retained a certain intellectual vigor, although it had long since passed its period of greatness. As will be seen below, reformist ideas were already filtering into Morocco during the nineteenth century from the Arab East, and by the end of the century Fez was undergoing something of an intellectual renaissance.[65] Evidence of direct Western intellectual influence is much more difficult to find. Under Muḥammad IV (1859–73) a sort of administrator's academy was established at Fez to produce qualified personnel for the reformed makhzan. This palace school, or madrasa dār al-makhzan, was the only effort at nontraditional education, however, and it offered but a rudimentary training in secular subjects and did not produce an identifiable modernizing segment of the elite.[66] The absence of a group of Western-trained government officials crippled the hopes of a thoroughgoing reform movement. When ideas of reform did begin to take solid root among the Moroccan elite around 1900, they were filtered through Near Eastern writings and experience on the subject.

The Jewish population of Morocco alone had access to Western education, through the schools established under the auspices of the Alliance Israélite Universelle. Beginning in 1862, with the founding of a school for boys at Tangier, the AIU established schools in the chief ports of Morocco. Instruction was offered in both French and Hebrew for a range of modern and traditional subjects. Until the 1880s the AIU schools experienced indifferent success because of the opposition of traditional religious circles. Thereafter they played an important part in forming a group of French-speaking Jews, ready to serve as local commercial representatives for European firms when the economic penetration of Morocco began in earnest around the turn of the century. A wealthy Jewish bourgeoisie with strong ties to France began to develop in the ports; as in the Middle East, where minorities also served as middlemen, this group began to excite the jealousy and suspicions of the local Muslim population.[67]

While the major attention of the Moroccan reformers was addressed to the army and the administration, there were tentative efforts in several other directions which, although they were not immediately followed up, served to point the way to later developments. One of these was a brief flirtation with a more fundamentalist interpretation of Islam derived from the fourteenth-century Arab scholar Ibn Taymīyah and inspired by the doctrine of the puritanical Wahhabīya sect of Arabia. Under the sultans Sīdī Muḥammad ibn ʿAbdullāh (1757–90), and especially his son Mawlāy Sulaymān (1792–1822), an attempt was made to reinvigorate the traditional theology and purge it of heterodox influence. Mawlāy Sulaymān launched a campaign against the Sufi brotherhoods and local saint cults, and strove to prevent religious shrines from granting protection to refugees from makhzan justice. The Sufi orders themselves were attacked as decadent and prone to excesses. The fact that they also constituted potentially divisive foci of local power against the centralizing makhzan undoubtedly had something to do with this effort. After the death of Mawlāy Sulaymān, the current of Islamic modernism appears to have weakened for a time. It was briefly revived in the 1870s with the appointment of ʿAbdullāh ibn Idrīs al-Sanūsī to the Royal Learned Council of Mawlāy al-Ḥasan after al-Sanūsī's return from a voyage to the Middle East. In his travels al-Sanūsī had become strongly influenced by the ideas of the Al-Azhar modernist theologians. He propounded these views on his return to Morocco and received the backing of the sultan against the harsh criticism of the more traditional elements. Eventually he was forced to resign under pressure and left Morocco and went into exile in the Middle East. He did not return until after the death of al-Ḥasan and the development of a more receptive attitude toward reformists' ideas after 1900.[68] Thereafter Islamic modernism under royal sponsorship was to become one of the main strands of Moroccan resistance to the West and an engine of the movement to strengthen and centralize the makhzan.

For the individual Moroccan, the complex and powerful new currents of change which engulfed his country after 1860 were perceived as marking a sharp break with the experience of previous generations. Economic change, especially the ruinous inflation of the period, was taken as a symbol of the new order by the historian al-Nāṣirī, whose feelings evidently mirrored those of many of his contemporaries among the educated elite. He regarded the power of the West, especially the insidious side-effects of European commercial penetration in the port cities, with growing alarm. There, so it seemed, all manner of vice and immorality flourished unchecked, including an increase in alcoholism and drug addiction.[69] Tangier, the largest port and main center of contact between Morocco and the West, was viewed as hopelessly contaminated by the presence of a large resident European population. It appeared to learned and pious Moroccans as the fountain of iniquity and was much celebrated in pessimistic verse.[70] Even the drinking of tea was viewed as something subversive. The sharif Muḥammad ibn ʿAbd al-Kabīr al-Kattānī was so alarmed by the spread of the consumption of tea that he forbade it to the followers of his religious brotherhood. He perceived the importation and sale of large quantities of tea and sugar as the start of a European takeover of the Moroccan economy and a prelude to colonization.[71] A concern with economic independence was a trend in the thinking of ʿulamā and notables that characterizes the period.

The revelation of the military weakness of Moroccan armies and the growing power of the West was undoubtedly the single most significant item in opening the eyes of Moroccans everywhere to the danger which threatened. The sting of military defeat accomplished what the collapse of the economy was unable to accomplish—it shocked the elite into recognizing the need for thoroughgoing military reforms to transform and strengthen the state. Again al-Nāṣirī appears to have best articulated the dilemma of Moroccan reformers. Reforms, for him, were tainted by their connections with Christianity. He remarked, apropos of the new military cadets, "They want to learn how to fight to protect the faith, but they lose the faith in the process of learning how."[72] More clearly than most "traditionalists," those of Morocco appear to have perceived just how much was at stake in even external modernization of a few aspects of the state. Accordingly, they favored a continuation of the policy by which Morocco had capitalized upon the rivalries of the powers and played them off against one another. In the changed diplomatic circumstances after the turn of the century, the impossibility of continuing this policy soon became evident to all.[73]

Conclusion

The considerable abilities and energy of Mawlāy al-Ḥasan prevented most European observers from recognizing the nature and extent of the undermining of the old society. After Ḥasan's death in 1894 and until 1900 the fate of Morocco lay in the hands of the grand vizir and regent, Si Aḥmad ibn Mūsā. He continued the policies of his former master, although he was lacking in his tremendous drive. When the youthful and inexperienced ʿAbd al-ʿAzīz came into his majority in 1900, all of the weaknesses in the old regime became glaringly apparent.[74]

If we contrast the beginnings of modernization in Morocco with the experience of other Middle Eastern countries, some interesting contrasts emerge. To begin with, there were the external forces at work, European commercial penetration and the diplomatic and military struggle for hegemony throughout the region. In the Ottoman empire, Egypt, and Iran, European military pressure was felt from early in the nineteenth century and continued to be an important factor throughout. In Morocco, on the other hand, European military pressure was felt but intermittently and provided no continuous stimulus to reform. The French victory at Isly in 1884 failed to spark a serious effort at reform. While the Tetouan War demonstrated the weakness of the army, the absence of a continuous threat muted the initial impetus for change.

European commercial penetration of Morocco was similarly retarded. Not until after mid-century was the country drawn into the economic orbit of Europe, and then only incompletely and unevenly. By way of contrast with Egypt, Morocco, despite its strategic position, remained relatively unattractive to potential investors. It had no known natural resources of much importance, poor port facilities, and a reputation for turbulence. As a result, Morocco, already more backward than the other countries of the Middle East at the beginning of the century, lagged still further behind at its close, despite having experienced many far-reaching changes. These changes were most advanced along the coast, but much of the interior remained little affected.

In the Middle East modernization produced important reforms in the bureaucracy and the army. In Morocco no such dramatic progress can be noted, although the work of demolishing the old system made some advances. As in the Middle East, military reforms remained vulnerable to the manipulation of the powers and the criticisms of the tradition-minded elites. Mawlāy al-Ḥasan was relatively successful at dismantling the jaysh military system but was much less so in creating a new army that would outlive him. No coherent bureaucracy was created in Morocco, despite progress in the functional separation of tasks within the makhzan. The traditonal makhzan families continued to dominate government offices at the higher levels of the bureaucracy until after 1900. The forty years of grace which followed the Tetouan War (during which the country did not have to face a major military threat from the West) were thus largely wasted. Morocco entered the twentieth century with only a small group within the elite favorable to reforms and a traditional system which was on the verge of severe testing. The results were not long in becoming known.

3

THE ERA OF THE TRAVELING SALESMEN

Morocco in 1900—The Legacy of Bā Aḥmad

On May 13, 1900, with the death of the grand vizier and regent, Sī Aḥmad ibn Mūsā, Morocco came to the end of an era.[1] The cautious diplomatic policies and conservative domestic stance which had marked the last years of Mawlāy al-Ḥasan no longer seemed appropriate to the new makhzan that took over the reins of government. The antireform viziers who managed to survive the cholera epidemic which carried off the grand vizier were soon swept to one side by a younger makhzan with different attitudes toward the efficacy of internal reforms. With British diplomatic support, Morocco soon embarked upon a long overdue program of administrative reforms and internal improvements that were intended to strengthen the ability of the state to withstand the pressures of French diplomacy. By 1903, however, the optimistic dreams of a renewed Moroccan state had been destroyed by the outbreak of a major rural movement of protest against reforms and by the changed diplomatic circumstances which placed France in an uncontested position of dominance. The present chapter deals with the period of reforms under British backing.

Mawlāy al-Ḥasan's death occurred on June 7, 1894, while he was on campaign in the Tadla region. He had been ill constantly ever since his return to Marrakech from his exhausting previous trip to Tafilalet, and his death amidst hostile tribes posed a grave problem to the royal caravan, which risked being attacked and pillaged if the death became known. It was also perceived as a remarkable opportunity by the chamberlain (Ḥājib), Sī Aḥmad ibn Mūsā, who utilized the situation to bring about the accession of Ḥasan's youngest son, ʿAbd al-ʿAzīz, and arranged for himself to be regent. The incumbent makhzan, notably the Jamaʿi family who were archenemies of the new regent, was ousted, and the family of Ibn Mūsā came to power. The death of the sultan was concealed until the *maḥalla* had reached safety, and the proclamation of the ʿulamā of Rabat was obtained without much difficulty.[2]

The accession of ʿAbd al-ʿAzīz was not viewed with favor in much of Morocco. Many of the ʿulamā resented the irregular manner in which the proclamation had been handled and the fact that they were confronted with a fait accompli, rather than given the opportunity to give their formal assent free from constraint. While they signed the *bayʿa* announcing their adherence to the selection of young ʿAbd al-ʿAzīz, it was only after a great deal of grumbling. There were, moreover, other sons of Ḥasan with a claim to the throne and support among the people, notably Mawlāy Bilgīth and Mawlāy Muḥammad. Mawlāy Bilgīth was the oldest son of the late sultan.[3] He possessed some support among the tribes of the Chaouiạ province, but an attempted revolt on his behalf was quickly suppressed by the new government. Mawlāy Muḥammad, on the other hand, represented a real threat to the plans of Bā Aḥmad, for he had shown himself to be a vigorous leader and a just ruler and had acquired strong support among the tribes and a segment of the ʿulamā. Accordingly, one of Bā Aḥmad's first decisions after ʿAbd al-ʿAzīz had been proclaimed sultan was to place Mawlāy Muḥammad under house arrest in one of the palaces in Meknes. For the remainder of the reign of ʿAbd al-ʿAzīz he stayed there, closely guarded by trusted makhzan servants and prevented from communicating with his many supporters. Mawlāy Muḥammad's appeal was enhanced by the religious reverence with which he was regarded by the superstitious tribesmen, allegedly due to his physical deformity and the fits of madness to which he was subject. Periodic tribal revolts broke out during the years that followed, the tribes declaring support for Mawlāy Muḥammad, but he never managed to escape, and they were all eventually suppressed.[4] The dubious legitimacy of the proclamation of ʿAbd al-ʿAzīz as sultan continued to be productive of unrest during the remainder of his reign.

The internal political situation of Morocco in 1900 was less secure than it appeared on the surface. Three years of almost ceaseless campaigning from 1894 to 1897 had managed to bring the tribal dissidence which followed the interregnum under control, and the court had retired to Marrakech. While the court was in the south, the tribes in the north around Fez had profited from the absence of close supervision to adopt a semiautonomous stance. The jaysh tribes of the north grew increasingly used to enjoying the privileges of their status without having to perform their military duties.[5] In the south, the presence of the court at Marrakech for five years enabled the ambitious chiefs of the Western High Atlas to greatly expand the number of tribes under their domination in return for services rendered the makhzan. It was after the death of Mawlāy al-Ḥasan, in effect, that the fiefs of the great qāid-s attained their fullest development. Chiefs like al-Faqih Madanī al-Glawī gained notoriety by supplying contingents of troops to the makhzan for its expeditions in the Sous valley, and elsewhere.[6] As part of the effort to gain control of the situation in Tafilalet after the fall of Touat in 1900, for example, when the tribes were threatening independent action against French border posts, a thousand-man force had been dispatched under Madanī al-Glawī to prevent actions that would incite French reprisals.[7] In return for similar services the other great qāid-s received vast additions to the number of tribes under their authority, as the Glawa had done. These included concessions of tax-farm privileges over some of the wealthy tribes of the Marrakech plain. Any taxes collected from *sība* tribes could be retained by the great qāid-s. The creation of a number of very powerful semifeudal chiefs directly contradicted Mawlāy al-Ḥasan's policy of dividing tribal governorships among a great many lesser figures. It also made the makhzan heavily dependent on the great qāid-s for the administration of large portions of the south and therefore made it vulnerable to pressure from them.

Because of his great skill at sowing division among the tribes and the great qāid-s, and in using them against one another to attain his ends, Sī Aḥmad ibn Mūsā was able to maintain some semblance of political stability in the empire. Thus although he neglected the tribes of northern Morocco and those of the Algerian frontier region, by 1900 no cracks had yet appeared in the edifice fashioned under Mawlāy al-Ḥasan. His successors continued most of the same internal policies but without the skill of the old grand vizier. The northern and eastern frontier tribes began to assume more autonomous positions without being recalled to order, and the great qāid-s continued to expand their domains virtually unchecked.

One policy of Bā Aḥmad which was continued under his successors and which was eventually to have important repercussions was the gradual weakening of the *zawiya*-s as loci of regional power. Bā Aḥmad had worked consistently to curb the temporal power of religious shrines and the lodges of religious brotherhoods through an attack on their privileges, such as the right to own vast tracts of land and herds, and the right to grant sanctuary to those accused of a crime.[8] The movement against the religious brotherhoods and the saint cult had its origins in the traditions of the dynasty (which naturally sought to increase its power at the expense of regional concentrations of power) and in the influences of ideas of Islamic modernism from the Arab East.[9]

The most important deviation by the new makhzan from the internal political policies of Bā Aḥmad was to be in attitudes of groups within the makhzan toward the adoption of a program of internal improvements and administrative reform. Sī Aḥmad ibn Mūsā had himself been one of the principal opponents of reforms, on the grounds that it was neither desirable nor feasible for Morocco to engage in reforms.[10]

Morocco's international situation was also less brilliant than it seemed in 1900. Bā Aḥmad's general policy was to prevent any one European power from gaining a disproportionate influence. Otherwise, he limited relations to the settling of outstanding grievances. This isolationist policy was not to last. The Moroccan frontier was menaced by French military penetration at two points: to the south, where there was danger of French encroachment from Mauretania, and to the east, where the oases of Touat, Figuig, and Tafilalet presented an inviting opportunity to expansionist-minded French Algerian officials. In both of these areas, the new government sought to maintain the general policy which had been followed under Bā Aḥmad.[11] The shifting diplomatic context, however, worked to undermine these efforts almost before they were begun. Only to the south, where the Moroccan government had supported resistance activities against French expansion, could this policy be said to have been even temporarily crowned with success. There too, French power and influence eventually transformed the situation.

Along the eastern frontier with Algeria, the policy of the grand vizier had proved a failure even before he died. From the late 1880s, French commercial and political circles in Algeria had begun to become interested in further expansion to the south. Several different projects for a trans-Saharan railroad were broached at one time or another. By 1890 French interests were beginning to fasten upon the Touat oasis complex, together with its lateral access route, the Saoura valley, as the specific object of French expansion.[12] This renewed interest in the Sahara was translated in Morocco into the increasingly uneasy attitude of the tribes along the frontier. Even after the death of Sī Muḥammad al-ʿArbī al-Darqāwī in 1892, which removed one of the most vigorous proponents of a jihād from the scene, and the visit of Mawlāy al-Ḥasan to Tafilalet in 1893, tensions were only partly alleviated. In an effort to take the bull by the horns, a makhzan ambassador, Muḥammad ibn Mūsā (brother of the grand vizier) was dispatched to Paris to treat directly with the French government on the matter. While Ibn Mūsā was well received in Paris, he was nonetheless politely informed that, if he wished to discuss Moroccan territorial claims in the Sahara, it was not with the government of the Republic but with French officials in Algeria that he should take up the matter.[13] The rebuff was little calculated to reassure the Moroccan government as to French intentions.

By the end of the century Morocco still lacked assurances that its claim to Touat would be given diplomatic backing by any of the powers. The outbreak of the Boer War in October 1899 temporarily weakened Great Britain's ability to intervene and opened the way for the French offensive which followed. In January 1900 news reached Marrakech that a French military column had marched into Touat and that the entire oasis was in their hands. Further reports brought word of French troop movements elsewhere along the frontier which threatened the oasis of Igli, at the junction of the Saoura and Guir valleys.[14] The tribes between Figuig and Tafilalet urged prompt military retaliation. Despite strong sentiment within the makhzan for such a response, Bā Aḥmad, who knew only too well the real weakness of the Moroccan state, decided to stay within the regular diplomatic channels and solicit international diplomatic support. The qaḍī of Marrakech, Sī al-ʿArbī al-Manī, was sent to Tangier as a special envoy to deliver the protest of the Moroccan government to the powers. He was also to sound them out on their response to a Moroccan initiative to guarantee the integrity of the sharifian empire. Due to lack of response, the idea of an international conference died stillborn, but the idea remained active in government circles.[15]

The weak response of the makhzan to the loss of Moroccan territory excited the anger and contempt of various groups of Moroccans. The Touat crisis thereby contributed to the undermining of the legitimacy of the government in the eyes of many Moroccans. The ʿulamā of Fez were among the most upset by the inability of the government to respond vigorously to the loss of part of the Moroccan *Dār al-Islām* to a Christian nation. The anonymous author of the *Ḥalāl al-Bahīya* no doubt expressed the attitude of most of the ʿulamā of Fez. A sultan worthy of the name, he scornfully remarks, would have been ashamed to appeal to the Christian powers of Europe for assistance when a vigorous military campaign was the only honorable course of action. There was thus a certain justice in the fate of the sharifian envoy, Sī al-ʿArbī al-Manī, who suffered a curious "accidental" death—soon after the completion of his mission.[16] Under the circumstances it is probable that he was murdered by the proponents of a more unyielding response to French aggression, perhaps as a warning to other would-be collaborators.

Predictably, the most vigorous response to the loss of Touat came from the tribes of the southeast, who saw themselves directly menaced by the French advance down the Zousfana valley toward Igli. The Moroccan viceroy in Tafilalet, Mawlāy Rashīd, refrained from taking an exposed position on the issue. Seeing themselves thus unsupported, the tribes of the region began to plan an offensive against the French at Igli.[17] Volunteers were sent from as far away as the Middle Atlas tribes of Ait Ndhir, Ait Yusi, and Ait Njild to help defend Moroccan territory, and the price of gunpowder on the market at Fez rose sharply in response to the crisis.[18] The issue of the defense of the frontier thereafter became one of the principal targets of the opponents of reforms within the makhzan. The ʿulamā of the principal cities and makhzan partisans of a firmer attitude began to press for a military campaign to preserve the "Abode of Islam" from Christian defilement. Other groups within the makhzan saw the lesson of the loss of Touat as the necessity of reforming and strengthening the state. The battle within the Moroccan elite between the partisans of jihād (composed mainly of the rural notables and a part of the ʿulamā) and those who favored an extensive program of reforms to strengthen the state (chiefly the makhzan officials and the remainder of the ʿulamā) was joined from this point onward.[19]

To the south, following the lead taken under Mawlāy al-Ḥasan, Bā Aḥmad had pursued a somewhat more militant policy by supporting the resistance movements in Mauretania, which were directed by Shaykh Mā al-ʿAynayn ibn Muḥammad Fāḍil and his numerous family. Mā al-ʿAynayn had been received at the court of Mawlāy al-Ḥasan, and possessed a considerable reputation for piety and religious learning in Morocco. Bā Aḥmad had gone beyond this religious sympathy to materially assist Mā al-ʿAynayn and the resistance activities in the Seguia el Hamra (Saqiya al-Ḥamrā) and southern Morocco.[20] Under the new policy, the smuggling of arms to the tribes in the extreme south received the blessing of the makhzan. After the death of Bā Aḥmad, this alliance was further reinforced. Mā al-ʿAynayn made several visits to the court.[21] Lodges of the ʿAynaynīya were opened at Marrakech and Fez and gained many members of the makhzan as adepts. In 1906 an uncle of the sultan, Mawlāy Idrīs, was sent as the makhzan representative to the Wadi Dra region, jihād was proclaimed against the French in Mauretania, and supplies of arms to the tribes in the extreme south were regularized.[22] One of the claims to legitimacy which ʿAbd al-ʿAzīz retained to the end of his reign was his support of resistance in the south. Close relations between the ʿAlawī dynasty and the family of Mā al-ʿAynayn persisted until 1912.

The Sultan and the Makhzan

It has often been claimed that the rapid deterioration of the Moroccan government after 1900 was due primarily to the incompetence of the young sultan, Mawlāy ʿAbd al-ʿAzīz. The prevailing view portrays ʿAbd al-ʿAzīz as an inexperienced and gullible youth who was systematically victimized by unscrupulous European speculators and confidence men, and through them induced to squander the Moroccan treasury on an endless variety of European gadgets, each more useless than the last.[23] That ʿAbd al-ʿAzīz had weaknesses and that he spent more freely than he ought is not open to question. But, as should become clear from the pages that follow, this view is considerably oversimplified. The broader currents of the age—imperialism, European commercial expansion, the rivalry of the powers, and the influence of reformist ideas in Morocco—had more to do with the collapse of the Moroccan state after 1900 than has generally been acknowledged.

When ʿAbd al-ʿAzīz came into his majority in 1900 upon the death of the regent, he was only nineteen years old and had spent most of his young life within the confines of the royal harem.[24] His mother was Lālla Raqīya, a beautiful and intelligent Circassian slave woman who had been the favorite wife of Mawlāy al-Ḥasan during the last years of his life. She had originally joined forces with Bā Aḥmad to insure the proclamation of her son and continued to have considerable influence over his decisions until her own death in 1902.[25] The education of ʿAbd al-ʿAzīz had been supervised by the grand vizier and had emphasized religious subjects rather than the art of command and the practice of government affairs. Among his teachers was al-Faqih Mufaḍḍal al-Sūsī, a reform-minded religious scholar from Marrakech who was later to provide legal rulings on the legality of the proposed reforms.[26] As a child ʿAbd al-ʿAzīz was encouraged to take up painting and other European pursuits. It was allegedly a toy railroad which provided the inspiration for introducing modern reforms to his country.[27] One aspect of his education which was to have important consequences in the years after the death of Bā Aḥmad was his isolation from his people. He never did acquire a realistic sense of what behavior was appropriate for the sultan to display on state occasions and thus was constantly to scandalize his subjects at inopportune times.

Europeans who came in contact with ʿAbd al-ʿAzīz were much impressed by his desire to be a good ruler. His intelligence (a characteristic of the dynasty) was equally remarked. As he was to demonstrate later on, he could be firm, and he did not lack political ability. His chief handicap initially was his inexperience, coupled with a lack of taste for the ceremonial and religious functions of his position and his inability to focus his attention on the affairs of state for very long.[28] But over the course of his short personal rule he matured a great deal and after 1903 no longer made the mistakes he had made in his first years. He acquired the habit of referring all decisions of state to an informal panel of advisors and thereby avoided further errors.[29] Unfortunately, after 1903 Morocco no longer possessed much diplomatic or economic room for maneuver.

The makhzan that was appointed by ʿAbd al-ʿAzīz after the death of Sī Aḥmad ibn Mūsā and his two brothers, who were also viziers, was in many respects a new one. In the new makhzan the balance was tipped in favor of those who favored a program of reforms as the best means of preserving Moroccan independence. Initially a cousin of Bā Aḥmad, al-Ḥājj Mukhtar ibn ʿAbdallāh was appointed grand vizier in an effort to retain continuity, but he was soon ousted and replaced by Muḥammad al-Mufaḍḍal ibn Muḥammad Gharnīṭ (Fr. Gharnit), an elderly official of Andalusian extraction. The vizier al-Baḥr (or minister of foreign affairs), Sī ʿAbd al-Karīm ibn Sulaymān, a proponent of reforms, and the Amīn al-Umanā (minister of finance), Sī ʿAbd al-Salām Tāzī, an opponent, were both retained in the new makhzan. The major figure in the government, however, was the royal favorite, the ʿAllāf al-Kabīr (roughly, minister of war) Sī al-Mahdī ibn al-ʿArabī al-Munabbhī (Fr. Mehdi el Menebhi), a strong supporter of the need to reform and strengthen the administration. Al-Munabbhī possessed family connections with al-Glawī and showed an ability to forge alliances with powerful patrons throughout his career. He had a strong personality and a good sense of humor; moreover, he was young and vigorous. This combination of qualities soon enabled him to win the confidence of ʿAbd al-ʿAzīz. It was through his intervention that Gharnīṭ was appointed and also through him that the sultan was introduced to Harry Maclean.[30] It was during the brief period of his ascendancy (1900–1903), although only partially through his influence, that

Morocco embarked on an ill-fated program of bureaucratic reform and internal improvements.

The times were not especially favorable to the implementation of a broad series of internal reforms. In the first place, the status quo which had prevailed among the powers for almost twenty years with regard to the Mediterranean was beginning to show signs of breaking down.[31] Although Great Britain was still tied down in South Africa in a very costly and exasperating war, she still sought, through her representative at Tangier, Arthur Nicolson, to gain predominance in Morocco by encouraging reforms under British aegis. The presence of two influential British citizens at court—Egbert Verdon, a medical doctor, and "Qaid" Harry Maclean, a British military instructor of the makhzan army—provided Nicolson with important privileged access to the sultan and his officials.[32] France, the other major contender, was emerging from the prolonged and bitter conflict over the Dreyfus affair. Its vocal colonial lobby in parliament was anxious to add to the prestige of the government by a dramatic colonial acquisition. Morocco, the chief prize sought after by the colonial interests in the Chamber of Deputies (especially by Algerian military and commercial interests) could admirably perform this function. The French also possessed influential representatives at the court in Marrakech. These were Dr. Ferdinand Linarès, who had been for many years in the service of Mawlāy al-Ḥasan, and Dr. Felix Weisgerber, who had first entered the service of the makhzan in December 1897, when he had been called to treat the ailing grand vizier.[33] There was in addition a French military mission which had little influence. Until 1901 it was headed by Major Burckhardt, thereafter by Lieutenant Colonel de Saint-Julien.[34] The renewed interest in Morocco by the two powers best placed to achieve predominance promised a further deterioration of Morocco's diplomatic position. Still, as long as Moroccan diplomats proved adept at playing upon the conflicts of interest among the powers, Morocco might have avoided undergoing the fate of Egypt, Tunisia, and most of the rest of Africa. But this depended on England and France remaining unable to resolve their differences. In 1900, this seemed like a good bet. Two years later, to those adept at reading the changes in the diplomatic winds, it was no longer so certain.

Reforms, 1901–1903

The first crack in the fragile edifice so carefully maintained by Bā Aḥmad was not long in appearing. In March 1901 the Moroccan government decided to adopt a program of reforms for its provincial fiscal and administrative systems and to request British assistance in the task. The circumstances surrounding the decision remain obscure. Despite French allegations to the contrary, it is likely that the reform impulse originated within the makhzan and that British involvement was requested only later. It is known that there were numerous strong proponents of reforms within the makhzan. They were alarmed by growing Moroccan weaknesses and convinced that a *tanzimat*-style reform program was the only way of avoiding a European takeover. The support of Sir Arthur Nicolson and "Qaid" Maclean was soon gained, and through their good offices British support was requested.[35] Since major financial commitments were necessary to insure the success of the reform program and London was reluctant to bear the risk alone, the Moroccans were counseled to first resolve their outstanding diplomatic disputes and to obtain French support.

Accordingly, during June and July 1901, two Moroccan diplomatic missions were dispatched to Europe. The first, headed by the royal favorite al-Munabbhī, went to London and Berlin to more directly test the financial waters. In neither place was the reception enthusiastic. Berlin was reluctant, although German arms manufacturers did seize the opportunity to make some sales.[36] The British were occupied with the Boer War and events in the Far East, and turned a deaf ear.[37] The other mission, under foreign minister Ibn Sulaymān, was sent to Paris and Berlin. In Paris, the Ibn Sulaymān delegation entered into negotiations to resolve the difficult Algerian-Moroccan frontier question, and to head off further flare-ups of violence. On July 20, an accord was concluded which at least temporarily resolved the situation.[38] The French government refrained from committing itself on the Moroccan reform program, however. After a ceremonial visit to St. Petersburg, the Ibn Sulaymān mission returned to Morocco.

During the two months that al-Munabbhī was abroad, the antireform elements at court led by Muḥammad Gharnīṭ convinced the sultan that he should abandon his favorite and, with him, the reform program. Only by some very clever maneuvering was al-Munabbhī able to restore himself to favor and rekindle the ardor of the sultan for reform. A month after his return a council to consider the entire question of reform was established. The council was composed of Sī Mufaḍḍal Gharnīṭ, al-Munabbhī, Ibn Sulaymān, Qaid Maclean, two other viziers, and two notables who had lived for a number of years in Egypt and knew something of the reforms there.[39] This group soon produced a comprehensive plan of reforms which received the backing of the sultan. In order to discern the feasibility of the project, it was decided that it should first be given a pilot application in the Marrakech area, and several tribes, including the Rehamna, were selected for the purpose.[40]

The reforms consisted of two separate but interrelated parts. The first was an overhauling of the Moroccan administration, especially the rural administration. By the terms of the reform, umanā were to be appointed to serve alongside the rural qāid-s and prevent abuses in the collection of local taxes. Both the umanā and the qāid-s were to receive salaries large enough to obviate the kind of tax-gouging and corruption which had been one of the hallmarks of the traditional system.[41] The umanā were to register the assessment and collection of all taxes and were empowered to recommend the censure of rapacious qāid-s. The tribal governors, for their part, were forbidden from raising exceptional taxes or other extraordinary levies and were not to accord exemptions to anyone, including the traditionally privileged groups like sharifs, protégés of European commercial firms, jaysh tribes, and certain religious brotherhoods.[42] The scheme represented a renewal and rationalization of reforms proposed earlier under Mawlāy al-Ḥasan but never systematically pursued.

Linked to the administrative reform was a second major innovation, the substitution of a new universal tax on agriculture and livestock, the *tartīb,* for the old Koranic taxes. This too had its antecedents in the reign of Ḥasan I in the so-called tertib (Fr.) of Article 13 of the Madrid Convention of 1880. The new tartīb differed from its predecessor in that it made a clean break with the old Koranic taxes.[43] The traditional levies, *ushr* and *zakāh,* were abolished. The new unique impost provided that a certain percentage of each taxpayer's income from agriculture or livestock would be due as tax. The umanā would register the number of animals a man owned and the size of his harvest, and would assess taxes in proportion. The rate of taxation was set relatively low to encourage increased compliance. The reformers expected that, because all tax exemptions had been done away with, the total amount of tax revenue collected by the treasury would actually increase, even though less tax was being exacted from the peasants. Rural unrest was expected to decrease since the major cause of rural rebellions, tax-gouging, would be eliminated.

Since the tartīb was to involve the abolition of all tax exemptions, including those of the Moroccan protégés of European powers, the powers were naturally interested in the manner of its application. France in particular was anxious about how its protégés and interests would be affected by the new measures. The tertib of the Madrid Convention had provided for the ratification by the powers of reform measures which touched their interests closely. Because it suspected that the 1901 tartīb was directed against the sharifs of Wazzan, who were French protégés, France imposed a temporary veto on the reform project until adequate guarantees could be worked out.[44]

Since the makhzan had already announced the reforms, together with the abolition of the old taxes, the delay in obtaining French ratification meant that many districts were able to escape all taxation. Some tribes, particularly those of the Chaouia province, paid virtually no taxes until 1903, when formal ratification was finally secured.[45] These tribes were able to accumulate wealth at a time when the government was starved for revenue and was taking on new obligations to finance the ambitious program of reforms and internal improvements. As if all of this were not enough, by eliminating the traditional exemptions, the reformers succeeded at one stroke in alienating the major special interests. The jaysh tribes, the religious brotherhoods, government officials, sharifs, and protégés all possessed considerable power and wealth, and all had been traditionally tax-exempt. Threatened with the loss of their privileges, they promptly began to agitate under the banner of religious orthodoxy against the "Christian" reforms of the sultan. Taxes laid down by the Koran, they argued, could not be tampered with by anyone, including the sultan. Some hastened to become protégés to preserve their fortunes, while others began to dabble in political intrigue against the regime.[46]

The reforms were first instituted in the Marrakech region, then after the court moved to Rabat in December they were extended to the Chaouia. While the court was at Rabat, prominent merchants and former customs officials were summoned from all of the northern ports to give advice on other reforms. A vast new program of internal improvements was the result. These included the modernization of port facilities and the construction of roads, bridges, and a telegraph system. Bids were solicited from interested European firms. Also at this time provincial governors were called to Rabat and made to swear an oath on the Koran that they would neither give nor receive gifts and that they would refrain from extorting "supplementary taxes" from those under them.[47] To reduce the temptations for graft, it was announced that all government officials would receive a salary. In the case of those of vizierial rank, this was the equivalent of four pounds sterling per day.[48]

By not seeking first to win the support of the powers, the reformers had made a serious mistake. This they had further compounded by not first explaining the reforms to the tribes and soliciting a recommendation from the ʿulamā. As a result, the government was deprived of a considerable portion of its income during a period when its expenses were rapidly increasing, making bankruptcy inevitable. If the reform measures had been successfully carried out, they would have amounted to a radical social revolution, leading to the destruction of privileged groups and semifeudal powers, the curtailing of much of the influence of the religious elite, and the transformation of the system of administration from an officially sanctioned rapacity to a responsible bureaucracy based on Western standards of efficiency and honesty. The efforts of the would-be reformers resemble in their intention and their failure those of the similarly minded financial officials in eighteenth-century France, like d'Arnouville and Turgot. The vingtième, like the tartīb, was to be a universal tax on agricultural revenue, with no exemptions permitted. It ran afoul of feudal interests, the lack of trained officials, and royal impatience when quick results were not forthcoming. But eighteenth-century France did not have the added worry of needing to have the reform proposals ratified by its neighbors.[49] If the reforms failed in Morocco, therefore, we should not be surprised. The odds against success, in the changed international circumstances after 1900, made it quite unlikely that the powers would approve of a regenerated Moroccan state. The great naiveté of the reformers, more than anything else, adds a ring of credibility to the French accusation that British machinations lay at the origins of the reform scheme. A panicky, last-ditch attempt to strengthen the state, the reforms of 1901 ended up by accomplishing the opposite.

The Era of the Traveling Salesmen: Economics

The rapidity of the collapse of the Moroccan economy after 1900 had no parallel in the Middle East, although the same general processes can be observed in motion. In four short years Morocco changed from a country with a substantial treasury balance to one owing almost 100 million francs and saddled with an international debt commission. The same phenomenon in Egypt took place over many years. The sudden opening of the economy attracted a great influx of legitimate businessmen but also many unscrupulous types.

In Egypt, under the Khedive Ismail, this period was known as "Klondike on the Nile."[50] In Morocco, it was called the era of the traveling salesmen. In the rush to modernize the country, there was much conspicuous wastage, with enormous profits for well-placed European middlemen. Already under severe pressure as a result of the botched reform program, the old system collapsed with remarkable rapidity. Economics therefore lies at the base of our explanation of this period of remarkable change.

By 1900, the Moroccan economy was already in the process of transformation. Thereafter, however, the pace of change was to accelerate greatly. The crisis had a number of dimensions. One was an enormous balance-of-trade problem. Whereas between 1878 and 1900 the trade deficit had averaged 4 million francs a year, from 1902 to 1909 it averaged over 14 million francs annually.[51] At the death of Bā Aḥmad the treasury contained 60 million Hasani pesetas.[52] Two years later came the first foreign loans, and two more years brought the debt commission. It is not known what proportion of Moroccan imports during this period was due to public expenditures. The share of private consumption undoubtedly increased, as a result of the increased disposable income given to many of the rural population by the temporary tax holiday. But it seems safe to say that most of the deficit was generated by government expenses. As nearly as can be estimated, court expenses made up only about 10 percent of total public expenditures. The bulk of the increase was thus the result of the reform program.[53]

Most explanations of the collapse of the Moroccan economy focus upon the role of the sultan. ʿAbd al-ʿAzīz had lived a relatively sheltered life before 1900 and was thus quite unprepared for the pressures which he would have to confront. He was also uncommonly curious about European technology and inventions. European salesmen were able to play upon this weakness. Soon objects both strange and curious filled the Marrakech palace, ranging from an authentic London taxi to a solid gold camera.[54] Starting in 1901, ʿAbd al-ʿAzīz began to surround himself with Europeans capable of keeping him amused with new games and inventions. At the outset, this entourage consisted of Englishmen introduced by Maclean. Later, after the court moved north, businessmen of all nationalities became common.

The enthusiasms of the sultan, expensive though they undoubtedly were, are insufficient to explain the very rapid draining of the royal treasury. It was the substantial sums necessary to finance the program of internal improvements which ultimately were more significant sources of difficulty. As long as makhzan purchases were confined to expenses for the court, the major European banking and commercial interests would have little to do with Morocco. But when bids began to be accepted in 1902 on port construction works, they immediately pushed the "traveling salesmen" aside and began to move in. Closely associated with them in this activity were their informal Moroccan associates, often officials or retainers of the court. Many of the viziers who had been most favorably disposed toward reforms were prominent in their efforts on behalf of different European commercial houses. Al-Munabbhī, as noted above, was closely identified with German and especially British interests. He profited handsomely from commissions and bribes on the makhzan purchase of surplus British and German arms.[55] Ibn Sulaymān was reputed to be pro-French during this early period. He too collected substantial *pots de vin* for favoring French business concerns with makhzan contracts. This of course was in addition to the bribes he received while in Paris to negotiate the border accord in 1902.[56] The list could be extended, but the essential point is the significant role which Moroccan officials played in the elaboration of the schemes of the financiers and the large profits which they made from this service. As the French colonial offensive gathered momentum after 1903, the partisans of reform found themselves seriously compromised in the eyes of the ʿulamā for their corrupt dealings and accused of having paved the way for a French protectorate.

Among the most successful firms to have dealings with the makhzan during this period was the French concern of Gautsch, a subsidiary of Schneider and Company, which later became part of the Compagnie marocaine. Gautsch possessed solid connections at court through the friendship of Fabarez, a son-in-law of Gautsch, with al-Munabbhī's principal secretary, al-Jāʾī. Fabarez was aided by his compatriot Gabriel Veyre, the court photographer, who had an excellent relationship with ʿAbd al-ʿAzīz due to the latter's interest in photography.[57] Qaid Maclean of course served as the chief representative for the major British concerns. When the Moroccan government was about to take out its first loan in 1902, Maclean made a special trip to London to try and prevent the loan from going to a French banking consortium. Despite this effort, the trip was to no avail and the loan went to the French.[58] The expenses of the makhzan during the 1902–1903 period were extraordinary: total imports came to 62 million frances.[59] In February, 1903 Gautsch estimated that it alone had sold 20 million francs worth of goods, against 5 or 6 million francs for Maclean and the British. Gautsch realized an average profit of 25 percent on these transactions.[60] The sales of the French firm of Brunschvig and Company, the major rival of Gautsch in Morocco, although unknown, were certainly substantial.

By 1902 Morocco had built up such debts that a foreign loan became necessary. After considerable negotiation the makhzan and the Banque de Paris et des Pays-Bas signed an agreement for 7.5 million frances at 6 percent interest on December 31, 1901.[61] This first loan was regarded by the French banks and the Quai d'Orsay as the opening wedge of a long-term process which would eventually place the Moroccan treasury completely in the hands of French finance. For this reason the terms on this loan were relatively easy, and the makhzan was not obliged to provide substantial security. In accordance with prior agreements, in April and May additional loans were contracted, this time with British and Spanish private banks, both in the same amount as the first loan, on substantially the same terms. With this, Morocco discovered, as the Ottoman empire, Egypt, and the other countries of the Middle East had before, the very dangerous illusions of living on credit. Within two years the makhzan found itself in financial difficulties of even greater magnitude. While Morocco was losing its economic room to maneuver as a result of its fiscal difficulties, a particularly severe monetary crisis was affecting the lives of most Moroccans. Essentially the monetary difficulties which Morocco faced after 1900 were similar to those which it had encountered earlier. The same mechanisms which had operated to the detriment of the dirham during the nineteenth century and the same basic errors in monetary policy by the makhzan continued to operate.[62] The post-1900 situation was complicated by ʿAbd al-ʿAzīz's introduction of a new silver coin, the Azizi douro or "sufficient dirham" (*dirham rājib*), intended to replace the older Hassani dirham. The Azizi was a twenty-five-gram dirham rather than the traditional twenty-nine-gram one, and was intended to thwart speculators who had earlier exploited the difference with the twenty-five-gram Spanish douro.[63] Excessive minting of the Azizi (300,000 kilograms of silver in 1902 alone) largely undermined many of the expected benefits. Since the Azizi was of higher silver content than the debased Spanish douro, moreover, there was still ample attraction for speculators. The nontraditional form and weight of the Azizi excited the opposition of many of the ʿulamā, and pious Muslims refused to use it except at a discount of 12 percent and then only after repeated government injunctions to accept it.[64] The overminting of bronze coin (500,000 kilograms in 1902), which set off speculation against the older bronzes, further upset the monetary situation.[65] At Fez in 1896 one pound sterling was worth thirty Hassani pesetas, while ten years later the exchange rate had fallen to forty Hassani pesetas, after allowing for changes in the pound.[66] Thus the Moroccan currency suffered an average of a 25 percent depreciation between 1896 and 1906. Since Fez was fairly isolated from the coast, and since by 1906 some of the stabilizing measures taken by the state bank had begun to take effect, there is reason to believe that the figures just quoted for Fez seriously understate the effects of the crisis, even for the cities of the interior. On the coast, due to the European presence in the ports, the exchange rate must have undergone more radical transformations, especially during the crisis years of 1900–1905.

Parallel to the general monetary crisis of these years was a second, closely related, and no less severe inflationary crisis. Between 1896 and 1906 the average increase in the prices of a list of fifty common consumer items prepared by J. M. Macleod, British vice-counsel at Fez, was over 300 percent, after deducting the depreciation in the Moroccan currency.[67] This by no means provides a full picture of the rate of inflation, for it discounts seasonal and regional variations (often extreme in a country like Morocco where internal communications were problematical) and averages out the increase over a decade, when it is known that some years were worse than others. From 1900 onwards, indeed, Morocco had suffered an abnormally bad series of agricultural years. There were locally poor harvests in 1901–1902, and a more severe and generalized famine during 1904–1905 that affected the entire country.[68] On the eve of the First Moroccan Crisis, the price of grain stood at five times its normal rate. In general, the cities of the interior were harder hit than the ports because of the transportation factor.

The impact of this devastating economic crisis was disproportionately heavy on those who could least afford it: artisans, day laborers, petty makhzan employees, and those living on fixed incomes (on, for example, revenues from pious foundations). Their misery was increased by wealthy merchants and officials who took advantage of food shortages to hoard grain and manipulate prices in the marketplace.[69] The wealthy also sought to preserve their riches and increase their local competitive advantage by becoming protégés of European firms. In a period of economic downturn this was to create powerful resentments among the people. There was an upsurge of banditry along the major roads. Merchants tended to compensate for the increased risks by raising prices, thereby further exacerbating the situation.[70] The longer the crisis continued, the more these various factors fed upon one another. What had begun as primarily an economic crisis had become by 1905 a general crisis of Moroccan society.

The Era of the Traveling Salesmen: Politics

In order to understand the wave of anger and disgust which swept over the Moroccan people after 1901 as a result of the personal conduct of ʿAbd al-ʿAzīz, it is important to have a clear picture of the central position of the sultan in the Moroccan state. The sultan was the chief possessor of *baraka* and paramount sharif, as well as the chief patron and source of benefits. There was a strong religious component to this position, along with its political aspects. Since the prosperity of the realm was commonly held to depend on the baraka of the sultan, his outward behavior was a sign of his continued possession of it. Unusual public actions on his part could (and frequently did) give rise to rumors that the grace had left him. In a country where public gestures received immediate and widespread comment, he had always to be on the alert, lest an unguarded remark give rise to damaging rumors. In the continual tug-of-war to maintain and expand the number of tribes paying taxes to the treasury, the illusion of strength counted almost as much as strength itself. The behavior of Mawlāy ʿAbd al-ʿAzīz, insofar as it did not correspond to the customary image of how a sultan should act, thus became a source of scandal and helped to weaken the political authority of his government. Although important in bringing on the crisis of 1902–1903, it was by no means the principal cause for the widespread rural unrest which came over Morocco after 1901, however.

The loss of the oasis of Touat to France in 1900 generated a considerable distrust among the tribes of the frontier that ʿAbd al-ʿAzīz was willing to defend them—a distrust which was shared by some of the urban elite as well. It certainly was not to the young sultan's advantage that his qualifications should be critically commented upon so shortly after coming into his majority. This was especially true in light of the fact that there was already an undercurrent of unrest and resentment against him among the tribes who felt that Mawlāy Muḥammad had been cheated out of the throne by the guile of Sī Aḥmad ibn Mūsā.

Accordingly the highly idiosyncratic conduct which the sultan began to exhibit in 1901, while the court was still at Marrakech, was little calculated to assuage the currents of distrust and incipient opposition which were beginning to manifest themselves. Under the influence of Qaid Maclean and al-Munabbhī, ʿAbd al-ʿAzīz was introduced to a variety of European games, pastimes, and curiosities. Being young and impressionable, he was soon caught up in their pursuit. Tales soon began to spread beyond the walls of the palace of the sultan riding a bicycle, eating with Europeans, being photographed in European costume, and playing foolish and demeaning games rather than attending to affairs of state.[71] The number of persons who witnessed such antics were few, confined chiefly to makhzan employees while the court was at Marrakech. But public occasions, like the mammoth fireworks display at the Jemaa el-Fna (the central square in Marrakech), did much to spread the word that the sultan had been bewitched (*majnūn*), or had gone mad (*mahbūl*).[72]

In December 1901 the court left Marrakech for Fez, urged, it is asserted, by the conservative members of the makhzan who hoped to counterbalance the dangerous influences of the reformers and the British with those of the powerful ʿulamā of the city of Fez.[73] On the way, the court stopped for several months at Rabat, where ʿAbd al-ʿAzīz successively received in audience the ministers of Great Britain, France, and Germany. In receiving the foreign missions, the traditional ceremonial ritual was abandoned that required the visiting minister to prostrate himself and then to remain standing during the interview while the sultan was seated. The change was immediately and unfavorably remarked by many of his subjects.[74] The oath which the qāid-s were required to swear on the Koran when called into Rabat was also an innovation. It too provoked unfavorable comment.[75]

At first there was little change in ʿAbd al-ʿAziz's conduct after the court reached Fez. A large group of European adventurers, speculators, and commercial agents followed the court to Fez, and the sultan continued to frequent their company, to spend great sums on foolish entertainments, and to affront venerable Moroccan beliefs about the sacredness of the person of the sultan. This time, however, he was under the surveillance of the religious scholars of Fez, so the impact of his actions was greatly magnified. ʿAbd al-ʿAzīz was not entirely oblivious to the vulnerability of the reform program to the attacks of the ʿulamā, and he therefore sought to allay the suspicions of the people by having *fatawā*-s, or legal opinions, issued in support of the reforms. In Marrakech his personal religious advisor, al-Faqih Mufaḍḍal al-Sūsī, issued these opinions until his death in July 1902. After the court reached Fez, the qāḍī of

Fez al-Jadīd, Sīdī Muḥammad al-ʿIraqī (who was a friend of al-Munabbhī) issued justificatory fatwā-s favoring the tartīb.[76] But these measures do not appear to have had any appreciable effect in counteracting the protests which the reforms stirred up in Fez. The scandalous public behavior of ʿAbd al-ʿAzīz, moreover, added fuel to the flames of disaffection and helped discredit the sultan's good intentions. When, for example, ʿAbd al-ʿAzīz became negligent in performing his religious duties and showed up several hours late for the ʿId al-Kabīr ceremonies, his behavior became a source of grave scandal to all.[77] This behavior, taken in conjunction with the anger in some circles over his handling of the border problems and the affront to customary interest groups by the reforms, caused increasing numbers of both urban and rural elites to question seriously ʿAbd al-ʿAzīz's fitness to be sultan.

It is to be doubted, however, whether it was the rumors about the behavior of the sultan, distorted though they undoubtedly were, which provoked the opposition of the tribes around Fez and led to the collapse of rural security. Much more significant in alienating them was the attempt to implement the tartīb and to begin a telegraph line between Meknes and Fez as the first step toward a railroad to the coast. This incited the Ait Ndhir and Gerrouan, Berber transhumant tribes whose land the telegraph was to cross, to begin raiding along the Fez to Meknes road. Several rural markets in the district were plundered, and Meknes itself was attacked by the tribes in the ensuing disorders. The attempt to implement the new tax reform induced the tribes north of Fez to come together in ad-hoc alliances to resist the imposition of the tax.[78] Even more significant was the opposition of the sharifs of Wazzan, whose political and religious influence in the strategic Jabala region and in the north generally rivalled the sultan's own. By abolishing their traditional tax exemptions, the tartīb threatened their considerable wealth. In addition, the sharifs of Wazzan were French protégés, and the whole affair threatened to have unhappy international repercussions. In the meantime, the French delayed ratifying the tartīb until the status of their protégés was cleared up. Long and complicated negotiations between the makhzan and the Wazzānī sharifs, which were moderated by Walter B. Harris, a prominent Englishman resident in Morocco, eventually ended in an agreement. By its terms, the makhzan would give the house of Wazzan an annual gift equivalent to the tax receipts which it received from them.[79] The reforms were thereby eviscerated in the north before they were ever applied. A tense political atmosphere was generated in the region around Fez which a chance incident could easily turn into a danger to the throne.

The precipitating event—the sultan's mishandling of the Cooper affair—took place in October 1902. David J. Cooper was a British missionary who was killed at Fez while there on a visit. Understanding no Arabic and knowing nothing of the customs of the city, he blundered down a street which took him past the sanctuary of Mawlāy Idrīs, the founder of Fez, whose shrine was one of the most revered in Moroccan Islam. There he encountered a tribesman, who, enraged by the presence of a Christian so near the holy shrine, assaulted and killed him. The murderer then took refuge, in time-honored Moroccan custom, in the shrine and refused to turn himself in. In view of the great number of Europeans at the court, the affair took on the aspects of a test case. After much argument, the tribesman was finally convinced to come out and explain himself before ʿAbd al-ʿAzīz, but he did so only on condition that he be accompanied by the *muqaddam*-s of the shrine, and that he retain the protection of the saint. The sultan heard the man's case, consulted with his *majlis,* or informal council of advisors, and with Walter Harris, and decided that as an example to all, the man should be executed. The sentence was immediately carried out in the presence of the sharifs and muqaddam-s of the shrine, Harris, and Hastings, a representative of the British vice consul.[80]

This incident immediately became a cause of much vociferous and hostile criticism at Fez and drove into opposition most of the ʿulamā who had any connection with Mawlāy Idrīs. Because the murderer had been under the protection of the shrine and its custodians at the time of his apprehension, the sultan's action was taken as a direct challenge to the right to give sanctuary and as a test of the power of the ʿulamā. The *haram*, or sacred zone around the tomb of the holiest saint of Fez, if not of all Morocco, had been desecrated by a Christian. The intruder had, then, rightfully been slain. What was worse, the sultan had flagrantly disregarded the fact that the killer was under the protection of Mawlāy Idrīs, and had him executed. It is difficult to imagine a sacrilege which could have produced a greater effect upon the Moroccan mind or been a more direct challenge to traditional religious vested interests. The news of the event spread rapidly to the tribes, fanned vigorously by the efforts of the enraged custodians of the shrine. It produced an immediate explosion. All of the accumulated resentment and frustration over the reforms, the weak temporizing on the frontier issue, and the unconventional behavior of the sultan burst to the surface.

Some weeks earlier, a pretender to the throne claiming to be Mawlāy Muḥammad had appeared among the tribe of Ghiata near Taza and openly proclaimed the *jihād* against ʿAbd al-ʿAzīz. In the wake of the Cooper affair, his cause attracted much increased support.

The Revolt of Abū Ḥimāra and the End of Reforms, 1903–1904

The protest movement of Abū Ḥimāra (colloq. Bū Ḥmara, literally, "the man with the she-ass"), as the pretender was known to his enemies, needs to be viewed within the context of the long-smouldering spirit of revolt among the tribes near Taza. These tribes, whose principal wealth was in the cattle and horses that they raised, were seriously affected by an 1898 makhzan ruling which had the effect of banning the export of cattle to Algeria, one of their chief markets.[81] During the seven years the court was in residence at Marrakech they had adopted a semiindependent stance. They had received the rumors of the new "Christian" ways of the sultan with alarm and had come to share in the opinion held by some that the reforms were but a prelude to a British protectorate. Abū Ḥimāra therefore found a responsive audience among the Ghiata in particular. The breaking of the *ʿar* of the tomb of Mawlāy Idrīs merely gave increased appeal to their revolt, and soon led to a major crisis for the regime. In another time, the appearance of a minor pretender intent on ousting the incumbent sultan would have received little attention from Europe. In the circumstances of 1902 it attracted the attention and apprehension of European diplomats and was the immediate signal of the failure of the British-sponsored reforms.

In origin the pretender, or el-Rogui (Ar. al-Rūkī) as he was sometimes known, was a former minor makhzan secretary and an ex-*ṭālib al-muhandis* (student engineer) who had been jailed in 1894 by Bā Aḥmad for forgery. His real name was Jilālī ibn Idrīs al-Zarhūnī al-Yūsufī, and he was from the Awlad Yūsuf, an Arab clan settled in Jabal Zerhoun.[82] He was released from prison in 1901 after the death of Bā Aḥmad and spent the next year or two traveling in Algeria and Tunisia. He became a good mimic and an amateur magician and thaumaturge, so that when he returned to Morocco in mid-1902 he had little difficulty in convincing the superstitious Ghiata tribesmen that he was Mawlāy Muḥammad, the elder brother of ʿAbd al-ʿAzīz. After the Cooper affair he proclaimed himself to be the precursor of the *mahdī*, "the expected one," de-

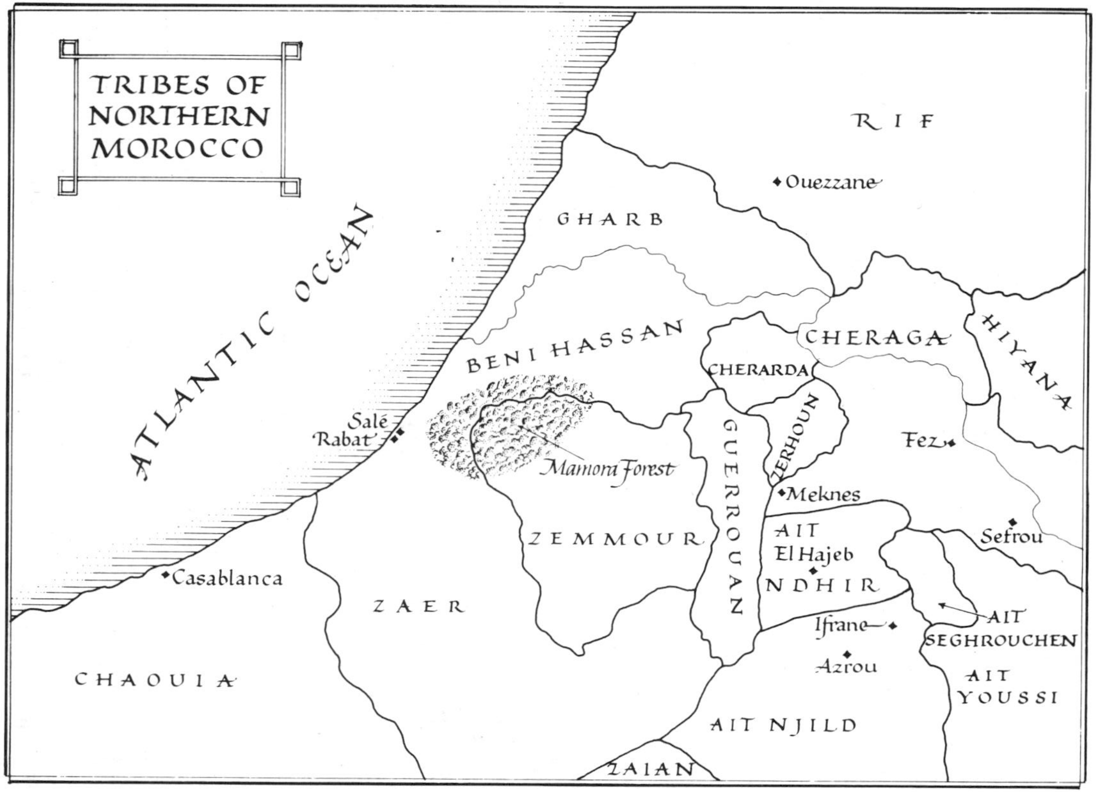
TRIBES OF NORTHERN MOROCCO
ATLANTIC OCEAN
RIF
Ouezzane
GHARB
BENI HASSAN
CHERAGA
HIYANA
CHERARDA
ZERHOUN
Fez
Salé
Rabat
Mamora Forest
GUERROUAN
Meknes
ZEMMOUR
AIT
El Hajeb
NDHIR
Sefrou
Casablanca
ZAER
Ifrane
AIT
SEGHROUCHEN
Azrou
CHAOUIA
AIT
YOUSSI
AIT NJILD
ZAIAN

clared a jihād against the sultan and his impious supporters, and swore to expel the Christians from Morocco. He solidified his local political base by marrying the daughter of a Ghiata qāid and began to constitute a rival makhzan.[83]

At first the government in Fez did not fully appreciate the seriousness of the situation. A rather hastily assembled maḥalla was sent to the borders between the Tsoul and Hiaina tribes where it "ate" the land in the manner of makhzan military expeditions but was unable to register a convincing triumph. Still unaware of the potential danger (the capital was still in a ferment over the Cooper affair), ʿAbd al-ʿAzīz decided that this was victory enough. As he was anxious to leave the restrictive atmosphere of Fez, he gave orders that the court should prepare to leave for Marrakech. The tribes along the route to Rabat manifested some restlessness at the passage of the imperial caravan and delayed its progress. In the meantime, Abū Ḥimāra had managed to lure the makhzan army to attack the Ghiata and recorded a victory. This he managed to present as proof of the authenticity of his mission, and other tribes began to listen to his message. Under the circumstances ʿAbd al-ʿAzīz was compelled to return to Fez to deal with the threat. A new and better equipped makhzan force was sent against the pretender in December. After several desultory skirmishes it came into conflict with Abū Ḥamāra's main force on December 22 and was defeated, with the troops fleeing in disorder. The way to Fez was wide open, but the pretender temporarily withdrew to Taza, where he celebrated the *ʿId al-fiṭr* with great pomp, reorganized his makhzan and received tribal delegations in an effort to establish his legitimacy in the eyes of the tribesmen.

When hostilities resumed toward the end of January 1903 ʿAbd al-ʿAzīz was much better prepared. For the first time the major political resources of the makhzan were used; bribes and false information were widely employed in an attempt to divide Abū Ḥimāra's forces, and the sharifs of Wazzan used their powerful influences in the Taza area to support the sultan. These measures paid off when the Ait Ouarain (B. Ait Warrayn) deserted the forces of Abū Ḥimāra at a critical point in the battle on January 29.[84] The Rogui was driven into the hills in disorder, and from this point onward he ceased to be a direct threat to Fez, although he was able to consolidate his influence in eastern Morocco until his capture in 1909. By 1904 he was driven from his headquarters at Taza to a less vulnerable position near Selouan in the eastern Rif Mountains, not far from Mellila. Until 1908 he remained in that area, governing in haphazard fashion the region between the Moulouya and the Rif, raising taxes and appointing qāid-s as if he were sultan. During this period he entered into dealings with European interests seeking mining concessions in the Rif. When the Spanish tried to import European labor to work the mines in 1908, this led to a rising by the tribes of the region against him.[85] The end of Abū Ḥimāra's story—he was once again to intrude into central Morocco—is given below in chapter 5.

Although it has often been suggested that Abū Ḥimāra's movement was of French inspiration, or that it was financed by the French government, no trace of such official participation has been yet uncovered.[86] The origins of the revolt are impeccably Moroccan and fall within the usual pattern of the emergence of pretenders to the throne. But later on, sometime in 1903, Abū Ḥimāra added Gabriel Delbrel, a French soldier of fortune, as his military advisor. By this time it was clear that he was being supported covertly by the business circles of Oran, who felt betrayed by the absence of a vigorous French government policy toward Morocco. Uniforms for the army of the pretender were supplied by the Oranais firm of Storta. Visitors to his camp reported no shortage of modern weapons or equipment, and he even had several cannon and two machine guns in his arsenal.[87]

Probably the most important result of the revolt of Abū Ḥimāra was that the French, led by their foreign minister, Delcassé, were able to capitalize on the defeat of the "British" reforms and launch their own policy of "peaceful penetration" (see below, chapter 4). Related to this was the overthrow of the royal favorite, al-Munabbhī, who was compelled to quit his post in the makhzan and go on a pilgrimage to the Middle East to preserve his life. Only by strenuous intervention on his behalf were the British able to preserve some of his property from repossession by the makhzan.[88] The ruinous effects upon the royal treasury of the financing of successive military campaigns to defeat Abū Ḥimāra marks a third consequence of his revolt. With tax receipts reduced because of the abortive reforms and expenses already at a record high because of the internal improvement projects, the addition of heavy military expenses proved to be too much for the treasury to bear. The rising of Abū Ḥimāra thus paved the way for the British and Spanish loans of 1903. With the makhzan tied up with the threat posed by the pretender, other regions of Morocco tended to adopt a more flexible relationship with the government of Fez. The trend toward the emergence of regional strong men was thereby enhanced.

One such regional leader who deserves to be mentioned, since his activities were to generate international complications, was the sharif Aḥmad ibn Muḥammad al-Raysūnī, who enjoyed great prestige among the tribes near Tangier and Beni Arous. Early in 1903, following the revelation of the weaknesses of the makhzan by Abū Ḥimāra, al-Raysūnī began to encourage Moroccans living in and around Tangier to demonstrate their hostility to the Europeans living in the city. There were a number of incidents in the months which followed, including several stonings of Europeans.[89] Al-Raysūnī appears to have been motivated by a number of things in his rise to power in the region, including personal ambition, an old feud with the pasha of Tangier, Sī ʿAbd al-Salām, and the fact that the attention of the makhzan at Fez was diverted by events around Taza. Not until May 1903, after several stiff protests from the powers, was the Moroccan government able to take action. A maḥalla was sent to try and capture the sharif but was only able to secure five of his men as hostages. In retaliation, al-Raysūnī captured Walter Harris, correspondent for the *Times* of London, and held him for ransom. Only after Raysūnī's men were released and an indemnity paid for the damage which the maḥalla had done to his property was Harris released. This episode appears to have suggested to al-Raysūnī the great leverage which he might exert by kidnapping Europeans. His next target was the wealthiest man in the Tangier expatriate community, Ian Perdicaris, a Greek-born naturalized American citizen. Perdicaris and his son-in-law Varley brought al-Raysūnī a large ransom and, through a private deal with the makhzan, the governorship of the province of Tangier.[90] His actions also established his credentials as a Moroccan patriot with the militant elements at Fez. He became linked with al-Munabbhī (who had settled at Tangier) and eventually played a discreet, though important, role in the movement to overthrow ʿAbd al-ʿAzīz. He then became a leader of the resistance against the Spanish after 1912. His activities during 1903 and 1904 were significant because they greatly damaged the international reputation of the Moroccan government, and served to add substance to the French claim that only thoroughgoing reforms, carried out by Europeans, had any chance of taking effect in Morocco.

In retrospect, the Abū Ḥimāra rising can be seen as the first of a series of radical movements of rural protest in Morocco between 1900 and 1912.[91] The chief motivating factors, in the case of Abū Ḥimāra as with the movements which followed, were the opposition of the tribes to the increasingly extortionate tax demands of the makhzan and to its weakness in the face of European penetration. These two strands of opposition would continue to fuel movements of protest in the countryside throughout the period under study. The form which these movements took varied but little: all aimed at constructing a broadly based coalition of rural and urban groups, and all were built around a pretender to the throne.[92] Crucial to the success of these movements was the degree to which they could solve the problem of scale. In particular, the intersection of rural and urban resistance groups, which appears first in the Abū Ḥimāra rising, seems to have been a determining factor. When the shurafa and guardians of the shrine of Mawlāy Idrīs returned to Fez in January 1903, Abū Ḥimāra was condemned to being a rural power with limited appeal outside northeastern Morocco. A final characteristic of all of the major movements of rural protest during the period is their transitional quality. Neither fully modern nor fully traditional, such movements contained elements of both worlds. The movement of Abū Ḥimāra is illustrative of this tendency. On the one hand it drew upon the existing traditions of popular protest in Morocco and in its appeals utilized the religious rhetoric of such movements. But on the other hand the organization of the army of the pretender, his skillful interviews with visiting journalists, and his dealings with French and Spanish business interests betray an acute awareness of the complications of international politics. Abū Ḥimāra thus represents a new figure on the stage of Moroccan history, and in this sense he foreshadows the kinds of movements which would emerge after him. Morocco, in more than one respect, would never be the same after him.

4

THE CRISIS OF 1905 AND THE EMERGENCE OF RESISTANCE

Big Banks and Great Power Diplomacy: Round One

As long as the stalemate between Great Britain and France persisted, the fate of the sick man of Morocco was left unresolved. Occasional differences of opinion had arisen in the past to temporarily cloud relations between Morocco and the powers, but these had always been worked out. When Algerian interests demanded action by the French government after a border incident, or when Manchester businessmen complained to Whitehall about Moroccan interference with British trade, the protests by the French and British governments had been duly noted by the makhzan and then ignored. The complex diplomatic minuet which constituted the chief survival mechanism of the Moroccan government enabled it to emerge more or less unscathed from each new crisis. All of this was changed by the revolt of Abū Ḥimāra and the French loan agreement of 1903, which signaled the failure of reforms under British inspiration. The era of diplomatic stalemate and of the small-time dealings of petty businessmen had come to a close. That of great-power diplomacy and international finance was beginning.

The failure of reforms under British inspiration left the way open for a French diplomatic offensive in Morocco. Under the direction of French foreign minister Theophile Delcassé a complex strategy which aimed at securing Morocco for France was devised. If successful, it would pave the way for a French protectorate and fully justify the risks it would entail. A failure, on the other hand, would certainly bring down the government and might even provide the pretext for a general European war. The humiliation which France had suffered in 1898 at Fashoda had convinced Delcassé that, despite the risks, the game was worth it. However the obstacles which lay in the path of a successful French initiative in Morocco appeared, at least initially, formidable.

The most important was the opposition of the powers to changes in the status quo. Nothing could be done until this opposition was somehow overcome.[1] The French internal political situation was also a source of concern to Delcassé. The political position of the Combes government was none too secure. Strong opposition to colonial ventures existed among both the Radicals and the Left in the Chamber of Deputies. The extreme Right tended to oppose anything which distracted attention from "la ligne bleue des Vosges" and the recovery of the lost provinces. The colonial lobby, as might be expected, was in favor of the acquisition of Morocco. But it was split on how this might best be accomplished. Algerian settler interests led by Eugène Etienne, a prominent politician, urged a more militant stance on the Moroccan question, notably the piecemeal conquest of the tribes along the frontier. The major industrial and financial interests were somewhat hesitant to become involved in Morocco without adequate guarantees of continued support. They, along with the remainder of the "colonial lobby," favored a more diplomatic approach to the question. The splits between the "Algerians" and the "diplomats" had recently been increased as a result of the appointment of General Louis-Hubert Lyautey as commander in the frontier region. The French domestic political situation, in sum, was in a rather delicate state, and whatever policy toward Morocco was finally decided upon would have to take it into account.[2]

The Delcassé policy of "peaceful penetration" which emerged in the fall of 1903 was explicitly devised to fit these international and domestic political conditions. The solution was to be twofold: the disengagement of the powers from their interests in Morocco would be obtained through a series of bilateral accords, while France simultaneously built up its influence in Morocco through a major loan agreement and the introduction of reforms in cooperation with the makhzan.[3] By this "makhzan policy" as it was called—in opposition to the "tribes policy" being urged by Algerian interests—Moroccan officials would be conditioned to look to France for financial support and assistance in the modernization of their country. French influence would slowly be developed through the creation of such institutions as the Contrôle de la Dette, customs inspectors, port police, medical missionaries, and the French military mission. France would pursue the British reform policies, but with greater insistence and resources, and would thereby achieve hegemony in Morocco. Moreover, this would be accomplished without provoking either the opposition of the powers or the ire of the Radicals and the Left in the Chamber of Deputies.[4]

At first things appeared to go well. A series of diplomatic accords between 1900 and 1904 removed Italy, Spain, and Great Britain from the list of possible opponents. Negotiations with Italy were begun in 1899 in a series of private discussions with Italian foreign minister Visconti-Venosta. In 1901 by an exchange of letters France obtained a free hand in Morocco in return for granting the same to Italy in Libya.[5] Negotiations with Spain proved less susceptible to a rapid conclusion. A tentative agreement was reached with Spanish premier Francisco Silvela in November 1902. By its terms Spain acquired extensive territories in southern Morocco (a tract running from the Sous valley to Rio de Oro) and in the north of the country (the city of Fez, together with the territory between it and the Mediterranean, and between the Moulouya River and the coast). Fortunately for Delcassé, the Spanish cabinet fell before the accord could be ratified, and his generosity was not put to the test. The new Spanish government, fearful of British opposition, dropped the matter. It was under greatly changed diplomatic circumstances that a Franco-Spanish accord was eventually concluded on October 3, 1904. By this time Delcassé was much less inclined to make substantial concessions, and the new accord limited Spain to a zone north of Larache and the Oueghra River. The accord also precluded Spain from acting in its sphere of influence until after France had acted in its own.[6] In keeping with Delcassé's passion for secrecy, both the Italian and the Spanish accords were private arrangements between governments, rather than formal treaties.

The heart of Delcassé's diplomatic strategy was the rapprochement with Great Britain. Initial approaches were made in 1902 but, owing to the mistrust which existed between the two traditional rivals, nothing came of them. By 1903 however the shifting international diplomatic situation and the failure of British reform efforts in Morocco had resulted in a more favorable conjuncture. Serious negotiations resumed in the fall of 1903, and the final bargain was struck soon thereafter. The Cambon-Lansdowne agreement, as the resulting accord was called, was signed on April 8, 1904, in London. By its terms, France agreed to renounce her latent claims to Egypt and received in return freedom of action in Morocco. Other lesser territorial points of contention between the two countries, including disputes in Newfoundland, Africa, and Siam, were resolved at the same time.[7] The *entente cordiale* signified the beginning of a major rearrangement of the European alliance system. It also brought about a transformation of the diplomatic posture of Morocco, leaving the way clear for a major French initiative. Delcassé moved swiftly to take advantage of the situation.

For France to mount a reform program, it had first to obtain sufficient leverage upon the makhzan to compel cooperation. This could only come through the conclusion of a major loan agreement that would give French financial and industrial interests a privileged position in the execution of Moroccan internal improvements. The consortium of banks headed by the Banque de Paris et des Pays-Bas seemed to Delcassé the proper instrument for the task. Having taken up the 1902 loan without receiving any substantial guarantees from the makhzan, the banks were prepared to impose extremely stiff terms this time. These would certainly include the establishment of a debt commission, a large part of Moroccan customs revenues, and possibly the creation of a state bank. As soon as it became apparent that an agreement with Great Britain was likely in the fall of 1903, Delcassé discreetly made known his approval of a new Moroccan loan by the consortium.[8]

The Paris banking consortium was not the only important French group with interests in Morocco. We have already observed the role played at court by the Compagnie marocaine (through its affiliate, Gautsch et Compagnie). Behind the Compagnie marocaine stood the major French industrial power, Schneider et Compagnie and a syndicate of industrial concerns and lesser banks. The Schneider combine, although excluded from participation in the 1902 loan, still possessed a strong position at court and continued to cherish hopes of important public works contracts from the makhzan. In economic difficulties due to makhzan tardiness in paying off its debts, Schneider resolved that it would contest the decision of Delcassé to accord a de facto monopoly to the consortium headed by the Banque de Paris on a new Morocco loan and on the juicy public works contracts which would flow from it. The aggressive attitude of the banks could not be tolerated. While the consortium conducted discussions on the loan agreement with Moroccan officials in Paris, Schneider prepared to launch its challenge.[9] Delcassé's decision to ignore the Compagnie marocaine in the 1904 loan was later to return to haunt him, and narrowly missed upsetting all of his calculations.

By the end of 1903 circumstances in Morocco were favorable to a new loan. The struggle against Abū Ḥimāra continued to make heavy inroads upon the royal treasury (and to provide a fertile source of graft for a few well-placed individuals), while persistent difficulties in extracting taxes from the rural population further hampered government efforts to right the economy. At the same time, the disgrace of al-Munabbhī and the decline of British influence within the makhzan left the way clear for the rise of a new group of viziers more favorable to a French loan. The new royal favorite, and an opponent of British influence, was Ḥājj ʿUmar Tāzī, the Amīn al-Mustafad. His ascension had been followed by the rise of his two brothers, ʿAbd al-Salām, the finance minister, and Muḥammad, the muḥtasib of Fez. French diplomatic observers, noting the penchant of members of the Tāzī clan to ingratiate themselves with whomever seemed most likely to guarantee their continued enjoyment of the fruits of office, put them down as "pro-French."[10] The young ʿAllāf, or minister of war, Muḥammad Ghibbās, was similarly described since he had helped handle the negotiations of the 1902 frontier accords.[11] There was less certainty about the grand vizier, Muḥammad Gharnīṭ, and the vizier for foreign affairs, ʿAbd al-Karīm ibn Sulaymān. But the latter was known to favor a new loan and had previously combatted British influence.[12] The favorable disposition of the majority of the new makhzan toward a new loan convinced French diplomats that the loan negotiations were assured of a favorable issue. The way to a French protectorate seemed to lie open.

Initially, matters seemed to go very much as planned. Under the leadership of Muḥammad Ghibbās and Ibn Sulaymān discussions were opened at Paris in November with the representatives of the banks. Negotiations were temporarily interrupted by the crisis which arose following the outbreak of the Russo-Japanese War but were resumed early in the new year with the encouragement of the Quai d'Orsay. Preparations were made in Paris to dispatch a representative of the consortium, M. Zangarussiano, to conclude the final document at Fez.

At about the time that the Zangarussiano mission was getting ready to depart, rumors of the Anglo-French agreement reached Morocco. When these were subsequently confirmed by an angry and bitter Qaid Maclean on his return from London, the effect was electric. Overnight the old diplomatic game, by which successive Moroccan governments had been able to play off the powers against one another came to a close. No longer could the makhzan count upon the existence of irreconcilable differences between the major contenders to help preserve it from harm. The unthinkable had happened. Already the news was spreading to the tribes: "England has sold Morocco to France," and signs of increasing unrest in the countryside were becoming manifest. At Fez, opposition developed within the makhzan between those viziers who continued to favor the French loan (Ghibbās and Ibn Sulaymān) and those who opposed it (Gharnīṭ and the royal chamberlain, Ibn Yā'ish, and others). Talk of resistance to France filled the air, and even the sultan was alleged to have become enraged upon hearing the news.[13]

In view of the relative ease which the French experienced in overcoming makhzan anger at the entente, it is easy to underestimate the importance of the crisis which broke out in April 1904. Yet it is possible to date subsequent makhzan efforts at resistance to this period. The flood of rumors generated by word of the Anglo-French agreement seems for the first time to have impressed the sultan and his ministers with the full seriousness of the French threat. Within the makhzan a group favoring a policy of opposition to France began to crystallize around the grand vizier, Muḥammad Gharnīṭ. The French minister at Tangier, in an effort to preserve a rapidly deteriorating situation, sent a special envoy to Fez to explain the terms of the entente and smooth the way for the completion of the suddenly jeopardized loan agreement. A secretary of the French legation, the Count de Saint-Aulaire, was selected for this task. He arrived at the sharifian capital on April 28 to discover a greatly distraught ʿAbd al-ʿAzīz and a badly shaken makhzan.[14]

Plagued by rumors, lacking certain knowledge of the French intent, and divided over what course of action to take, the makhzan was split into warring factions. The pro-French viziers, their position suddenly undermined, counseled prudence. But the sultan, still profoundly upset by this unexpected turn of events, seemed more inclined to listen to those urging resistance. Some proposed that the court should be transferred to Marrakech immediately, so as to place it beyond the range of French influence. Others resurrected the idea that the government should undertake the reform of the customs administration itself with the aid of European advisors recruited by the makhzan. Finally, still others recommended that the makhzan send to the powers a strong letter of protest that would make public its dissatisfaction with the Anglo-French entente.[15]

While Saint-Aulaire deployed all of his diplomatic talents to smooth over the affair, the situation continued to deteriorate. In early May the Zangarussiano mission arrived at Fez to begin discussions on the loan agreement. The overbearing manner of the representative of the banks and the surprisingly harsh terms which he demanded succeeded in arousing new currents of opposition. The realization began to dawn that the proposed loan would fundamentally alter the situation which the makhzan had to face. In place of a multiplicity of petty creditors with limited ability to exact payment, the 1904 loan would substitute a single all-powerful creditor holding substantial guarantees (through its control of Moroccan customs). The old makhzan game of playing its various creditors off against one another would be jeopardized. At the same time, the profits from kickbacks and bribes which had made the fortunes of many officials would be greatly restricted. It should therefore come as no surprise that the French loan of 1904 was perceived as a threat by the makhzan officials. Threatened both in their pocketbooks and in their patriotism, Moroccan officials began to move toward resistance. The various European commercial agents and concession hunters still at court, seeing their business interests endangered by the interjection of Parisian high finance on the scene, spared no effort to discredit Saint-Aulaire and the consortium.[16]

As the situation continued to evolve, two main threats to the French position slowly began to appear. The first was the possibility that the makhzan might conclude a loan agreement with the Compagnie marocaine. Unbeknownst to either the consortium or the Quai d'Orsay, secret negotiations had been going on for several months between the makhzan and the Schneider combine through the combine's agent at Fez, Fabarez. Incited by news that the consortium, with the apparent blessings of the ministry of foreign affairs, was prepared to exclude the Compagnie marocaine from all public works projects, the Schneider group resolved to get the loan for itself. Alleging that the terms of the contract carried by Zangarussiano would virtually deprive Morocco of all control over its finances, Fabarez managed for a time to turn the sultan against Zangarussiano's mission.[17] Stiff pressure by Saint-Aulaire at Fez forced a modification of the clauses of the loan contract. Eventually a compromise settlement was arranged after additional action at Paris. By its terms the consortium was compelled to admit the Compagnie marocaine to a share of the public works which were expected to follow the conclusion of the loan.[18] The agreement between French financial and industrial interests paved the way for the future organization of the French protectorate.

While the contest between the Schneider group and the consortium was at its height, resistance to the French position emerged from still another quarter. On May 10 Saint-Aulaire learned that the sultan had ordered Ibn Sulaymān to prepare a letter of protest against the Anglo-French declaration. The letters were intended for all the heads of state represented at Tangier and would have constituted a serious embarrassment to the French government at a time when public opinion was still unprepared as to the significance of the entente. This time it was ʿAbd al-ʿAzīz himself who had taken the initiative, against the wishes of his viziers (notably Ḥājj ʿUmar Tāzī, the royal favorite). Saint-Aulaire was required to exercise all of his persuasiveness to have the letters of protest withdrawn before they could be sent. Still more persuasion was necessary to get the loan negotiations put back on a solid footing.[19]

On June 12 after more than a month of strenuous negotiations, the loan contract was officially signed by the Moroccan government. A loan with a face value of 62.5 million francs was the result, bearing an interest rate of 5 percent, reimbursable in thirty-five years. As a public loan it would be carried on the French financial market. Sixty percent of the Moroccan customs revenues were given as collateral. In order to guarantee the orderly collection of customs duties the Contrôle de la Dette was created and empowered through a staff of European agents to oversee the functioning of the customs administration. An official representative of the bondholders (Henri Regnault, a career civil servant with previous experience in Tunisia) was nominated by the consortium and subsequently appointed by the sultan. The creation of the Contrôle de la Dette was a significant development, for it possessed great economic leverage and gave France a favored position from which it might later move, much as the Caisse de la Dette had done in Egypt. The contracting banks were also assured priority on all future loans. Finally, groundwork was laid for the establishment of a state bank and a massive program of public works. No action was to be taken initially, however, pending the elaboration of French plans for reforms.[20]

The loan agreement of 1904 marked the logical culmination of a series of events that began with the first loan in 1901. The right of the French government to freely intervene in the financial affairs of the kingdom was officially confirmed. It would require an extraordinary effort by the Moroccan government to break out of the desperate situation in which it found itself. As word leaked out of the program of reforms which the French were preparing for presentation to the sultan, alarm increased greatly at Fez. The coming round of negotiations would decide the fate of the country.

The Crisis of 1904–1905

Moroccan confidence in French intentions was seriously undermined in the six months which followed the approval of the loan agreement. One of the primary sources of friction between the makhzan and the French Republic had long been the ill-defined Algéro-Moroccan frontier. The accords of 1901 and 1902, far from resolving the difficulties, seemed to increase them. Incidents between Moroccan tribesmen and French troopers continued to occur with regularity during the months which followed the 1902 accord. The appointment of the ambitious General Lyautey to oversee the maintenance of security in the *confins* region in 1903 was in fact the signal for the launching of a more aggressive policy by the Algerian colonial interests. Tension along the frontier inevitably led to strife at Paris between the Quai d'Orsay and the Gouvernement Général d'Algérie and reactivated the struggle between the proponents of a makhzan policy and those who favored a "tribes" policy of piecemeal conquest along the Algerian frontier. Lyautey quickly developed for himself a reputation for bold and unconventional activism in French diplomatic circles. His frequent defiance of government orders to maintain a low profile along the frontier produced cries of outrage from the Quai d'Orsay.[21]

In June 1904 troops acting under Lyautey's orders occupied the Moroccan oasis of Berguent (also known as Ras el Ain). Alleging the need to protect French forces on the Algerian side of the frontier, Lyautey refused to recall his men despite protests from Delcassé. Not until August was a compromise solution worked out by which the oasis was returned to makhzan control through a gradual phased withdrawal. In itself insignificant, the timing of the Ras el Ain incident (as it was called) nonetheless convinced makhzan officials of the insincerity of French promises to respect Moroccan sovereignty and the established procedures of the government. The anti-French faction in the makhzan drew new strength from what they claimed was clear evidence of the aggressive intent of the government of the Republic. Efforts by the Quai d'Orsay to better coordinate Moroccan policy with the Algerian army helped to reduce the likelihood of future clashes of this sort. A diplomatic apology at least partially served to patch things up between the two governments. But a basic distrust of France continued at Fez.[22]

This distrust was greatly deepened over the summer as rumors of secret negotiations between France and Spain for the partition of Morocco reached the ears of makhzan officials. On October 7 Parisian papers published news of a joint Franco-Spanish declaration of the integrity of the Moroccan empire. The same document announced the adherence of Spain to the Cambon-Lansdowne agreement of April 1904. As Moroccan officials deduced from the language of the joint declaration when they heard of it a few days later, the public statement was buttressed by a secret convention which delimited French and Spanish spheres of influence.[23]

In September 1904 a series of meetings were held at Paris to elaborate the program of reforms which would be presented to ʿAbd al-ʿAzīz early the next year. Chaired by Delcassé, the meetings were attended by Saint-René-Taillandier, Charles Jonnart (the Algerian governor general), General Pendezec (chef d'état-major of the army), and General Lyautey. Discussions were held on various aspects of the Moroccan question. A comprehensive program for the military, economic, and financial reconstruction of Morocco was elaborated, and the strategy which would govern the mission of Saint-René-Taillandier to Fez was decided upon. The remaining legacy of mistrust and bitterness between the Quai d'Orsay and the Ministère de la Guerre arising out of the Ras el Ain affair was also resolved at this time. Saint-René left the meetings convinced that Delcassé had underestimated the possibilities of Moroccan resistance. He was also disturbed by Delcassé's resolute opposition to the use of force in Morocco in the event that difficulties should be encountered along the way. At the same time he recognized that, given the present state of French opinion on Morocco, a military expedition would excite great opposition at home unless it appeared to come only after all other expedients had been exhausted.[24] There is reason to believe that the unwillingness of Delcassé to consider military intervention was known to Moroccan officials. The onset of the crisis of 1904–1905 was thus predicated upon a sophisticated makhzan awareness of the vagaries of French domestic politics.

As the time drew closer to the start of discussions about the French reform proposals, anxiety as to their probable result increased in Moroccan official circles at Fez. Those who urged that the makhzan defy the French became more vocal, their hand strengthened by Ras el Ain and the suspicious nature of the Franco-Spanish joint declaration. It was under these circumstances that in early October ʿAbd al-ʿAzīz convoked members of the *ʿulamā, aʿyān,* and *shurafā* of Fez to seek their counsel on the current political situation. They recommended against acceptance of the French reform proposals and opposed French attempts to interfere in Moroccan domestic affairs. The consultations had been suggested by the grand vizier, Gharnīṭ, in an effort to counter the pro-French group within the makhzan.[25] A certain collegiality in the makhzan decision-making process can be observed throughout the remainder of the crisis of 1904–1905.

The ʿulamā of Fez began to play a leading role in the crisis starting with the informal canvassing of opinion begun in October. Additional voices were added to those calling for a reappraisal of makhzan policy by the return of a number of prominent Moroccans from the pilgrimage to the Near East. Among them was Muḥammad ibn ʿAbd al-Kabīr al-Kattānī, an Idrīsī sharif and the head of an important *ṭarīqa,* the *Kattānīya,* with many adherents at Fez and in the environs.[26] Kattānī possessed considerable religious prestige throughout the country. Now, fortified by his experience in the

Arab East and confirmed in his hostility to French imperialism, he stepped forth as one of the chief opponents of the French reform proposals. Together with other members of the ʿulamā, he pointed out that while there might be a need for certain reforms, there were real difficulties in employing European advisors to assist in the task. He urged that, in place of Europeans, qualified Muslim Egyptian or Turkish personnel be employed where advisors were needed. Drawing a parallel between the experience of the bey of Tunis and that of the Ottoman sultan, al-Kattānī pressed for a firmer stand on the proposed French reforms. The bey of Tunis, he claimed, had been uncertain of how best to maintain the independence of his country and, as a result, bit by bit he surrendered it to the French. The Ottoman sultan, on the other hand, had avoided making concessions on major issues and thereby preserved his country. It was up to ʿAbd al-ʿAzīz to preserve Morocco from the fate which had overtaken Tunisia.[27]

Discussions at Fez continued throughout the remainder of the fall about the forthcoming negotiations with France. In early December the sultan requested a formal legal opinion (*fatwā*) from the ʿulamā at Fez on the question of European advisors. Their response is worth considering in detail. After asking the question, "What is the cause of our present decadence?" the ʿulamā replied: "It seems to us that the foreigners are the original cause of our misfortunes. It is to them that our decadence, our anarchy, our internal strife, the disappearance of our independence and our downfall must be imputed." Accordingly, they recommended the immediate dismissal of all European advisors to the makhzan and their replacement by qualified Muslims from the Near East.[28] On December 17, on the eve of the departure of Saint-René-Taillandier for Fez, a letter was delivered to the French minister announcing the peremptory dismissal of all European employees of the Moroccan government, including the French military mission. The letter alleged the high cost of such advisors to the makhzan and the need to conserve money.[29] Needless to say, both the timing and contents of the note produced consternation in French diplomatic circles. A challenge to the Delcassé program had been launched.

There were other signs of a new disposition to oppose the French reform proposals in Morocco. Where formerly the makhzan had been cooperative, suddenly a host of petty obstructions loomed in the French path. The genial Ḥājj Muḥammad Turrīs (Fr. Torres) was replaced as Moroccan representative to the powers at Tangier by a known opponent of French influence, ʿAbd al-Salām Tāzī. The routine installation of new French military advisors at Rabat and Fez drew an unaccustomed letter of protest for violations of protocol. Next, it was let out that Muḥammad Ghibbās, the pro-French minister of war, was to be sent to the south on a tax-collecting expedition at just the time that Saint-René-Taillandier's mission would be at Fez. An urgent French note of protest was required to retain Ghibbās at court.[30] Finally, in a move regarded with particular suspicion by the French, on December 21 a makhzan functionary named Muḥammad al-Muqrī (Fr. el-Mokri) left Tangier on a journey to Paris, London, Berlin, Mecca, and Istanbul. The Quai d'Orsay saw in the al-Muqrī trip a covert attempt by the makhzan to obtain military instructors in the Near East to replace the Europeans recently dismissed at Fez. Although French pressure did get Berlin and Istanbul dropped from al-Muqrī's itinerary, he did get as far as Cairo. The mission does not appear to have produced any concrete results, however.[31]

The idea that Morocco should look to the Ottoman empire for support against the demands of the powers first clearly began to attract the interest of Moroccan officials in the fall of 1904. Previous attempts to bring about cooperation between the two states had always foundered on the rock of Moroccan suspicions of the Porte.[32] Contrary to the prevailing belief that Morocco was cut off from the rest of the Islamic world, the nineteenth century was a period of intense contact between Morocco and the Near East. Relations with the Ottoman empire were facilitated by a vigorous pilgrimage traffic to the holy cities of Mecca and Medina. Merchants and scholars in particular profited from the possibilities for material and spiritual enrichment presented by the *ḥājj*. Egypt, with al-Azhār mosque university and an important commercial network, became the main point of interchange. Egyptian books and newspapers began to find an audience at Rabat and Fez among the newly rich bourgeoisie. In this way the principal trends in Near Eastern thought came to have Moroccan proponents.[33]

While the French government debated its response to the suspension of the French military mission, the political situation at Fez continued to harden. On December 22, a delegation of ʿulamā and aʿyān led by the venerable Jaʿfar al-Kattānī (author of the famous *Salwāt al-anfās* and a cousin of Muḥammad ibn ʿAbd al-Kabīr) called upon the sultan at the Dār al-makhzan. Warning him not to interrupt, they presented a list of demands. The makhzan was urged to (1) break relations with France, (2) dismiss all foreign military instructors and replace them with Turks, (3) cancel the forthcoming

French mission to Fez, and (4) fire the pro-French viziers, Ghibbās and Ibn Sulaymān.[34] The public participation of the ʿulamā of Fez in the political struggle was a significant departure from their traditional aloofness. As the ultimate arbiters of the legitimacy of the regime, their opinion was closely watched throughout the country. The radicalization of opinion among the Fāsī elite since October was reflected in the sharpness of the demands submitted to the sultan. For the moment, ʿAbd al-ʿAzīz was able to take these demands under advisement, without having to commit himself more directly. As the crisis deepened, however, he found himself having to contend increasingly with an aroused public opinion.

Meanwhile at Tangier, Saint-René-Taillandier had been coping with the problems created for his mission by the December 17 dismissal notice. The same day as the Fez delegation was meeting with the sultan, he informed the sharifian representative at Tangier of the postponement of his trip to Fez and threatened to withdraw all French citizens from Fez as the first step in breaking relations. Delcassé, correctly seeing continued Moroccan resistance as fatal to his program of "peaceful penetration," wrote to his minister at Tangier demanding that he bring an end to the crisis as soon as possible, even if he had to "buy" all of the leading French opponents at Fez.[35] Under the French pressure ʿAbd al-ʿAzīz abandoned the idea of hiring Turkish advisors, and the Saint-René mission was rescheduled. The French mission had originally been bent on travelling by land all of the way from Tangier to Fez, but rumors of a plot to kidnap the entire mission when it passed through the district of al-Raysūnī forced a change in plans. On January 11, Saint-René-Taillandier and his suite embarked for Larache by ship and then pursued their course inland from that port city.[36]

There is little question that, left to its own devices, the makhzan would never have been able to maintain its determination to oppose the Saint-René mission. The entrance of Germany into the struggle, however, fundamentally altered the situation. For reasons which have more to do with European great-power rivalries than with the intrinsic importance of Morocco, the German attitude had undergone considerable change in a few months' time.[37] Reluctant to respond to Moroccan appeals for support in the fall, the German Foreign Ministry suddenly switched its position in early January to become a resolute champion of Moroccan independence and of the most-favored-nation provisions of the Madrid Convention. This transformation was the function of a number of considerations. The accords and loan of 1904, together with the growing arrogance of

French pretensions in Morocco, had produced a mounting pressure for a strong German initiative among German industrialist and colonialist circles. The situation in the Far East and the failure of negotiations with Russia offered an occasion and a justification. Morocco, threatened by a French protectorate, seemed the most promising place to make a stand. On January 2, 1905, Foreign Minister Bulow telegraphed the sultan of German support for continued resistance to French demands.[38]

It should be noted that German intervention was predicated upon the fact of Moroccan resistance. The emergence of an anti-French movement within the makhzan provided Germany with a means of taking action without directly opposing France and risking a European war. German support remained slow to develop due to uncertainty about the Moroccan determination to resist. For its part, the makhzan responded cautiously to the new German policy as long as it remained at the level of discreet diplomacy. The two parties gradually felt their way toward a more concrete understanding during the next few months. France remained unaware of the new developments for the time being.

On January 26, 1905, Saint-René-Taillandier made his entry into Fez in the company of his official party. In a letter to Delcassé he pronounced himself as well satisfied with his reception by Moroccan authorities. Apparently the makhzan had returned to its senses. Still, there were disquieting signs. On presenting his credentials several days later, the French minister noted that the sultan had studiously avoided engaging himself beyond a few polite formulas in his ceremonial address of welcome. The next few weeks seemed to go well enough. Saint-René had several private meetings with the sultan at which he outlined the general ground which he hoped would be covered by the forthcoming negotiations. In his analysis of the present situation of the empire, he sought to justify the need for a comprehensive program of reforms. He also made an effort to allay the fears of the sultan as to the extent of French demands.[39]

At the meeting of February 11, however, the French minister was presented with a surprising new Moroccan request. ʿAbd al-ʿAzīz asked that the French reform proposals be presented not only to the relevant makhzan officials, but also to a specially convoked *majlis al-aʿyān,* or council of notables. Since the Moroccan people had a direct interest in the kind of reforms adopted, the sultan argued, it was important that they (through their representatives) understand what their government was being asked to assent to.[40] The council was to be composed of forty-two members, of whom twenty-six were from Fez, and the remainder were drawn from the other cities of Morocco and from the provincial elite. With the exception of a few members of the Fāsī ʿulamā (notably Muḥammad al-Kattānī), and the three qāḍī-s of Fez, most of the appointees were merchants and secular notables.[41] The individuals selected appear to have been moderate in their political orientation, and even Saint-René-Taillandier had to admit himself to be satisfied with them on the whole.[42]

A later generation of Moroccan nationalists has seen in the *majlis al-aʿyān* the beginnings of representative government in Morocco, the prototype of a senate.[43] Some of those who supported the creation of the Council of Notables may have thought of it as a first step in a sweeping series of political reforms. The immediate origins of the majlis, however, are to be found in the panel of notables who were invited to advise the sultan the preceding October. Under similar circumstances Mawlāy al-Ḥasan had convoked the notables of Fez to seek their opinions on the reform proposals of Sir Charles Euan-Smith in 1892.[44] The grand vizier Mufaḍḍal Gharnīṭ had been involved in that earlier assembly as a young official in the makhzan of Bā Aḥmad. He seems to have been a chief architect of the policy of consultation which began in October 1904. In fact the consultation of the sultan with members of the elite, known as *mushawara* in Arabic, had ample precedent in Moroccan history and had often practiced in times of stress or uncertainty. There should be no doubt about the impeccably Moroccan origins of the majlis idea.

Saint-René-Taillandier was at first inclined to see the sultan's suggestion of a council to hear his reform proposals as evidence of a renewed Moroccan will to resist. But on further reflection he was inclined to see some solid advantages in the scheme. He insisted however that only fifteen delegates from among those assembled in the majlis be allowed to hear his proposals and that they not be allowed to speak in the session. Under this reservation, negotiations went forward without further delay. The first meeting of the French minister with the augmented Moroccan delegation took place on February 22. For the first time it became apparent that ʿAbd al-ʿAzīz himself, and not his makhzan, intended to take the leading role in the negotiation process. Saint-René limited his opening remarks to some general observations on the necessity of reform and the weakness of the makhzan. Still unaware of German intervention at this point, he looked forward to the speedy conclusion of his mission.[45]

Before the first meeting of the council with the French minister, the opposition, led by Sīdī Muḥammad al-Kattānī, sought to further pressure the sultan to adopt an anti-French attitude. In a letter to the sultan, al-Kattānī demanded that Ibn Sulaymān and Ghibbās be dismissed and summarily executed. To replace them, he proposed two of his allies, Sī ʿAbdullāh ibn Saʿid, and ʿAbd al-Ḥakīm al-Tūnisī. The former had gained a reputation for his hostility to France while he was a secretary to Turrīs at Tangier. The latter had been a favorite of ʿAbd al-ʿAzīz prior to 1900 and was known for his support of Turko-Moroccan rapprochement. In early 1905 al-Tūnisī was in France, from whence he kept al-Kattānī informed of the state of French public opinion by regular letters.[46] The sultan steadfastly resisted this request to dismiss two of his viziers, although he continued to demonstrate his new patriotic proclivities. At an interview with Vassal, the German consul at Fez, he broached the idea of joint action against the French on the frontier with Abū ʿAmāma and dissident tribes of the *confins,* and solicited German support.[47] Ibn Sulaymān became more openly pro-German under the impact of events.

On February 26, soon after the first meeting of the French ambassador with the majlis, a gathering took place at the house of Gharnīṭ to discuss the Moroccan attitude to the reform proposals. It was attended by the viziers and notables who were members of the majlis, including known opponents of reforms like Muḥammad al-Kattānī. After hearing a summary of the private meetings between the sultan and Saint-René-Taillandier, those in attendance were asked to state their views. Some members of the ʿulamā, like Ibn Khadrā, the Qadi of Old Fez, favored a more moderate stance. They were bitterly opposed by al-Kattānī and the hard-liners. The struggle between the moderates and the extremists grew steadily more intense during the months which followed.[48]

While the French minister continued outlining the proposed reforms to the makhzan at Fez, the international and French domestic contexts continued to change. The Far Eastern situation required the constant attention of Delcassé and, as news of the difficulties of Russian military forces continued to arrive, became a source of increasing anxiety. Public opinion in France remained resolutely opposed to the use of force in Morocco. The weak political position of the Combes government and the imminence of new elections compelled the foreign minister to use caution. On a number of occasions he had pointedly to urge Saint-René-Taillandier to moderate his desires for a test of force with the makhzan and his sense of vexation at the petty obstacles placed in his path.[49] A policy of peaceful penetration would be hard to justify to a suspicious Chamber of Deputies if it entailed the occupation of Moroccan ports and the seizure of the customs.

As the German diplomatic offensive developed during February and March, the Moroccans became more steadfast in their resistance to France. Through Philip Vassel, the German counsel at Fez, the Wilhelmstrasse sought to convince ʿAbd al-ʿAzīz of the serious interest which the Imperial government placed in the continuing independence of Morocco and of its opposition to the accords recently concluded between France, England, and Spain. They also assured the sultan of the opposition of German public opinion to French ambitions in Morocco. In return for its moral support of the Moroccan position, the German government sought to exact a series of economic concessions from the makhzan. These included the construction of a submarine telegraph cable, port works, a railroad, and mining concessions in the Rif. They also sought the right to extend their assistance in the reform of the country, assistance that would include a German military mission. The viziers received the German offers of assistance with enthusiasm, while prudently seeking to elicit a firm guarantee of continued support in the event of French armed intervention. Vassel's skillful handling of the situation was largely responsible for the way in which the Moroccan government was able to continue its policy of resistance despite considerable French pressure.[50]

At a time when the German government was searching for a means of making a public demonstration of its support for Morocco, the idea of a visit of Kaiser Wilhelm to Tangier appeared to offer considerable advantages. Not so bellicose as to run the risk of provoking an intemperate French response, a landing of the Kaiser served at the same time to dramatize the concern of the imperial government with the course of events in Morocco. First conceived in early March by Kühlmann, the German minister at Tangier, plans for the landing went rapidly ahead. By March 18 the adhesion of the Kaiser himself to the project had been obtained and that same day the makhzan was informed of the pending visit. A press campaign was simultaneously begun in Germany which sought to spell out the intentions of the government. As a result of the happy effect which the news of the visit produced upon the makhzan, a number of pending concessions and commercial deals were concluded.[51] On March 30 the Kaiser debarked briefly at Tangier. He was welcomed by a Moroccan delegation headed by the uncle of the sultan,

Mawlāy ʿAbd al-Mālik, and a suite of other officials and makhzan secretaries. A dazzling reception was held, and the Kaiser was treated to the enthusiastic responses of the crowd. Jubilation characterized the reactions of the makhzan, while ʿAbd al-ʿAzīz promised to entertain any reform proposed by Germany.[52]

Despite French protestations that the landing of the Kaiser had changed nothing, it was soon evident that the Delcassé policy had overnight been placed in jeopardy. A challenge had been launched to the French position in Morocco which was only gradually comprehended in its full gravity. Suddenly Delcassé's passion for secrecy, his studious neglect of German interests in Morocco, and the contradictions latent in his policy of peaceful penetration came to be seen by French public opinion as both dangerous and foolhardy.

The landing of the Kaiser virtually assured the rejection of the French reform proposals. Saint-René-Taillandier struggled against this impending result, though now with a rising sense of exasperation. The formal announcement of failure did not come until May 28, after two months of bitter debate with the makhzan. ʿAbd al-ʿAzīz notified the French minister of the decision with the words, "It has not been possible for His Majesty to oppose the people. . . ."[53]

At the same time a Moroccan appeal for an international conference of all of the signatories of the 1880 Madrid Convention was issued. The conference originated from a proposal of ʿAbdullāh Ibn Saʿīd, a member of the majlis. Subsequently taken up by Germany and given broad publicity, the conference was intended to give comprehensive attention to the entire question of Moroccan reforms.[54] It was anticipated that by placing the reform question in an international context it would be possible to ward off French claims to predominance. Any decisions which were reached by such a meeting would probably be unenforceable because of the need for international agreement and controls. While Delcassé remained in office, France continued to oppose the idea of a conference, but after his fall the new ministry withdrew its opposition. The Algeciras conference was the result.

Algeciras and After

The proposal of an international conference on Morocco which would bring together the signatories of the Madrid Convention of 1880 to consider the question of reforms was slow to gain acceptance among the powers. Even after France agreed in principle in June, intense discussions continued about the format, scope, and location of the conference. The German position that Moroccan reforms should be internationalized found little backing among the other powers, and the agenda which was eventually decided upon confirmed the victory of French diplomacy. Although making a few gestures toward international opinion, the final agenda essentially affirmed that what would be discussed was not the question of French predominance but the way in which it would be exercised, Algeciras, a sleepy little port town in the shadow of Gibraltar was decided upon as the conference site. Fully six months were consumed in preparatory talks. It was not until January 16, 1906, that the opening session of the conference was held.[55]

Against the background of intense diplomatic activity over who was to control the conference and what questions it would take up—a debate to which the makhzan had little to contribute—events continued to evolve in Morocco. A broad and systematic sampling of opinion from throughout the country was decided upon to assure unity on the position that would be taken by the Moroccan representatives. Letters were dispatched to the tribes inviting them to send delegates to Fez to discuss the matter. Mahdī al-Wazzānī, a member of the Fez majlis, was sent to sample opinion at Tangier and in the surrounding area.[56] He was later also sent to sound out the views of Moroccan merchants living in Algeria and Tunisia.[57] Strong support was received for the idea of a conference and for opposition to the French reform proposals. Only after the results of this extraordinary consultation process were in did the makhzan officially agree to take part in the conference. Discussions on the position that would be taken by Morocco at the conference occupied the summer and fall.

It is difficult to speak in any detail about the Moroccan strategy at Algeciras, given the continued inaccessibility of makhzan archives. ʿAbd al-ʿAzīz appears to have expected that the conference would sustain the German (and therefore Moroccan) position with regard to reforms, thus blunting the French offensive. Considering the record of ineffectiveness of previous international conferences on Morocco, there was little reason to expect anything of Algeciras. By permitting a return to the old ways of playing the powers off against one another, the conference would insure that whatever reforms were agreed upon would remain dead letters. Either the proposed reforms would be parcelled out among all of the powers or there would be no machinery to insure Moroccan compliance. It was anticipated that the conference would also reaffirm the sovereignty and legal rights of Morocco.[58]

As it turned out, the conference established an international control body dominated by France, which had the power to intervene broadly in the political and economic life of the country, especially in the major port cities, which now passed de facto largely out of the control of the makhzan. A special port police force was created to insure security for European interests. It was to be composed of Moroccans but officered by Frenchmen and Spaniards. A state bank, dominated by representatives of the consortium headed by the Banque de Paris et des Pays-Bas, became the sole financial agent of the Moroccan government. The bank would negotiate all future loans. It also received the sole right to issue currency and sweeping powers to stabilize the shaky monetary situation of the country. All revenues not hitherto committed to the payment of outstanding loans were to be deposited in the state bank, which would make disbursements for all mahkzan expenses. The main source of revenue not controlled by the bank was the tartīb, but with the difficulties that had been experienced in collecting this tax since its institution, this was small comfort indeed. With the establishment of the Banque d'Etat, the Moroccan government became the virtual prisoner of the Paris banking consortium, dependent upon it for its daily existence.[59]

The results of Algeciras came as a distinct shock to the makhzan and to most informed Moroccan citizens. The immediate feeling was one of betrayal. The conference, which had been entered into with such great expectations, had instead resulted in an almost complete victory for France. At Fez, the militants counseled continued resistance to French demands and rejection of the Act of Algeciras. For a time ʿAbd al-ʿAzīz appears to have considered submitting the act to the *majlis al-aʿyān* for its consideration.[60] Such a step would have led to certain refusal by the notables and might have enabled the sultan to claim that the representatives of the people had spoken. By mid-May Morocco had still not ratified the act. The Moroccan strategy during the conference had been to reserve all major matters for the decision of the sultan. This was done with the apparent intent of enabling the makhzan to claim later that the conference decisions were in fact but the basis for further negotiations.

In order to cut short this line of retreat, French diplomats at Tangier provoked the dispatch of a special delegation to Fez, charged with obtaining ratification of the act by Morocco. The delegation was headed by Giulio Malmusi, the dean of the European diplomatic corps in Morocco. On May 24 the Malmusi mission departed for Fez. Its official purpose was to present formal notification of the decisions of the conference to the sultan and to obtain his ratification.[61] Initial discussions with the sultan were not promising. But patient French diplomatic efforts soon persuaded him of the folly of further resistance and put an end to his haggling over details. The Act of Algeciras was finally signed by Morocco on June 18, 1906.

The ratification of the Act of Algeciras consummated the break between the sultan and those Moroccans who favored continued resistance to France. From this point onward a marked increase in anti-French and anti-European feelings can be observed throughout Morocco. ʿAbd al-ʿAzīz was accused of having forfeited all claim to allegiance by bowing to French pressure. His ministers were denounced for having sold out the country for their own personal gain. A coalition began to form which sought to depose ʿAzīz and substitute a sultan more committed to resistance.

Two developments characterized the period after Algeciras. They were the rapid growth of French influence in Morocco (and of European influence generally), and the no less rapid increase in the number of incidents involving attacks of Moroccans upon Europeans.

French policy toward Morocco after Algeciras continued in the same general path laid down by Delcassé. France remained attached to the program of peaceful penetration and the institution of reforms in cooperation with the makhzan. The French policymakers who followed Delcassé, however, showed themselves to be much more cautious in asserting their rights in Morocco. The risk of a general war in Europe and continued apprehension about German aims in Morocco dictated prudence. The French domestic situation, including labor unrest and turmoil over the policy of military conscription, further restricted the possibilities for bold action in Morocco. The dull-minded and timid Foreign Affairs ministers who followed Delcassé proved incapable of either designing a more effective policy toward Morocco or of showing the determination necessary to make a success out of the old one. From 1905 until 1911, therefore, the forward party among the French colonial lobby had to mark time, waiting for a solution of the diplomatic impasse with Germany. French penetration of Morocco continued unchecked, yet France was unable to reap the fruits of its labors.

The policy of peaceful penetration consisted of a number of different elements. One was the establishment of an internationally sanctioned port police, already begun at Tangier before Algeciras. It was to be extended to the other ports. When completed, the garrisons of Tangier and Casablanca were each to consist of two tabors, while those of the other six ports were to have one tabor, officered by French and Spanish personnel (there were between one hundred and five hundred men in a tabor). The installation of police units in fact lagged considerably due to problems of organization and recruitment.[62] The right to inspect the Moroccan customs administration and to place European agents to supervise the work of the Moroccan customs officials, or umanā, had been established along with the Controle de la Dette in 1904. Development of the system of customs inspection had gone slowly until Algeciras because of bitter opposition by the umanā. Thereafter, the installation of European (chiefly French) agents proceeded more rapidly, although grumbling persisted. By 1907 their presence had already led to noticeable increases in customs revenue and efficiency of operation. At Casablanca, the opposition of the umanā was to be one of the stimuli for the July 30 rising.[63] One aspect of the Delcassé program of peaceful penetration had been the establishment of medical dispensaries in the major cities of Morocco. Medical missionaries were perceived as having an important political as well as humanitarian role to play in extending French influence in the country. By 1906 there were dispensaries at Larache, Rabat, Casablanca, al-Jadida, Safi, and Essaouira, as well as Marrakech in the interior. The doctors were appointed by the French Foreign Ministry, and were selected for their knowledge of Arabic and familiarity with Arab customs.[64] A final component of the program of peaceful penetration was the French military mission. It was resumed in 1906 after an interruption of a year and a half. Its primary role was as a listening post at the capital, since it was deprived of all control over the organization, equipment, and payment of the Moroccan army. (It might be noted that both British and German officers were also in the service of the makhzan at this time.)

At first it appeared that ʿAbd al-ʿAzīz, and indeed many among the makhzan elite, were anxious to cooperate with France in the extension of the new reforms. Troops were recruited to fill the Franco-Moroccan police force at Tangier and encouraged to submit themselves to the commands of their French officers. During the fall of 1906 Tangier witnessed an influx of a considerable number of unemployed *kātib*-s (secretaries) and other educated men from Rabat, Fez, and Marrakech. Most were attracted by the possibility of obtaining employment in the Banque d'Etat or one of the other organizations established by the Algeciras Act.[65] The expectation of a dramatic increase in trade possibilities also attracted a great many French and other European business firms to Morocco in 1906 and

1907. For the most part they confined their activities to the port cities of the country, and the European population of these cities, especially Tangier and Casablanca, grew in consequence. The makhzan willingness to consider reforms remained high during 1906. As a demonstration of good will, the governorship of the city of Tangier (but not its hinterland) was placed in the hands of Ibn al-Ghāzī, known as a tough proponent of maintaining public order.[66] For a moment it looked to French observers as though it might be possible to continue the Delcassé policy without having to use force.

While the makhzan reformers pressed ahead on military and administrative reform, ʿAbd al-ʿAzīz made an effort to regain some credit with the opposition group. The Mauretanian warrior-saint Mā al-ʿAynayn was received with pomp and honor at Fez on one of his regular visits. He was lodged at the government's expense and accorded several interviews with the sultan. On his departure, Mā al-ʿAynayn was given a quantity of rifles from makhzan stores.[67] The passage of the shaykh through Casablanca, Marrakech, and Mogador, before he boarded a ship to return to the Seguiat el Hamra, was marked by a series of incidents between his followers and Europeans.[68] At about this time a makhzan representative was sent to establish at least the facade of Moroccan sovereignty in the extreme south. He was given hospitality by Mā al-ʿAynayn, a fact which provoked a formal French protest. The sultan nonetheless refused to recall him.[69]

Despite makhzan efforts to put a good face on the post-Algeciras period, it had lost all control over events. An economic slump produced widespread bitterness and unrest. There was an upsurge in the number of attacks on Europeans. Experienced Moroccanists, like the ethnologist Edmond Doutté, were stunned by the polarization of opinion after 1903. Whereas earlier the rural populations had been receptive to Europeans, by 1905 they manifested an attitude of noncooperation and sullen hostility.[70]

The recession which prevailed from 1905 to 1907 aggravated the already bad political climate.[71] The crisis began in 1905 with major crop failures and a sharp upswing in livestock mortality. There was little rain in 1906 and only local improvement in 1907. The result was a widespread famine and severe outbreaks of epidemic disease. Fortunately, the country was spared the kind of demographic catastrophe which it had experienced in 1878–84. At Fez rioting was averted only by the massive importation of grain from Marseilles.[72]

At Marrakech and in the port cities depressed economic conditions prevailed. The misery of the poor was increased because speculators had sold for export the meager 1905 grain harvest. Everywhere trade slumped badly. There was an influx of peasants to the cities, where they swelled the mass of unemployed and discontented.[73]

For the wealthy in Moroccan society the recession of 1905–1907 was but a momentary inconvenience. Urban protégés merely shifted from exporting grain and wool to exporting animal skins and hides (these were in abundance owing to the heavy livestock mortality). Wealthy officials continued to have richly ornamented palaces constructed, and the jobs which were thereby provided helped, ironically, to alleviate the distress of the poor.[74] European firms engaged in land speculation around the ports with increased boldness. Vast agricultural domains and commercial production for the market gradually transformed the countryside. The combination of economic distress and makhzan impotence at curbing French expansion intensified the post-Algeciras insecurity.

The deterioration of Franco-Moroccan relations after 1906 was in large measure the result of a wave of attacks on French citizens. At Tangier the political climate was particularly threatening as a result of a series of riots and affrays in the marketplace between Andjera tribesmen and the supporters of al-Raysūnī. On May 27, a young Frenchman named Charbonnier was murdered just outside the city.[75] The deed was ascribed to al-Raysūnī's men. The French government demanded immediate satisfaction from the makhzan. When this demand was slow in producing action, France entered into conversations with Madrid on a possible joint naval demonstration.[76] (This occurred only in December, after the crisis had passed.) The Moroccan government finally moved to fulfill the terms of the French ultimatum. It also dispatched a military expedition to the north in a fruitless effort to sieze al-Raysūnī. The expedition did restore some semblance of order, however.[77] But by tying down troops who were to be badly needed elsewhere, it hampered the ability of the makhzan to reply to future crisis situations.

There were also serious anti-French outbreaks at Fez and Marrakech. At Fez a French tourist named de Gironcourt was set upon by a mob and severely beaten on March 6, 1907, when he sought to photograph a group of natives. Only the chance passing of a soldier of the pasha prevented him from being killed.[78] In Marrakech the situation was more serious. The pasha, ʿAbd al-Salām al-Warzāzī, was an adherent of the Kattānīya ṭarīqa well known for his anti-French attitude.[79] After a series of minor incidents, an employee of the Compagnie marocaine was attacked on the road to Safi just outside the city and almost killed. The climactic event was the brutal murder of Dr. Emile Mauchamps, a French medical missionary, outside his dispensary on March 19 by a crowd of angry Moroccans.

The Mauchamps murder has generally been ascribed by French sources to the intrigues of the pasha, al-Warzāzī, and Dr. Judah Holzmann, a German physician.[80] The truth is more complex. Although Mauchamps was a devoted and patriotic official and even appears to have known some Arabic, some observers found him headstrong and irritable.[81] After a year at Marrakech he departed for Paris in December 1906. During his absence the political climate continued to deteriorate. One aspect of this deterioration was widespread alarm over attempts to establish wireless telegraph installations in the interior.[82] Mauchamps returned from France in March 1907, accompanied by the geologist Louis Gentil. He became the focus of immediate concern. Local officials perceived Gentil's bulky geological instruments as telegraphic equipment.[83] The morning after his arrival Mauchamps was attacked and killed by an angry mob, probably after further provocative acts. The volatile atmosphere at Marrakech made such an event likely; the insensitivity of Mauchamps made it inevitable.

The murder of Mauchamps provoked the French government into immediate action. The Moroccan city of Oudjda was occupied by an expeditionary force commanded by General Lyautey. A French ultimatum demanded the payment of indemnities, the dismissal of the pasha of Marrakech, and the arrest of the guilty parties. The French government declared that, until such incidents came to a halt, it would continue to retain possession of the city.[84] For the first time since Algeciras the French government had taken forceful action in Morocco in defense of its interests. Whether or not it would have the desired effects upon the behavior of the Moroccan government, however, remained to be seen.

The seizure of Oudjda placed the Moroccan government in serious difficulties. Unable to counter the French action and increasingly dependent upon France for its financial survival, the makhzan was in no position to protest. Whatever credit the government might have possessed among the powers had been largely dissipated in the disastrous turn which events had taken at Tangier and the increasing collapse of security throughout the empire. A letter sent by ʿAbd al-ʿAzīz which blamed the Moroccan people for the recent series of attacks upon Frenchmen generated angry comments when it was read in mosques through the country. "We have insistently warned you many times," the letter read in part,

> of events which might result from the conduct of the population, but you haven't paid attention to our recommendations and the present events are your fault. Now we are going to make an effort to settle this affair in paying, if necessary with our men and goods, in order to reestablish good relations between the French government and us, and to put an end to the occupation of Oudjda. We inform you of the preceding so that you [may] abstain from all agitation.[85]

In the face of this tepid response, the opposition to ʿAbd al-ʿAzīz daily gained more recruits. The political difficulties of the regime, already severe due to acceptance of the verdict of Algeciras, steadily worsened.

The Chaouia Jihad: Anatomy of an Explosion

Until 1907 the rural populations had been but little involved in determining the fate of Morocco; thereafter they became increasingly involved. How did this transition come about? While some details of the process remain unclear, the broad outlines are known. Most important was the growing interpenetration of city and country and the consequent disruption of the structures of rural life. This process can be observed most closely in the Chaouia province.

The crisis in the Chaouia was a complex affair. One dimension of the changing situation was the striking growth of the city of Casablanca. From a sleepy port town of 9,000 in 1884 Casablanca developed into a bustling commercial center of 25,000 in 1907, by which time it had also become the first port of the country both in tonnage and value of merchandise.[86] This expansion was accompanied by a remarkable transformation in the relationship between the city and the countryside. Prior to 1900 the tribes appear to have had little contact with the city. The governor was selected from among the most important rural families and did not reside in town.[87] There were relatively few quasi-feudal appanages (jaysh lands or *ʿazzabā*) in the province, though in most other respects the agrarian system resembled that which prevailed elsewhere in central Morocco.[88]

European business interests were among the main beneficiaries of the newly emerging agrarian system. They acquired major holdings of real estate in the countryside. The Compagnie marocaine is said to have held over 7,000 hectares,[89] while according to Guillen German interests controlled an additional 2,000 hectares.[90] British merchants owned substantial flocks and herds through local intermediaries.[91] The actual dimensions of European holdings in the province remain unclear.

Moroccan agricultural associates and protégés constitute a second major group which benefited from the emerging new order. In 1907 they numbered about 10,000 for a total population of 300,000.[92] While they battened on their tax-exempt status and privileged access to European credit, the lot of the poor in the Chaouia steadily worsened. By 1898 countryfolk were being jailed at Casablanca for defaulting on debts owed European merchants.[93] The incipient class antagonisms between rich and poor in Chaouia society intensified greatly.

The emergence of a centralizing government constitutes a second major aspect of the crisis. As the revenue needs of the makhzan increased, so too did friction between the local agents of the makhzan and the rural notables. Given the inefficiencies of the tax system, the qāid-s charged with collecting the taxes on agriculture benefited more from the increased revenue demands than did the makhzan treasury. In the Chaouia they began to fortify their houses and to hire large numbers of armed retainers. Not surprisingly, this increased pressure provoked rebellions in 1894, 1898, and 1900.[94] By 1903 the rural notables were at the breaking point.

Makhzan self-strengthening efforts had as their main result a sharp rise in taxes, then, in the absence of an army able to collect them, the collapse of its authority in the countryside. The decline of makhzan authority in the Chaouia had some special features, as well. Casablanca lacked a solid and cultured merchant class such as existed at Tangier, Rabat, and the other major cities. Neither did it have an influential group of ʿulamā and sharifs able to oversee the conduct of affairs. Makhzan presence in the city was confined to the pasha and a small garrison. It was therefore easy for the European powers to dominate the city. In 1894, for example, a dispute which threatened to lead to an attack by the tribes was mediated by a British merchant after the pasha had failed ignominiously in an attempt to restore order.[95] In the boom-town conditions which prevailed after 1900, Casablanca was more than ever vulnerable to gunboat diplomacy. Eventually the consent of the local diplomatic corps was necessary before the makhzan could make major appointments, as for the pasha of the city.

The makhzan decision to institute the tartīb in 1901 constituted one of the immediate precipitants of revolt. The suspension of the traditional agricultural taxes, pending the authorization of the tartīb, provided a heaven-sent opportunity for the rural notables to lay in stocks of grain and build up their private arsenals. Unable to collect any taxes, the qāid-s encountered serious difficulties in the exercise of their functions.[96] At the end of 1902, the Chaouia qāid-s were summoned, together with their nāiba contingents, to take part in operations against Abū Himāra. This was the signal for a jacquerie. With the qāid-s away, bands of rebellious peasants, known as *jawqa,* began to assemble with the aim of overthrowing the local makhzan government. The movement began in the fall of 1902 among the Oulad Bou Ziri and the Oulad Bou Said. By the beginning of 1903 it had begun to spread. The *qasba*-s at Settat and Bir Rachid were attacked and put to the torch. The refugees flocked into Casablanca, Azemmour, and Boujad.[97]

In spite of the anarchic manner by which the revolt seemed to spread, the jawqa operated in more or less coordinated fashion. Tribes residing closer to Casablanca tended to be less engaged than those further away. The rebels grouped themselves in bands of ten to thirty horsemen, each with its own chosen leader who was held responsible for the acts of his men. Internal discipline was maintained by a collective oath binding the heads of all the jawqa. Abū Azzāwī, a prominent local sharif, was the overall head of the revolt. A nucleus of several hundred men whose commitment was greater than the others constituted the core of the insurrection.[98] For a social movement of this amplitude, we know surprisingly little of its inner workings.

The aims of the rebels were the destruction of all qasba-s in the province and the ransoming of wealthy prisoners. The jacquerie was thus primarily directed against the local agents of the makhzan, who alone were allowed to construct qasba-s. Like the peasant revolts studied by Roland Mousnier,[99] it was not a rising of the poor and the downtrodden but rather a rebellion of a rising new class of rural notables and protégés against an encroaching central government. If we consult a list of the heads of jawqa-s among the Oulad Said (seemingly typical of the rebel tribes), it is striking to note the number of times we find the phrases "rich native" and "censal" after their names. Only six of forty-one names do not clearly belong to the local ruling class. No poor peasants are to be found.[100]

One aspect of the struggle which bears mention is that it seems to have provided the chance for families who had long been subordinate to overthrow their rivals. The careers of two of the leaders, Abū Azzāwī and Ḥājj Muḥammad Wuld al-Ḥājj Ḥāmū, may serve to illustrate this point. Abū Azzāwī was born into a humble sharifian family in the tribe of Mzab. After studying at Fez he returned home in 1877. In the intervening years his religious influence and his ambitions grew considerably. The revolt provided him with a chance to play a national role.[101] Ḥājj Muḥammad Wuld al-Ḥājj Ḥāmū was the nephew of the governor of the Oulad Hariz at the outbreak of the revolt. He was able to successfully contest the headship of the tribe. By 1906 his vaulting ambitions led him to seek the governorship of the Chaouia, and, when ʿAbd al-ʿAzīz chose the lackluster Abū Bakr ibn Abū Zayd instead, to join forces with Abū Azzāwī and preach the ouster of ʿAbd al-ʿAzīz himself.[102] A principal result of the siba of the Chaouia was the growing militance of the tribes.

The post-Algeciras mood of the Europeans was not one of putting up with extortion by tribal toughs. The succession crisis over the governorship of the province had called forth protests from the local representatives of the powers. In response to another incident in April 1907, involving an attack on a Portuguese protégé, the diplomatic corps of Casablanca requested a show of force to repel a threatened tribal attack on the city. A French cruiser was dispatched, and the crisis dissipated.[103] The incident bore a striking resemblance to the uprising which was to occur at the end of July.

The Act of Algeciras gave European inspectors the right to oversee the collection of the 60 percent share of customs revenues which belonged to the Debt Commission by dint of the 1904 loan. This set up a conflict with the umanā of the ports, who were the responsible Moroccan officials. The arrival of French customs inspectors at Casablanca in July 1907 jeopardized the opportunities for graft of the local umanā, who promptly sought to rally support against the French agents. Although most of the Casablanca umanā were of Fāsī origin, they had strong ties to the local merchant community and through it with the countryside. Disputes which involved them could thus quickly become serious incidents. Rumors were spread that the French were not only collecting customs duties but that they were also laying hands upon the revenues of the shrine of Sidi Billiut, the patron saint of the city. (Since the umanā had traditionally administered the sanduq of the shrine, the charge had some semblance of truth.) Allegations of Christian interference soon excited a powerful current of anti-French feeling which spread to the tribes. The governor of the Oulad Hariz, Wuld al-Ḥājj Ḥāmū, led a large tribal delegation on the city on July 29. They demanded the immediate removal of the French customs agents, and cessation of work on the harbor jetty. Otherwise they threatened to pillage the city.[104]

Construction of a jetty for the port of Casablanca had been begun in March by the Compagnie marocaine. They had constructed a narrow-gauge railroad to a rock quarry several kilometers outside of the city to get rock for the jetty. In the process, they had violated a Muslim cemetery which stood across the right of way. Not surprisingly, this generated considerable adverse comment from the traditional religious circles. When the train began making regular trips to and from the quarry, accompanied by much whistle-blowing, noise, and confusion, the opposition increased. The tribes, who had never before seen a steam locomotive, were greatly alarmed by this frightening new apparition and resolved to take action.[105] Finally, as if all of this were not enough, the harbor works were plagued by labor difficulties. The overseers employed by the Compagnie marocaine were mostly of French Algerian origin, and few of them spoke Arabic. They tended to be harsh and brutal in their treatment of the workers and paid them low wages. Most of the labor force was not recruited locally but instead was composed mostly of poor Sūsī-s hired in the south by labor contractors. The importation of outside labor only intensified the grievances of local people.[106]

In view of all of these developments, it was only a matter of time before a chance spark would set off the politically highly combustible environment and lead to an outburst of anti-European violence. This occurred on July 30, 1907, when the railroad was attacked by some tribesmen and townspeople on the outskirts of Casablanca, and eight Europeans on board a train were killed. A wave of pillaging and killing then spread over the town, and a number of other Europeans were set upon by bands of Moroccans. After some sporadic firing, the situation began to quiet down and the town authorities began to regain control of the situation. At this point further imprudent actions, notably by the commander of the French cruiser *Galilée*, blocked further negotiations. The key error was the premature landing of an inadequately armed shore party of sailors to reinforce the French consulate, an action which incited a second wave of fighting and pillaging in the town. When the cruiser then shelled the town in reprisal, the resulting terror and destruction united the townspeople with the tribesmen against the French.[107] Several days later a two-thousand-man French expeditionary force under General Drude arrived to restore order, and the action in the Chaouia entered a new phase.

The landing of large numbers of French troops at Casablanca immediately provoked a kind of *levée en masse* among the tribes of the surrounding region, who moved to attack the French and expel them. For reasons of domestic and international politics, the French government had forbidden General Drude to penetrate inland to break up the concentrations of hostile tribes. To do so would make the French expeditionary force look like it intended the conquest of the whole of Morocco. But by limiting Drude in his possibilities of movement and response, Paris policy-makers unwittingly made his task much more difficult. Each time French units repulsed a Moroccan attack and the enemy began to withdraw, the French would have to break off the engagement. This convinced the Moroccans that they, not the French, were winning, since it was the French who broke off and retreated first.[108] The illusion of success enabled the number of resisters to grow rapidly as men came from all over Morocco to take part. By the end of August more than ten thousand Moroccans faced the French at Casablanca.

The French policy of "peaceful penetration" had by the summer of 1907 come to a halt. Serious incidents and expressions of hostility against Europeans, Frenchmen in particular, had broken out all over the country at an accelerating pace from 1906. Because the policy had been designed by men who were more concerned about the possible international and domestic political consequences of French action in Morocco than they were about the effects of that policy in Morocco, the strong Moroccan response which it provoked was almost inevitable. A strong French proponent of the "tribes policy" like Alfred LeChatelier was therefore justified when he wrote in 1908, "France sincerely believes that it is following a policy of peaceful penetration [in Morocco]: it is accomplishing in reality a work of methodical provocation."[109] The Moroccan reaction to an accelerated program of French penetration was to call into question not only the nature of French policy but also the continuation of ʿAbd al-ʿAzīz on the throne.

5

THE ORIGINS AND DEVELOPMENT OF THE ḤAFĪẒĪYA, 1905–1908

Prelude to Rebellion

By the beginning of August 1907 Morocco had reached the parting of the ways. A simmering conspiracy which involved the great qāid-s of the Atlas was publically unveiled in that month. It aimed at placing ʿAbd al-Ḥafīẓ upon the throne in place of his lackluster brother. Soon it spread to include the cities of thc North. How arc we to explain the development of a powerful opposition movement among the rural notables of the south? It is well not to take too teleological a view of the evolution of the Ḥafīẓīya. The account which follows has been pieced together from European sources and will no doubt be modified when makhzan records become available.

It may be useful to begin our exploration of the Ḥāfīẓīya with a brief consideration of the personality of the leader of the movement, Mawlāy ʿAbd al-Ḥafīẓ. Earlier accounts have found him something of a mystery. Praised by French visitors to Marrakech prior to 1907 for his openness of mind and accessibility, he was thereafter excoriated by many of the same people for his bloody-minded fanaticism. The key to this complex individual is to be sought, I would suggest, in an examination of his early career and experience.

Of all of the sons of Mawlāy al-Ḥasan, the one who allegedly most resembled him was his fourth son, Mawlāy ʿAbd al-Ḥafīẓ. The photographs which we possess of him show a tall, well-built man of middle age with a full dark beard, and an intelligent if somewhat haughty face and an imposing bearing. ʿAbd al-Ḥafīẓ was born in 1876.[1] His mother, ʿAliya Sattātiya, was from the rural gentry of the Chaouia. (Her grandfather, al-Ghāzī ibn al-Madanī had been governor of Rabat, the Chaouia, and Tadla under Mawlāy Sulaymān.)[2] From an early age ʿAbd al-Ḥafīẓ appears to have had strong intellectual interests. He also demonstrated considerable aptitude as an administrator. From 1897 to 1901 he served as *khalifa* at Tiznit in the extreme south of the Sous province, while operations were con-

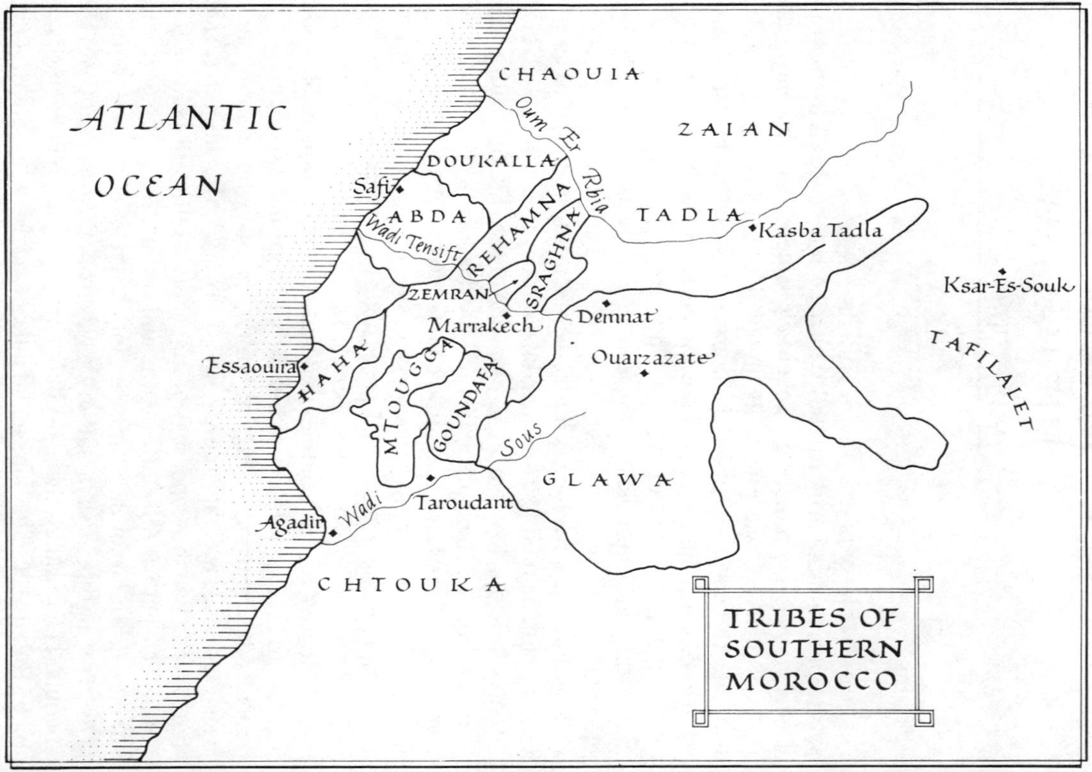
TRIBES OF
SOUTHERN
MOROCCO
ATLANTIC
OCEAN
CHAOUIA
ZAIAN
Oum Er Rbia
DOUKALLA
Safi
ABDA
Wadi Tensift
REHAMNA
SRAGHNA
TADLA
Kasba Tadla
Ksar-Es-Souk
TAFILALET
ZEMRAN
Marrakech
Demnat
Ouarzazate
Essaouira
HAHA
MTOUGGA
GOUNDAFA
Sous
GLAWA
Taroudant
Agadir
Wadi
CHTOUKA

ducted there by the makhzan in an attempt to restore order. Little is known about this period of his life.[3] Later, when the court left Marrakech in November 1901, he became khalifa for his brother there. He was to serve in this position until 1907 when he stepped forward to challenge ʿAbd al-ʿAzīz for the throne.

In contrast to his brother the sultan, ʿAbd al-Ḥafīẓ was an intellectual with a reputation for being a scholar in Muslim theology and law. He was something of a poet, and wrote a number of books, including one which was a vehement attack upon the Tijāniya brotherhood.[4] At various times in his career he studied with some of the most famous scholars in Morocco. He possessed a diploma (*ijāza*) from Shaykh Mā al-ʿAynayn dated 1904,[5] and after becoming sultan was instrumental in recalling Abū Shuʿayb al-Dukkālī from his exile in Medina to become a member of his Royal Learned Council. (Later known as "the Moroccan ʿAbduh," al-Dukkālī was one of the founders of the Islamic modernist Salafiya movement in Morocco.)[6] Under the influence of al-Dukkālī he became a militant Salafī and a strong opponent of heterodox religious practices. ʿAbd al-Ḥafīẓ was a regular subscriber to the Arabic press of Egypt, as well as to *al-Saʿada,* a French-financed Arabic newspaper published in Tangier.[7] He took a strong interest in the latest developments in the Arab East, and (as will be seen below) was something of a pan-Islamist. ʿAbd al-Ḥafīẓ was also keenly interested in European affairs, and appears to have had a shrewd appreciation of the rivalries of the powers and the strength of the opposition parties in France. He had the chief European newspapers translated for him regularly so that he could keep up with foreign opinion toward Morocco.[8] In sum, he was a man of great cultivation and intellect, with a sophisticated understanding of the outside world.

ʿAbd al-Ḥafīẓ possessed other qualities which made him more acceptable as a sultan than his brother to most of Morocco.[9] He had considerable abilities as an administrator, his period as khalifa having made him adept at dealing with the complexities of tribal politics. He possessed the respect of the merchants and religious leaders of Marrakech and knew the proper symbolic gestures to make to reinforce his image among the rural population. At home in the cultivated ambiance of the bourgeois salon, he was also capable of being extremely forceful when he wished. Lacking the playful spirit which was always one of the most noted qualities of ʿAbd al-ʿAzīz, ʿAbd al-Ḥafīẓ was dignified and reserved in his public demeanor. His vices were those of the urban notables: private self-indulgence and a measure of greed. He also possessed a cruel streak and was rather nervous and high-strung. Under the pressures of office his less admirable qualities appear to have become exaggerated.[10] He displayed a selectivity toward European ideas and inventions which had been absent in his predecessor. With his resemblance to his father, and his many impressive qualities, there was reason for the strong popular response which his candidacy evoked.

According to A. G. P. Martin, our principal source on the origins of the Ḥafīẓīya, the conspiracy grew out of several meetings between ʿAbd al-Ḥafīẓ and Madanī al-Glawī during the fall of 1904. The subject of their talks was the deteriorating political situation and certain projects aimed at "assuring the security of Islam."[11] It will be noted that this was also the time when opposition to the French reforms was emerging at Fez. Nonetheless, there seem to have been no significant connections between the two movements, and it was not until 1906 that the backers of ʿAbd al-Ḥafīẓ sought to build a national movement. Further, as will be seen, the Ḥafīẓīya was not a stable coalition but a shifting pattern of alliances in which the main participants constantly recalculated their interests and commitment. This fact made it vulnerable to makhzan divide-and-rule tactics.

In early 1905 Si ʿAissa ibn ʿUmar al-ʿAbdi was invited to join the intrigue. Instead, he refused to cooperate and warned ʿAbd al-ʿAzīz of what was in the wind. Already under pressure from the *aʿyān* of Fez over the French reform proposals, the sultan could ill afford a rebellion. He therefore resolved to take action. In the spring of 1905 he sent a maḥalla under his uncle Mawlāy al-ʿAbbās to collect taxes in the south. In fact ʿAbbās had been given a secret mission: to arrest ʿAbd al-Ḥafīẓ and conduct him to Fez. But word of the plot was leaked to Ḥafīẓ in advance, and with the aid of al-Glawī he was able to thwart his brother's designs.

During the reign of Mawlāy al-Ḥasan, Madanī al-Glawī had been content to build his power base in the south with the support of the makhzan. Already he was interested in the world outside his mountain fastness and was a subscriber to the Arabic press of the Arab East.[12] His experiences during the ill-fated makhzan expedition against Abū Ḥimāra in 1903 appear to have definitively soured him on ʿAbd al-ʿAzīz. A visit to French Algeria seems to have impressed him with the extent of Morocco's backwardness.[13] Soon thereafter he began to speak openly of the need for a crash program to modernize the country. Like many Middle Eastern nationalists, he was much impressed with the victory of Japan in the Russo-Japanese war (1904–1905), which he saw as demonstrating that non-European peoples could achieve progress.[14] His movement into opposition was thus motivated by a sincere patriotism, as well as hopes of personal gain.

While the Moroccan crisis occupied the attention of the elite in the north, ʿAbd al-Ḥafīẓ set about raising money for the campaign. From makhzan properties at Marrakech that were in his charge some money was raised.[15] Loans were obtained locally from Joshua Corcos, the wealthy head of the Marrakech Jewish community, a man later to become known as al-Glawī's banker.[16] But in order for there to be any chance of overthrowing ʿAbd al-ʿAzīz, very substantial sums were required, and these, despite the wealth of the great qāid-s, could not be supplied from local sources alone. Accordingly, Ḥafīẓ dispatched his personal physician, a Syrian Jew named Judah Holzmann, to test the money markets of Europe. Paris showed little interest, but in Berlin Holzmann secured promises of support from the Mannesmann Brothers in return for mining concessions in the Atlas Mountains. Although the German government does not appear to have facilitated the transaction, it does not seem to have sought to discourage it either. In this fashion was initiated what was to blossom into a continuing relationship between ʿAbd al-Ḥafīẓ and the Mannesmanns.[17] Having secured his foreign loan, Ḥafīẓ was free to devote his attention to strengthening the coalition of Glawa and other forces which was the backbone of the Ḥafīẓīya.

From the sources at our disposal it does not appear that significant advances were made in the conspiracy until mid-1906, when ʿAbd al-ʿAzīz finally signed the Algeciras Act. There is even some evidence that for a time there was a cooling of relations between ʿAbd al-Ḥafīẓ and Madanī al-Glawī.[18] While the movement was temporarily stalled, the principals involved explored other options. During this period ʿAbd al-Ḥafīẓ sought to ingratiate himself with the European population of Marrakech. It was at least partly at the invitation of Ḥafīẓ that Dr. Mauchamps opened his clinic there in 1906.[19] The khalifa, no doubt in an effort to protect himself from the intrigues of ʿAbd al-ʿAzīz, covertly solicited the protection of the French government under the auspices of Mauchamps.[20] While ʿAbd al-Ḥafīẓ was cozying up to the Europeans at Marrakech, al-Glāwi was adopting a similar strategy. During a visit of the Marquis de Segonzac, a French explorer, he approached his visitor with the proposal that the French government accord him a patent of protection similar to that which had earlier been granted the Sharif of Wazzan.[21] Neither his request nor that of ʿAbd al-Ḥafīẓ was accepted by the French.[22]

The fierce rivalries of the great qāid-s were to constitute a continuing threat to the possibilities of forging a dependable coalition with which to challenge ʿAbd al-ʿAzīz. The sultan, for his part, was adept at playing upon the jealousies of the qāid-s to keep them off balance. The principal contest was that which pitted Si Tayyib al-Goundafī, qāid of Tagontaft and a long time makhzan ally, against both Madanī al-Glawī and ʿAbd al-Mālik al-Mtouggui. The territory of al-Goundafī extended in both directions down the valley passes of the Tizi N'Tichka which connected Marrakech with the Sous valley. On the east he was pressed by Glawa expansion into the upper Sous (Ras el Oued), while on the west al-Mtougguī contested his control of tribes in the Marrakech plain and along the slopes of the Atlas west of Wadi Nafīs.[23] In 1905 al-Mtougguī forcibly seized the lands of the Ouled Bou Sbaa, a tribe of the Hawz. Unable to oppose al-Mtougguī in the field, al-Goundafī sought redress at Fez. The sultan, who continued to be alarmed by rumors of plots being mounted against him in the south, gave al-Goundafī all that he wanted and more. Tribal governorships were taken from both al-Mtougguī and al-Glawī and given to al-Goundafī. At the same time, ʿAbd al-ʿAzīz secretly ordered al-Goundafī to arrest ʿAbd al-Ḥafīẓ upon his arrival at Marrakech. Once again, however, word of the royal plot was leaked in advance, and al-Goundafī was lucky to make it back to his qasba alive.[24] In the ensuing fight al-Goundafī lost still more tribes to his chief rivals and was effectively eliminated as a major force in the region.

By the spring of 1906, there were signs that ʿAbd al-Ḥafīẓ was once again actively seeking support for his candidacy. In May he held a series of talks at Marrakech with one of the leading political figures of the Chaouia, Abū ʿAzzāwī. He allegedly told Abū ʿAzzāwī that the time for the holy war was fast approaching and urged him to inform the tribes of the Chaouia that they should begin to prepare themselves for the coming struggle. He also allowed himself to be inducted into the Rimāiya, a *ṭarīqa* long associated in the Maghrib with the fifteenth-century resistance to the Portuguese. Upon his return to the Chaouia, Abū ʿAzzāwī convoked the tribes and passed on this grave information.[25] From about this time we can date the recrudescence of agrarian disorders and occasional anti-European incidents in the province that were to culminate in the attack on European workers at Casablanca a year later.

By the end of the summer it was open knowledge that ʿAbd al-Ḥafīẓ was actively preparing for his proclamation as sultan. There were rumors from Marrakech that he had sold arms and ammunition from makhzan stores to the nearby tribes.[26] In September

Mahdī al-Munabbhī revealed in conversation with Regnault at Tangier that ʿAbd al-Ḥafīẓ was in correspondence with his uncle Mawlāy al-Rashīd, the khalifa at Tafilalet. While Mawlāy al-Rashīd had not yet committed himself to support Ḥafīẓ, it was regarded as likely that he soon would.[27] The support of the ʿAlawī sharīfs at Tafilalet, the guardians of the tombs of the dynasty, could be of importance in establishing the legitimacy of ʿAbd al-Ḥafīẓ's claims to the throne.

The cold war of the two brothers continued. In December ʿAbd al-ʿAzīz made yet another attempt to arrest ʿAbd al-Ḥafīẓ. This time he sent five makhzan qāid-s to the south with orders to link up with local forces to capture the khalifa. Again, however, the plan was prematurely disclosed and came to naught.[28] In order to restore himself to favor at Fez, Mawlāy ʿAbd al-Ḥafīẓ took care to send 100,000 pesetas as his gift for the ʿĪd al-Kabir ceremonies. He also sent a letter which protested his innocence of the base suspicions which were directed against him.[29]

The murder of Dr. Mauchamps on March 19, 1907, led to an exacerbation of tensions in the Marrakech area. When the sultan, in an effort to regain control of the rapidly deteriorating situation, sought to appoint a new pasha, the rural populations, led by the Rehamna, banded together to prevent this. The new pasha was to be Ibn al-Ghāzī, a man who had proven his toughness by restoring law and order at Tangier after the Charbonnier affair. ʿAbd al-ʿAzīz had given him secret orders to arrest ʿAbd al-Ḥafīẓ and conduct him to Fez.[30] In early May the Rehamna called a meeting of the tribes in the Hawz and demanded (1) that al-Warzāzī, the present pasha, remain at his post; (2) that the prisoners not be handed over; (3) that all Europeans should leave Marrakech; (4) that the guards at the city gates be withdrawn; and (5) that the Jews be compelled to once again remove their head coverings and go barefoot in the city.[31] A ground swell for the proclamation of ʿAbd al-Ḥafīẓ spread throughout southern Morocco.

The developing radicality of the demands of the tribes of the Hawz placed ʿAbd al-Ḥafīẓ in an awkward position. The French demands for the punishment of the murderers of Mauchamps and the French occupation of Oudjda had focused international attention on Marrakech. A rash move might bring further French reprisals. Yet negotiations for the cooperation of the great qāid-s in the projected rebellion had not yet been completed, and premature action might well jeopardize the possibility of gaining the support of those, like Sī ʿAissa ibn ʿUmar, who continued to waver in their commitment to the cause until assured of its success. Discretion seemed for the moment the best strategy to pursue. With the aid of al-Glawī, ʿAbd al-Ḥafīẓ succeeded in secretly transferring the prisoners taken in the Mauchamps affair to Essaouira, whence they were subsequently moved to Fez for safekeeping.[32] Faced with the continued opposition of the tribes, Ibn al-Ghāzī was unable to advance beyond al-Jadida.

Things dragged on in this state of tension for some months. The outbreak of widespread fighting in the Chaouia, following the landing of French troops, provided the spark which set off the public unveiling of the Ḥafīẓīya. With Abū ʿAzzāwī playing a leading role, the Chaouia tribes held several important assemblies. One result of their deliberations was a letter to ʿAbd al-Ḥafīẓ which urged him, as the best qualified of men, to take action to restore Islam from the low estate into which it had fallen.[33] It is at this point that the tangled history of the origins of the Ḥafīẓīya rejoins our main story.

The Civil War of the Two Sultans

On August 16 the letter of the Chaouia tribes to ʿAbd al-Ḥafīẓ reached Marrakech. The notables and ʿulamā were convoked to the Dār al-Makhzan to discuss the situation and to consider alternative courses of action[34] ʿAbd al-Ḥafīẓ began with a brief statement of his willingness to serve as sultan, stressing his personal reluctance. A number of speakers dwelt upon the desperate situation of the country and the sufferings of the people of the Chaouia. (At the mention of the latter, ʿAbd al-Ḥafīẓ's mother, who was from the region, broke into tears.) The ʿulamā were asked whether it was licit to depose ʿAbd al-ʿAzīz and select another. When they replied in the affirmative, Muḥammad Wuld Mawlāy al-Rashīd (son of the khalifa of Tafilalet) arose and stated, "The only one who is fit for the dignity of king, who is already khalifa, son and grandson of sultans of the imperial dynasty, learned, capable, intelligent, is Mawlāy Ḥafīẓ. May God give him victory!" Madanī al-Glawī then stepped forward and intoned: "May God prolong the life of Mawlāy Ḥafīẓ, our sultan!" All those assembled repeated the invocation. Then the ʿulamā, sharifs, and *aʿyān* all signed the *bayʿa* (the act of allegiance) signifying the accession of a new sultan.[35] The first act of the civil war was over.

The rest of the day and the following one were taken up with public rejoicings. ʿAbd al-Ḥafīẓ was occupied in receiving delegations of the various groups inhabiting the city, including the pasha, the notables, the Fāsī merchants, and the Jews. Over 400,000 pesetas in gifts were collected. Makhzan properties were seized and the revenues from the pious foundations (*hubūs*) diverted to the treasury of the pretender. In accord with established traditions, ʿAbd al-Ḥafīẓ made the ritual pilgrimage to the *zawiya* of Tamesloht in the Atlas to the south, where he was received by the sharifs. On the return journey the party visited also the shrine of Sidi Bel Abbes.[36] By these acts he further solidified his religious legitimacy in the eyes of the tribes.

The new makhzan which was appointed by ʿAbd al-Ḥafīẓ in the first few days after his proclamation was a reflection of the basic forces that had been behind the movement from its early stages. Madanī al-Glawī was named *ʿAllāf al-Kabīr,* or minister of war, since this was the most important position at the time.[37] The grand vizir was Ibn Kabbūr, the pasha of the qasba of Marrakech. He had been named to the makhzan because his loyalty was in doubt and a hostage was needed. He lasted only until May 1908, when al-Glawī took over the formal title—the functions had been his from the beginning.[38] ʿAissa ibn ʿUmar al-ʿAbdī was the Wazīr al-Baḥr, or minister of foreign affairs, although the functions of the office were exercised by his principal secretary, ʿAbdallāh al-Fāsī.[39] Sī ʿAissa was pasha of Safi and the head of the powerful and wealthy Abda confederation; next to al-Glawī, he was able to mobilize the most numerous cavalry force. Al-Mtouggui was Wazīr al-Shikāya, or minister of complaints. The important position of minister of finances went to Sī Tayyib al-Tāzī, a long-time makhzan employee and an Arab.

The insurgency which developed in August 1907 was in many ways unprecedented in the history of Morocco, for it linked in close collaboration a prince of the ʿAlawī house and the Berber chieftains of the Western High Atlas. As such it represented a drastic change in the social composition of the makhzan (hitherto largely confined to Arab makhzan families and the aʿyān of the major cities of the north). By basing his government upon semifeudal Berber chiefs, rather than on an effete clerkly class, ʿAbd al-Ḥafīẓ created a regime which represented real and potent interests in the country and not just an isolated constituency of urban Arab bureaucrats.[40] Such a change opened up possibilities for real reform and ensured that the new regime, were it to succeed in establishing itself, would be markedly stronger than the fragile government of ʿAbd al-ʿAzīz. But should reform begin to cut athwart the interests of the great qāid-s, it could place the new government in a vulnerable position once again.

If it was to develop into a truly national movement, the Ḥafīẓīya would have to obtain the backing of the ʿulamā and aʿyan of Fez. The dominance of the new government by the lords of the Atlas was, however, hardly calculated to reassure these groups.[41] Cementing this alliance would occupy most of the latter half of 1907.

Within a matter of weeks after the proclamation at Marrakech most of the important tribes of the Marrakech plains region had rallied to ʿAbd al-Ḥafīẓ. During the same period, one after the other, the cities of the south proclaimed the pretender. Both Azemmour and El Jadida came over before the end of August.[42] In the latter city, a veritable panic sent the European population to seek refuge in their respective consulates. Wealthy Moroccans (for the most part protégés) fled the city for safer quarters at Tangier. It required bold action by the French consul to prevent the contents of the makhzan armory there from being turned over to the insurgents.[43] Safi, after some initial wavering, proclaimed ʿAbd al-Ḥafīẓ on September 7. On the same day Sī ʿAissa ibn ʿUmar departed for Marrakech with a sizable group of Abda horsemen to take up his position in the government of the pretender.[44] Further north, only the arrival of two French cruisers at Rabat prevented that city and its neighbor, Salé, from erupting in violence and proclaiming Ḥafīẓ.[45] Along the southern Atlantic coast of Morocco, the port of Essaouira alone managed to escape the storm. For the moment, at least, Morocco was divided into two kingdoms, one centered on Marrakech and the south, the other based at Fez and including most of the north.

Even before the proclamation of ʿAbd al-Ḥafīẓ at Marrakech, the political situation of ʿAbd al-ʿAzīz was desperate, and the treasury was empty. A projected move of the court to Marrakech had already been indefinitely postponed due to lack of funds.[46] More embarrassingly, Muḥammad al-Ghibbas had been obliged to take out a personal loan at Tangier in order to pay his troops operating against al-Raysūnī.[47] To regain the initiative, on August 18 ʿAbd al-ʿAzīz caused the ʿulamā of Fez to issue a *fatwā* in which they reaffirmed his legitimacy and denounced the machinations of ʿAbd al-Ḥafīẓ.[48] He also desperately tried to convince the tribes in the Chaouia to make peace before things became too inflamed.[49] Neither effort seemed to work. On August 24, the Europeans resident in Fez departed for the coast to avoid incidents.[50] It was open knowledge that ʿAbd al-Ḥafīẓ had many supporters at Fez. ʿAbd al-ʿAzīz resolved to transfer the court to Rabat, where it would be in greater safety. An advance was needed from the state bank to permit the trip. It was granted, and on September 12 the royal maḥalla departed for the coast.[51] It was the last time ʿAbd al-ʿAzīz would lay eyes upon Fez as sultan.

Before leaving Fez, ʿAbd al-ʿAzīz had asked that a French diplomatic mission be sent to Rabat, to undertake discussions with the makhzan on a variety of outstanding matters. He hoped in the process to secure promises of a new major loan, desperately needed if his regime was to survive the challenge of ʿAbd al-Ḥafīẓ. He was to be disappointed. The mission duly arrived on October 7. It was headed by Henri Regnault, the head of the Contrôle de la Dette, and included in its party General Lyautey, the French commander at Oudjda.[52] The negotiations were long and tedious. By December ʿAbd al-ʿAzīz had agreed to a broad range of French demands. France and Spain were to be permitted to install without delay the port police laid down by the Algeciras Act. On a variety of other matters the sultan made important concessions, including the customs regime, the ownership of property by Europeans, and compensation to European commercial interests for losses suffered at Casablanca in the rioting.[53] Only by pawning the crown jewels was ʿAbd al-ʿAzīz able to raise even a small (1,800,000 francs) short-term loan at Paris.[54] About the only concrete thing which he received from Regnault was the *grand cordon* of the Legion of Honor (which rumor soon transformed into the baptism of the sultan). The pusillanimous attitude of the French government disgusted Lyautey, who felt that a golden opportunity to secure a protectorate had been let slip away.[55] Instead of strongly supporting ʿAbd al-ʿAzīz, the French government, under fire domestically, declared a policy of strict neutrality between the two sultans.

The forces that were unloosed by the landing of the French in the Chaouia were only with difficulty channeled and controlled by the proclamation of ʿAbd al-Ḥafīẓ. The turbulent tribes of the Hawz of Marrakech, in particular the Rehamna and Seraghna, threatened the city with attack unless forthright steps were taken to implement the mandate of the new sultan: *jihād*.[56] The pretender was placed in a cruel dilemma. As long as his regime was not securely seated in the south, he remained vulnerable to defections in his rear and could not risk leaving Marrakech for the Chaouia. Not all of the great qāid-s had joined his cause. Soon after his proclamation at Marrakech, al-Goundafi had retreated to his qasba in the mountains to wait out the struggle.[57] Alone Goundafi could do little, but the qāid who controlled the region around Essaouira, Sī Aḥmad al-ʿAnflūs, had also rallied to the cause of ʿAzīz in the expectation of substantial reward. ʿAnflūs was the mortal enemy of al-Mtougguī, and as long as his rival remained in the pretender's camp he would pick the opposite side.[58] Then too, ʿAbd al-Ḥafīẓ was reluctant to have himself too closely identified with the cause of jihād as long as there remained a chance of garnering support in Europe, or at least in convincing the French that he was not a direct threat. In September he dispatched two notables to Hamburg, there to seek firm commitments from sympathetic business enterprises. The group was also to make a tour of the European capitals to sound out the governments on possible support.[59] Until they returned, ʿAbd al-Ḥafīẓ was obliged to follow a policy of restraint.

In order to occupy the energies of the tribes, who were showing increasing anxiety about the fate of their brothers in the Chaouia, ʿAbd al-Ḥafīẓ allowed a maḥalla of about 3,000 men to be formed at Marrakech under the direction of Muḥammad Wuld Mawlāy al-Rashīd.[60] On September 16 it departed for the Chaouia, joined by tribesmen from the Rehamna and other Hawz groups. On the twenty-sixth it camped at Settat on the fringes of the Chaouia. While ibn al-Rashīd adopted an attitude of restraint, his tribal auxiliaries immediately joined forces with the Chaouia resistance bands.[61] During the months which followed he himself would become very deeply involved in the struggle. At about the same time as the arrival of the maḥalla in the Chaouia, there came the text of the formal *bayʿa* of ʿAbd al Ḥafīẓ, which had been signed by the ʿulamā of Marrakech on September 4th. It was circulated throughout Morocco during the weeks which followed and stimulated a further wave of support for his cause.[62] Several weeks later, ʿAbd al-Ḥafīẓ strengthened his ties with his chief allies by marrying daughters of Madanī al-Glawī and Sī ʿAissa ibn ʿUmar at Marrakech.[63]

In the Chaouia the fighting went through several stages during the first months after the French landing.[64] French troops under General Drude were able to pacify the zone immediately surrounding Casablanca by the end of September, due primarily to their superior firepower. But the French government in Paris, anxious to avoid charges of preparing the military conquest of Morocco, had specifically restricted General Drude's freedom of operations to fifteen kilometers from the coast.[65] Thus French victories like the September 11 attack on the rebel camp at Taddert were never followed up, and the tribes were always able to regroup beyond the range of French cannon and return to the offensive. The ponderous and methodical style of combat favored by Drude, who had his troops maneuver in the classic square formation, was ill-suited to deal with lightly armed but highly mobile tribal forces. French search-and-destroy operations served principally to antagonize the Chaouia population further. But through the efforts of mediators sent by ʿAbd al-ʿAzīz at least the tribes of the immediate hinterland were briefly convinced to submit and provide hostages. On September 25 and 26 representatives of the Awlād Ziyān, Awlād Harīz, Ziyāda, Zenata, and Madiuna agreed to lay down their arms and to resume their dealings with the markets at Casablanca.[66]

The arrival in the Chaouia on September 26th of the maḥalla of ibn Rashīd and its combative tribal auxiliaries soon reversed the trend toward a cooling of hostilities. Emissaries began to circulate among the tribes of the eastern edge of the province, encouraging them to redouble their efforts. They also threatened to attack any group which made peace with the French. In the face of the rekindling of enthusiasm for the holy war, those tribes who had been engaged in negotiations broke off immediately and withdrew to the hills beyond the range of French attack.[67] Several engagements between the forces of General Drude and the resistance forces marked the month of October, as volunteers began to flock to the scene from all over Morocco.

The authority of ʿAbd al-ʿAzīz, which had been momentarily strengthened by the submissions of September was placed once again in jeopardy by the renewal of hostilities. Vigorous action was called for to reestablish the royal prestige, but the penury of the treasury precluded more than a token effort. By dint of desperate expedients, a sharifian maḥalla of about 4,500 men was finally assembled at Rabat in late October under the command of Abū Shatā al-Baghdādī. Al-Baghdādī announced that his mission was the pacification of the Chaouia and requested that General Drude allow him to proceed without inconvenience. The rainy season had begun by the time that al-Baghdādī's forces set out for the Chaouia. After some initial successes they became bogged down in difficult terrain among the Ziyada. Despite further reinforcements from Rabat, which swelled the numbers of the maḥalla to 7,000, it was only with the greatest difficulty that the column could advance. Both officers and men were lacking in experience and were ill-trained. As they had not been paid for weeks, they began to sell their rifles and ammunition to the Chaouia forces. On November 24 al-Baghdādī's forces came under heavy attack while in the process of defending submitted *duwār*-s in Ziyada territory. They came into conflict with rebel forces commanded by ibn Rashīd. After a day-long struggle, Baghdādī's ragtag forces were utterly routed.[68] The prestige of ʿAbd al-ʿAzīz had suffered a major blow.

Several important developments marked the remainder of the fall. ʿAbd al-ʿAzīz succeeded in recouping much of what he had lost by the defeat of al-Baghdādī with the aid of France. On October 23 a force of 700 men under Ibn al-Ghāzī was landed from French ships at Essaouira. The city, which had managed to resist the blandishments of Ḥafīẓīya propaganda thus far, was reported to be threatened by a maḥalla sent from Marrakech. Through quick action, the city was saved and the maḥalla eventually defeated by Ibn al-Ghāzī's men in alliance with the forces of ʿAnflūs.[69] A month later, the pattern was repeated as another sharifian force was landed at al-Jadida. While several French cruisers sat just offshore, the town fell without a shot being fired.[70] Only the port of Safi remained in the control of ʿAbd al-Ḥafīẓ. With the assent of ʿAbd al-ʿAzīz, the French set about organizing police contingents in the newly recaptured ports, as well as in those of the north. There were some protests from local notables, but on the whole the organization of the port police was able to proceed freely.[71]

Several important gains were made by the Ḥafīẓīya after the defeat of al-Baghdādī. In November Moha ou Hamou, chief of the powerful Zaian confederation, emerged from his neutrality and sent his formal adhesion to the cause. At about the same time Shaykh Abū ʿAzzāwī escaped from custody at Rabat and rejoined the resistance forces in the Chaouia. Volunteers from all over the country swelled ibn al-Rashid's forces to over 10,000.[72] Reports from Tafilalet, where ʿAbd al-Ḥafīẓ had been recognized early, indicated that the tribes were planning to attack French posts along the Algerian frontier.[73] To the north, around Oudjda, a sudden flare-up of hostility against the French indicated that in that quarter, too, the unrest had penetrated.[74] At Fez, the intensification of the struggle between avowed Ḥafīẓists and partisans of the existing government showed signs of coming to a head.[75] The tendency of the rebellion to spread beyond the borders of the Chaouia and the province of Marrakech was a severe blow to ʿAbd al-ʿAzīz. It was becoming clear even to hostile French observers that ʿAbd al-Ḥafīẓ was more than just another rebel like Abū Himārā.

At Marrakech in the meantime, preparations for the departure of the court for the Chaouia dragged on. ʿAbd al-Ḥafīẓ occupied himself with a last attempt to convince the French government that his intentions were not hostile. He gave several interviews to French journalists to that effect, but the die was by this time already cast.[76] The return of the emissaries who had been sent to Europe earlier only underlined this conclusion. Although they had been well received in Germany, no firm commitments had been made.[77] For the moment ʿAbd al-Ḥafīẓ hesitated between marching to retake Essaouira and proceeding directly to the Chaouia. In the end the latter objective proved more compelling, and the court set out on the route north. By December 5, it was encamped in the hill country on the edge of the Chaouia plain.[78] There, with some shifting of site, it would remain until April 1908.

Finally, mention should be made of the outbreak of a jihād against French posts near Oudjda on November 23. The insurrection was led by the Berber tribe of Beni Snassen (Ait Iznāsin), and was initially successful, forcing the French to give ground. But French troops, commanded by General Lyautey, soon regrouped and went on the offensive. By January 12, after a series of deft political and military maneuvers had fragmented and demoralized them, the Beni Snassen rebels sued for peace. This remarkable achievement dramatically underscored the advantages of the Lyautey system of pacification as opposed to the more static approach of Drude in the Chaouia. It no doubt served to reinforce the French government's resolve to replace General Drude. The Beni Snassen rebellion was significant for other reasons as well. Although apparently primarily local in character, it in fact was clearly connected with the general movement in favor of ʿAbd al-Ḥafīẓ throughout Morocco. It appears to have been sparked by news of the success of the forces of Muḥammad ibn al-Rashīd in the Chaouia.[79] More dramatic demonstrations of the national scope of the Ḥafīẓīya were soon to follow.

The Triumph of Mawlāy ʿAbd al-Ḥafīẓ

The intersection of popular sentiments for the jihād and agrarian disorders with the pro-Hafīẓ attitudes of the urban notables, which had provided the motor of the Ḥafīẓīya revolution in the south was dramatically intensified as a result of developments at Fez in the month of December 1907. The bitter opposition of much of the aʿyān of Fez to ʿAbd al-ʿAzīz had originally been responsible for the decision of the sultan to transfer the court to Rabat. After the departure of the sultan, Fez had gradually drifted into a state of virtual civil war. ʿAbd al-ʿAzīz was represented at the city through the governor of Fez, al-Jadid. An important group of notables (among which the Tāzī and al-Baghdādī families stand out) remained firmly committed to his cause. But the forces that opposed the sultan, led by Muḥammad al-Kattānī were numerous and grew steadily bolder during the fall. In order to preserve security under such tense circumstances, the regular municipal administration of the city was set aside, and a three-man committee selected by the notables of the various quarters was put in its place. Fortified by strong social and religious sanctions against breaches of order, it was charged with governing the city until the political situation should became stabilized.

By November, the rural populations living near Fez began increasingly to escape the control of their qāid-s. Agrarian unrest had been more or less endemic in the region since the ill-fated decision to implement the tartīb. The subsequent difficulties of ʿAbd al-ʿAzīz further exacerbated the situation. Finally, on December 15 came the explosion. Peasants from the Oulad el Hadj district burst into Fez, armed with rifles and clubs. They angrily denounced the maks, a tax on goods entering or leaving the city. Once within the gates, they joined forces with the urban mob and set about breaking open the nearby strongboxes in which the maks was deposited and attacking the umanā charged with its collection. The crowd then proceeded into the heart of the city where it burned and laid waste the building which housed the Tobacco monopoly. In the *sūq*-s a minor panic ensued. Merchants frantically closed their shops to prevent looting. One establishment, owned by a wealthy Jew, was thoroughly pillaged. Then, after attacking the French post office, where they were repulsed, the rioters descended upon the Jewish quarter, which hastily closed its gates. For the next two days the revolt continued. Eventually the merchants were able to regain control by organizing a kind of civil guard made up of their employees and slaves. Calm gradually returned to the city, although the *mallāḥ* remained threatened by isolated groups of rioters for several days afterwards. A day or two later the same scene was repeated at Meknes, some seventy-five miles away, where Beni Mtir and other tribesmen descended upon the city.[80] The disturbances at Fez and Meknes were only suppressed with difficulty by the forces of order.

The people of Fez had long been known for their rebellious spirit. Several times during the nineteenth century they had revolted, often in conjunction with rural uprisings. In 1873, they had taken advantage of the death of Muhammad III to protest against the maks. It was only after much difficulty that Mawlāy al-Ḥasan managed to restore order. One feature of this insurrectionary tradition was the opposition between Old Fez and New Fez, the latter being the area where the sultans resided when they were at Fez. The riots of December and January thus took place within a well-defined tradition of popular protest.[81]

On December 30 an envoy from the court at Rabat, Sī Idrīs al-Fāsī, arrived at Fez with a message from ʿAbd al-Azīz. Rumor had it that he carried secret correspondence to the ʿulamā requesting them to issue a *fatwā* authorizing another major foreign loan. He was soon surrounded by an angry crowd which demanded that the letter be read in public. The letter turned out in fact to be merely a message of thanks to the aʿyān of Fez for the way they had handled the disturbances of December 15–17. For the moment the crowd withdrew. But it soon reassembled near the tomb of Sīdī ʿAbd al-Qādir Tāzī and, now thoroughly aroused, proclaimed itself independent of the sultan and ʿulamā. Then it ordered seven of the ʿulamā of Fez to appear before it and demanded that they secure the secret correspondence and read it to them. Denying still the existence of such letters, the ʿulamā accompanied the crowd (which by this time numbered about 20,000) to the Qarawīyīn mosque. There they were asked to render a formal legal opinion (*fatwā*) on the suitability of ʿAbd al-ʿAzīz to continue as sultan. The ʿulamā requested a one-day delay in order to consider their response. Other members of the ʿulamā had by this time come to the mosque, including Mawlāy Idrīs al-Zarawtī, a member of the three-man interim municipal government. Again they sought to postpone their decision, and again they were shouted down by the crowd. By now some 40,000 people were jammed into the mosque and the adjoining side streets. After a brief consultation, the qādī of Fez pronounced the opinion of the ʿulamā: "This man, ʿAbd al-ʿAzīz, must be deposed right away." The ʿulamā all signed the fatwā to the acclamation of the crowd. Public criers spread the news throughout the city, announcing the deposition of ʿAbd al-ʿAzīz. The next several days were followed by rejoicings and attempts to intimidate known supporters of ʿAbd al-ʿAzīz remaining in the city.[82]

On January 3 another mass meeting was held, this one at the Mawlāy Idrīs mosque. The chiefs of neighboring tribes, notables, and ʿulamā all gathered together with a very numerous crowd to sign the formal proclamation (*bayʿa*) of ʿAbd al-Ḥafīẓ. It had been written by Aḥmad ibn al-Mawāz, a secretary of al-Gharnīṭ's and an early member of the Ḥafīẓīya at Fez. It included a number of conditions which the new sultan would be expected to fulfill. According to its terms ʿAbd al-Ḥafīẓ would be required to (1) abrogate the

Algeciras Act; (2) do his utmost to restore Morocco's territorial integrity; (3) bring about the evacuation of French troops from Casablanca and Oudjda; (4) undertake no agreements with foreigners except with the approval of the people; (5) abolish the maks; (6) restore and revivify the practice of Islam; (7) abolish foreign privileges and capitulations; (8) seek a closer cooperation with other Muslim powers, especially the Ottoman state; and (9) repudiate the debts which had been contracted by ʿAbd al-ʿAzīz.[83]

There is some dispute over what happened next. Most sources agree that the attempt to name ʿAbd al-Ḥafīẓ in the conditional bayʿa was opposed by many who doubted if the pretender would accept such a document. At this juncture, Muhammad al-Kattānī allegedly intervened and declared that, if there was any question about whether the conditions would be acceptable to ʿAbd al-Ḥafīẓ, he, for one, was willing to abide by them himself. In the face of Kattānī's threat to accept the conditions of the bayʿa himself, the backers of Ḥafīẓ immediately agreed to the conditions on behalf of their candidate. French sources, which are inclined to underscore the demagogy of al-Kattānī, have claimed that the incident represents an abortive coup d'état by the fanatical shaykh.[84] While there is considerable evidence that attests to the rivalry between al-Kattānī and ʿAbd al-Ḥafīẓ, the French interpretation is not the only one possible. It may be that al-Kattānī merely wished to get ʿAbd al-Ḥafīẓ put on record as favoring the demands of the aroused peasants and common people. The incident remains obscure.

The signing of the bayʿa document was the result of the convergence of a number of forces, not all of them compatible in the long run. The conditions reflect the interests of the main elements of the coalition—the ʿulamā, makhzan officials, and merchants of the city. Its author, Ibn al-Mawāz, was a makhzan employee and a known supporter of ʿAbd al-Ḥafīẓ. The document can also be read as an explicit statement of the program of jihād. It breathes the spirit of religious revival and calls for the rigorous application of the *sharīʿa* in all realms of life. Provisions for the abolition of uncanonical taxes, the restrictions placed on Europeans, even the injunction to seek alliances with other Muslim powers can be interpreted in this way. An attempt to turn back the clock to the days when Islam commanded respect, the bayʿa could only be rejected by the pretender.

The signing of the bayʿa by the ʿulamā of Fez virtually ensured the success of the Ḥafīẓīya. In the space of a few weeks the position of ʿAbd al-ʿAzīz underwent a dramatic shift, as one by one the chief cities of the interior went over to his rival. On January 17 Mawlāy Ḥafīẓ was proclaimed by the populace at Sefrou. On the eighteenth, the qāḍī and ʿulamā of Meknes, confronted by a large and angry crowd, added their signatures to the bayʿa. Soon thereafter, the sharifs of Wazzan, threatened with the loss of their economic privileges in and around Fez by aroused tribesmen, proclaimed ʿAbd al-Ḥafīẓ at Wazzan in turn.[85]

After the proclamation of ʿAbd al-Ḥafīẓ by the ʿulamā of Fez on January 4, 1908, the Ḥafīẓīya made no further advances until March. The bulk of the pretender's forces remained concentrated upon the combat with French troops in the Chaouia, and both sultans used the time to attempt to foment disorder and unrest in the camp of the other by means of false letters, dramatic defections, and declarations of intent which placed the opposition on guard. The marabout of Boujad, Sīdī Muḥammad ibn Dawūd, who had been won over to the cause of ʿAbd al-ʿAzīz by promises of French subvention, succeeded in fomenting disorders among the Sraghna in the Houz of Marrakech, thereby temporarily creating a barrier to communications between ʿAbd al-Ḥafīẓ and the tribes of the Tadla region.[86] In the Fez region, rumors that ʿAbd al-ʿAzīz was about to dispatch a maḥalla to Fez to chastise those who had deserted his cause led to a certain weakening of support for the pretender. The tribes of the region, especially those, like the Zemmour, along the strategically important route from Rabat to Fez either wavered in their attitudes or accepted bribes from one side or the other (occasionally from both).[87] The pasha of New Fez, ʿAbd al-Karīm Wuld Abī Muḥammad Sharqī, qāid of the jaysh tribe of Cheraga, remained covertly loyal to ʿAbd al-ʿAzīz while making gestures of support for ʿAbd al-Ḥafīẓ.[88] This kind of maneuvering for position was characteristic during the cold war of the two sultans.

In the Chaouia, the situation had changed considerably since General d'Amade had taken command of French forces. Throughout the months of January and February the French took the offensive. The constant circulation of military columns, active political propaganda, and the creation of dispensaries and markets near French posts at crossroads split the main Moroccan force into smaller groups.[89] D'Amade then pursued these in turn, and by March had driven the maḥalla of Muḥammad ibn al-Rashīd across the Oum er Rbia River and out of the Chaouia. The main body of resistance forces under Abu ʿAzzāwī was driven from Settat to the high country at the southeastern edge of the province. The tribes in the vicinity of Casablanca and within the range of French posts presented their submission to the French commander.[90] Since many tribesmen from outside the Chaouia had come to participate in the fighting, their return home with tales of French invulnerability did much to discourage more active support of ʿAbd al-Ḥafīẓ in their home areas.[91]

The series of offensives which d'Amade launched against the Chaouia maḥalla placed ʿAbd al-Ḥafīẓ in serious jeopardy. The best strategy would have been for him to proceed on to Fez, then raise additional forces and attack ʿAbd al-ʿAzīz at Rabat. The French attacks required him to concentrate all of his men in the Chaouia and leave thoughts of other things aside. In this way ʿAbd al-ʿAzīz gained several precious months, while his brother was compelled to strain his resources to the utmost and in this way to further augment existing tensions within his coalition.[92]

A dramatic stroke was clearly needed by ʿAbd al-Ḥafīẓ to restore confidence in his cause. To retreat to Marrakech would imply the abandonment of all hope of ousting his brother, while to continue the murderous combat in the Chaouia was equally unthinkable. Even though severely pressed by the French, he had one choice that remained open—to make the difficult journey to Fez along the seldom-used interior route and to link up with his supporters in the north.

He began negotiations with the Berber tribes between the Chaouia and Fez along the dangerous interior route. Protracted discussions with Moha ou Hamou Zaiani, leader of the very powerful Zaian tribe, concluded in an agreement that the Zaian would guarantee the passage of ʿAbd al-Ḥafīẓ and his force to the north. The alliance was sealed by the marriage of Ḥafīẓ to a daughter of Zaiani.[93] To insure that the tribes of the south would not revolt against him immediately after he left, Ḥafīẓ adopted the device of keeping notables from each tribe along the route as hostages.

Having first insured safe passage, ʿAbd al-Ḥafīẓ set out for the north in April. After passing through the territory of the Zaian (where he was received by Moha ou Hamou in person) and the Oulmès plateau, he made his triumphant entry into Meknes on May 16.[94] By this trip he became only the third of the sultans of modern Morocco to have accomplished the journey from Marrakech to Fez by traversing the territory of the Middle Atlas Berbers.[95] The political reverberations of this important accomplishment were considerable, especially in the north where the power of the Middle Atlas Berbers was known and feared.

The participation of the Tafilalet oasis and the region of the southeast in the struggle has already been noted. Initially the region was content to send contingents to fight in the Chaouia.[96] But by early 1908 the focus of anti-French militancy had switched to the upper Guir valley. There, at the Darqawa zawīya of Douiret Sbaa (Ar. Da'ira Sabaʿ), Mawlāy Aḥmad Ḥasan al-Sabaʿ emerged from a lifetime of asceticism and prayer to preach the jihād. Mawlāy al-Ḥasan had great prestige in the area owing to his undoubted religious charisma. In February 1908, a force composed of men from the tribes of Ait Izdig, Ait Seghrushin, Ait Aissa, and from the *qsār*-s in the upper Guir valley began to assemble. Over 4,000 individuals took part. By April they were ready to take action and had decided upon Colomb-Béchar as their objective.[97]

On April 16 they attacked a French column at Menabha, a point between Colomb-Béchar and Ain Chaīr. Heavily outnumbered and surprised, the French fought desperately. After a lengthy engagement they succeeded in driving off the attackers by dint of their superior armament and discipline but not before they suffered heavy casualties. The *ḥaraka* withdrew to the west, pursued by French reinforcements who had been hastily assembled. Near Bou Denib the Moroccan force paused to give battle. On May 14 the French column attacked and chased the *ḥaraka* from the oasis, which was then occupied. Thereafter the tribes dispersed and returned to their homes. The resistance effort of the tribes of the upper Guir was over.[98]

The news of the French occupation of Bou Denib sent shock waves throughout the region. Armed banks from the High and Middle Atlas set off for the frontier to assist their brothers in expelling the French. The tribes of the Ziz valley, notably the powerful Ait Khabbash, sent several thousand men north to join in the struggle. From as far away as the Chaouia, Moroccans are alleged to have come for one final effort. Mawlāy ʿAlī Amhawsh, a leading religious figure in the Middle Atlas, urged a jihād against the French assembled at Bou Denib. After several false starts the ḥaraka (which by now numbered 20,000 men) moved against the French blockhouse on September 1. The ensuing battle lasted sixteen hours. When it was over, the Moroccans had suffered devastating losses, and France had won a great victory. A French relief column completed the rout, fragmenting what remained of the ḥaraka and driving the remnants back down the Ziz valley and into the Atlas. Thereafter France was able to move virtually unchallenged to the pacification of the entire region of the upper Guir.[99]

Events on the southeastern frontier, culminating in the battle of

Bou Denib have generally been seen as forming part of Algerian history, not the history of Morocco. However, recent studies have extablished their close connection with events in central Morocco at this time.[100] As in the case of the jihād of the Beni Snassen to the north, events in the upper Guir in 1908 must be seen in a wider Moroccan context. (It is likely that the series of attacks upon French forces in the Saqiyāt al-Ḥamra and Mauretania in the same period are also to be seen in the light of events in central Morocco.)[101]

The decision to move to the north brought about the first significant defection from the Ḥafīẓīya. In early April, right after the decision had been made, ʿAbd al-Mālik al-Mtouggui left camp for the south, taking with him all of his supporters.[102] The great coalition appeared ready to disintegrate before the pretender was fairly launched. In the meantime, the merchants and traders of Marrakech became seriously upset by the incessant tax demands of the pasha, al-Ḥājj Tahamī al-Glawī. A rumor began to circulate that they might welcome the return of ʿAbd al-ʿAzīz. Al-Mtouggui, in the meantime, remained aloof and temporarily inactive at his qasba in Bouaboud. Emissaries sent to him by ʿAbd al-Ḥafīẓ urging that he rejoin him failed to achieve their purpose; similar missions which tried to win over the ʿAzīzist great qāid, Sī Aḥmad al-ʿAnflūs (Fr. Anflous), who controlled the region around the port of Essaouira also failed.[103]

While al-Mtouggui adopted an enigmatic position and the bourgeoisie of Marrakech became restless under Glawa rule, ʿAbd al-ʿAzīz was reaching a decision to march on Marrakech and his brother was preparing for his formal entry into Fez. On July 12 ʿAbd al-ʿAzīz left Rabat at the head of a maḥalla of 4,000 men. Several military instructors were attached to his forces to assist in the operation of the imperial artillery. After a brief stop at Temara, the advance continued; by July 24 his forces had reached Sokhrat Ed-Djeja on the border between the Chaouia and Tadla. The Oum er Rbia was crossed on August 8, and the maḥalla appeared likely to continue its advance to Marrakech with little difficulty. The only force of note which remained to be dealt with was that of ʿAlāl al-Glawī, the qāid of Demnat, which advanced rapidly. On August 19 a battle took place at a place called Bou Ajiba. ʿAbd al-ʿAzīz was totally defeated as a result of the defection of his tribal auxiliaries at a crucial moment in the battle. He was able to escape back to the Chaouia relatively unharmed, although his jellaba was pierced by bullet holes in half a dozen places. On August 21 ʿAbd al-ʿAzīz reached Casablanca and abdicated the throne.[104]

From the beginning of the Ḥafīẓīya revolt, French students of Morocco had blindly insisted upon its localized character, denying that it represented anything more than an isolated handful of fanatics. Now, with their sultan defeated in the field, there were still some whose hopes continued to mount. The object of their enthusiasm (quite misplaced as it turned out) was ʿAbd al-Mālik al-Mtouggui, who stubbornly persisted to hold out in the south.[105] Al-Mtouggui's men still subjected Marrakech to a loose investment. But French attempts to mount an expeditionary force to join up with him were doomed before they started. Madanī al-Glawī and ʿAissa ibn ʿUmar soon arrived from the north with substantial reinforcements. After lengthy negotiations, the three entered Marrakech on October 1, and the crisis came to an end.[106] For the moment the three great qāids returned to their family domains, apparently determined to have nothing further to do with ʿAbd al-Ḥafīẓ or his government. Not until early 1909 were they to return to Fez with their private armies. Their prolonged holdout caused considerable anxiety to ʿAbd al-Ḥafīẓ but caused little damage to his short-term ability to govern.

The confusing reversal of political loyalties in the south had almost resulted in the bizarre exchange of capital cities by the two sultans. From March 1908 events in the north revealed no less strikingly the great divisions which existed within the Ḥafīẓīya movement there. The leader of the anti-ʿAzīz faction at Fez, al-Kattānī, met ʿAbd al-Ḥafīẓ at Meknes with many of the notables of the region. Al-Kattānī had been preparing to go with a large volunteer force from the region to fight against the French in the Chaouia. The rather moderate language which ʿAbd al-Ḥafīẓ used with him came as a sharp disappointment. Al-Kattānī did not delay long in making his discontent known at Fez.[107] This soon increased when Ḥafīẓ rejected the conditional bayʿa by which the ʿulamā at Fez had proclaimed him sultan, and demanded one without conditions attached.

Significantly, the great financial needs of Mawlāy ʿAbd al-Ḥafīẓ moved him to take actions that soon exposed the fragile basis on which his rule in the north rested. Upon his arrival at Meknes he was unable to pay his troops. To raise the necessary revenues he was compelled to reestablish the maks and the tobacco monopoly and even to double them, this despite the fact of their abolition by the conditional bayʿa. When even this was insufficient, he seized the property belonging to the families of prominent ʿAzīzist officials at Fez.[108] These measures generated great displeasure among the merchants of the city.

While still at Meknes, ʿAbd al-Ḥafīẓ made two appointments of makhzan officials which aroused further opposition. Sī Aḥmad al-Jāʾī was named *muḥtasib* of Fez, and Tayyib al-Muqrī was made the new minister of finances. When the news of this became known at Fez, a riot almost broke out, for both men were infamous former supporters of ʿAbd al-ʿAzīz. The news of the deteriorating political situation at Fez decided Mawlāy Ḥafīẓ to advance the date of his arrival in the city. On June 2 he left Meknes, and after the traditional visit to the shrine of Mawlāy Idrīs at Jabal Zerhoun, he made his solemn entry into the capital on June 7.[109] At this time he adopted as his regnal title the device "al-Ghāzī," that is, "victor in the holy war."[110] He also named a son of Moha ou Hamou al-Zaiani as pasha of Fez al-Bali, in spite of further grumblings from the population.[111] The great gamble had paid off. ʿAbd al-Ḥafīẓ had reached Fez and established his rule there. A new wave of support for his cause was the result.

For the next several months ʿAbd al-Ḥafīẓ ruled uneasily at Fez. His financial needs and his moderation continued to stimulate splits within the movement that had supported him in the region. The merchants were outraged by the way in which he was obliged to reinstitute taxes and erode their privileges. Ardent opponents of ʿAbd al-ʿAzīz were angered by his appointment of known ʿAzīzists to high office. The ʿulamā objected to his moderation and were scandalized by his attempt to introduce innovations such as the sale of decorations in imitation of European powers. The tribes, who had been partisans of a militant anti-French stance, continued to show their disappointment at his renunciation of the jihād. Much the same thing was true of the partisans of al-Kattānī at Fez. A smouldering discontent enveloped the region. It looked as if the Ḥafīẓīya was in the process of disintegration, its many successes notwithstanding.[112]

All of this was changed by the dramatic news from the Chaouia of the rout of ʿAbd al-ʿAzīz's maḥalla on August 19 at Bou Ajiba. The subsequent reconciliation of the great qāid-s completed the triumph of ʿAbd al-Ḥafīẓ. While many difficulties remained before his regime would be fully secure, the extent of his accomplishment was already remarkable. Against great odds, the Ḥafīẓīya had been able to depose one sultan and establish another upon the throne. For a comparable episode in Middle Eastern history one has to look to the

Iranian constitutional revolution of 1906–1909. But in neither range nor intensity does the national struggle in Iran appear to have equalled that in Morocco.

The Ḥafīẓīya in the Perspective of Time

Any explanation of the Ḥafīẓīya must begin with the particular conjuncture of political and economic forces within which it evolved. By 1907 the long-term commercial penetration of the West, drastically accelerated at the end of the nineteenth century, had largely undermined the bases of the existing economic system. The French colonial offensive since 1903 (and more generally the international control exercised since 1880) exerted a pressure which gradually produced a situation of generalized political crisis. The incapacities and mistakes of ʿAbd al-ʿAzīz further magnified all of these difficulties and raised grave doubts about his suitability to continue as sultan. The severe economic downturn in 1905–1906 and the signing of the Act of Algeciras constituted the final elements in this steadily worsening situation. By 1907 Morocco confronted a situation of multiple and intersecting crises. If the existence of these strains provided the essential context within which the Ḥafīẓīya revolt could develop, it is important to realize that the international conjuncture (and that of French domestic politics) made unlikely a determined French effort to conquer Morocco. This fact ultimately enabled the Ḥafīẓīya to achieve success, safe from vigorous counterattack.

If we can account for the existence of a revolt in Morocco in 1907–1908 in this fashion, how are we to explain the form which it took? Various answers suggest themselves. To the historian of Morocco one likely response might be that in the Ḥafīẓīya we are witnessing a repetition of that intransigence in the face of European attack first displayed in the widespread resistance to the Portuguese and Spanish in the fifteen and sixteenth centuries.[113] Certainly the old heroes were very much in the minds of Moroccans who responded to the call of jihād in the Chaouia in 1907. Whatever other similarities may exist, and there are several, including the vitality of the rural populations and the role of popular Islam, there are several crucial differences between the two movements. One is the nationwide character of resistance in 1907–1908, the fact that all over Morocco individuals responded to the appeal of ʿAbd al-Ḥafīẓ to combat the French and overthrow ʿAbd al-ʿAzīz. While far from unitary, this response was to an extent centralized and directed by the pretender. The fifteenth-century resistance movements on the other hand were highly fragmented, with a variety of regionally based centers and much competition among the different movements. No conception of *la patrie en danger* motivated the fifteenth-century groups. Further, the Ḥafīẓīya provoked fierce divisions in Moroccan society down to the local level; all were forced sooner or later to take sides, and their positions were noted. It was a truly national political event of major importance, perhaps the first in Moroccan history to affect so many people. At times the lines of division pitted brother against brother. Years later old men still remembered, with a flickering of passion, who had been the ʿAzīzists and who the Ḥafīẓīsts. The Ḥafīẓīya therefore constituted a new phenomenon in Moroccan history.

With an eye to seventeenth-century France, another explanation of the Ḥafīẓīya might be attempted, one which sees it as a latter-day Fronde.[114] All of the ingredients are there: agrarian disorders, corruption in high places, an incompetent king, a scheming provincial nobility, and—most important of all—a prince of the blood to lead the insurrection. But this resemblance is only superficial. The revolt of ʿAbd al-Ḥafīẓ occurred in the context of the twentieth century at a time when an expansionist Europe was completing the colonial subjugation of Africa and Asia. The eruption of French imperialism, therefore, sets the Ḥafīẓīya on another plane. Without French support, ʿAbd al-ʿAzīz could not have lasted three months. (But also, without the fact of French intervention, the crisis might never have come to a head and he might have avoided at least this particular fate.)

A second factor which makes the Fronde analogy less convincing is the specifically Islamic context within which the events of 1907–1908 are situated. In particular, I wish to draw attention to the ideology which fueled the insurrection and helped shape the direction which it took, the Muslim concept of jihād. The term has often been misunderstood in the West. "Holy war" is an inappropriate gloss: the full resonance of the term goes much deeper. According to John R. Willis, Islamic doctrine distinguishes three levels or types of jihād: of the heart, of the tongue and the hands, and of the sword.[115] Self-purification, preaching against unbelief and heresy, these precede the launching of the military aspects of jihād. Of the three, the first, which has been called the "interior jihād," was regarded as the greatest. The aim of jihād was to transform and revitalize one's own faith and that of the community of Muslims through the reenactment of certain key episodes in the life of the

Prophet and his companions. There was a strong populist and egalitarian thrust to jihād. It was to restore the rule of the sharīʿa and to overthrow injustice that Muslims declared jihād. Characteristically jihād-s appeared only in times of great and multiple stresses upon society.

If we turn from this brief outline of the concept of jihād to the unfolding of the Ḥafīẓīya during 1907 and 1908, we note that, from the outset, the Moroccan movement was closely bound up with the idea of *jihād*. The meetings of ʿAbd al-Ḥafīẓ with Abū ʿAzzāwī at Marrakech in 1906 and the charge which he gave him to deliver to the Chaouia tribes is freighted with meaning in this context: "Prepare for the jihād, the time has come." His proclamation in August 1907 as sultan "for the cause of the *jihād*" further underscores his mandate. The great majority of the communications of the pretender with the tribes emphasize his strong commitment to the jihād.[116] The spread of the fighting to eastern Morocco (under the patronage of ʿAbd al-Ḥafīẓ) also took place under the aegis of this concept. Note, finally, the regnal title adopted by ʿAbd al-Ḥafīẓ upon his entry into Fez—"al-Ghazi," that is, "the victorious in combat against the unbelievers."

Yet there is an ambivalence in the way ʿAbd al-Ḥafīẓ dealt with this formidable legacy and charge. Constantly we see him trying to moderate the radicality of his supporters, to tone down their militancy. Thus, for example, he rejected the conditional bayʿa of the ʿulamā of Fez. Fully aware of the stakes, he refused to risk all in a murderous headlong assault on French positions in the Chaouia and elsewhere in the country. In his dealings with the powers he consistently sought to allay fears that he was a sanguinary fanatic. A letter written to Herbert White, British chargé d'affaires at Tangier, dated January 29, 1908, makes clear his attitude toward jihād:

> As regards to any reports which may have reached you of the proclaiming of the Holy War, we merely employed that as a strategm to tranquillize the excitement of the people on seeing their land occupied by force, the slaughter of their kin on their own territory, and their being prevented from ruling in their own country. We had the intention to place Governors over the Showia Province in order to put an end to the disorder, but the troops which have penetrated into the centre of the country stood in the way of that course being followed, as possibly had we gone to the Showia it is not improbable that these troops would have employed some strategem to bring about a battle, which we do not want; our object being merely to tranquillize

> our subjects and firmly establish security in the country and on the roads.[117]

The actions of ʿAbd al-Ḥafīẓ largely bore out his words. Throughout the tumult at Fez in December and January, an Algerian Frenchman lived unmolested in the city. The same was true at Safi, which although solidly Ḥafīẓist, placed no impediments in the way of resident Europeans, and at the other ports in the south over which he briefly reigned.[118]

The story does not end here, however. Lurking beneath the saga of an inchoate national revolution which was both anticollaborationist and anti-French is another tale. It concerns the revolution which did not happen, the social revolution. Everywhere the Ḥafīẓīya was strongest—in the Chaouia, Marrakech, and Fez—there was a great *journée,* a rising of the lower classes, the oppressed peasants, urban day-workers and artisans, which preceded the proclamation of ʿAbd al-Ḥafīẓ. The demands of the crowd (abolition of the maks and government monopolies, implementation of the rule of the sharīʿa, and stringent controls on European presence) appears in every case to have been diverted by the proclamation of ʿAbd al-Ḥafīẓ as sultan and the declaration of the jihād. We need to know much more about the circumstances of each of these major episodes of the revolt if we are to come closer to unraveling the puzzle of the *révolution manquée.* The available evidence, admittedly neither as detailed nor as reliable as we might wish, suggests the following conclusions.

The landing of French troops in the Chaouia provided the catalyst for a vast popular movement which narrowly missed its objectives, coming closest at Fez. Grievances that had long been seeking an outlet welled up to the surface. But because different groups within the society had different diagnoses of their own difficulties, the remedies also varied. Faulty communications and inadequate articulation of the interests of the poor especially helped to contain the explosion. The absence of an ideology other than that of *jacquerie* prevented the popular movement from achieving any substance. A glance at the list of the principal backers of ʿAbd al-Ḥafīẓ should help clarify what happened next: the active courting of jihād-ist sentiments by the pretender. By means of this *fuite en avant* the ambitious provincial notables, merchants, and religious scholars who were the leadership of the Ḥafīẓīya (and the privileged of Moroccan society) were able to preserve their positions.[119]

If the Ḥafīẓīya was neither a reenactment of the resistance of the fifteenth century, nor a Fronde, nor entirely a jihād, nor yet a popular revolution, what are we to make of it? The answer, I would suggest, lies in the coming together of elements from each of these explanations. The Ḥafīẓīya was rooted in a conspiracy of some provincial notables with a royal prince and was fed by the staunch opposition of the ʿulamā, profound economic grievances, and a strong sentiment for jihād. The coalition which they temporarily produced, although fragile, was able to accomplish its chief objective: the deposition of ʿAbd al-ʿAzīz and the elevation to the throne of his brother, ʿAbd al-Ḥafīẓ.

Morocco would never be the same thereafter.

6

ʿABD AL-ḤAFĪẒ IN POWER

Pressures for Change

Although the victory of ʿAbd al-Ḥafīẓ freed new political forces to participate in government, the same intractable problems continued to confront Moroccan officials. The financial prospects of the makhzan remained bleak. French forces continued to occupy large areas of the country, including Oudjda and the Chaouia. The countryside was in turmoil and, without a reliable army, little could be done to restore order. Most important, as long as ʿAbd al-Ḥafīẓ refused to accept the Act of Algeciras, the European powers would refuse to recognize his government. This meant that he was deprived of access to the customs revenues, which were currently being deposited in the state bank. Negotiations with France were thus inevitable, but French terms promised to be harsh (amounting to a repudiation of all that the Ḥafīẓīya had stood for). If they suspected a sellout, the tribes would cause further trouble.

During the civil war of 1907–1908, French relations with ʿAbd al-Ḥafīẓ had steadily deteriorated. The pretender was regarded as a sanguinary fanatic at Paris, and as long as any hope remained of refloating the candidacy of ʿAbd al-ʿAzīz the French refused even to consider opening relations with Fez. For his part, the new sultan was reluctant to make concessions. Eventually, however, the inevitable could no longer be avoided. Diplomatic relations between Morocco and the powers would have to be normalized. The arrival of a German consul at the sharifian capital in early September necessitated a French response. Thus it was that soon thereafter a French emissary, Si Kaddour Ben Ghabrit (Fr.) was dispatched to Fez, ostensibly for the purpose of putting the French consular post office back in operation.[1] Ben Ghabrit discreetly entered into contact with the sultan. From this initial meeting serious negotiations eventually resulted. With the assistance of Mahdī al-Munabbhī a letter was drafted and sent to the powers at Tangier. In it the sultan promised to honor the debts of his predecessor, accept the Act of Algeciras, and pay indemnities and the costs of the Chaouia and Oudjda campaigns.[2]

With the sultan's letter in hand, the powers sought to work out the terms of the recognition of his regime. At first the French insisted that ʿAbd al-Ḥafīẓ be required to publicly renounce the jihād in a letter to be read in all of the principal mosques of the country. British diplomats, aware of the danger this would constitute for the stability of the regime, were able to obtain a modification of this clause.[3] By a joint note of September 14, France and Spain announced their provisional recognition of the government of ʿAbd al-Ḥafīẓ.[4] During the remainder of the autumn the Franco-Spanish note was circulated among the powers for comment and approval. In January the French and Spanish missions to Fez were expected to clear up all other outstanding grievances. Until then, ʿAbd al-Ḥafīẓ continued to be blocked from drawing upon Moroccan customs receipts collected by the state bank. Finally, on January 5, 1909, official notification of the recognition of the new regime was communicated to the makhzan representatives at Tangier.[5] The way was open for a normalization of relations between Morocco and the great powers.

The most vocal of the groups that sought to influence ʿAbd al-Ḥafīẓ in the fall of 1908 was the militants at Fez. Led by Muḥammad al-Kattānī and composed of a portion of the ʿulamā and the aʿyān, with a large following among the poor of the city and the surrounding tribes, the militants were still smarting from the rebuffs which they had received after ʿAbd al-Ḥafīẓ had arrived in the north. The appointment of notorious former supporters of ʿAbd al-ʿAzīz, instead of stalwart Ḥafīẓists, to positions in the new government angered them. Now the suspicion that ʿAbd al-Ḥafiz was prepared to make substantial compromises in negotiating with the powers placed them on their guard. Nothing less than one of the cornerstones of the legitimacy of the new sultan, his image as the sultan of the jihād, was in jeopardy. Obliged by the needs of the state treasury to seek European recognition and, inevitably, to accept the Act of Algeciras, but compelled by the exigencies of internal politics to maintain a militant posture, ʿAbd al-Ḥafīẓ found himself caught in the same political vise as his predecessor.

The militants at Fez, led by al-Kattanī, were in no mood to accept further compromise of the principles of the Ḥafīẓīya. During the summer they continued to urge the sultan to adopt a more vigorous strategy of resistance. ʿAbd al-Ḥafīẓ, however, refused to listen to them. The notables met on October 3 to consider the various options available. In the end they rejected al-Kattānī's insistence on further resistance and agreed that the Act of Algeciras would have to be accepted. But they recommended that, if there were to be reforms, then at least German assistance (rather than French) should be sought. The next few weeks brought additional signs of trouble at Fez. A deranged tribesman attempted to proclaim Mawlāy Muḥammad sultan during the Friday prayer at the mosque of Mawlāy Idrīs. The man was arrested and beaten, and the cafés of the city were closed down subsequently, but grumblings of dissatisfaction persisted.[6]

Given the unsettled state of opinion and the insecurity which prevailed in wide areas of the country, the possibility of an insurgency by a prince of the royal blood presented the main threat to the new regime. Mawlāy Muḥammad, the eldest son of Mawlāy al-Hasan, was the biggest potential source of danger because of his great popularity among the rural populations. Toward the end of October (just after the incident at Mawlāy Idrīs) he escaped from the makhzan force which was conducting him from Marrakech to Fez. He sought asylum among the turbulent tribe of Zaer outside of Rabat, where he was proclaimed sultan. He had allegedly been encouraged by certain Frenchmen in his entourage at Rabat.[7] Further difficulties were avoided, however, when he was rapidly recaptured by the sultan's representative at Rabat, Ḥājj Ibn ʿAissa. Had he succeeded in getting away, there is no doubt that Mawlāy Muḥammad would have become the immediate center of a powerful insurgent movement and a threat to the life of the regime. Following his arrest he was safely transferred to the palace at Fez, where he was placed under tight security.[8]

Not all of the attempts made to influence ʿAbd al-Ḥafīẓ's policies came from the militants. A group of prominent officials and ex-officials residing at Tangier who were well acquainted with dealing with Europeans made a number of suggestions embodied in a memorandum on how the new government should deal with the powers. This group included al-Munabbhī, al-Ḥājj Muḥammad Turrīs, and al-Ḥājj Idrīs ibn Jalūn (Fr. Benjelloun). Their suggestions combined leniency toward ʿAbd al-ʿAzīz and his former officials with a rather firm policy toward relations with Europe. Ibn Jalūn personally delivered the memorandum to ʿAbd al-Ḥafīẓ in early September 1908. A number of its proposals were subsequently acted upon.

The chief recommendations in the memorandum were as follows.

(1) No Europeans should be received at court unless recommended by their legations. (2) No Europeans should be hired by the makhzan. (3) No concessions of any kind should be granted. (4) No grants of makhzan houses should be made at any of the ports. (5) All diplomatic correspondence should be cleared first at Tangier with those knowledgeable on the subject. (6) Mawlāy Ḥafīẓ should announce his willingness to abide by the Act of Algeciras and all other treaties. (7) Mawlāy Ḥafīẓ should accept responsibility for all loans previously made. (8) He should agree to pay the debts of ʿAbd al-ʿAzīz after they have been examined and passed by the state bank. (9) Amnesty should be granted to all former officials. (10) ʿAbd al-ʿAzīz should be generously treated.[9]

The ubiquitous al-Munabbhī enjoyed something of a resurgence during the autumn of 1908. He was named Friend and Counselor of the Makhzan by ʿAbd al-Ḥafīẓ and himself drafted, or suggested changes in, several letters to the powers during this period.[10] He served as intermediary between the French and the sultan in the negotiations which preceded recognition of the regime. As the brother-in-law of Madanī al-Glawī he also acted as mediator in the discussions between the sultan and his chief vassal in the south. In addition, he acted as a clandestine agent in the exchange of letters between ʿAbd al-Ḥafīẓ and the German minister at Tangier, Dr. Rosen.[11]

It was through al-Munabbhī's mediation that ʿAbd al-Ḥafīẓ was able to negotiate a settlement with the sharif al-Raysūnī. In November al-Raysūnī assembled a delegation from the tribes under his command and journeyed to Fez, where he was well received. After prolonged negotiations with ʿAbd al-Ḥafīẓ an agreement was worked out by which al-Raysūnī would renounce his British protégé status and the unpaid two-thirds of the ransom of Qāid Maclean, in return for which he would be named governor of Arzila and all of the tribes in the district. As part of the arrangement al-Raysūnī promised to raise 300,000 douros in taxes from the tribes. Before leaving Fez, he swore an oath with ʿAbd al-Ḥafīẓ to defend Morocco from the Christians.[12] In this manner the sultan gained valuable military and financial support at a time when it was much needed, and a potential enemy was appeased.

Another group also sought to influence ʿAbd al-Ḥafīẓ in planning the orientation of his policies. Through the Tangier Arabic-language weekly, *Lisān al-Maghrib* (The Tongue of Morocco), edited by two Lebanese brothers, Farāj Allāh and Artūr Nimūr, an appeal was made to ʿAbd al-Ḥafīẓ in the issue of October 11, 1908, to institute the reforms which his subjects demanded of him.[13] These were to include state-sponsored universal elementary education, the establishment of a consultative assembly (*al-muntada al-shurā*), and the promulgation of a constitution. The assembly was conceived of as completing the experiment in representative government that had begun in 1905 with the *majlis al-aʿyān*.[14] The constitution was modeled upon the restored Turkish constitution of July 1908 and reflected the connections between the young Moroccan nationalist elite of Fez and Tangier and the Committee of Union and Progress.[15] The arguments used by the proponents of the constitution invoked the example of Japan, a nation which had shown that a stronger state might result from handing over power to the people. While it now appears likely that the constitution was substantially drawn up by the Nimūr brothers, a group of young Moroccan intellectuals have been identified as supporters. According to ʿAlāl al-Fāṣī their names include ʿAbd al-Ḥafīẓ al-Fāṣī, Muḥammad al-Muqrī, al-Mahdī ibn Ṭālib al-Fāṣī, Saʿid al-Fāṣī, and Aḥmad al-Zabdī.[16] It is likely that other lesser-known members of the ʿulamā and makhzan officials were also among the backers of the proposed constitution.

Since the sources on the draft constitution of 1908 are few, it is well not to read too much into the project. In view of the fact that little was made of it either at the time or until well into the nationalist period, it is best seen as an isolated proposal which gained support only from a small group of young intellectuals. There is no evidence that those who suggested its adoption had given much thought to the difficulties of implementing it without a long preparation of public opinion. In this they resemble the small group of officials who persuaded ʿAbd al-ʿAzīz to adopt the tartīb in 1901. Had they been successful in getting ʿAbd al-Ḥafīẓ to adopt the constitution, the consequences for Morocco would no doubt have been more severe than those which flowed from the tartīb. Still, the publication of the proposed constitution does serve as further tantalizing evidence of connections between Morocco and the Arab East in the early twentieth century. It demonstrates the extent to which Morocco was beginning to be drawn into the Arabic cultural revival, *al-Nahda,* and to participate in some of the new currents of thought then sweeping the region.

The Arabic press of the Middle East was well known in Morocco, and the new sultan had come to appreciate the power it exercised over public opinion. He therefore resolved to establish an official newspaper to serve as the main organ of his government. In July a pro-Ḥafīẓ paper named *al-Fajr* (The Dawn) began publication at Tangier. It was edited by a Syrian Christian named Niʿamet Allāh Daḥdaḥ. When it was closed at French insistence, the sultan invited the editor to reestablish his paper at Fez under makhzan auspices. With the assistance of Ernest Vaffier-Pollet, two issues of *al-Fajr* were eventually published at Fez in December 1908. Although ʿAbd al-Ḥafīẓ was pleased with the results, the shortage of funds soon led to the abandonment of the project.[17] The establishment of an official Moroccan newspaper, like the enactment of a draft constitution, remained unrealized. In truth the time was not yet ripe for them.

The Search for a Political Base

The initial omens for the continued health of the regime, despite important gains, were not good. The search for a political base was to occupy most of 1909. In December Ibn Sulaymān, the former foreign minister of ʿAbd al-ʿAzīz, died at Fez, allegedly the victim of poisoning. Since he had been identified as a notorious collaborator by the extremists at Fez, there was much concern in makhzan circles. This increased when his grave was profaned soon thereafter, and his head was disinterred and hung over one of the gates of the city with a legend attached to it which warned of a similar fate to all those who compromised themselves with the Christians. Clearly this was an attempt to intimidate the sultan. As if to give evidence of this view, a tribesman shortly afterward attacked ʿAbd al-Ḥafīẓ while he was going to the mosque. The attempt failed and the assailant was summarily executed, but there could be no denying the dangerous deterioration of the political atmosphere in the capital.[18]

In view of the circumstances, ʿAbd al-Ḥafīẓ resolved to return to Marrakech as soon as possible, where he would be in greater security. The imperial tent was pitched outside the walls preparatory to the departure of the court. It was widely rumored that in order to prevent a rebellion at Fez in his absence, the sultan intended to take certain Fāṣī notables with him as hostages. One of those allegedly selected for this "honor" was Muḥammad al-Kattānī. When news of his impending arrest reached the head of the militant faction, he decided to flee from Fez and seek sanctuary among the Berbers of the Middle Atlas, where he had numerous clients.[19]

It was the evening of March 19 when al-Kattānī and members of his immediate family secretly left Fez for the safety of the hills. His escape was made easier by the incessant rains of the previous several weeks, which kept the roads deserted and his movements unnoticed. Upon reaching the territory of the Ait Ndhir, he made an *ʿar* sacrifice at the tent of one of the leaders of the Ait Harzalla clan, imploring protection.[20] ʿAbd al-Ḥafīẓ reacted energetically as soon as he heard the news. Orders were sent to the qāid-s of the Ait Ndhir for the arrest of al-Kattānī and his detention until the special makhzan force which was on its way could arrive. Otherwise, it was threatened, every village of the tribe would be burned to the ground. On March 20, orders were given that all Kattānīya lodges in Morocco should be closed immediately. On March 22, news reached Fez that al-Kattānī had been caught just as he was about to cross into the territory of the Ait Njild and the safety of the mountains.[21] He was subsequently brought back to Fez, jailed, and beaten so badly that he died as a result. From this point onward the intransigent party retreated into the background at Fez.

In order to follow up his victory, ʿAbd al-Ḥafīẓ resolved to make a lesson of the Ait Ndhir for having accorded their protection to the fugitive. A maḥalla was assembled and dispatched to the territory of the tribe, where discussions were begun over the terms of submission. The sultan demanded a large payment in kind and 100,000 douros in cash as an indemnity. After consultation the tribe rejected this demand and hostilities were initiated. The Ait Ndhir, like most Middle Atlas Berber tribes, were extremely jealous of their right to accord protection, and it was this right which the makhzan had violated when al-Kattānī had been betrayed. The first battle ended in a resounding victory for the Ait Ndhir, who had been given assistance by some of the other tribes of the district. This created a potentially dangerous situation in the north, and the makhzan had to quickly assemble another force to achieve a victory before the dissidence had a chance to spread.[22] Strong reinforcements were sent under the French military instructors LeGlay and Pisani and the Algerian artillery expert Ben Sedira. After the usual dilatory maneuverings by both sides, the makhzan forces won a few victories and the Ait Ndhir finally agreed to surrender. The terms were more severe than those which had been first demanded: payment of the fine, acceptance of makhzan-selected qāid-s, and the supply of 300 men to serve in the Moroccan army. This marked the first time in recent history that a Middle Atlas Berber tribe had been induced to supply men to the sharifian army and was regarded as an important political victory for Mawlāy ʿAbd al-Ḥafīẓ.[23] It also unwittingly helped lay the groundwork for the insurrection of 1911.

The open breach between the sultan and al-Kattānī had not arisen solely from a dispute over how best to resist the West. There were important religious differences between the two men as well. ʿAbd al-Ḥafīẓ was a recognized theologian and intellectual, and he had come to believe that Islam was in need of purification from alleged non-Muslim accretions, such as saint cults and heterodox religious brotherhoods.[24] While khalifa at Marrakech, he had come under the influence of Mā al-ʿAynayn, who as a religious scholar preached the need to purify Islam and to make the brotherhoods into one.[25] Moreover, when ʿAbd al-Ḥafīẓ reached Fez, he wrote to Abū Shuʿayb al-Dukkālī, a Moroccan theologian then teaching at Mecca, inviting him to return to Morocco. Al-Dukkālī was a proponent of the Salafīya doctrine that taught the need to purify Islam and reform it in order to better withstand the challenge of the West. When al-Dukkālī returned in 1907, he became a member of the sultan's royal learned council and was admitted to teach a course on Koran exegesis (*tafsīr*) at the Qarawīyīn mosque university at Fez. Through his influence ʿAbd al-Ḥafīẓ became a fervent supporter of many of the ideals of the Salafīya and began to try to put some of them into practice.[26] This religious motivation further explains ʿAbd al-Ḥafīẓ's attack upon the Kattānīya religious brotherhood. At one stroke an important potential rival was removed and a corrupt *ṭarīqa* shut down.

The Kattānīya were not the only brotherhood to attract the sultan's reformist ire. At about the same time he directed his attention to the prestigious Tijanīya ṭarīqa, to which many of the urban bourgeoisie and officials belonged. In 1909 he published a book in which he chastised many of the beliefs and practices of the brotherhood as being incompatible with true Islam.[27] As part of the same campaign, the sultan also attempted to assert makhzan authority in the city of Wazzan by appointing a non-Wazzani as qāid and requiring the sharifs of Wazzan and those under their protection to pay taxes to the makhzan. This was part of a general effort to abolish traditional privileges that saw regular taxes imposed on the jaysh tribes around Fez.[28] By doing away with the potentially divisive influences of the religious brotherhoods, Mawlāy ʿAbd al-Ḥafīẓ sought to strengthen the state's control over its citizens. To the end of his reign he remained convinced of the baleful effect of the brotherhoods on Morocco.[29] He must be rated the first Moroccan sultan to make serious efforts to implement Salafīya doctrines.

The successful suppression of the rebellion of al-Kattānī was only the first in a string of notable political victories for ʿAbd al-Ḥafīẓ during 1909. Sometime in the spring, agreement was reached with the great qāid-s on the terms of their renewed participation in the government. In April Madanī al-Glawī, ʿAbd al-Malik al-Mtouggui, and ʿAissa ibn ʿUmar traveled north, accompanied by a sizable retinue. They traversed the Chaouia with the authorization of the French command and eventually reached Fez on May 15, 1909. Their entry into the city was the occasion of celebration, with an honor guard lining the route and the sultan waiting to greet them. The fanfare was very much in order.[30] The great qāid-s brought with them important military forces, enough to tip the balance in the north in the favor of the makhzan. As a result ʿAbd al-Ḥafīẓ was able to substantially dispense with the services of the jaysh tribes, and makhzan control over the Ait Ndhir soon improved noticeably.

Two days after the arrival of the great qaid-s at Fez, Mawlāy ʿAbd al-Ḥafīẓ had an opportunity to demonstrate his strong support of resistance activities in the extreme south of Morocco. On May 17, Mawlāy Aḥmad Haybat Allāh (Fr. el-Hiba), a son of Mā al-ʿAynayn, arrived and was accompanied by a group of "blue men" from the Sahara. He was accorded the same honors and attentions that had been given the great qaid-s and stayed as a guest of the sultan. Like his predecessor, ʿAbd al-Ḥafīẓ found it politically useful to associate himself with resistance forces in the south, thereby strengthening his regime without seriously compromising himself with the powers.[31] With his credit somewhat restored among the militant faction, and strengthened by the arrival of reinforcements from the south, ʿAbd al-Ḥafīẓ was in a much better position to deal with challenges to his regime by June 1909.

There was one other potential crisis in the spring of 1909, but it soon proved less ominous than had appeared initially. On May 3, while en route from Rabat to Fez, Mawlāy al-Kabīr, another royal prince and brother of the sultan, escaped from his makhzan escort and sought refuge among the turbulent Zaer. While willing to accord him hospitality, the Zaer prudently refrained from taking up his cause. For over a year Mawlāy al-Kabīr managed to elude makhzan forces sent to capture him. During the latter part of his adventures, he languished as an exile among the Ghiata tribe near Taza.[32] Influenced by the treatment accorded the Ait Ndhir, the tribes of the Fez region refused to back would-be insurgents.

The most impressive example of the sultan's new political influence was the defeat and capture of Abū Ḥimāra in August 1909. The pretender had eluded (and often defeated) makhzan forces for seven years. The expense of mounting expeditions against him had been a major drain on the treasury of ʿAbd al-ʿAzīz (and a minor bonanza for corrupt makhzan officials charged with outfitting the expeditions). After 1904 Abū Ḥimāra no longer presented a direct threat to government administration in central Morocco, but he was able to seriously disrupt communications with the northeast. He established his rule over the tribes of the eastern Rif mountains, with the tacit consent of the Spanish in Melilla. There he remained with varying degrees of success for five years.

In 1909, in an effort to supplement his revenues, the pretender began to let out mining concessions to European interests. When they began to import European labor to work the mines, this excited the tribes against Abū Ḥimāra. They revolted and drove him back into the Jabala north of Fez. From there the pretender was attracted by the continuing disorder among the Ait Ndhir and began to march toward Fez. Despite a victory over the first makhzan force sent to subdue him, the pretender failed to press his advantage. By August, thanks partly to the intervention of the sharif of Wazzan (who convinced the Jabala tribes to remain neutral), the tide had begun to turn. After a defeat at Moulay Bouchta on August 11, he was eventually captured and brought back alive to Fez. There he was exhibited to the population in a small iron cage.[33] News of the astonishing defeat and capture of the pretender rapidly spread throughout the country. A rebel who had defied two sultans since 1902, and whom many had come to think of as invulnerable, had been convincingly vanquished. The tribes were enormously impressed with this achievement, and the personal prestige and political strength of ʿAbd al-Ḥafīẓ reached an all-time high.

The departure of Abū Ḥimāra from his headquarters near Melilla left the eastern Rif in a politically unstable situation. Despite the growing danger, Spanish mining interests decided to construct a railroad from Melilla to the chief mineral deposits in the hills to the south. Construction began in June and at first proceeded smoothly enough. But on July 9, the Spanish railroad workers came under attack from the nearby tribes. What happened thereafter looked like a replay of the scenario which had been enacted at Casablanca in 1907. Spain sent an expeditionary force to restore order, and a bitter struggle ensued. A jihād was declared by the tribes of the area, and a major new diplomatic crisis resulted.[34] (The incident may in fact have been deliberately provoked by Spanish partisans of a more aggressive policy toward Morocco.)

At first, ʿAbd al-Ḥafīẓ adopted a moderate position on the affair, but this soon played directly into the hands of the militant faction at Fez, who accused him of not fulfilling his duties as sultan.[35] A delegation of Rifian leaders visited Fez to solicit makhzan military assistance. They were warmly received by the sultan but obtained little or no tangible support from him. However, soon thereafter ʿAbd al-Ḥafīẓ did take a series of steps to curry favor with the militant group at Fez. He appointed *imām*-s to serve as chaplains for each tabor of the makhzan army and also sought to resurrect the practice of compelling the local Jewish community to provide forced labor to the makhzan.[36] (The latter effort predictably attracted immediate protests from the powers.) Finally, in a striking gesture, he gave public recitations of anti-French poems of his own composition—poems which were subsequently assigned for use in the *madrasa*-s at Fez.[37] Not until December was the Melilla affair resolved. Despite his attempts to retain at least some credibility with those elements that continued to favor the jihādist program of 1908, however, ʿAbd al-Ḥafīẓ's image suffered from his moderate stance.

Great-Power Diplomacy and the Big Banks: Round Two

The official recognition by France of the government of ʿAbd al-Ḥafīẓ on January 5 paved the way for a French diplomatic mission to begin negotiations aimed at clearing up outstanding grievances between the two powers. These included the unpaid indemnities demanded by France at the time of the Mauchamps affair and the regularization of the situation in the Chaouia. On January 31 a French embassy arrived at Fez under the leadership of the French minister at Tangier, Henri Regnault.[38] Discussions went more rapidly than anticipated. By March 14 a provisional accord relative to French evacuation from the Chaouia had been drafted.[39] It was followed two weeks later by a second accord on the Algerian frontier districts.[40] Finally, a point of interest to French industrialists, Regnault obtained the sultan's agreement to appoint a European technical advisor to draw up an integrated public works program.[41] Still, many of the Moroccan concessions were more apparent than real, and to put teeth in the agreements it was decided that a Moroccan diplomatic mission to Paris would be necessary.

By prior agreement, the French mission was joined at Fez in early March by a Spanish one, under the direction of the Marquis Merry del Val. Whereas negotiations with France had moved smoothly, the sultan remained adamant in refusing all concessions to Spain because of alleged Spanish violations of Moroccan territorial integrity around the presidios of Ceuta and Melilla. Combined pressure from Regnault and Merry del Val soon forced ʿAbd al-Ḥafīẓ to relent, however, and within a few weeks matters had advanced far enough so that procès-verbaux of the discussions could be drafted.[42] Further discussions to work out the details of the agreement were scheduled for later in the year. There was no illusion on either side that relations between Spain and Morocco had been much improved by the Merry del Val visit. The dynamics of Spanish expansionism around the presidios (especially Melilla) ensured that these relations would continue to deteriorate. The outbreak of fighting at Melilla in July, therefore, capped a lengthy period of strained relations.

The needs of the Moroccan treasury and the weak domestic political position of the sultan guaranteed that the negotiations with France would be soon resumed. ʿAbd al-Ḥafīẓ was in no position to risk a rupture. Thus a Moroccan diplomatic mission departed for Paris in early April to continue discussions on the proposed accords. It was composed of the minister of finances, Muḥammad al-Muqrī, the minister of foreign affairs, ʿAbdallāh al-Fāsī, and two other makhzan officials.[43] During the interim, the French government had stiffened its negotiating posture. Several additional demands were made. (One called for the makhzan to sever all connections with Mā Al-ʿAynayn and to refrain from supporting resistance in Mauretania.) Nonetheless, substantial agreement had been reached between the two parties by August, and a note summarizing the French position on the Chaouia evacuation, the frontier question, and the liquidation of makhzan debts was prepared for submission to ʿAbd al-Ḥafīẓ. ʿAbdallāh al-Fāṣī was sent to deliver the note to the sultan and await further instructions.[44]

The conclusion of the second stage of the Franco-Moroccan negotiations at Paris coincided with a change in the attitude of ʿAbd al-Ḥafīẓ toward France. The capture of Abū Ḥimāra left his rule virtually unchallenged in central Morocco. For the first time he could afford the luxury of a bolder and more intransigent posture in his dealings with France and with Europeans more generally. Thus the accord was allowed to wait while the sultan sought to curry favor among the militants at Fez. The growing anti-French sentiment on the part of the sultan was accompanied by numerous incidents involving attacks upon French protégés. These called forth a stiff French note of protest in October. The protest was rejected by the makhzan.[45] The absence of diplomatic support for the Moroccan effort to resolve the Melilla affair further angered the sultan. He sought to fight back by taking steps to break out of the diplomatic isolation the country had been in since Algeciras. He began to cultivate relations with potentially sympathetic powers, Germany, Italy, and Turkey. The French monopoly on furnishing technical advisors came under attack—as it had in 1905. Italian and Turkish advisors were solicited, and a loan was concluded with a German private business concern.

The stranglehold which the Paris big banks had upon the Moroccan treasury by virtue of their dominance of the Banque d'État posed a grave threat to the new regime. Unless the makhzan could escape from the crushing embrace of the consortium by developing alternative sources of foreign capital, it would eventually be compelled to renounce all possibility of an independent policy. In its early stages the Ḥafīẓīya movement had been able to generate funds by promising mining concessions to European firms that sought to evade the jealous controls of the Paris consortium. The most important of these firms was the German Mannesmann combine, which had helped finance the rebellion despite the coolness of the German government toward the combine's ambitions. Thus it was no surprise that during a period of straitened economic circumstances, ʿAbd al-Ḥafīẓ once again turned toward the Mannesmann Brothers in hopes of alleviating the strain on the royal treasury. In July 1909 the Mannesmanns advanced two million francs to the makhzan in return for additional promises of mining concessions in the Atlas mountains.[46] Such cash advances, while they might temporarily relieve the strain upon the treasury, were no solution for the long-range financial problems of the government. Only the French capital market was in a position to provide a large enough loan, while the Algeciras Act gave France the diplomatic leverage to prevent interloping by rivals. Despite short-term success, therefore, the makhzan was forced inevitably into negotiations with the consortium.

In the meantime, the Moroccan diplomatic offensive continued. Discreet soundings convinced the makhzan that approaches to Italy might yield fruit. During the summer ʿAbd al-Ḥafīẓ invited the Italian government to resume its military mission to Fez. (Under Mawlāy al-Ḥasan the Italian government had provided the technicians who directed the *makina,* or arms factory, at Fez.) The sultan appears to have hoped that improved relations with Italy would give pause to French statesmen contemplating direct action in Morocco. In November an Italian officer named Giuseppe Campini took up his post as director of the makhzan repair shops at Fez. (Campini had earlier served in that capacity under Mawlāy al-Ḥasan.) His arrival alarmed Commandant Mangin, the head of the French military mission. Inquiries at Rome, however, convinced the Quai d'Orsay that there was nothing to fear. Questioned by ʿAbd al-Ḥafīẓ about the attitude of his government soon thereafter, Campini seems to have discouraged the sultan from expecting support for any new makhzan diplomatic initiative.[47] At any event, rebuffed by Italy, the Moroccan government began to look elsewhere for diplomatic backing.

One of the results of the victory of ʿAbd al-Ḥafīẓ was a renewal of strong sentiments within the Moroccan urban elite for closer relations with Turkey. The impact of the Young Turk revolution had produced a wave of sympathetic response in Morocco. One of the ways in which this expressed itself was the resurrection of earlier projects which looked to the Ottoman empire to supply trained Muslim military advisors to Morocco. The makhzan could thereby avoid heavy dependence upon French or other European advisors in the training of the Moroccan army. Following the Turkish revolution in 1908, the Young Turk regime adopted a policy of support for Muslims outside the empire engaged in resisting the West. Thus when Moroccan overtures were made to the Young Turk government at Istanbul in 1909 for a military mission, they encountered an immediate favorable response. Although we are not as fully informed on this episode as we would like to be, the following outline can be pieced together.[48]

At some point during 1909 Aḥmad al-Muqrī, brother of the Moroccan minister of finance, contacted officials of the Young Turk government. Discussions resulted in the dispatch of a twelve-man Turkish military mission to Morocco in November.[49] The mission was drawn from Turkish and Syrian officers of the Ottoman army and commanded by Captain ʿĀrif Bey. Upon their arrival at Fez the Turks were received by al-Muqrī and presented at court. Over the protests of the French military mission, they were attached to the makhzan army as advisors and soon began accompanying the troops on maneuvers against dissident tribes to the north of Fez. Until March 1910 they continued to act in this capacity. On that date they were compelled to leave by French diplomatic pressure.[50] The arrival of the Turks coincided with renewed attention at Paris to the unratified accords. It also came at a moment when the emptiness of the makhzan treasury was once again becoming a matter of grave concern at Fez. In dire need of a major French loan and threatened by the Quai d'Orsay with a rupture in normal diplomatic relations, the makhzan had no recourse but to dismiss the Turkish military mission. A number of the members of the group were destined to see further action in Morocco.

During its brief stay in Morocco the Turkish military mission was involved in a number of activities not connected with their official function. A pan-Islamic youth group, "Young Maghrib," was created, with which young Muslims in the other countries of North Africa (including Egypt) were also affiliated. A German correspondent estimated in 1911 that the organization had 10,000 members. Its purpose was to instill a sense of solidarity in the youth of Morocco and to support the army.[51] It is probable that claims of broad membership in the organization were highly inflated, and that Young Maghrib existed primarily on paper. The Turkish military mission sent numerous reports to the Turkish embassies at Madrid and Paris, urging that a Turkish consulate be established in Morocco. Nothing came of this effort, either.[52] The episode of the Turkish military mission testifies to the continued development of Pan-Islamic tendencies among a certain segment of the urban elite in Morocco. While of marginal importance in its impact upon the course of events, the tendency of some Moroccans to look to the Middle East for inspiration and assistance persisted.

The attempt of ʿAbd al-Ḥafīẓ and his government to break out of the diplomatic isolation in which Morocco found itself was therefore ultimately a failure. The French position was unassailable. Practical demonstrations of this fact served only to increase the pessimism of makhzan officials and to reveal the true impotence of the government in the face of events. Neither Germany nor Italy was willing to do anything which might be construed by France as a challenge to the French position of predominance. Turkey, while willing, was incapable of taking effective action under the circumstances.

While Moroccan relations with France deteriorated and the makhzan embarked upon a search for diplomatic support, the status of the Franco-Moroccan negotiations on the Chaouia and Algerian frontier languished. At Paris Muḥammad al-Muqrī waited for further instructions from the sultan on how next to proceed. French protests in October against attacks on French citizens and protégés marked the start of a get-tough policy by the Quai d'Orsay. The conclusion of a major loan agreement was now directly tied to the signing of the Franco-Moroccan accord. Evidence was demanded that the makhzan seriously desired to improve relations with France. The episode of the Turkish instructors served as an admirable pretext for the French government to bring pressure to bear upon the makhzan to sign the accord, since the engagement of the Turks was an obvious slap at France. ʿAbd al-Ḥafīẓ for his part desired to delay signing the accord as long as possible, so as to avoid compromising himself in the eyes of his countrymen.

By early February French diplomats in Morocco had become thoroughly disgusted with the perpetual stalling of ʿAbd al-Ḥafīẓ. They resolved to take measures to ensure that the accord was signed by the sultan without further delay. On February 14 Foreign Minister Pichon requested Regnault to fix a date by which a favorable reply would have to be received or France would initiate steps toward a break in relations.[53] Similar tactics had been envisaged during the crisis of December 1904 but were never carried out. When Gaillard delivered the French ultimatum on the twenty-first, he was informed that the sultan had already written to al-Muqrī at Paris authorizing him to ratify the accords. Suspecting a ruse, the French consul announced the suspension of the military mission and the evacuation of all French citizens from the city. The same day the sultan's letter arrived in Paris. Pichon telegraphed Tangier immediately to countermand the evacuation orders. By the time runners from Tangier reached Fez with the news, preparations were already well advanced. On February 25 ʿAbd al-Ḥafīẓ yielded to the French ultimatum and handed Gaillard a letter indicating his willingness to ratify the accord.[54] The final signing ceremony took place several weeks later, on March 4 at Paris. In this fashion the long-drawn-out negotiations were brought to a successful conclusion —one which was heavily in the favor of France.

As a result of the accords the makhzan achieved what had been a principal objective, a promise by France to evacuate its troops from the occupied provinces, on condition that a Moroccan police force capable of maintaining order first be installed. The Moroccan government also committed itself to defray the entire cost of French military operations in the Chaouia and Oudjda, to pay all fines and indemnities demanded, and to recognize the right of France to organize government in the occupied territories on behalf of the makhzan. The Moroccan government agreed to implement articles of the 1901 and 1902 border accords relative to the organization of markets and the collection of taxes. It also agreed publicly to disavow its support for resistance in the Sahara, including the connection with Mā al-ʿAynayn. Finally it authorized the implementation of article 60 of the Act of Algeciras, which granted foreigners the right to own land in Morocco.[55]

By surrendering a present sovereign right of administration of the Chaouia and Oudjda in return for a future evacuation of French troops to be decided upon by France, the accords can be said to have weakened the Moroccan legal case for the speedy restoration of the occupied territories. In any case, the de facto presence of European occupying forces and Morocco's diplomatic isolation rendered any resort to the niceties of international law futile. On the majority of the issues makhzan negotiators were compelled to accept the French interpretation. The weakness of ʿAbd al-Ḥafīẓ's regime was exposed for all to see. Such was the desperate financial position of the Moroccan treasury that almost any French demands would have been accepted, if doing so would make possible a loan agreement. The capitulation of ʿAbd al-Ḥafīẓ to French pressure in 1910 had an effect rather like that of ʿAbd al-ʿAzīz's acceptance of the Algeciras Act in 1906: it served to compromise him in the eyes of his people and to make inevitable yet another insurrection.

Following the ratification of the accords, the stage was set for the resumption at Paris of negotiations over a new Morocco loan.[56] On the French side the negotiators consisted of the representatives of the big banks and officials of the Ministry of Finance and the Quai d'Orsay. The Moroccans were represented by al-Muqrī. By March 21 the preliminary outlines of the loan arrangements were already clear. On May 13 the loan contract was signed by al-Muqrī and the representatives of the Moroccan state bank (the official contracting party). The loan had a face value of 90 million francs. The terms were severe for Morocco: the makhzan pledged as security the remaining 40 percent of Moroccan customs revenues, all of the indirect taxes (like the maks), the receipts from state monopolies on tobacco and *kīf* (cannabis), and the income on state lands within ten kilometers of the coast. The Controle de la Dette was authorized for the first time to collect customs duties, not merely to oversee the umanā in the exercise of their functions. The disposable revenue of the makhzan was limited to 3 million francs, assigned by the state bank from the taxes under its jurisdiction. The bondholders rigorously deducted the payments due on the outstanding loans and indemnities before turning the remainder of the proceeds over to the government. The only sources of revenues not assigned after the conclusion of the 1910 loan agreement were the tax on agriculture (the tartīb) and the gifts traditionally offered to the sultan on the principal feast days (*hadiya*). In the case of the occupied territories even the tartib revenues were withheld by France, to be applied to the costs of occupation.[57] Whatever financial autonomy Morocco still possessed was eliminated by the conclusion of the loan agreement of 1910. The deterioration in the financial position of the state led to a growing ruthlessness in the collection of taxes, since its receipts from customs revenue and the indirect taxes were now sharply limited. The tribes naturally resented the increased pressure by makhzan representatives and became more inclined to revolt. The familiar Moroccan cycle of "squeeze," "revolt," and "repress," which had helped lead to the downfall of ʿAbd al-ʿAzīz, was begun once more. On the local level, the economic condition of Morocco was on the whole much improved over what it had been under ʿAbd al-ʿAzīz. For this the state bank and the stringent measures which were taken to correct the disastrous monetary situation were at least partially responsible. Between 1906 and the end of 1909 the dirham remained stable in its relation to the British pound at 40 to 1.[58] Prices of the most common consumer items rose only slightly during the same period. The only monetary problem was the localized one of too much depreciated bronze currency in circulation.[59]

With affairs between France and Morocco at last settled, the diplomatic focus turned again to Spain. Relations between the two countries had steadily grown more sour during the period since the outbreak of hostilities at Melilla in July 1909. An early Moroccan attempt to resolve the disputes outstanding between them had gone awry from the beginning. The Spanish government was in no mood to be flexible with a war going on and was further vexed by word of a Franco-German agreement in which it had not been consulted. The terms submitted by the Spanish foreign minister were rejected by ʿAbd al-Ḥafīẓ as far too greedy. Moroccan counterproposals submitted in August were in turn immediately rebuffed by Madrid.

A new diplomatic initiative was made by the makhzan with the arrival of Muḥammad al-Muqrī at Madrid in late September. Fresh from the successful conclusion of the Franco-Moroccan accords at Paris, al-Muqrī set to work immediately. The good offices of the French government, which was by this time becoming concerned about deteriorating Franco-Spanish relations, enabled an accord to be worked out with minimum difficulty. By November 16 the text was ready for signing. It was composed of sixteen articles, plus a letter which spoke of the future disposition of the Ifni enclave south of Agadir. (Spanish rights to Sidi Ifni, a tiny fishing way-station had been recognized by the 1860 accords but never implemented.) Three major provisions distinguished the new accord: the amount of the Melilla indemnity was fixed, a police force charged with maintaining order in the vicinity of the presidios was established, and a customs post at Ceuta was created to handle the transit trade.[60] In its broad outlines the Madrid accord paralleled the Franco-Moroccan accord. With its ratification the major sources of diplomatic friction with Spain were cleared up, and the legacy of bitterness dating from the accession of ʿAbd al-Ḥafīẓ was at least temporarily dissipated. Best of all from the Moroccan point of view, al-Muqrī had been able to arrive at a settlement without yielding any Moroccan territory.

The Impossibility of Reform

The signing of the 1910 accords and the loan agreement gave a temporary respite to the sultan. But if the new regime were to survive, it would need a tranquil countryside and a stable fiscal base. The key to both was a modern army. The Moroccan army, despite impressive victories during 1909, remained little changed from the traditional makhzan forces. As such, it was a weak reed upon which to lean. Military reform thus loomed large on the agenda in 1910.

While the urgency of military reform was clear, the context for reform was not promising. Although temporarily cowed, the tribes around Fez were seriously disaffected and awaited only the chance for revenge. More important in the long run was the attitude of the elite of Fez. The policies pursued by ʿAbd al-Ḥafīẓ seemed almost deliberately designed to alienate and intimidate them. Not content with repudiating the conditional bayʿa and reinstituting the maks, the sultan had gone out of his way to bring the militants to heel. The execution of al-Kattānī was but the most drastic of the measures which he took in his first year and a half in power. He reinstituted Koranic punishments for transgressions of the holy law, including mutilation. These were applied to captured servants of Abū Ḥimāra. The pretender himself was brutally tortured and killed. His body was thrown to the palace lions.[61] The lesson did not go unnoticed among the Fāsī bourgeoisie.

It was the Ibn ʿAissa affair which most clearly showed ʿAbd al-Ḥafīz's intentions to brook no opposition at Fez. In May 1910, Ibn ʿAissa, the pasha of Meknes was arrested together with other members of his family, allegedly for inciting the Zemmour to revolt. Since he had been a loyal Ḥafīẓist from the first hour and had been the one to recapture al-Kattānī following his escape attempt, there were expressions of disbelief when news of his jailing became known at Fez.[62] For several months there was no news. Then in early June rumors began to spread that Ibn ʿAissa and his family had been savagely beaten. It was learned that one of his wives had been tortured in an effort to force her to divulge the hiding place of her jewels. By this time the Fāsī community was considerably alarmed.

If a highly placed and trusted official could be subjected to such indignities, and even his women were not spared, then no one was safe.

Among the European community of Morocco, the Ibn ʿAissa affair became a veritable cause célèbre, instantly confirming stereotypes of the sultan as a bloodthirsty tyrant. Newspaper editorialists inveighed against the barbarity of the punishments and called for the intervention of the powers. The French and British consuls vigorously protested the treatment accorded Ibn ʿAissa and his family and demanded that medical attention be given his wife. Under pressure, the sultan was forced to comply. Ibn ʿAissa was kept under arrest pending trial, but the other members of his family were freed, on condition that they live at Marrakech.[63] The affair came on the heels of a series of attacks on French protégés elsewhere in Morocco and provided a convenient justification for increasing French interventionism.

In the months which followed, French military officers began to press harder in their efforts to expand their zone of influence. This was particularly the case among the tribes who bordered on the Chaouia. Applying a fallacious distinction between ʿAzīzist and Ḥafīẓist local leaders, these officers encouraged the formation of pro-French groups within tribes like the Zaer and the Rehamna.[64] As a result local feuds were inflamed and the tribes became increasingly turbulent.

There were two areas of conflict to the north of the province, the fertile Gharb plain north of Rabat and the hill country inhabited by the Zaer to the south. There were substantial French investments in the Gharb, and French protégés were increasingly bold. This incited a backlash of anti-French sentiment from local officials and soon led to a series of petty incidents. These in turn called forth several strongly worded French protests during the course of 1909 and 1910. Overzealous local French agents caused further troubles by attempts to take the law into their own hands.[65] One particularly flagrant incident occurred in the fall of 1910 when several vacationing French officers on their way as "tourists" to Fez arrested a number of Beni Messara tribesmen alleged to be ringleaders of the local anti-French resistance forces.[66]

More serious was the situation in the Zaer territory. French officers showed increasing anger at the alleged provocations of Zaer troublemakers, who occasionally raided the villages on the northern fringe of the Chauouia and harassed local would-be collaborators. A French patrol was ambushed in 1910 by dissident tribesmen. Yet nothing was done by the makhzan to redress the situation.[67] By the end of the year plans were under way for a French punitive force to be sent into Zaer country to give the local hotheads a taste of their own medicine. By the end of 1910, a stiffening of French attitudes and intentions could be observed all around the rim of the Chaouia.

The province of Marrakech was one area which was especially affected by continued French encroachment. Because of the military importance of the tribes just across the Oum er Rbia from the Chaouia (tribes like the Sraghna, Rahamna, and Doukkala), French native affairs officers were especially anxious to win support among them. One project sponsored by the French military administration of the Chaouia that had some success in this direction was the construction of a bridge across the Oum er Rbia in March 1910. The bridge did much to develop commerce between the two neighboring provinces and brought tribes from the Marrakech region into regular contact with the tribes under French administration in the Chaouia, exposing some of the benefits of French rule to their inspection.[68]

French administration in the Chaouia served as a highly successful advertisement of the benefits of collaboration. The improvement of roads, the establishment of markets, and the policy pursued by the occupation forces of purchasing from local merchants led to great prosperity in the region.[69] Fāsī merchants, who by this time were numerous at Casablanca, were well placed to appreciate the contrast with the mediocre business climate at Fez.[70] Already intimidated by the bullying tactics of ʿAbd al-Ḥafīẓ and worried by growing social unrest, many of them embarked at this time on the process of evolution which would put them in the French camp by 1912.

The transformation of the French position in Morocco manifested itself also in the sphere of military reforms. During the early years of the reign of ʿAbd al-Ḥafīẓ the military mission under Colonel Emile Mangin had remained in the background. Its activities had been restricted to the training of troops and the giving of advice while on campaign. The mission had had no power to alter the kind of training given or to update it, nor did it have control over the payment, recruitment, or outfitting of the troups, who remained under the command of their makhzan qāid-s. Following the signing of the Franco-Moroccan accord, Colonel Mangin came forward with a comprehensive plan for the reform of the makhzan army and presented it to ʿAbd al-Ḥafīẓ. It was this proposal, with some modifications, which was subsequently adopted by the makhzan.[71]

The new military reforms were put into effect during November

1910. In their broad outlines they were inspired by the strict regulations of the French Army in Algeria, the system which had given rise to the Chaouia goum. All of the troops currently serving in the makhzan army were discharged. Then those who wished to be considered for service under the new regulations were given a medical examination, further tested for aptness, and enrolled. Numerous changes were made in the new army. The term of service was extended to four years, and the men were to be regularly paid the equivalent of five English pence each day. The French instructors were given authority over the issuance of equipment and the payment of the troops. It was the disciplinary regulations which were to be the greatest cause of difficulties. The easygoing methods of the traditional Moroccan army contrasted most unfavorably with what the soldiers perceived as the harshness of the new system. Under the old system, theft of government property was a time-honored tradition, officers habitually embezzled the pay of their men, and it was common for the men to absent themselves periodically for the harvest or spring plowing in their villages. Under the new regulations both robbery and desertion became crimes punishable by death. The new regulations, moreover, were poorly explained to the recruits, and no breaking-in period for gradually reeducating the men was allowed for.[72]

The size of the French military mission was increased to provide an adequate number of instructors. They leaped to their task with a new vigor. There was much optimism that they would soon be able to make a disciplined, modern army out of the undignified rabble which had hitherto made up the Moroccan army. With a modern army ʿAbd al-Ḥafīẓ would be able to bring the countryside under much tighter control from the capital and perhaps regain much of the confidence which he had lost from his people. Further, a new army might enable him eventually to replace French forces in the occupied territories and thereby restore the territorial integrity of his kingdom. Unfortunately the new army regulations were to produce results rather different from those anticipated. The political mistakes in instituting the military reforms of 1910 were to emerge as one of the chief grievances behind the tribal insurrection of 1911.

Morocco and the Middle East: A Balance Sheet on Change

The financial condition of the treasury and the diplomatic isolation of Morocco were the most important long-term factors in undermining the reform efforts of ʿAbd al-Ḥafīẓ. In the face of them his political victories proved finally ephemeral and lacking in substance. Other factors can be distinguished, however. Here, contrast with patterns of political development in the Middle East can usefully serve to highlight the internal weaknesses of the Moroccan political system.

The army, which in the Middle East had played a major role in the overthrow of the traditional system, played none at all in Morocco. The jaysh tribes, which constituted the core of the Moroccan armed forces, continued to enjoy their tax-exempt status without having to provide contingents to the makhzan. In the Middle East such traditional military units had been forcefully disbanded. In Morocco they remained an obstacle to reform long after they had ceased to perform a useful purpose. The creation of a more modern force was systematically hamstrung by lack of resources, lack of personnel, and the rivalries of the powers.

The role of agents for change that had been occupied in the Middle East by the modern army officers was filled in Morocco by the provincial notables. The Moroccan equivalent of the Turkish valley lords, al-Glawi, al-Mtouggui, and company, provided the military force necessary to place ʿAbd al-Ḥafīẓ upon the throne and restore order. They thereafter dominated the chief posts in the new government. If there was to be reform, they would be its principal support. Here the weight of rural forces in the Moroccan context shows most clearly. Divided by their rivalries, lacking all discipline, and unable to visualize the kinds of changes needed, it is no surprise that the great qāid-s proved unable to stomach reform. Morocco paid a high price for the failure of military reforms to take hold.

Although the Moroccan ʿulamā were more widely acquainted with Middle Eastern intellectual currents than has been previously recognized, the weight of traditional beliefs and practices was heavy indeed. The Moroccan ʿulamā never occupied the formal positions of power that their Middle Eastern cousins enjoyed in the state apparatus. Their traditional privileges and immunities did give them a powerful set of vested interests which stood athwart the path of reform, and they were thus well placed to threaten governmental plans. The attempt by ʿAbd al-Ḥafīẓ to apply Islamic modernist doctrines was aimed at sapping their power. Instead, it only further alienated important groups from his government.

There were also differences between the Moroccan bureaucracy and that of the Ottoman empire. In the nineteenth-century Ottoman empire, for example, some modern-minded bureaucrats developed into critics of further internal improvements or reforms and eventually joined with the modern army officers to overthrow the old regime (the Young Turk movement). In Morocco, bureaucratic support of ʿAbd al-Ḥafīẓ was also an important factor in the success of his movement. Bureaucrats alone possessed the necessary skills to conduct the elaborate diplomatic and financial negotiations with the powers upon which the survival of the regime depended. But Moroccan bureaucrats with some experience of the world, like Muḥammad al-Muqrī, lacked a formal Western-style education and were therefore unencumbered by much of the intellectual baggage which weighted down their Ottoman counterparts. They formed a much less cohesive group, bound together by little more than common opposition to French penetration and a vaguely common outlook. The functionally rudimentary Moroccan bureaucracy was ill-adapted to assisting in the rapid transformation of the political structure of the government. As a result it could not serve as one of the primary carriers of ideas of political change as the Middle Eastern bureaucracy had done.

The situation which confronted the Moroccan elite in 1908 was symptomatic of the more general problem of other countries in the Muslim East during the precolonial period. Ideological appeals to Muslim solidarity and jihād were one thing, and the fashioning of some institutional means of keeping factions in line and maintaining discipline was another. The organization of the Ḥafīẓīya, which had operated through ad-hoc groups of partisans had been quite successful in building local followings during the period of the insurgency. What was lacking for longer-term political viability was some institutional mechanism (a party, perhaps) capable of achieving a more lasting organization and purpose. It was therefore inevitable that the early hopes many had vested in the Ḥafīẓīya would be disappointed.

A final area of important Moroccan structural weakness in comparison with the nineteenth-century Middle East is that of education. It was through the translation of Western books and manuals and the creation of schools for the training of a new elite on a Western model that Egypt, Iran, and the Ottoman empire were able to move rapidly on a broad series of reforms. The nondevelopment of schools on a Western model in Morocco helps explain why a cohesive, modern, educated elite failed to emerge. (The schools of the Alliance Israélite Universelle constitute a partial exception, but their clientele was exclusively Jewish.) Such ideas of reform as appear to have filtered into Morocco were brought by individuals who had spent time traveling in Europe and the Middle East or through the diffusion of Arabic books and newspapers from the Middle East. It now seems clear that the weakness of the currents of reform, Islamic modernism, and pan-Islam in Morocco is to be ascribed to the rudimentary level of the system of education.

The failure of the Ḥafīẓīya movement to bring about permanent change in Morocco was in a sense inevitable. The forces which composed the movement were too diverse, regional interests were too strong, and existing governmental structures too fragile for any other outcome to have been possible. The political sophistication of a tiny portion of the elite could not overcome the heritage of the past or the overwhelming rural and tribal character of the country. The rural elite, which was opposed to both governmental reforms and European penetration, became alienated from the regime it had placed in power as soon as the new sultan's policies on these two issues became known. With the urban resistance forces cowed, this elite began to pursue an increasingly independent strategy.

7

REFORM AND REBELLION

THE OUTBREAK AND ORGANIZATION OF THE REBELLION OF 1911

The inability of ʿAbd al-Ḥafīẓ to forge a new and more viable kind of state, based upon a closer integration of the various segments, meant that, despite short-run gains in political stability, all of the old splits and discontinuities within the Moroccan elite would once again reassert themselves. The persistence of strong currents of hostility to French penetration and to the centralizing drive of the makhzan among a broad spectrum of people placed a limit on the program of reforms adopted in 1910. Once more the major impetus for armed resistance was to come from the countryside, and the rebellion of 1911 was the result.

In order to understand the collapse of rural security, it is important to realize the consequences of the reshuffling of posts in the makhzan which took place in July 1910. Prior to this date the major governmental offices had been divided by some of the old makhzan families and the great qāid-s from the south. Essentially the traditional pattern of rural administration was followed, with tribal governorships being parcelled out among clients of most of the major factions. Thereafter, however, all of this was changed. The families of al-Glawī and al-Muqrī divided all of the important *baniqa*-s among themselves, and al-Mtouggui was definitively excluded from the makhzan. Under the new arrangement, the al-Muqrīs obtained the vizierates of foreign affairs and finance, while the al-Glawīs were accorded the positions of ʿAllāf al-Kabīr and grand vizier (thereby giving them a virtual control of the rural administration). In addition, the governorship of Fez al-Bali (old Fez) went to al-Ḥājj Aḥmad al-Muqrī (Fr. Hamed el Mokri), and the pashalik of Marrakech to al-Ḥājj Tahamī Glawī.[1] The new system was intended to give ʿAbd al-Ḥafīẓ a solid base of support by reliance on the military strength of the family of al-Glawī, while the special talents of the al-Muqrī family were utilized to restore the diplomatic and financial position of the country. Naturally there were important material advantages for the two families concerned in addition to the glory of joining together to combat French ambitions. For al-Muqrī, there were the substantial bribes which came from the negotiation of the 1910 accord, the loan, and arms purchase orders, while for al-Glawī there was a slice of the tax receipts collected from the tribes around Fez and Meknes (in addition, of course, to the income from his vassals in the south).[2] To solidify this alliance, ʿAbd al-Ḥafīẓ and Madanī al-Glawī each married a daughter of Muḥammad al-Muqrī.[3] During the rest of 1910 the control of the key positions in the makhzan by these two families became steadily more complete, with devastating consequences.

By concentrating extensive power in the hands of a single family, the sultan can be said to have given hostages to fate. The traditional makhzan strategy had been to play off the various factions and alliances of the provincial notability. Under the new makhzan this strategy was largely subordinated to the imperious necessity of raising revenue, no matter what the political cost. The Marrakech region had been for some time the most populous and wealthy part of Morocco, and by relying extensively upon the most powerful and successful of the great qāidal families, ʿAbd al-Ḥafīẓ was only recognizing the facts of life.[4] Yet by their very ruthlessness the methods employed by the agents of Madani al-Glawī in the north of Morocco promised in the long run to upset the calculations of the sultan. The traditions and way of life of the tribes of the north were quite different from those of the more sedentary tribes in the region around Marrakech. Jaysh tribes like the Cherarda and Middle Atlas Berber tribes like the Ait Ndhir were used to a more independent life-style and were very jealous of their traditional liberties. When Glawa henchmen began executing a series of extraordinary levies at gunpoint, there was bound to be major opposition. The Ait Ndhir complained of extortion on a large scale, the Cherarda protested that as a jaysh tribe they had never before had to pay taxes, and in the Gharb there were rumors of an impending rebellion led by the Beni Hassen.[5] North of Fez, conditions were not much better. A qāid of a small Arab tribe along the Sebou River was made to pay a total of 150,000 pesetas in bribes in order to obtain his post, with Madanī al-Glawī pocketing much of the amount.[6] The inevitable outcome of this state of affairs was a massive backlash from the heavily pressured tribes. By early 1911 all that was needed to set off a general rising in the north was a precipitating event.

Mawlāy ʿAbd al-Ḥafīẓ was not entirely oblivious to the dangers of placing too much power into the hands of the Glawa family. He also perceived that for the court to remain at Fez only increased the likelihood that one day his grand vizier might be tempted to launch a coup against him. Accordingly, in order to provide himself with greater room for maneuver, the sultan began to make plans to transfer the court to Marrakech sometime in March. The royal tents were pitched outside Fez on January 23 as a sign of the impending move, and on February 19 some of the women of the royal harem left Fez for the south.[7] News of the impending change was greeted by Madanī al-Glawī with considerable anxiety. As long as the court remained at Fez he and his brother, the pasha of Marrakech, could jointly dominate the makhzan, since it relied extensively upon their military strength. With the court at Marrakech, however, the situation would be changed. ʿAbd al-Ḥafīẓ could freely play upon the jealousies between the two brothers, as well as profit from the reinvigorated competition for the favors of the makhzan among the other great qāid-s. If the reform of the Moroccan army embarked upon with French aid in 1910 was successful, moreover, the sultan would no longer be dependent upon Glawa contingents for his main backing. He would then be in a position gradually to weaken his dependence upon the family of al-Glawī and assume a more active personal role in internal politics.[8]

The political situation in the south, while not as precarious as that in the north, was still dangerous. In early 1911 there were risings among the Doukkala and Sraghna tribes of the Haouz of Marrakech against the heavy exactions of their qāid-s.[9] Excessive taxation had begun to produce a current of unrest among the other tribes of the region as well. A joint Glawa-Mtougga ḥaraka into the Sous valley met with only mixed successes in the early part of 1911, and there were signs that a coalition of anti-Glawa tribes was beginning to emerge, led by the Chtouka.[10] The Sous valley was in a period of political transition. The death of Shaykh Mā al-ʿAynayn on October 28, 1910, at Tiznit removed a stabilizing force from the region and provided an opportunity for ambitious tribal qāid-s. The successor of Mā al-ʿAynayn was his son Mawlāy Aḥmad Haybat Allah (known as El Hiba). While El Hiba sought to preserve as much as he could of the family patrimony against the depredations of the tribes, leadership in the Sous Valley was taken by Haida ou Mouis, the pasha of Taroudant. By early 1912 El-Hiba had largely succeeded in reestablishing the position of his family in the region.[11] Conditions in the Sous were favorable to a revolt against the established authorities. A famine in 1910–11 had already driven the price of grain out of reach and had resulted in many deaths. Thousands had flooded north to seek relief in the cities along the coast.[12]

Finally, the political situation along the northern border of the Chaouia should be mentioned. There the activist role which the French native-affairs officers had begun to adopt was a source of increasing resentment, especially among the Zaer tribe. The Zaer were a transhumant Arabic-speaking tribe who inhabited the rolling hill country between Rabat and Casablanca. They were bordered on two sides by powerful Berber confederations, the Zemmour (located inland from Rabat) and Zaian (situated to the southeast).[13] The tribe had gained a reputation for feuding and banditry, and this combative tradition had earlier drawn them into participation in the Chaouia resistance effort. After the French victory, diehard elements from the Chaouia tribes continued to find a privileged sanctuary among the Zaer from which to engage in occasional raids and sniping against French forces. At the same time, some of the weaker Zaer clans, in an effort to counterbalance their rivals within the tribe, began to appear at French posts in the Chaouia and accept French patronage. Once such contacts were established, French native-affairs officers began to patrol beyond the Chaouia to show the flag and give heart to their Zaer supporters. Such intervention in the internal affairs of Moroccan tribes was of course against the Algeciras Act, but the French officers on the spot found it increasingly hard to resist getting involved. French patrols into Zaer territory were perceived by the majority of the tribe as hostile acts and were resisted. It was only a matter of time before a major incident occurred.[14]

The rebellion of 1911 was the response of the tribes of the district around Fez and Meknes to the multiple crises which had undermined the legitimacy of the government of ʿAbd al-Ḥafīẓ during 1910. The application of the new French military reforms further intensified what was already regarded as an intolerable situation. The catalyst which set off the rebellion was the public execution on January 28 at Fez of two tribesmen for violation of the new military regulations.[15] It was followed by a wave of anger in the countryside. Since most of the tribes of the region had sent contingents to the makhzan army, they all saw themselves affected by the new regulations. The stories which had circulated for weeks in the rural markets about the way the troops were being compelled to adopt Christian ways, and how even the sultan was becoming a creature of the French were instantly confirmed.[16] These intersected with existing grievances, the ruthless plundering by al-Glawī and his agents, resentments against the expanding power of the makhzan and against French encroachment, and a generalized feeling that bold action was necessary if Morocco was to avoid slipping under French control.

Exploratory talks had been held between the major tribes of the district during the fall of 1910 about the possibilities of combined action to redress the situation at Fez if the political situation continued to deteriorate. Toward the end of the year a delegation of prominent rural notables from the area had gone to Tangier to make known their discontent in high places and to solicit the intervention of the French legation on their behalf with ʿAbd al-Ḥafīẓ. The leader of the delegation, Qāid ʿAqqa al-Bubidmāni of the Ait Ndhir, sought to utilize his friendship with al-Mahdī al-Munabbhī to have the latter mediate with the French to have restraints placed upon the authority of al-Glawī. When the French refused to enter into the game, al-Munabbhī told the notables to fend for themselves.[17] From this point onward, the likelihood of some sort of joint demonstration by the tribes was inevitable. The executions at Fez on January 28 therefore merely hastened its arrival.

The leadership in planning the rebellion was taken by the Ait Ndhir, a Berber tribe which occupied the foothills of the Middle Atlas mountains and a portion of the plain south of Meknes. The Ait Ndhir were transhumants and by their way of life were thrown into frequent contact with the other Middle Atlas Berber tribes of the area, the Gerrouan, the Zemmour, and Ait Njild (Fr. Beni Mguild). Like the other tribes of the region, they had been active supporters of ʿAbd al-Ḥafīẓ in 1907 and 1908, and had sent contingents to join in the Chaouia fighting. Muḥammad al-Kattānī had exercised considerable influence over them, and they had been briefly tempted to back him in 1909 when he fled from Fez to the mountains. Thereafter, a makhzan military expedition had been sent to punish them for having joined with al-Kattānī. The terms of their surrender had been severe: they had been compelled to pay a large indemnity in addition to back taxes, and had been forced to provide a three-hundred-man contingent to the makhzan army. In order to guarantee their continued submission, a number of notables and sons of notables had been taken as hostages to Fez. By early 1911 the hostages had still not been released.[18] There were thus ample grievances which propelled the Ait Ndhir to take a leading role in the rebellion.

On February 25 a meeting was held at Agourai, a small market village to the south of Meknes. It was planned by the Ait Ndhir and was attended by notables from the other Berber tribes of the area, the Zemmour, the Ait Njild, and the Gerrouan. In the presence of several sharifs a temporary truce on feuding and raiding between the tribes present was decided upon.[19] Messengers were sent to the powerful Zaian confederation to encourage them to form a common front with the Zaer against the likely French incursion in force from the Chaouia.[20] Still others were sent to the Arabic-speaking tribes of the Meknes region to solicit their participation in joint action at Fez. Talks continued among the tribes of the region during the weeks which followed. Eventually a plan of action began to crystallize from these conversations. It called for the tribes to go to Fez for the ceremonies marking the birth of the Prophet (*ʿId al-Mawlid*) on March 14, at which time it was the custom for the sultan and his court to formally receive delegations from the tribes and to accept their gifts. On a prearranged signal, the conspirators would attack and kill the viziers (al-Glawī being a special target), kidnap the sultan, and offer to lead the jihād on his behalf. Those in on the plot included the Beni Hassen and the Cherarda, in addition to the four Berber tribes that had been present at the Agourai meeting.[21] It should not escape notice that what was initially being planned was a kind of ritual rebellion rather than a revolution. Events would soon compel the rebels to adopt a more radical course of action.

Before the tribes were able to complete their plans, a revolt broke out prematurely among the Cherarda at the end of February. It had been triggered by the attempt of agents of al-Glawī to collect taxes from them, although the Cherarda by virtue of their jaysh status had long enjoyed exemption from makhzan-imposed levies. The revolt soon spread to tribes in the surrounding district, fanned by a generalized spirit of opposition to the exactions of al-Glawī. To put down the revolt ʿAbd al-Ḥafīẓ dispatched a maḥalla led by the ʿAllāf, Muḥammad al-Glawī, and the head of the French military mission, Colonel Emile Mangin.[22] The expedition was to be the first test for the reformed makhzan army and was not expected to occupy much time. The plans to move the court to Marrakech were to be delayed until the return of the maḥalla but were not cancelled. No word of the intended coup d'etat had apparently reached the sultan, and the makhzan continued to display optimism in its ability to surmount the crisis. Events, however, did not go as hoped. The other tribes of the region joined with the Cherarda to put up stubborn resistance to the maḥalla, which soon found itself surrounded and under siege. A month of heavy rain next intervened, with the result that the maḥalla became deeply mired in the mud, unable to move, and communications with Fez became very difficult.

With the makhzan force thus occupied, the stage was set for the bulk of the conspirators to take action. On March 11 the Ait Ndhir and their allies proceeded to Fez and established camp, preparatory to laying siege to the town.[23] Their original plan was by now abandoned. Instead, the rebels sought to use the siege as a means of pressuring the sultan into dismissing all European military instructors, releasing all of the Ait Ndhir hostages held by the government, and returning to the tribes all of the money which had been unjustly extorted from them.[24] By the end of March the besieging forces had increased their demands to include the dismissal of Madanī al-Glawī. It became difficult for Fez to communicate with the coast, and ʿAbd al-Ḥafīẓ became increasingly apprehensive about the future.[25] To relieve the siege, he requested France to allow a maḥalla to be formed in the Chaouia from among the French-trained Chaouia *goum* and sent to Fez under the command of Muḥammad al-ʿAmrānī. Permission was also requested for a 1,500-man relief force raised in the Marrakech region to be permitted to cross the Chaouia on its way to Fez.[26]

By the beginning of April the rebels began to harden their position. For the first time a number of important tribes to the north of Fez began to be drawn into the rebellion, threatening the city with being completely cut off. Makhzan attempts to foment dissension within the rebel camp consistently failed to attain their objective. Contact continued between the tribes surrounding the city and the makhzan, but there was no longer much hope that negotiations could solve the dispute. The rebels began to look for a viable pretender from among the princes of the royal blood as a means of legitimizing their revolt. Their demands now included (1) dismissal of the grand vizier, (2) the abolition of the military mission, (3) an end to the new military regulations, (4) only a fixed amount to be required of each tribe in taxes, (5) all qāid-s to be selected by their own tribes, and (6) the return of sums recently extorted by the makhzan.[27]

The rebellion entered its final phase on April 19, with the proclamation of a pretender to the throne by the ʿulamā of Meknes. The new candidate to the throne was Mawlāy Zayn al-ʿAbadīn ibn al-Ḥasan, a brother of the sultan, whose very name conjured up radical visions from the distant Islamic past. A rival makhzan was appointed which fully reflected the Berber origin of the movement.

The grand vizier was Abū Ziyān al-Milūdī of the Ait Ndhir; the ʿAllāf was ʿAqqa al-Bubidmānī, also of the Ait Ndhir; Aḥmad Mikwār, a British protégé and Fez merchant was the vizier for foreign affairs; and Mawlāy Ibrahim was named khalifa of the new sultan for the rebel army.[28] The city of Meknes became the headquarters of the new rebel government. There was some pillaging of the Jewish quarter by the tribesmen, but order was eventually restored. Mawlāy Zayn was clearly a reluctant dragon, and the non-Berber members of his makhzan allowed themselves to be appointed only after casting about for assurances from France and Great Britain that they would be leniently treated if the movement was defeated.[29] Nonetheless, the new government set about trying to win other tribes and cities in the region to the cause and also sought to gain European support and understanding of its aims.

At about the time that the tribes were proclaiming Mawlāy Zayn at Meknes, ʿAbd al-Ḥafīẓ was coming to the conclusion that French military assistance would be necessary if his regime was to survive the challenge. The circumstances of French intervention are recounted below. Here it is sufficient to say that Ḥafīẓ was encouraged to seek French support by Gaillard, who played upon the sultan's fears with considerable skill. Accordingly, on April 27 an official request was made that French troops be sent to support the Chaouia maḥalla under al-ʿAmrānī in its mission to relieve the siege of Fez and disperse the rebels.[30] On the same day the Cherarda maḥalla returned to Fez to reinforce the garrison there. The city was now almost completely cut off from the coast, and French dispatches had to pass via Taza to French forces on the Moulouya River.[31]

The new government of Mawlāy Zayn also sought to obtain European backing, but the international circumstances were no longer as favorable to a successful insurgency as they had been in 1907. Exploiting an old acquaintanceship, ʿAqqa al-Bubidmānī wrote several letters to the London *Times* correspondent at Tangier, Walter B. Harris, in which he pleaded the cause of the rebels. He denounced al-Glawī's depredations in the area, and urged that France refrain from backing the corrupt and unpopular government of ʿAbd al-Ḥafīẓ.[32] Subsequently Mawlāy Zayn wrote numerous letters to both the British and German representatives at Tangier, seeking the support of their governments for his cause. Neither government saw fit to reply to the letters, however, and this attempt to rally diplomatic support for the government of the pretender was a complete failure.[33]

There was also support for the pretender from an unexpected quarter. Several former members of the Turkish military mission arrived in Morocco in May and sought to enter into contact with the insurgents. They later turned out to have been financed by a Cairo-based pan-Islamic group called *al-ittihād al-maghribī*. The Turkish agents were to have provided military advice and financial backing to Mawlāy Zayn.[34] They were arrested and deported by the French in early June and never did accomplish their objectives.[35] Some of the same individuals were to return in 1912 for another go at support for resistance forces.

Within Morocco the cause of the rebels went better during the first two weeks of May. While the besieging forces were still unable to constitute a military threat to Fez, the political climate in the region was steadily growing more uncertain as the economic effects of the siege made themselves felt. On May 2, the city of Sefrou officially proclaimed Mawlāy Zayn to be sultan. When the news reached Fez, there was fear within the makhzan that Fez al-Bali might be tempted to follow suit.[36] The price of grain stood at 50 percent above normal, and the prices of other necessities, like livestock and charcoal, were also very high.[37] The makhzan treasury began to run low, and there was a question as to whether it could continue to pay the army. Rumors of contacts between the insurgents and the people of Fez al-Bali only made the makhzan more nervous. To preserve the situation from further deterioration several steps were decided upon by the sultan, with the advice of Gaillard and Ben Ghabrit. French protégés among the Fāsī merchant community were persuaded to advance enough cash to the government treasury to cover the wages of the troops. In return, the French firm of Brunschvig, through its Fez branch, agreed to cover the advance.[38] To guard against the possibility of a revolt by Fez al-Bali, the makhzan and Gaillard arranged for a controlled insurrectionary regime to be proclaimed under Mawlāy Idrīs al-Zarawtī.[39] To this end al-Zarawtī was chosen as *shaykh al-rabī*ʿ, a position he had held during the similar situation in 1907. The threat of major disturbances appears to have died down following this bold stroke. The influence of Gaillard over the sultan reached a high point during this period.

The last weeks of the siege of Fez were marked by continued sporadic attacks by the tribes. At the height of the action, there were three rebel camps around Fez, with an estimated total of 6,000 men taking part. In fact the number of tribesmen involved was probably greater, for most of them disliked being away from their lands for more than a few days at a time, and there was a steady stream of men coming and going to Fez.[40] While the core of the rebel forces consisted of contingents from the Middle Atlas Berbers, included were such unlikely allies as the Arab clans settled in the Sais plain near Fez, jaysh tribes like the Oudaia and the Cherarda, some of the upland Berber tribes like the Ait Saddin and the Ait Warrayn (Fr. Beni Ouarain), and even some contingents from the Jabala and from Jabal Zerhoun. Although primarily a rural movement, the rebellion also enjoyed considerable support among the urban populations at Meknes, Sefrou, and Fez. It was never able successfully to appeal to the ʿayān of the cities in the way that the Ḥafīẓīya had been able to do, however, due to the traditional fear and distrust of the Middle Atlas Berbers among this class.[41]

In the perspective of modern Moroccan history the achievement of the movement of Mawlāy Zayn was considerable, despite the eventual failure of the rebellion. For the first time, a pan-tribal coalition which embraced most of the tribes of the north was assembled. The rebels were able to coordinate their activities over a wide area and to keep together for three months. They were well armed and showed considerable political skill. The program which they advanced and the grievances to which they responded were similar in broad outlines to the program and grievances which had motivated the rebels in 1907–1908. They were able to keep their coalition intact through the use of traditional religiously sanctioned alliance mechanisms, such as the ritual exchange of turbans and *silhām*-s. The dispatch of letters to enlist diplomatic support displays a considerable degree of political sophistication. As an effort to overcome the problem of the limited scale of political action in the precolonial world, the rebellion of 1911 stands in the line of development which leads from the Chaouia resistance of 1907 to the more widespread effort at mass resistance in 1912. It points up the persistence of widespread opposition among the rural populations of Morocco to the threat of encroaching makhzan centralism and to French imperialism.

If the rebellion of 1911 was in some measure a success, was it merely a protest movement or did it look forward to a reformed and reinvigorated makhzan? The question is difficult to answer in a clear-cut fashion, due to the scarcity of sources that deal with the movement of Mawlāy Zayn. The attempts to attract European support do not necessarily imply a progressive program. One looks in vain, for example, for evidence of the influence of reformism, of pan-Islam or Islamic modernism upon the leaders of the movement.

One cannot help concluding, finally, that the rebellion of 1911 was irrevocably more provincial in outlook than that of 1907. Outside of northern Morocco, none of the important tribes or cities appear to have been tempted to join. The rebellion of 1911, to be sure, took place with the experience of French occupation behind it, and it might be argued that the French presence in the Chaouia greatly limited the spread of the movement to the south. But no such attempt to spread it appears to have ever been made. The rebellion remained within the Moroccan tradition of secular insurgencies headed by a prince-pretender. In contrast to the final convulsive rebellion against French imperialism in 1912 (the *jihād* of El Hiba) it had no millenarian overtones. Profoundly rooted in the traditional context of ritual rebellions, the 1911 tribal rising was fated to be overcome and outrun by events.

The last attack of the rebels on Fez took place on May 18 and was warded off without too much difficulty by the garrison. The long months of siege had taken their toll upon the besiegers almost as much as upon the besieged. Only a fraction of the original complement of rebels remained to harry the arrival of the French relief column. The others had melted away during the final weeks, exhausted. Three days later, on May 21, the 8,000-man French expeditionary force arrived from the coast and delivered the city from the last of its Berber attackers.[42]

The Diplomacy and Politics of Intervention, 1911

The rebellion of 1911 was of lasting significance in Moroccan history primarily because of the role which it played in speeding the establishment of the French protectorate. French intervention in Morocco in 1911 has long been portrayed as an inevitable outgrowth of deepening French involvement in Morocco after 1900, and in a sense it was. Careful attention to the circumstances of that intervention, however, raises a number of questions about its normal and inevitable character. There are indeed important reasons why French action in 1911 should instead be seen as at least partly the result of a deliberate policy of deceit practiced by the activist elements of the French colonial group against both the French and Moroccan governments, in the face of largely unfavorable European opinion. In the final analysis, no doubt, opportunism had more to do with the timing and success of the activists' thrust than careful and concerted action. This however should not obscure the fact that what was inevitable about the crisis of 1911 was not so much French intervention as the coming to power of a French government that was weak and inexperienced enough to be taken advantage of by the colonial lobby.

If we would understand the 1911 rebellion and the subsequent French decision to intervene, we must begin with an analysis of the circumstances in which French action took place. In the first instance, this means a study of the diplomatic position of the makhzan at the beginning of 1911. Although the loan of 1910 and the decision to embark on a major program of military reforms by the makhzan might perhaps be expected to have improved the diplomatic position of the regime by strengthening its internal stability, in fact the opposite was the case. The loan of 1910 was exhausted almost as soon as it was made, and the impact of the military reforms was rather to undermine governmental authority than to strengthen it. Indeed, as we have already seen, the military reforms were to serve as one of the causes of the rebellion of 1911. Diplomatically, Morocco fell more completely than at any time since 1907 into the embrace of France. The possibilities of a diplomatic opening to the East were frankly abandoned by the major makhzan officials, who now contented themselves with being able to restrict French penetration and to exact benefits as substantial as possible both for the country and for themselves.

After the conclusion of the Hispano-Moroccan accord of 1910, Muḥammad al-Muqrī returned to Paris in November, where he began discussions with the French government and the representatives of the banks on yet another loan. This time, however, the banks were no longer in so generous a mood and were determined to extract the maximum possible concessions before agreeing to pump still more money into keeping the Moroccan government afloat financially. In December 1910 negotiations on the new loan began between al-Muqrī and a team of experts drawn from the ministries of Finance and Foreign Affairs. The loan was intended to pay outstanding makhzan debts and to finance the military reforms and some new public works projects (including the Tangier and Casablanca port works and a railroad concession).[43] The initial face value of the loan was set at 30 million francs. To encourage the banks to take up the loan, the French government agreed temporarily to forego the 2,740,000 franc annuity assigned to cover its military expenses under the terms of the previous loan.[44]

By early February only slight progress had been made, and al-Muqrī protested that the makhzan had need of immediate action on the loan, or else serious internal difficulties would result.[45] This intervention appears to have accelerated things somewhat, for by February 18 the text of the proposed loan and reform agreement was ready for submission to the two governments. An analysis of its provisions gives us an interesting index of the extent to which the makhzan had become more willing to engage in a large-scale program of reforms since 1910. In addition to the provisions already noted above, the agreement included a formal undertaking on the part of the Moroccan government that it would implement the tartīb in progressive stages and that it would permit a railroad concession to be granted to France (apparently without first requesting general bidding as required under the Algeciras Act), for the sections Oudjda-Taourirt, Casablanca-Settat, and Tangier-El Ksar.[46] That this shift in the makhzan's position represented the opinion of ʿAbd al-Ḥafīẓ himself is confirmed by the conversation which the sultan had with French consul Gaillard on February 14.[47] This new willingness of ʿAbd al-Ḥafīẓ to consider propositions which he would earlier have rejected out of hand testifies to the increasing leverage which France possessed at court since the approval of the 1910 accord on the one hand, and to the search for a new, more efficient, and disciplined administration on which to base his authority on the other hand.

In the face of the opposition of Spain and Germany, France was to pursue the Moroccan loan slowly and carefully. The principal cause of objections was the railroad concession. Both Spain and Germany were concerned lest they not be given a right to bid on the concession, as prescribed by the Algeciras Act. Spain in addition was alarmed by the extension of the influence of the French military mission without a parallel increase in the level of Spanish military authority in Morocco. Fundamentally, the difficulty between Spain and France was the result of persistent Spanish fears of French duplicity. Before France could be permitted to act, therefore, Spain wished to receive solemn assurances that its own rights under the 1904 accord and the Algeciras Act would be safeguarded.

On March 13, 1911, al-Muqrī officially indicated his willingness to sign the combined loan and reform agreement, before submitting it to the sultan for his ratification.[48] In an accompanying letter he elaborated on his understanding of Moroccan obligations not included in the text of the accord itself.[49] These included statements of the seriousness of the makhzan's resolve to carry out long-needed reforms and public works projects, a renunciation of the brutal methods which had been the occasion of scandal in 1910, and an agreement to name and revoke officials according to the principles of order, justice, and humanity. The letter concluded with this remarkable passage:

> In case troubles take on a sufficiently grave character as to imperil the general security, His Majesty, recognizing the preoccupation of your government to see peace and tranquility established in the Empire, given the common interests which bind these two countries from the fact of their being neighbors, will examine with the Government of the Republic the means appropriate to employ to eliminate the origin of these troubles.
>
> His Majesty Moulay Hafid has confidence that if he is led in these conditions to demand the support of France, the Government will assure him it, with the aim of maintaining his Throne and the independence of his sovereignty in conformity with the principles of the Act of Algeciras. . . .

While the importance of this letter has not previously been remarked, it was later to provide (together with the Act of Algeciras itself) one of the legal bases for French intervention. It is curious to reflect that it was written a scant two days after the siege of Fez began.

From late 1910 one can observe a growing spirit of interventionism in the attitudes of the French government toward Morocco. The focus of much of this concern was with the situation in the Zaer. The climax of several months of continued small incidents between French forces in the Chaouia and the Zaer came on January 24, 1911. A small French patrol was ambushed near the hamlet of Merchouche deep inside Zaer territory, while on a reconnaissance mission. There were five French casualties, including one officer. From this time onward the French military command argued energetically for the need for a punitive expedition. Reinforcements of two battalions were requested from Paris. In a break with the previous pattern of rivalry, the request received the support of the legation at Tangier.[50] French military preparations in the Chaouia during February and March alarmed ʿAbd al-Ḥafīẓ and the Moroccan government and produced several diplomatic protests to the French.[51] They also stirred up a hornet's nest along the borders of the Chaouia, causing a temporary alliance to be made between the Zaer and the powerful Berber Zaian confederation, its neighbor to the southeast. The movements of the tribes and the apprehension of the makhzan also caused diplomatic actions to be taken by Germany to warn the French from taking precipitate action in Morocco that risked provoking major tribal unrest.[52] To the protests of ʿAbd al-Ḥafīẓ the Quai d'Orsay tended to respond with cool statements disclaiming any responsibility for what happened if the makhzan was unable to preserve order in its own house or to punish the perpetrators of the attack of January 24.[53]

The proponents of a more aggressive policy toward Morocco within the French government had been very disappointed with the course of events since 1907. What was needed, they were certain, was a spectacular gesture to break the existing political stalemate and confront French domestic and international opinion with a fait accompli. The downfall of the Briand cabinet and the formation of a new government under Ernest de Monis on March 2, 1911, provided a favorable environment for the *parti colonial* to lobby for a more energetic policy toward Morocco. At the same time, the anarchy in northern Morocco appeared to them to present a splendid opportunity for the carrying out of such a policy. The Franco-Moroccan loan negotiations provided a means of bringing pressure to bear upon the makhzan to acquiesce in French intervention. A temporary unity of aim among the diplomats and military in Morocco further completed the favorable circumstances.

In Paris, the change of ministries brought to power a government of unusual mediocrity, even by the rather low standards of the time. The prime minister, Ernest de Monis, was a career politician with little interest in the intricacies of foreign policy. His foreign minister, Jean Cruppi, was a neophyte in diplomacy who had been included in the new cabinet to provide political balance, while the new war minister was Maurice Berteaux, an intensely ambitious man who, it was alleged, had not scrupled in the past to sell his political favors. The product of a particularly farfetched exercise in cabinet coalition-building, the de Monis government was to prove vulnerable to the pressures of a newly resurgent *parti colonial.*[54] Finally, a change in the sensitive position of director of the Bureau du Maroc within the Foreign Ministry signaled a move to a more aggressive Moroccan policy. The new director was Henri de Marcilly, formerly on the staff of the French legation in Tangier, a close friend of Cruppi's and a close collaborator of Regnault, the French minister in Morocco.[55]

The key individuals in Morocco were the acting head of the French legation, Edouard de Billy, who was known to be attracted to the hard line and had shown it by his support for the Zaer expedition, and Henri Gaillard, the French consul at Fez. Gaillard had just returned to Morocco in early January from a vacation in France.[56] While there, he had conferred with the chief Foreign

Ministry officials about the situation in Morocco, and it is plausible to assume that contingencies were explored for what he should do in the event of a sudden deterioration of internal security in Morocco. During the years he had been at Fez Gaillard had acquired an almost unrivaled understanding of the workings of Fāsī society and of its relations with the nearby tribes. His ample discretionary funds made him a major source of patronage in the region. Thus he was able to attract large numbers of clients. During the crisis of 1911, Gaillard's influence over the sultan and his standing as a major patron were to provide the essential context within which Moroccan acquiescence in French intervention was acquired. Finally, the enigmatic figure of Kaddour Ben Ghabrit, the Algerian councilor to the French legation who had earlier been utilized on sensitive diplomatic assignments to the Moroccan court, should be mentioned. Ben Ghabrit would play a significant role in convincing ʿAbd al-Ḥafīẓ of the necessity of calling for French assistance in the relief of the siege of Fez.

By the beginning of April, the Cherarda maḥalla was thoroughly mired in the mud and Fez was completely surrounded by the tribes. Communications between Fez and the coast became increasingly chancy, and Gaillard painted the situation of the city in gloomy tones. The sultan was reluctant to sign the combined loan and reform agreement as long as France was obligated to train only 5,000 men by its military provisions.[57] In order to facilitate the signing of the agreement the French legation decided to send Kaddour Ben Ghabrit secretly to Fez. Although the road between Tangier and Fez was supposedly blocked by the rebels and impassable because of the weather, Ben Ghabrit was able to make the journey without great difficulty, arriving at Fez during the first week of April.[58] His persuasive qualities were very soon turned to advantage. After being closeted with ʿAbd al-Ḥafīẓ on April 7 for most of the day, Ben Ghabrit finally managed to convince him of the need to sign the financial accord along with the covering letters, and to agree to apply the tartīb (under French supervision) as soon as the rebellion was suppressed.[59] The first essential step toward laying the legal groundwork for French intervention had been taken.

In the meantime, the political situation in Paris was gradually evolving in a direction favorable to the colonial lobby. While most of the cabinet was away from Paris during the Easter recess, an important meeting was held on April 17 at which it was decided to send an expeditionary force to Fez. Present at the meeting were Cruppi, Berteaux, and the head of the colonial bloc, Eugène Etienne. According to the testimony of Caillaux and Messimy, Etienne used the occasion to take advantage of the inexperience of Cruppi and the ambition of Berteaux to convince them of the need to make a decision immediately. When the full cabinet reconvened on April 23 they had no choice but to approve the initiative.[60] To avoid unduly exciting the opposition of French public opinion, the relief operation was still officially described as a joint Franco-Moroccan expedition. In fact, the ʿAmrānī maḥalla was now almost completely disregarded, and the Moroccans were distinctly the junior partners in the new cooperative venture. Four French battalions were to be included in the relief expedition.[61] Not for the first time, the impetuosity of the French colonial lobby was to be the cause of a serious international crisis before the episode was completed.

By April 26, the Cherarda maḥalla had finally managed to return to Fez. The city was now almost completely isolated—or so it seemed.[62] While Ben Ghabrit and Gaillard tried to get the sultan to recognize the need for French troops to relieve the siege, they sent only the most pessimistic dispatches to Tangier to reinforce the claims of the government as to the gravity of the situation at Fez. The French plans were almost unmasked ahead of time when several copies of the April 29 issue of *al-Saʿada* arrived at Fez. The paper spoke of a planned French expeditionary force massing on the coast. Since this was the first that anyone at Fez had heard of such a plan, there was an immediate unfavorable reaction, and Gaillard had to spend the next few days reassuring nervous Fāsī notables.[63] Finally, on May 4, Gaillard managed to get the sultan to promise to write an official letter requesting French military support. The text of the letter did not arrive at Tangier until May 12, on the eve of the departure of the French expeditionary force. It was predated to April 27 to make it look like a confirmation of an earlier verbal request that the sultan had vaguely made.[64] It is however clear from the text of the letter itself, as well as from subsequent developments, that ʿAbd al-Ḥafīẓ had the impression that only a small French force would be sent and that the bulk of the relief force would consist of the ʿAmrānī maḥalla. The French commander at Fez, Mangin, recommended on April 30 that two columns be prepared, one to advance on Fez from the Chaouia, the other to feint an advance from French posts along the Moulouya River. In this way the attention of the rebels would be divided and the Chaouia force would be able to proceed at a more rapid pace.[65]

The expeditionary force began to assemble at Kenitra in the last week of April. While supplies were stockpiled and reinforcements

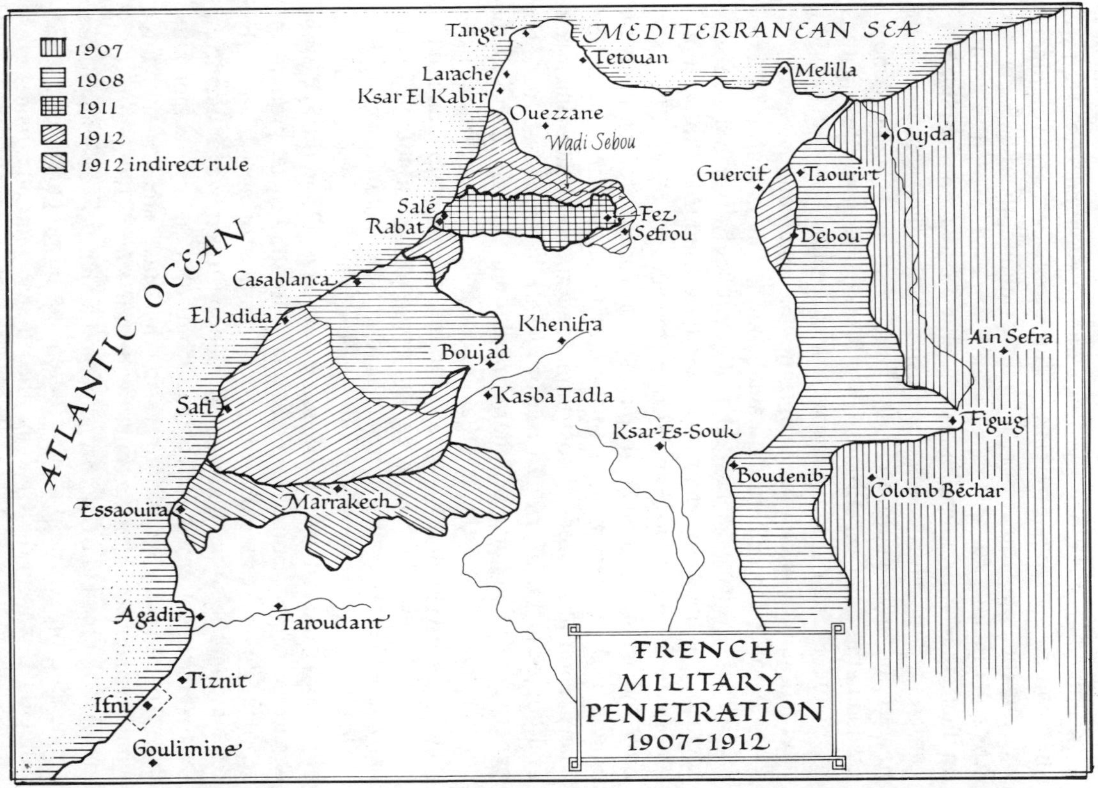

FRENCH MILITARY PENETRATION 1907–1912

continued to arrive (they would eventually total 20,500 men), the French government employed its efforts in seeking to convince the powers (and the French public) of the necessity of intervention. The official text of the request of the sultan arrived on May 21. The juridical status of the operation was thus assured, at least as far as the Quai d'Orsay was concerned. The progress of the expeditionary force was surprisingly rapid once it started out. It seems to have caught the tribes off guard: many of them were exhausted after several months of fighting, while others were already involved with the spring harvest. The relief force reached Fez on May 21 and delivered the city from the last of the besiegers.[66] The inhabitants of Fez, who had been led to believe until the last moment that it was al-ʿAmrānī's column which was coming, were much angered when they learned the truth.[67] Those in the relief force, for their part, were astounded to discover that, contrary to the stories which they had been told, the inhabitants of Fez were not starving and that the garrison was in relatively fit shape.[68]

The Aftermath of Revolt

Neither Germany nor Spain had shown any particular willingness to accept French claims of humanitarian intent during the relief of Fez. French diplomats had not chosen to attach particular significance to the German and Spanish attitudes at the time, perhaps out of a conviction of the self-evident correctness of their actions. They therefore reacted with astonishment to manifestations of German disapproval in June and to the news of Spanish military intervention at Larache in the northern Gharb. Thus began what has been called the Second Moroccan Crisis.

On June 3 Spanish diplomats gave the first concrete inkling of their pique at French unilateral intervention at Fez.[69] The Spanish Foreign Ministry reported that unrest in the Spanish zone of the Gharb created a dangerous situation, which might require Spanish intervention to safeguard its nationals and its interests in the region. A few days later a Spanish post in the town of El Ksar in the Gharb was attacked at night by rampaging tribesmen, as if to give substance to the Spanish concern. After an abbreviated press campaign about the need to act, Spanish troops were landed at Larache.[70] In justification, Spanish diplomats asserted their right to intervene according to Article 3 of the 1904 Franco-Spanish secret accord, namely, French prior intervention to alter the status quo. Thereafter, in the face of a mild French protest, Spain set about organizing the administration of its region until such time as a protectorate treaty regularized its diplomatic position.[71]

The Spanish were far from satisfied with their position, however, and continued to protest more or less openly that they should be treated as equal partners by France and that they would be satisfied with nothing less. The negotiations of the 1911 Cruppi-Muqrī Accords, which included a large loan and a concession to build a railroad line between Tangier and El Ksar, they regarded as prejudicial to Spanish interests. During the remainder of 1911 Spanish diplomats worked to obtain a more favorable share of the public works contracts and concessions in Morocco.[72]

The major diplomatic outcome of the occupation of Fez by Moinier's troops was not the Spanish intervention, significant as that was from a Moroccan standpoint. Rather it was the outbreak of the Second Moroccan Crisis between Germany and France, which brought Europe to the verge of war (although probably not so close as was thought at the time). On June 21, after several oblique comments to Cambon about the likelihood of some response by Germany in defense of its own interests, Kiderlen formally demanded compensation from France.[73] As a way of dramatizing this concern, the gunboat *Panther* was sent to Agadir, allegedly to protect Germans in the Sous who were endangered by the growing anarchy in the region.[74] In fact this allegation was quite as fraudulent as the Spanish protest about deteriorating security around El Ksar. The aim, however, was similar: to compel France to disgorge an appropriate compensation in return for acquiescence in the French action. The crisis grew still more complicated by the entry of Great Britain into the fray in defense of its ally, France. Relations grew tense between Britain and Germany for awhile. After long and complicated talks between Germany and France a bargain was struck. On November 4, 1911, an accord was signed which gave Germany two strips of territory in the French Congo with access to the Congo River. In return, Germany agreed to a French protectorate over Morocco.[75] The way was finally clear for the realization of the dream of a united French North Africa that had haunted a generation of colonial-minded Frenchmen.

In the ambiguous new preprotectorate period, serious difficulties once again emerged with the French government between the diplomats and the warriors. This time, the source of discord was confusion over which branch would direct affairs during the difficult transitional period. The dispute manifested itself at Fez in the persons of

Henri Gaillard, the French consul, and General Moinier, commander of the French expeditionary force to Fez, d'Amade's successor in the Chaouia. Gaillard favored a policy of subtlety and patience in dealing with the sultan and the makhzan, and his skill in ingratiating himself with ʿAbd al-Ḥafiẓ before, during, and after the siege gave him a very powerful influence on the makhzan. Moinier had been given a mission to perform, that of delivering the Europeans at Fez, pacifying the region, and restoring communications with the coast. Moinier was a cautious man. He had taken no unnecessary risks in the deliverance of Fez and intended to take none during the difficult transitional period. This meant, among other things, that all Moroccan officials who were not openly pro-French were to be regarded with suspicion. If the toleration of a few abuses was the price for securing loyal native collaborators, then this price must be accepted.

The relationship between Gaillard and Moinier was complicated from the outset by the fact that Moinier outranked the consul in age, experience, and by the dictates of the protocol manual, yet he was forced by circumstances to pay close attention to Gaillard's advice. In the event of a policy disagreement between the two men there was no satisfactory way of solving the problem, for neither possessed any clearly delimited authority of his own and, being of different and rival branches of government service, neither could impose his views upon the other. All that could be done was to refer the dispute to higher authorities, a course which naturally had a number of unpleasant consequences. It meant, for example, that the simplest decisions affecting makhzan appointments at Fez could not be solved without long delay. Problems arising out of local circumstances could no longer be settled on the spot; if they were, a protest might be lodged at Paris. In addition, local disputes between diplomacy and military could become magnified into full-fledged major battles between the Quai d'Orsay and the Ministère de la Guerre.

The French government, being none too strong at home politically, tended to take the easy way out and tried to avoid admitting that any problems existed. No clear lines of direction were ever laid down, and the government wavered back and forth in its attitude toward the proper policy to take in Morocco. To undertake a radical reorganization of the administration of the north, including the attribution of political responsibilities to the native-affairs officers was inadmissible, for this would make the French presence in the interior of Morocco look like outright conquest. But to go along with the whims of ʿAbd al-Ḥafiẓ, who was exhibiting extreme nervousness over his personal fate, would be to undercut the major gains in French influence. In either case the powers were likely to protest at the danger to the interests of their nationals and protégés. The dilemma was never satisfactorily resolved and did much to increase the possibility of serious difficulties arising out of the transition period before a protectorate treaty could be signed.[76]

After the relief of Fez, Moinier's troops had undertaken the pacification of the region on behalf of the makhzan. Military columns had been sent to circulate among the tribes, put down resistance, and submit the tribes to makhzan authority. A large force under General Ditte had left Fez in early June to deal with the Ait Ndhir, Ait Youssi, and Gerrouan, tribes which had been the heart of the 1911 insurrection. After several pitched battles along the way, the column arrived on June 9 at the gates of Meknes, where it received the formal surrender of the pretender, Mawlāy Zayn, and his makhzan.[77] In September operations were conducted against the Zaer and Zemmour. The lines of communication between Fez and the coast were secured by a line of military posts across the Gharb. Work was begun to join Fez with Rabat and Casablanca by wireless telegraph.[78] Forts of mixed French and makhzan troops were constructed at Sefrou and El Hadjeb as a means of keeping the turbulent Ait Youssi and Ait Ndhir under close surveillance.[79] In eastern Morocco, the diversionary activity had taken French troops under General Toutée from Taourirt to the village of Guercif on the other side of the Moulouya River. This had attracted the attention of the Taza hill tribes away from Fez as it had been intended to, and Toutée made no further effort to advance on Fez.[80]

Perhaps partly because the French intervention caught the tribes by surprise peace was restored with relative ease in the north of Morocco. In the surrender of the tribes Gaillard, the French consul at Fez, served as intermediary between the palace and the tribes.[81] By the procedure agreed upon with the sultan, representatives of tribes who wished to submit were to sign an undertaking that they would be personally responsible for the behavior of their clans and that, in the event of a resumption of hostilities, they would call upon French and makhzan forces for assistance. These representatives were also obliged to promise that they would not continue the old abuses in tax collection. In return they were to be given two signed statements, one by ʿAbd al-Ḥafīẓ in which he accorded them *amān* (security) and promised fair administration, and the other by General Moinier, guaranteeing the execution of the agreements.[82] There was one major flaw in the arrangement. The representatives who came forward were often without influence in their tribes, and only later did the French discover that they had often appointed as qāid-s men who were opportunistic nonentities. Predictably, the abuses of the "French-imposed" officials were blamed on France.[83] With the establishment of the "Pax Gallica," there was a general movement to settle old scores by denouncing enemies to the native-affairs bureau. Serious injustices were committed before the French discovered what was in fact going on.[84]

The French policy of administration, or at any rate their practice of it, did much to intensify the already smouldering resentment felt by many tribes. In this way, they paved the way for the tribal risings of May-August 1912. Many of the army officers stationed in the countryside attempted to get around the bother of referring everything back to Fez or Tangier by administering the tribe under their jurisdiction with as little reference to the makhzan as possible. Others sought to intervene more directly in the workings of the makhzan at Fez, or even to substitute the native-affairs bureau for the makhzan. One officer, for example, intervened to have makhzan-appointed qāid-s fired and his own candidates appointed. At the Fez native-affairs bureau, some of the officers tended to insist that all makhzan officials should report through them.[85] Ill-advised and hasty measures, like the expropriation of the Qasba Shararda (in which some three hundred families were living) lost the French a great deal of sympathy at Fez.[86] The impolitic directness and vigor with which French officers moved to put a stop to contraband in arms within the city of Fez led to several ugly incidents, because young officers who had recently arrived in Morocco and who spoke little Arabic pursued all rumors without attention to their source.[87]

The points of friction where the new regime chafed especially on Moroccan sensibilities should have been predictable, in view of recent events. Abuses in the system of taxation and rural administration, and the difficulties occasioned by the introduction of military reforms, had earlier sparked revolts. These once again proved to be major irritants. Much of this was foreseen by J. M. Macleod as early as July 1911:

> . . . there will be little but troubles all the time until some decent administration of the Finances of the interior is created and put into practice together with the elementary justice in various branches of the government which naturally result from a reasonable system of taxation &c. What else can one expect as long as the present cycle of 'squeeze' 'revolt' and 'suppress' (in

> practice raid and burn this district or that) goes on. That I am convinced is the real root of nearly all of the evils of the country and until this is recognized and resolutely dealt with no true start will be made with the development of the country or even of its pacification.[88]

The criticism remained generally valid until the arrival of Lyautey in May 1912. Although some measures were taken to try and bring some of the more crying injustices under control, a great many others went uncorrected.

Preprotectorate Unrest

A major demand of the rebels in 1911 had been the dismissal of the grand vizier, Madanī al-Glawī. Accordingly, one of the first steps taken by the French after their arrival was the summary firing of Madanī al-Glawī and all members of his clan holding makhzan office. Although it seems strange in view of the later notoriety that Madanī al-Glawī was to win as the pasha of Marrakech, considerable suspicion of his loyalties existed in French military and diplomatic circles at Fez. Mangin was convinced that he had intrigued against the military mission, and Gaillard held grave doubts as to his reliability.[89] His brother, al-Ḥājj Tahamī, was considered more favorable to France—he was, after all, a protégé of the Compagnie marocaine. But it was at first thought to be for the best if the entire family should lose power in a sort of general house-cleaning. The makhzan at Fez fell into the hands of Muḥammad al-Muqrī and his clan and was less influential in the new circumstances. At Marrakech, the chief candidate to fill the vacuum in the south left by the withdrawal of the Glawa was ʿAbd al-Mālik al-Mtouggui, longtime rival of the Glawa family and more militantly anti-French.

Rapid changes of fortune were relatively common in Moroccan politics, so at first the clan of al-Glawī accepted their fate with stoic resignation. But they later became apprehensive about whether ʿAbd al-Ḥafīẓ intended to seize their considerable properties in the south and sought British intervention on their behalf. In the meantime talk of jihād circulated in the Chaouia and the Marrakech region. In mid-June, after British representations on behalf of al-Ḥājj Tahamī, an agreement was worked out whereby he was allowed to make up a list of his relatives to whom French protection (and therefore immunities) would be accorded by the Quai d'Orsay.[90] After further negotiations between the makhzan, France, and al-Ḥājj Tahamī (with the British minister, Sir Reginald Lister, an interested party), a final settlement was worked out. By its terms al-Ḥājj Tahamī was permitted to retain his properties at Marrakech, and the Glawa agreed to pay the Moroccan treasury the equivalent of 20,000 pounds sterling.[91]

The settlement was at best a half-measure, for it left unresolved the tense and ambiguous political situation in the south. Al-Ḥājj Tahamī had not been reappointed as pasha of Marrakech, nor had any of the other Glawa chiefs received confirmation of their positions. Al-Mtouggui made several efforts to take over some of the tribes that had formerly been under Glawa sway, and the tribes at Demnat revolted against their Glawa qāid. The French aggravated the situation by refraining from openly favoring either candidate as a matter of principle, since the sultan was still the legal authority in the state and the French could only advise.[92] The new pasha eventually appointed for Marrakech was Idrīs Wuld al-Ḥājj Mīnū (Fr. Driss Menou), a notoriously corrupt retainer of ʿAbd al-Ḥafīẓ. From his arrival at Marrakech, Mīnū made himself an opponent of France, while collecting taxes with a vigor equal to that which al-Glawī had employed, and extorting additional contributions. In his capacity as the sultan's business associate at Marrakech, he began illegally to sell makhzan properties and engage in land speculation. This irritated many of the local merchants and resident Europeans.[93] He also engaged openly in anti-French propaganda and encouraged a display of open defiance to France by the populace. The appointment, from the French point of view, was clearly a disaster.

Efforts to get al-Ḥājj Tahamī reinstated were begun in October 1911, again with British sponsorship. Despite strong pressure by French diplomatic agents upon the sultan, however, he continued to procrastinate. The situation in Marrakech continued to grow more and more unstable, as tension mounted between al-Mtouggua and Glawa factions. Nothing in fact was done, and by April 1912 Mīnū was still firmly ensconced at Marrakech.[94] The situation of political instability in the south was to play an important role, following the signing of the protectorate treaty, in the rise of a new pretender in the south.

The behavior of Mawlāy ʿAbd al-Ḥafīẓ following the occupation of Fez set the tone for the rest of his people. Willfully obstructionist when it came to matters of administration like the Glawa succession imbroglio, the sultan maneuvered skillfully to exploit the ambiguities that surrounded his position. Of particular note is his sale of makhzan properties for his own benefit. Moroccan law made no clear distinction between lands which formed part of the national patrimony (and which were therefore inalienable) and the personal property of the monarch.[95] Working through a local agent at Marrakech, for example, he made great profits in land speculation.[96] There is no doubt that this practice, which he continued up to the eve of his abdication, undermined whatever legitimacy he might have retained in the eyes of his people. It also made him millions of Moroccan pesetas.

More significant politically was the attitude of ʿAbd al-Ḥafīẓ toward the indemnity and taxes owed by the tribes, since these added to their financial grievances. As part of the surrender terms, Moinier had gotten the tribes to agree that they should jointly pay an indemnity of 200,000 pesetas for the damages which they had caused at Meknes and Fez. The sultan high-handedly maintained that the claims for damaged property were in addition to the indemnity, and ultimately he got his way.[97] The 1911 loan agreement had called for the institution of the tartīb and the elimination of all tax exemptions. The tribes feared that during the transition period both old and new taxes would be collected, and this tended to predispose them against the French and the makhzan. Privileged groups and individuals who had been tax-exempt formerly were naturally upset at having to give up the exemptions, and some agitated covertly against the regime.[98] Unrest in the north was also encouraged by the heavy fines which were imposed on the Ait Ndhir and the continuation of old administrative abuses.

The combination of the attractions of French rule and the depressed condition of the Moroccan economy under ʿAbd al-Ḥafīẓ worked toward encouraging the urban bourgeois groups to abandon their resistance to a French protectorate. French policy at Fez, where the major Moroccan merchant families had their headquarters and the ʿulamā were the strongest, was therefore greeted with initial favor mingled with apprehension. The errors of that policy and the indistinct and confused impression which the French gave of their intentions during the months which followed the occupation of Fez began to erode the sympathy of the Fāsīs. By April of 1912 the indecision and alternating extreme indulgence and harshness of French native policy had alienated most of the aʿyān of Fez and made possible the mutiny and rising.

The reemergence of the tradition of rural unrest is the most important development of the period from June 1911 to April 1912. In northern Morocco, this meant the persistence of the movements of protest which had brought about the 1911 revolt. The relative smoothness of the transition at Fez was largely illusory. In the countryside the unevenness of the pace of change after June 1911 and the deficiencies of French native policy threatened to produce an explosive situation once again.

In all, for the first time in the recent history of northern Morocco, a joint coalition of Arab and Berber tribes (including for the first time several jaysh tribes) had joined in resisting the tax demands of the makhzan and of growing French influence. They had accomplished this out of common fear: fear that the makhzan would soon grow strong enough to dominate them, fear that France would gain predominant influence over the sultan. Out of this combination of patriotism and defense of local interests they had succeeded in forging an alliance which had lasted for three months under difficult conditions and had only succumbed to a vastly superior French force. Their defeat had not been a convincing one. The principal leaders of the rising remained at large in the mountains, and their tribes remained on the alert, ready to take advantage of the first sign of French weakness.

In general the growing deterioration of the French political situation in Morocco went unnoticed by all but a few specialists in native policy. Most eyes were turned toward the task of working out a diplomatic settlement with Germany (accomplished by the accord of November 1911), and the negotiation of a protectorate treaty and appointment of a resident-general.

8

THE FEZ MUTINY AND THE REVOLT OF EL HIBA

An important feature of precolonial Moroccan politics was the vitality of the rural areas. During the decade of rapid change which preceded the French and Spanish protectorates, rural groups were prominent at each major turning of the political wheel. The tribal movements of 1912, by their relative cohesion, organization, and discipline stand out from those which came before. They also make an interesting contrast with similar movements of popular protest and resistance in the Middle East.[1]

The Mutiny at Fez

During the winter of 1911–12, the ambiguous political situation continued to be productive of disputes between the occupying French forces and the local population. In the countryside, vague disquiet showed signs of turning into a more determined resistance effort. In the cities of the interior, especially at Fez, rumblings of discontent came increasingly to the attention of the Arab Bureau. Fāsī merchants who had assumed that the arrival of the French would facilitate the development of trade revised their calculations when new contracts failed to accompany the occupation forces. The laboring poor found themselves squeezed by the rise in prices and resented the presence of French troops in the city. The religious elements were alienated by an inopportune French decision to abolish their tax exemptions and to apply the tartīb to them.[2] Despite numerous indications that all was not well, plans went ahead for the signing of the protectorate treaty later in the year.

On March 24, Henri Regnault, the French minister at Tangier arrived at Fez, fresh from lengthy consultations in Paris. In his baggage was the protectorate treaty. Immediately upon his arrival Regnault closeted himself with the sultan. With the assistance of Gaillard and Ben Ghabrit, he was able to induce ʿAbd al-Ḥafīẓ to sign the treaty without modification. Elaborate guarantees for the future status of the sultan, including a substantial annual pension, eventually convinced him to sign.[3] Even then he did so under duress.

The sultan and his ministers had been for some time resigned to the inevitability of a protectorate. Discussions with Consul Gaillard and others, however, had led makhzan officials to believe that Morocco would be given a regime similar to that of British Egypt, with considerable autonomy in crucial areas like justice and the internal workings of the administration. What they received instead was a treaty modeled explicitly upon the treaty of Bardo, which had established the Tunisian protectorate. By its terms the sultan was to be reduced to a position approximating that of the bey of Tunis.[4] The insult was patent. As Mawlay ʿAbd al-Ḥafīẓ observed bitterly to Macleod, "who cares a farthing [sic] whether the Bey of Tunis is wise or foolish?"[5] A glance at the terms of the treaty reveals the source of the sultan's disquiet.

Article 1 of the treaty guaranteed the exercise of the Islamic religion, the preservation of the religious character of the sultanate, and the security of the pious foundations (*hubus*). Closer inspection showed the hollowness of such promises, however. No safeguards existed against later encroachment upon these rights by the protectorate government. Furthermore the same article excluded the sultan from the negotiations over the northern zone and the status of Tangier. Clearly, this amounted to the disposition of Moroccan territory without Moroccan consent. Article 2 could be read as authorizing the dispatch of troops anywhere in Moroccan territory without the approval of the sultan, as well as their commitment overseas. Article 3 was more straightforward. It obliged the French government to preserve the throne and dynasty. Through the legal fiction of delegation propounded in Article 4, virtually all powers were placed in the hands of the new protectorate government. Moroccan officials retained only symbolic authority, and their number was to be kept to a minimum. The resident-general now assumed all control over the foreign relations of the country (Articles 5 and 6). The sultan renounced the right to conclude financial agreements without the prior approval of the French government and agreed to join with France in working out the financial reorganization of the state (Articles 7 and 8). In effect, the financial affairs were now definitively handed over to the bondholders. The Treaty of Fez, in sum, emptied the authority of the sultan and the makhzan of all substance and created alongside their authority a highly ramified protectorate government with complete control in all the areas which counted.[6]

Regnault sought at first to keep news of the signing of the treaty a secret, pending the departure of the sultan for Rabat. It soon leaked to the French press, however, and before long was the subject of agitated conversation among the Moroccans of the city. According to Weisgerber, who was there,

> When it was known at Fez, there was general consternation. The protectorate treaty was considered as a bill of sale, and the whole city, from the sharifs and the *ʿulamā* to the least of the *baqqāl* [petty traders], disapproved of the transaction by which the *imām,* the Commander of the Faithful raised on the shield four years earlier as sultan of the *jihād,* had "sold" to the Christians a part of *Dār al-Islām.*
>
> A calm heavy with menace weighed upon the city but the warning signs of the storm were not yet perceptible, among the Europeans, except for the rare initiates to the intimate life of the capital. However, in the streets, no more smiling faces: the natives scarcely replied to words addressed to them, and yesterday's friends pretended not to recognize you.[7]

In the days which followed, changes were noted in the attitudes of the Moroccan court. Makhzan officials became noticeably more truculent in their dealings with the French. The grand vizier, Tayyib al-Muqrī, while refraining from publicly expressing his feelings of bitterness, made no secret of his true opinions to Consul Macleod. The sultan himself avoided a public statement about the treaty, but in circles whose opinions counted, his attitude was well known. He gave no clear direction or leadership during a time when such would have been greatly welcomed by Regnault.[8]

The political situation around Fez continued to deteriorate during the first weeks of April, although the French command continued to manifest the greatest confidence. Other French observers were less certain that this confidence was warranted. On the morning of April 13, Weisgerber was visited by a tribesman from the Zerhoun and warned of forthcoming action against the official party scheduled to conduct the sultan to Rabat. The tribes not only possessed precise intelligence of the date scheduled for the departure of the sultan, they were well organized and determined to act. The aim of the operation, said Weisgerber's informant, was "To take back from the ambassador his bill of sale." Alarmed by the news, Weisgerber went directly to Regnault to urge greater caution. The French minister was at first skeptical but was eventually persuaded to postpone his departure.[9] No further precautions were taken however. The old optimism had returned by the following day, even as fresh evidence of unrest continued to come to light.

The signing of the protectorate treaty and the ensuing deterioration of the political climate at Fez coincided with a French decision to press ahead with the drastic reform of the makhzan army. The excution of this decision provoked a mutiny of the makhzan troops at Fez on April 17, which in turn soon led to an insurrection of the popular classes against the French. The intersection of these two crises, one general, the other confined to the army, thus lies at the roots of the sudden reemergence of Moroccan resistance in the spring of 1912. In order to more fully understand the reasons for the Fez mutiny, it is necessary to explore the circumstances of the French decision to reform the Moroccan army at such a critical juncture and to investigate the manner by which French officers at Fez sought to implement their program for change.

France had supplied advisors to the makhzan army since the middle of the nineteenth century. In time, reform of the Moroccan army had come to be seen as an important means of "peaceful penetration" and the furtherance of the interests of France. The crisis of 1905 had prompted a rethinking of French national defense policy. French strategists, alarmed by the demographic advantage enjoyed by Germany over France, searched for alternative sources of military manpower. The conscription of native troops in the colonies seemed to offer the best possibilities of rapid gains.[10] Accordingly, the high command became interested in a project proposed by Colonel Charles Mangin for the recruitment of a black African army from French West African possessions. By 1912, the development of the "force noire," as it was called, was well launched.[11] At much the same time a campaign to conscript Algerian Muslims for service in the French army was initiated. The program was opposed, for different reasons, by both the Muslims and the settlers. It was continued despite protests.[12]

It is within the context of concern over the relative sizes of French and German armies, and experimentation with colonial troops to fill the gap, that the project for the reform of the Moroccan army should be situated. It had been estimated that the conquest of Morocco would be costly in French lives—a cost which critics maintained the metropolitan army should not be compelled to bear. To get around this difficulty, they proposed that Moroccan troops be substituted for European troops. Experiments had already been made in the Chaouia, beginning in 1909, to recruit native cavalry units, which would serve under French or Algerian Muslim officers and a modified French disciplinary code. This was the Chaouia goum (Ar. *qawm*) system and was modeled on Algerian irregular forces. The Moroccan troops had led the Moinier relief column to Fez in 1911 and had performed well under fire. In the fall of 1911 the goum system was extended to the Gharb.[13] Also about this time plans were laid to recruit a similar force at Marrakech, but because of the political situation of the region and budgetary difficulties little was done to follow through on this idea.[14] A third part of the reorganization of the Moroccan military was the rapid enrollment of volunteers for a new makhzan army similar to that created by the 1910 reform designed by Commandant Emile Mangin.[15] Continued reports of rural unrest made the reform of the Moroccan army seem especially urgent by early 1912. With limited numbers of French troops available, the Poincaré government counted on Moroccan forces to maintain order. But as long as Morocco was independent and the protectorate treaty remained unsigned, French instructors would have to go slow in introducing the planned reforms. The longer the delay, of course, the more precarious the French position became. During the winter of 1912, the stakes steadily increased for the planned military reforms.

The reorganization of the Moroccan army was not without peril. Despite a deliberate go-slow policy, French military instructors at Fez managed through their insensitivity to offend not only some of their Moroccan recruits but the population of the city as well. Lacking experience in the complex and sophisticated political world of Fez, many advisors committed serious breaches of local customs.[16] Further, the presence of large numbers of French troops in the city inevitably led to almost daily incidents in the markets. A kind of continuous feedback situation was created whereby news of alleged French mistreatment of Moroccan troops alarmed the Fāsī townspeople, while disturbances in the sūq-s provoked critical comment within the army.[17] On March 18, for example, a Lieutenant Guillass was shot and killed by a Moroccan soldier in his unit. Earlier the lieutenant had verbally and physically abused the man during drill, shaming him in front of his comrades.[18] The soldier's speedy trial and execution according to French (and not Muslim) justice was the object of bitter criticism among the troops as well as the Fāsī elite. No lesson appears to have been drawn from this unfortunate incident by the French. Instead it was perceived as a typical example of alleged Muslim fanaticism.

On April 9 and 10 there were several incidents of jostling in the crowded streets of Fez involving French officers and a visiting tribesman which further inflamed passions in the city. Upon the insistence of the French military command the man was arrested by the makhzan and jailed. On April 11 the sultan issued a letter very strongly critical of the obstreperous attitude of the population and calling for an end to such incidents. The letter was read in all the mosques and, because of its caustic and hectoring tone, was badly received by the people.[19] Some saw it as a clear indication that ʿAbd al-Ḥafīẓ had completely thrown in his lot with the French and was no longer to be looked to for leadership.

While the political atmosphere at Fez became steadily more poisonous, with rumors of imminent uprisings reported almost daily, French military advisors proceeded with their plans to introduce a comprehensive overhaul of the Moroccan army along French lines. Now that the protectorate treaty had been signed, there was not a moment to lose. Eventually it was decided to introduce the reforms on April 17. The selection of the date was remarkably inept, since it was known that there would be an eclipse of the sun on that day with all of the potential for confusion and panic it promised. Warnings indeed had been received by the native-affairs bureau. Nonetheless, with little or no explanation or prior preparation, on the morning of April 17 Moroccan troops were brusquely informed that new, more stringent regulations would henceforth be in effect. Among the items that caused the most resentment were provisions that commands would be given in French instead of Arabic and that the troops would be expected to carry regulation field knapsacks (which was regarded as a grave humiliation). Most important, a new system of payment was introduced under which salaries would be paid partly in kind, as well as in cash (previously it had been all cash). It was soon perceived that the new arrangements amounted to a de facto pay cut, and at a time of severe inflation at that! It did not take long for angry words to spill over into actions.[20]

The mutiny began among two tabors of infantry garrisoned at the Qasbah Cherarda outside the walls. The men protested vehemently against the new regulations, then attacked and killed their French instructors. Next they descended upon Fez al-Bali in great agitation, firing on any Frenchman they saw. The civilian population of the city soon became caught up in the movement. As the rioting spread, several other tabors of makhzan troops mutinied against their officers. An excited crowd of soldiers came to the palace to inform the sultan of what was happening and to solicit his advice. They were received in the garden by ʿAbd al-Ḥafīẓ but in all of the confusion received such contradictory impressions of what he said that many left with the idea that he favored the mutiny. In fact it appears that the sultan did make an effort to calm them but was himself badly rattled by the course of events and unable to express himself clearly. In any event, by this time the riot was already out of hand, and the mob had begun looting European businesses in the market. The offices of the Compagnie marocaine and the Crédit Foncier de l'Algérie, and the British post office were special targets. The European section of New Fez next came under attack, but by the efforts of loyal Moroccan troops and their French officers the rioters were repulsed without reaching their objective, the French consulate. In its frustration the crowd then moved upon the Jewish quarter, the *mallāḥ*, and attacked and pillaged it. Fighting lasted until April 19. It was only repressed after French artillery was turned upon the town and fired into the most affected quarters.

When it was all over, French troops had suffered losses of fifty-three killed, while some thirteen European civilians had been massacred. The Jewish population was especially hard hit. They had suffered losses of forty-two killed and thirty-seven wounded. More tragically, the mallāḥ had been virtually leveled in the course of the struggle, leaving more than ten thousand people homeless. As many as six hundred Moroccans may have perished in the rioting and the subsequent French repression.

Despite the firm conviction of many French observers, no evidence was ever found to substantiate the claim that a widespread conspiracy lay at the origins of the mutiny. The reports prepared by Regnault's staff, French military intelligence, the British consul Macleod all concurred that the events could more easily be explained as the result of French political blunders. Given the highly charged atmosphere which prevailed at Fez, the spread of the mutiny was deemed inevitable.[21] A more original theory was propounded by Phillip Vassel, the German consul. He saw the mutiny as the result of a plot to discredit Regnault that had been launched by the Fez native-affairs bureau but had somehow miscarried.[22] His theory remains unproved.

In a sense, we can say that Vassel's suspicions were vindicated by events. One consequence of the Fez mutiny was that it did effectively end Regnault's hopes of becoming the first resident-general of the protectorate. The split between the diplomats and the military was resolved in favor of the military. With renewed disorder in Morocco, the Poincaré government decided that a civilian would be inappropriate in the position and that the job must be given to a general. To soften the blow, Regnault was promised a major diplomatic post and publicly commended for the successful manner in which he had conducted his mission.[23] Under heavy attack in the Parisian press for vacillating under fire and emotionally devastated by the unforeseen turn of events, Regnault became increasingly bitter toward the military. Like a good civil servant, he agreed to remain on the job until his successor had arrived, but his letters during the weeks following the mutiny reveal the depths of his disappointment.[24]

The deteriorating political situation in Morocco necessitated a rapid decision on the new resident-general. During the last week of April and the first week of May the government conducted an intensive search for a military man with the right combination of suppleness and firmness and a strong talent for administration. Eventually the field narrowed down to three candidates, Generals d'Amade, Gallieni, and Lyautey. Gallieni's age was against him, while d'Amade lacked strong political support. Lyautey was supported by Eugène Etienne and the Comité du Maroc. On April 27 the decision was officially made.[25] The following day a meeting was held at Versailles, at which Lyautey was invited to review his plans for the new protectorate administration with Poincaré and officials of the Ministries of Foreign Affairs and War. Lyautey by all accounts put on a dazzling performance, reassuring the skeptical on his determination to economize French lives through the use of political action where possible.[26] By May 9 he was en route to Morocco, taking with him only a small personal staff. As a concession to the Quai d'Orsay, which had come to regard him as their special bête-noir during the period he had served in eastern Morocco, the Count de Saint-Aulaire was appointed secretary-general of the protectorate. Privately Saint-Aulaire was charged with preserving the prerogatives of the Quai d'Orsay and serving as unofficial watchdog on Lyautey. (In fact, the two men got along famously, and the bureaucratic rivalries were soon smoothed over.)[27]

The Second Siege of Fez

French reactions to the Fez uprising tended to mirror the preexisting lines of cleavage between civilian and military authorities. General Moinier and the officers of the Arab Bureau viewed the revolt as evidence of the seditious spirit of the city and urged stiff repressive measures as a needed antidote. For Regnault, on the other hand, the mutiny and ensuing events were simply the result of the errors of Moinier and the military. In the conditions of insecurity that followed the insurrection, the initiative passed to the military, and Regnault was forced to accept the measures adopted by Moinier, even though he might deplore them.[28]

The first step taken by Moinier was to declare a state of siege and to impose martial law. In making his decision he had consulted neither Regnault nor Mawlāy ʿAbd al-Ḥafīẓ. A strict curfew was instituted, and orders were issued that all weapons in the possession of Moroccans were to be turned in to the French authorities. A house-to-house search for contraband would follow in the event of noncompliance. The Fāsī bourgeoisie, already terrified by the shelling of the town during the suppression of the revolt, became thoroughly panicked by this turn of events. When wholesale arrests of suspected mutineers and rioters followed, their fear increased. Those arrested were to be judged by a military court martial, regardless of whether they were soldiers or civilians.[29] The trial of suspected mutineers dragged on during the month of May. Punishments were unusually severe—long terms of imprisonment or death by firing squad. By the end of the month over one hundred suspected rioters had been executed and hundreds of others jailed. Such French vindictiveness soon eroded whatever confidence Fāsī-s might have had in French justice.[30]

The worst excesses of the mob had been committed against the Jewish quarter, which had been destroyed and pillaged. Over ten thousand Jews had been forced to seek shelter in the palace. They were cared for by the sultan and the wealthy merchants of the city. Later, European relief assistance was also forthcoming. Although the merchants had not been involved in the rioting and had already done much to succor the riot victims, Moinier arbitrarily ordered that Fez al-Bali (in practice, the bourgeoisie) pay a fine of 200,000 pesetas over and above damage claims. The announcement of the fine, moreover, came not from the sultan but from the Arab Bureau. It therefore added substance to the contention that France intended to abolish the makhzan and rule the country directly. The bourgeoisie of Fez were willing to contribute to a relief fund, but they were incensed at being obliged to pay a fine which they judged grossly unfair and high-handed. Far from calming things, Moinier's intemperate actions risked provoking still further violence.[31]

The French military command kept a close watch on the development of resistance sentiment among the tribes. But they were unable to muster sufficient strength to intervene forcefully against the slowly crystallizing ḥaraka-s since most of the available troops were tied down in occupation duties at Fez, Meknes, Sefrou, and El Hadjeb.[32] The native-affairs bureau accordingly was reduced to the expedient of attempting to utilize the religious and political influence of some of the sharifs of Wazzan among the tribes north and east of Fez in an effort to dislocate the ḥaraka-s. Sīḍī ʿAbd al-Jalīl al-Wazzānī, Sīdī Muḥammad ibn al-Makkī al-Wazzānī, and Sīdī Muḥammad al-Muṣṭafā al-Kandūssī worked to convince the tribes to return to their homes and kept the French informed of developments. Ultimately all of their powers of persuasion proved of no avail, and oral evidence indicates that more than one of them may have been playing a double game, secretly supporting the movement in the countryside.[33]

The behavior of Mawlay ʿAbd al-Ḥafīẓ was a second factor which helped to erode the French political position. Alternately very much afraid of the tribes and terrified of the fate which he imagined that the French had in store for him, ʿAbd al-Ḥafīẓ failed to provide any clear direction or leadership which would encourage cooperation with France. Indeed, the confused signal which he emitted could be interpreted as a refusal to serve as a French tool under any circumstances. He proved to be very difficult for a dispirited Regnault to control. By delaying the appointment of qāid-s and continuing to engage in large-scale land speculation he seriously aggravated the French political problem.[34] The Fez Arab bureau sought to get around the necessity of dealing with him by circulating official documents under its own seal. This only made matters worse. By insisting that he sign all official correspondence and then delaying in doing so, ʿAbd al-Ḥafīẓ discovered that he had a powerful bargaining weapon for improving the terms of his abdication. There is some evidence that he was in discreet relations with the chief tribal groupings, such as the Zaian, and that he considered the possibility of slipping out of Fez and becoming once more the sultan of the jihād.[35] None of this went unnoticed by the population of Fez, and reports of his generally obstructionist attitude were spread throughout the region.

Prior to the Fez mutiny, resistance leaders in the countryside had been unable to rally much support. Distracted by their internal disputes and bickerings, they seemed incapable of mounting a serious threat to a French protectorate. Reports of the Fez uprising, no doubt greatly exaggerated in the retelling, suggested that the French might be more vulnerable than hitherto supposed. During the month of May there was a vast recrudescence of energies in the camp of the resisters. Alliance networks began to crystallize in a number of regions of the country. Banditry increased on the roads, and almost daily incidents against French troops were reported. Although even the southern part of the country was affected (the Sous valley and the Marrakech plains), it was the situation in the north which most preoccupied French intelligence experts at this time.

There were two main alliance networks in the north. Each was led by a hitherto obscure local religious figure. In the hilly country to the north and east of Fez was a group coordinated by Sīdī Muḥammad al-Hajjāmī, a sharif and Darqawa brotherhood leader from the tribe of Jaʿia. Elements of the Hiaina, Ait Saddin, Ait Warrayn, Branes, Ghiata, Beni Zeroual, and Cheraga (a mixture of Arabic- and Berber-speaking groups) composed the resistance force assembled by him. To the south of Fez, along the slope of the Middle Atlas near the towns of Sefrou and El Hadjeb, a second group was forming under the direction of Sīdī Rāḥū, a local sharif, and ʿAqqa al-Bubidmānī, war leader of the Ait Ndhir. It was made up of men from the Berber tribes of Ait Youssi, Ait Ndhir, Ait Njild, and Ait Segrouchen of Immouzer. The leaders of the two resistance coalitions exchanged letters and emissaries and sought to coordinate their forces for a decisive thrust.[36] To hold the fragile alliances together, a series of fines and symbolic punishments were proposed for slackers. In addition, the leaders reinforced their committment through the ritual exchange of turbans and silhām-s (a traditional method of sanctifying alliances). The military credibility of the tribal forces was greatly enhanced by the addition of some four hundred deserters from the makhzan forces at Fez. The deserters brought with them a knowledge of the rudiments of modern warfare and of the state of the French defenses. A few with special skills were able to direct the firing of the decrepit artillery pieces which had been left behind at Taza by Abū Ḥimāra. In this way the fortunes of the resistance fighters improved significantly in the weeks after the mutiny.[37]

On May 24 General Lyautey arrived at Fez to assume his duties as resident-general. He was escorted by two battalions under the command of Lieutenant Colonel Gouraud. The entry of Lyautey into Fez took place under the sullen gaze of the population. There was no fanfare, no greetings from the Moroccan government. One lone tabor of the Moroccan army was on hand to perform the military honors, and it was without arms because of French fears of further revolts.[38] It is not surprising that Lyautey felt that he was "camped in enemy country" as he indicated in a famous letter written at the time.[39] Perhaps partly to make up for the inauspicious entry and to belie insistent rumors of an impending attack of the tribes on the city, Regnault and his staff devoted most of the evening to seeking to convince the new resident-general that the political situation was less critical than it appeared and was in fact improving. Events were soon to reveal the falseness of such predictions.

Scarcely twenty-four hours after the arrival of Lyautey, the city of Fez came under sustained attack.[40] The besieging forces showed from the outset that they meant business. French posts all along the walls came under heavy fire starting at 10 P.M. Fighting continued almost without interruption until noon the following day. Several times the attackers came near to breaching French defenses, only to be driven back. The Moroccan forces maneuvered skillfully in compact groups, directed by signals from nearby hilltops. Each tribal unit taking part had been assigned a section of the walls upon which to concentrate its fire. Word was passed to the people of Fez that no harm was intended to them, as the attack was directed solely against French forces. The cohesion of the besiegers remained firm even under murderous volleys from French artillery fired at point-blank range. Here was no simulacrum of an assault, as occurred during the 1911 siege of the city.

After a day's respite, during which the tribes under al-Ḥajjāmī regrouped their forces, the fighting resumed on the morning of May 28. This time, to the consternation of the French defenders, several parties of attackers succeeded in breaching the walls and penetrating into the center of the city. Most were quickly dealt with, but some were able to exit from the city, taking with them several banners from the shrine of Mawlāy Idrīs as trophies of their bravery. Eventually, superior French firepower and discipline began to tell. By the afternoon, several French sorties had broken up the main body of the attackers and driven them several miles from the city. Sporadic fighting nonetheless continued for the next few days, and it was not until the arrival of French reinforcements on June 1 that it was possible to move in pursuit of al-Ḥajjāmī's forces. By a forced march, troops under the command of Gouraud were able to surprise the rebel camp. In the next few days, through a liberal use of artillery, the French forces were able to disperse the tribal groups. In the baggage of al-Ḥajjāmī's camp Gouraud discovered the battle plan of the siege operations and correspondence with most of the tribes of the region. These documents attest to the seriousness with which the campaign was prepared and organized.[41]

The attack on Fez was only one of a series: the plans of the tribes called for coordinated assaults on French posts at Sefrou and El

Hadjeb as well. Here the beseiging forces were drawn primarily from the surrounding Berber tribes and were led by Sīdī Rāḥū and ʿAqqa al-Bubidmānī. Once again the resistance forces were able to maintain their cohesion in the face of fierce opposition. French defenders later paid tribute to the well-planned nature of the attacks. As in the case of the siege of Fez, however, the tribes ultimately failed to accomplish their objectives, and French forces were able to restore some measure of security around the towns by concerted action. Most of the summer would be required to bring the outlying districts under French control.[42] A major source of concern for the French command was the situation in the strategically placed tribe of Hiaina (Ar. Ḥiyāna), which controlled access to Fez from the northeast. Political influence, bribes, and displays of force were employed to bring them under control. So large was the force under Gouraud in the area, and so lavish the distribution of five-peseta coins (known colloquially as douros) to the tribesmen, that one wag was moved to declare that he didn't see how the Hiaina could possibly hold out against such formidable opponents as Generals Gouraud and Douro.[43] The Hiaina proved a tough nut to crack. By mid-July only half the tribe was considered pacified.

The French command was alarmed by the persistence of organized resistance, for they had only a limited number of troops at their disposal, and vast areas of Morocco still escaped their control. The telegrams of Lyautey during the critical months from June to September reflect fully his conception of the gravity of the French political and military situation in Morocco.

> It can be affirmed that the column which operated June 1st and 2nd around Fez had to deal with an almost homogeneous army, having only one flag and one soul, whose various elements obeyed voluntarily to one discipline and affronted death for the same idea. This is the first time perhaps, since the beginning of our action in Morocco that as many tribes have been grouped together against us in a relatively intimate union, forgetful for a moment of their rivalries and quarrels.
>
> The continuity of the efforts, the simultaneity of the shots, the rapidity in the deployment and crossing of open areas were, on the side of the enemy, the positive signs of a real organisation and a complete entente.
>
> The actual battle plan . . . found in one of the tents of an enemy encampment during the day of June 1, which was addressed to more than twenty tribes (of whom several until recently had been traditionally hostile to one another) is a

> particularly eloquent sign of their agreement, of their common hatred of 'roumis', of their irreductability.
> If to this is added the mobility and endurance of these tribesmen, their great skill in the art of utilizing the terrain, one can appreciate the worth of the adversary whom we find ourselves confronting and against whom we will need more than ever before well trained and officered units in sufficient quantity.[44]

In 1911 nothing like this willingness to forego traditional factionalism for the common cause had been found amongst the tribes of the region. The remarks of Lyautey are an indication of just how much had changed in a year.

In Search of a Native Policy

The strategy devised in Paris by Lyautey and War Ministry experts had called for extreme caution. French direct administration would be limited to the zones already occupied: the Chaouia, the Gharb, and the narrow band of territory extending inland from the coast to Fez. The remainder of the country, including the Marrakech plains and the Middle and High Atlas would be subject to only indirect French influence. The Marrakech region would remain under the great qāid-s, who would govern with French advice.[45] Unfortunately the Fez uprising and the rapid spread of unrest throughout the country soon made this policy impractical. As a consequence, Lyautey, from the beginning, was forced to improvise as he simultaneously sought to implant the protectorate administration.

A major factor which hampered the French ability to deal with the widespread rural unrest was the limited number of troops available (about 32,000). There were scarcely enough men to conduct one important campaign (like that carried out by the Gouraud column) at a time, leaving the bulk of French forces tied down in occupation duties.[46] The numerical weakness of French troops was reinforced by the long, vulnerable lines of communication which stretched inland from the coast. Despite superior firepower and discipline, therefore, French forces were vulnerable to much less well-armed and trained tribal forces. Nowhere was this more true than in the large and strategic Marrakech region, which remained for the moment at least beyond French control.

The restoration of confidence in French rule at Fez was perceived by Lyautey and his key advisors as their first priority. The errors of the heavy-handed policy of Moinier were manifest. A more flexible policy was called for which would soothe the injured pride of the Fāṣī bourgeoisie. Clemency was shown to alleged rioters still under arrest, and the unpaid balance of the fine was cancelled. A talented young Arabic-speaking officer, Captain Charles Mellier, was appointed to head the Fez native-affairs bureau, and the more impetuous of the earlier staff were given alternative assignments elsewhere. Through the good offices of British consul Macleod, Lyautey was introduced to a number of influential sharifs and notables. To reduce the likelihood of incidents, French troops were ordered out of town, and fast riding on the narrow streets of the city was outlawed.[47]

A special effort was made to win over the religious classes at Fez. They were assured by Lyautey that the protectorate authorities would not tamper with their traditional privileges and immunities. No attempt would be made to interfere in affairs related to the practice of the Islamic faith. A shrewd bargain was struck with the students of the madrasa-s and the Qarwiyin mosque university whereby they were given an increase in their annual stipend in return for an agreement to refrain from politics. Those who persisted in opposing the French, on the other hand, were threatened with loss of privileges and arrest.[48] In August, as part of this policy, the *zawīya* of Mā al-ʿAynayn in Fez was closed down and its local head arrested. The building was made available to the notables as a meeting place. Simultaneously the *zawīya* of al-Kattānī, which had been closed by ʿAbd al-Ḥafīẓ in 1909, was reopened.[49]

Concern about the potential adverse impact of the press on the educated urban class led the French to introduce censorship. Lyautey personally argued for greater control. All of the chief figures of the makhzan, he wrote on July 6, "are at the center of everything which appears in the press, especially as . . . [they] are surrounded by foreign agents who are eager to communicate, translate and comment on it to them, especially if they can [thereby] find a means of detaching them from us." Accordingly, he urged that the protectorate administration be given the authority to censor the news. "We must not lose sight of the fact that we are 'at war' here against opponents who are very well informed and for whom publicity has the same disadvantages as in a metropolitan war."[50] Even after the 1912 emergency was over, Lyautey continued to invoke his authority to suppress all published commentary not in keeping with his views.

Since the harsh direct-rule methods of administration had proved so ill-adapted to the complex political world of Fez, an experiment with decentralization was decided upon. The old city of Fez was given its own budget, and the notables were allowed to elect a municipal council and to devise their own local administrative regulations. It was felt that, with the proper supervision by French authorities, this *majlis al-baladīya* (as it was called) would prove a far more supple instrument of control. Key notables were sounded out in June and convinced of the value of such an arrangement by Captain Mellier. With these preparations, elections were held on September 12.[51] There was a large turnout of eligible voters (franchise was limited to the notables), and the results were generally approved. The success of the venture did much to reassure the aʿyān of the city, and tensions eased greatly.

A final aspect of French policy in northern Morocco during the summer of 1912 is worth noting in passing. It concerns the French failure to make any headway in pacifying the tribal coalition under Sīdī Rāḥū to the south of Fez. While General Gouraud made slow progress in dealing with the remnants of al-Ḥajjāmī's ḥaraka in the territory of the Hiaina, the *tamazight*-speaking Berber tribes of the Middle Atlas presented difficulties of quite another order. Nothing in the French experience in Morocco had prepared them for the problems they were to face in this region. Unlike the sedentary Berbers of the Western High Atlas, with their great qāid-s and quasi-feudal regime, those of the Middle Atlas were pastoral transhumants, riven by feud but fiercely devoted to their way of life. More important, they were an acephalous society with a horror of centralized leadership of any kind. The Lyautey methods, which had been developed along the Algéro-Moroccan frontier where there were important notables to bribe and more coherent clan structures, were inapplicable to the Middle Atlas groups. Since the Middle Atlas tribes occupied a strategic position from which they could threaten communications between north and south, their submission to French authority was a key objective. Until the formulation of a Berber policy designed specifically to deal with these tribes in 1914, the French experienced nothing but frustration in their attempts to pacify the region.[52]

Further south, the occupied province of the Chaouia was plagued by insecurity. Incidents of banditry and political unrest multiplied alarmingly during the months following the siege of Fez. More dangerous still, the coalition of tribes in the Tadla region led by the Zaian was assuming a more menacing air, and the tribes along the eastern borders of the Chaouia, like the Beni Meskin, were less and less able to resist entreaties to join forces with the coalition against the French.[53] The lack of manpower greatly handicapped the ability of the French command to respond to this threat.

At Marrakech, the persistence of the incipient civil war between the partisans of al-Glawī and the supporters of al-Mtouggui continued to divide the population of the region and furnish a major source of anxiety to the French command. Already some of the tribes of the Marrakech plain were beginning to utilize the opportunity presented by the political deadlock to edge toward a position of greater autonomy. This was noticeable not only north of Marrakech, where the Sraghna, Doukkala, and Rehamna were plagued by internal dissension, but also to the southeast, where wealthy tribes like the Mesfioua showed themselves increasingly defiant of Glawa rule. The fact that some of the lesser qāid-s had been changed several times since the beginning of the year (with consequent tax-gouging by the officials involved) had increased the resentment of many of the tribesmen. They were led to seek relief in sība.[54]

From his arrival, Lyautey's strategy in the south was clear. In response to a British query, Lyautey emphasized his intention to rely upon Tahamī al-Glawī and Sī ʿAissa ibn ʿUmar come what may.[55] The policy of relying upon the great qāid-s had in fact probably been decided on before Lyautey left France. Delays in applying the policy were to cost them dearly before the crisis was over, but the outlines of the protectorate policy were already visible by the summer of 1912. With most of his troops occupied around Fez, Lyautey launched a politico-military campaign to shore up the French position in the south. An agent of the Compagnie marocaine, Vaffier-Pollet, who was on friendly terms with Tahamī Glawī, was sent to Marrakech to extract promises of support. When he failed to make any headway, other measures became necessary.[56] By early August, the political atmosphere in the south was openly turning hostile. Two further representatives were dispatched by Lyautey to build up sagging morale and to preserve the impression of makhzan authority in the region. Commandant Edmond Verlet-Hanus, a brilliant young officer with special talents in native affairs, was sent to Marrakech to compose the feud between al-Glawī and al-Mtouggui and to gain the backing of al-Goundafī. Dr. Felix Weisgerber was sent on a parallel mission to Sī ʿAissa ibn ʿUmar. Sī ʿAissa was promised firm support if he would seek to organize the defense of the region from the menace of El Hiba. The instructions issued to both men allowed them considerable latitude in promising the great qāid-s a privileged position in the protectorate regime.[57]

While Lyautey's special political agents were working on the chiefs of the south, the second part of his plan to restore French authority in the south was put into effect. Because of the tendencies toward anarchy in the Marrakech region, a climate of unrest had gradually spread among the tribes in the Chaouia. If these defected, then the French position would be in a very serious state. The object of the plan was to restore the French hold on the Chaouia and the neighboring tribes. An emergency force was hastily constituted and placed under the command of Lieutenant Colonel Charles Mangin, and given the task of patrolling the borders of the Chaouia. Garrisons in the Gharb and less affected portions of the Chaouia were depleted to assemble a force of sufficiently imposing size. Important Moroccan political figures, like Mawlāy al-ʿAmrānī, the sultan's uncle, accompanied French columns sent to persuade tribes whose loyalty was suspect, like the Doukalla, from joining the general dissidence. Pending the arrival of reinforcements, the offensive capabilities of the Mangin column remained restricted to the fringes of the Chaouia.[58]

A final political problem which confronted Lyautey during this period was the future of ʿAbd al-Ḥafīẓ. According to the terms of the protectorate treaty, official decrees had to bear the royal signature. By refusing to sign proposed ẓahīr-s unless certain concessions were made to him, ʿAbd al-Ḥafīẓ was in a position to block changes of which he did not approve.[59] For example, the French attempt to replace the qāid of Azemmour with a person less known for his militancy was successfully stymied by the sultan for a long time.[60] Suspicions and tension between Madani and Tahami al-Glawī were inflamed in similar manner by a series of calculated leaks. Naturally, this only further aggravated the political situation at Marrakech.[61] As long as ʿAbd al-Ḥafīẓ remained at Fez, moreover, he could always slip away to join the tribes and declare a jihād. It was to avoid just this nightmare that Lyautey arranged to have the court transferred to Rabat on June 6, leaving Mawlāy al-Yūsuf as khalīfa at Fez.[62] Lyautey came increasingly to feel that the continued presence of ʿAbd al-Ḥafīẓ on the throne threatened to compromise the protectorate from the outset. He would therefore have to go. Yet there was at first glance no obvious replacement among the royal princes, save perhaps ʿAbd al-ʿAzīz, and he demanded too many concessions to be acceptable. The others were insufficiently docile to be amenable to French purposes.[63] For a time the idea of an Idrissid restoration seems to have been briefly entertained by some, but it was dismissed as representing too radical a break with Moroccan traditions.

While the search for a new sultan continued, ʿAbd al-Ḥafīẓ was placed in the care of the experienced French diplomat the Count of Saint-Aulaire and Sī Kaddour Ben Ghabrit, the eternal *éminence grise* of French policy in Morocco. They were given the frustrating task of negotiating the terms of abdication while keeping the sultan out of trouble in the meantime. As Ḥafīẓ was known for the legendary quality of his tantrums and his epic sulks, they had their work cut out for them. Knowing the sultan's reputation as a lover of fine wines, Saint-Aulaire arranged a series of wine-tasting parties, drawing on the stocks of the French crusier *Du Chayla*.[64] Such tactics might have succeeded in rendering a lesser man more tractable. But ʿAbd al-Ḥafīẓ was known for his enormous physical capacities. It soon became known that he was taking nocturnal strolls in the city, unbeknownst to his French watchdogs. All the while he continued to block the negotiating sessions.[65]

By early August, as the French control continued to deteriorate in the south, Lyautey was determined to have done with ʿAbd al-Ḥafīẓ no matter what the cost. An acceptable prince to fill the royal office had been discovered in the person of Mawlāy Yūsuf. The eventual terms agreed to by ʿAbd al-Ḥafīẓ for his abdication were the result of months of haggling and were stiff indeed. The ex-sultan would receive an annual pension equivalent to 15,000 pounds sterling and would be permitted to reside at Tangier. Further, a long list of makhzan properties were recognized by the French government as part of his personal property, and not part of the national patrimony. In this way France associated itself with the land speculation and personal greed of the sultan in his last days. While the transition was being effected, the French further agreed to arrange a six weeks' tour of France for the ex-sultan.[66] Despite the agreement, the French remained apprehensive until the last minute, expecting duplicity. It was with a sigh of relief that Lyautey received the official signed letter of abdication from ʿAbd al-Ḥafīẓ just before the sultan boarded the *Du Chayla* on August 12. Before embarking, he destroyed the imperial seal and parasol, emblems of his authority, as a way of manifesting his consciousness of being the last sultan of an independent Morocco.[67] It was several days before Mawlāy al-Yūsuf could be proclaimed by the ʿulamā of Fez. A new era was beginning in Moroccan history, one in which the sultan was selected by the French and proposed to the ʿulamā for ratification. Many Moroccans learned to regard him not as the Commander of the Faithful but as the Sultan of the Roumis. The prestige of the office received a very damaging blow in the process.

Revolution in the South: The Jihād of El Hiba

Like the ominous rumblings of offstage thunder, news of the stunning development and spread of a radical Islamic resistance movement in the distant Sous valley came increasingly to preoccupy French authorities during the late spring. By July, the same officials were frankly alarmed. At attempt to mobilize the great qāid-s to oppose the movement had failed, and it was attracting support not only in the Sous but even in the Hawz of Marrakech. The radical social program of the movement had turned it into a force which threatened to overturn the political structures of the south. The Lyautey strategy was jeopardized, and with it perhaps the French position in Morocco. There are a great many misconceptions about this movement, known as the jihād of El Hiba. Some have claimed to see El Hiba as a sanguinary fanatic and his movement as a kind of freakish aberration or a throwback to the days of the Almoravids. What do we know about the origins and early development of El Hiba's movement? How can we explain the remarkable speed with which it spread? What were its aims and objectives? The answers to questions such as these will lead us to a deeper understanding of this remarkable social movement and its place in the history of modern Morocco.

A warrior saint in the style of the heroes of the Islamic past of the Maghrib, Shaykh Mā al-ʿAynayn was already a legend in Morocco and the western Sahara at the time of his death in October 1910. His combativeness, if not his scholarly proclivities, were fully shared by his many sons, among whom his fourth son, Mawlāy Aḥmad Haybat Allāh (known as El Hiba) was especially favored. It was El Hiba who succeeded to the leadership on the death of the old shaykh. The year which followed the death of his father El Hiba devoted to reestablishing the family influence around Tiznit.[68] The severely depressed economy of the Sous had served to aggravate an already volatile political situation. The exactions of the great qāid-s, and their stranglehold over trade between the Sous and the cities to the north provided an ample stock of grievances. The Agadir crisis of 1911 had heightened the political sensitivities of the tribes and made them conscious of the deteriorating position of the makhzan. During the fall of 1911, they had successfully come together to resist a joint Glawa-Mtougga ḥaraka sent to restore order in the area.[69] The Sous valley, in short, was undergoing a series of intersecting crises: a severe economic crisis, a political crisis, and a social crisis caused by the implantation of the regime of the great qāid-s. It is here that we must begin, if we are to understand the rapid spread of the movement of El Hiba.

The event which provoked a movement toward jihād in the Sous was the arrival of news of the Fez mutiny. It created consternation throughout the region. There were rumors that ʿAbd al-Ḥafīẓ had been killed and that the French had all been massacred. Into this atmosphere of political confusion stepped El Hiba. The time had come to expel the French from Morocco, he proclaimed. With the sultan either dead or a prisoner of the French, then he, El Hiba, was the logical choice to lead the community. After a brief, clever campaign to build support among the nearby tribes, El Hiba had himself proclaimed *Imām al-mujāhidīn* at Tiznit on May 3. There was some initial opposition to his pretensions, but it evaporated following the provocative arrival of several French warships off the coast of Aglou several days later. On May 9, Saʿīd Guellouli, a powerful qāid of the Haha confederation sent money and ammunition as a public demonstration of his backing. The following day, emboldened by his successes, El Hiba conducted the Friday prayers in the mosque at Tiznit with the full ceremonial pomp of a sultan. From this point his claims to the throne were clear. During the weeks which followed, letters were written to all of the tribes of the Sous, inviting them to adhere to his movement. Reports of the many miracles (*karamāt*) performed by El Hiba began to circulate among the more credulous people. Whoever dared oppose him, it was said, would be turned into a frog. El Hiba was reported to have the power to turn cannon shells into watermelons; he could give out an endless supply of grain from the same sack; a suspected traitor was struck with paralysis by him, and so on. Men began flocking to join El Hiba from as far away as the lower Dra and the Saqiyāt al-Ḥamrā.[70]

There is no question that timing had much to do with the early successes of El Hiba. The uncertainty caused by the struggle between al-Glawī and al-Mtouggui favored the progress of the movement in the Sous. The control which the great qāid-s could exert in the Sous was at a low ebb. During the months of May and June one tribe after another overthrew their Glawa- or Mtougga-imposed qāid-s and joined El Hiba. The advance of El Hiba was heralded by a crier who proclaimed: "Jihād against the Christians! Submission to El Hiba! No more qāid-s, no more jārī-s [tax collectors]! No taxes except the [Koranically sanctioned] ʿushr and zakāh!" As soon as it had joined the movement, the first act of the local population was to destroy the house of the qāid if he showed any signs of hesitating to come over himself. Everywhere the movement spread, tribal jamāʿa-s replaced qāid-s. The pasha of Taroudant Haida ou Mouis, an ally of Taḥamī al-Glawī, found himself unable to maintain his authority over the nearby tribes and was forced to accept the new regime.[71] Despite promises of substantial rewards and threats of punishment, nothing the great qāid-s or the French could do was able to stem the tide.

One place to go, if we would understand more about the ideology and program of El Hiba's movement, is the work of the Moroccan chronicler al-Marrākishī.[72] Here we have an image of the movement which is far closer to the way in which it sought to present itself than the picture of it we find in the European sources. A reading of al-Marrākishī establishes that El Hiba saw himself as engaged in a jihād to reform Moroccan society and restore the purity and integrity of Islam. One key to this interpretation is the first title adopted by El Hiba: *Imām al-mujāhidīn,* the religious leader of those who fight in the holy war. But this view is also evident in the program that he adopted, which showed particular concern with eliminating innovations that had corrupted the faith. For example, it called for the elimination of non-Koranic taxes—including the hated maks and other indirect taxes and government monopolies. It also focused on the need to combat vice and immorality of all kinds and therefore on the necessity for the precepts of the sharīʿa, the holy law of Islam, to be applied to the letter. Finally, El Hiba called for the overthrow of all makhzan-appointed qāid-s and the selection of tribal governors by the tribes themselves. The jihād of El Hiba might justly be compared with the jihād-s which rocked other parts of Africa in the nineteenth century, such as that of al-Ḥājj ʿUmar and ʿUsuman Dan Fodio in the western Sudan, ʿAbd al-Qadir in Algeria, and the Mahdī in the Sudan. Like them, al-Hiba doubled his appeal to jihād with a claim to temporal sovereignty over Muslims by having himself formally proclaimed sultan.[73] He was careful to surround himself with the symbols of that position and to comport himself as the legitimate sultan.

It is important, once again, to consider the context in which the movement of El Hiba emerged. The circumstances of famine and economic decline and the increasing rapaciousness of the great qāid-s had generated a state of severe stress in the society of the Sous. The Fez uprising, moreover, had produced a grave crisis of political legitimacy: the sultan was presumed dead, the country was being taken over by Christians. To the desperate and credulous peasants of the Sous the message of El Hiba must have sounded like the answer to a prayer. From the first, therefore, the movement took on a radical quality which sharply differentiates it from the others we have thus far considered. It was a revolution aimed at nothing less than the overturning of the existing political regime, that of the great qāid-s and the makhzan, and the substitution of a new society modeled upon the early Islamic community of Medina. The millenarian thrust of El Hiba's movement made it far more dangerous to the powers than earlier movements but also far more unstable.

The nucleus of El Hiba's strength was his more than thirty brothers (the number of Mā al-ʿAynayn's progeny was legendary throughout the region). They formed his bodyguard and through their marriage alliances among the prominent families of the Sous valley provided the beginnings of the political network which guaranteed the durability of the fortunes of the clan.[74] Initially El Hiba's forces numbered about 5,000 men. The size of the group reached 10,000 or so following the capture of Marrakech. In contrast to the relatively well-armed tribesmen who gathered about al-Ḥajjāmī in May, El Hiba's men, according to French intelligence reports, had only six ancient bronze cannon, one machine gun, and a thousand muzzle-loading rifles. The bulk of his men were armed with clubs and rocks. Most of the tribesmen who joined him in his advance up the Sous valley were totally without experience of modern warfare. Capable officers were almost nonexistent. Two renegade Senegalese artillerymen and a Spanish convert to Islam "of military bearing" named Sīdī Ḥamū were all we know of.[75] Again, the comparison with al-Ḥajjāmī is relevant: most of the Fez area tribes had seen action in 1911, and they were stiffened by the presence of some 400 makhzan army deserters. The major danger posed by the movement of El Hiba was that it might spread north of the Atlas mountains and gain the support of the numerous and wealthy tribes of the Marrakech plain.

That this danger was more than hypothetical became apparent to the French command as the summer wore on. Suspicions that, despite protestations of enduring loyalty, some of the great qāid-s were in secret communication with El Hiba were confirmed in August by the French consul at Safi. According to his informants, both al-Mtouggui and Idrīs al-Minū, the pasha of Marrakech, had sent gifts of money and arms to El Hiba as a testimony of their friendliness.[76] British sources established that Madanī al-Glawī was in clandestine relations with El Hiba.[77] More ominously, there were reports that Mawlāy ʿAbd al-Ḥafīẓ himself was in correspondence with the pretender. In addition, El Hiba was engaged in an intense letter-writing campaign with most of the leaders of resistance in the north, including al-Hajjāmī, Sīdī Rāḥū, and Moha ou Hamou al-Zaiani, urging cooperation in the common effort to defeat the French.[78] The emergence of El Hiba as the champion of the holy war in the summer of 1912 threatened to crystallize the regional tribal alliance groupings into a united front.

As the situation became more precarious, the European consuls sought to obtain guarantees from the great qāid's of the security of life and property of their administrative charges.[79] Throughout the region a complex political struggle between factions intensified, in which the settling of old scores and the double-crossing of friends form the essential backdrop. Wealthy protégés were attacked and their goods pillaged. Ambitious notables sought alternately to capitalize on their privileged connections with France and to ride the updraft of popular enthusiasm for resistance. In brief, things were coming to resemble the situation in the Chaouia during the insurrection of 1903–1906. The state of affairs in the large and strategically situated tribe of Rehamna may be taken as typical.[80] The tribe was split into pro-Glawa and pro-Mtougga factions. The first was headed by ʿAbd al-Salām al-Barbūshī, the second by al-ʿAyyādī ibn al-Ḥāshimī. Each group saw in the unstable situation a long-awaited chance to crush its rivals. While al-ʿAyyādī played the French card, his opponent sought to capitalize upon the popular enthusiasms for jihād by entering into relations with El Hiba, meanwhile hoping that word of his attachment would increase his value as an ally in the eyes of the French. In early July some of the Rehamna tribesmen descended on Marrakech, where they succeeded in extorting weapons from the makhzan stores. These they employed in raiding the farms of protégés. By this time, their qāid-s had completely lost control over them. In such circumstances, European attempts to organize resistance to El Hiba were doomed.

Lyautey's strategy for holding Marrakech, and with it the regime of the great qāid-s on which it was based, suddenly collapsed. On August 12, most of the European population departed for Safi to wait out the storm. French consul Maigret remained behind, still blindly confident of his ability to organize the defense of the city.[81] The hollowness of his dreams was revealed two days later when advance elements of El Hiba's "blue men" rode into the city. A popular insurrection broke out, the great qāid-s defected to the pretender, and the city fell without a shot being fired. Only later was it discovered that for the last month all of the great qāid-s had been playing a double game. Under the protectorate regime they stood to lose everything they had. Nine surprised Frenchmen including Maigret and Verlet-Hanus (Lyautey's personal representative) found themselves the captives of the Sultan of the South. On August 18 El Hiba made his formal entry into the city. He was immediately proclaimed sultan by the ʿulamā of the city.[82] The moment could not have been more propitious to his cause. Mawlāy Yūsuf had still not been proclaimed at Marrakech, although word of the abdication of Ḥafīẓ had already come. The throne could thus technically be considered vacant, and El Hiba could advance himself as the best-qualified claimant. In fact, as French agents pieced the story together later, El Hiba had been in regular correspondence with ʿAbd al-Ḥafīẓ and had been informed in advance of the date of the sultan's abdication. He had been able to coordinate his arrival accordingly.[83]

The fall of Marrakech placed El Hiba in a temporarily unassailable position. Using the city as a base, he could pose as the legitimate sultan to the populations of central Morocco and picture Mawlāy Yūsuf as a French puppet. His formal investiture by the ʿulamā of Marrakech lent further credence to that strategy. Already in regular correspondence with tribes in the Tadla and further to the north, El Hiba was in a position to capitalize on his spectacular success by forging a united front of resistance groups against a French protectorate. The nine French hostages gave him at least a temporary immunity from attack, and in the short run Mangin's forces on the borders of the Chaouia remained insufficient for a full-fledged expedition. Fully conscious of his delicate position, Lyautey tried offers of ransom money, as well as promises of nonintervention and what amounted to acquiescence in El Hiba's rule over southern Morocco.[84] In the meantime, he concentrated on building up Mangin's military strength by depleting garrisons all over the country. Through the good offices of the prominent Marrakech Jewish banker, Joshua Corcos, Lyautey entered into communications with al-Glawī and obtained a more exact picture of the situation in the city. In Paris, the War Ministry considered forbidding Lyautey from intervening at Marrakech.[85]

At about the time that El Hiba was advancing on Marrakech, French intelligence in Tangier uncovered evidence of a plot aimed at bringing about a general insurrection of the Moroccan population at the end of Ramadān (September 13).[86] Further investigation and cross-checking with the British confirmed the existence of the plot, and implicated *al-ittihād al-maghribī,* a Cairo-based secret political organization, as the chief sponsor. The plans for the uprising were to be coordinated by *al-ittihād al-maghribī* agents at Tangier who were in written communication with El Hiba and the other main resistance groups in central Morocco. Arms and money were to be smuggled to the tribes, and an attempt was even made to send five or six Egyptian and Turkish officers to advise El Hiba's forces. Among them were two veterans of the 1909 Turkish military mission to Morocco, ʿArif Ṭāhir and Muḥammad Ḥilmī. They were intercepted by the French before they could reach their destination.[87] Another Egyptian was arrested in Marrakech after the defeat of El Hiba and deported. The newspaper *al-Ḥaqq,* which was published at Tangier under the protection of the Spanish legation, maintained a steady stream of anti-French propaganda during the summer, culminating with a call for a general insurrection. It was disseminated through the Spanish consular post office to the major cities of the country. The Spanish consuls in several cities, including al-Jadida and Safi, were active in propagandizing on behalf of El Hiba.[88] They greatly frustrated the French authorities. In the end, the plot accomplished little, although it did throw a healthy scare into the French. It is doubtful that the conspirators would have been able to generate anything like a creditable threat in any event. The episode testifies nonetheless to the concern of Eastern Arabs for Moroccan independence well before the days of an ongoing nationalist movement.

After several weeks of stalemate, the situation of El Hiba began to deteriorate at Marrakech. By the end of August reports indicated that the puritanical ways of El Hiba and the uncontrollable wildness of his "blue men" were alienating the bourgeoisie of the city. The local populace was particularly aroused by El Hiba's effort to reform their morals. Since the practice of celibacy was forbidden to Muslims, he insisted that all unmarried women should immediately marry his men! The wrath of the merchants was stirred by the introduction of heavily depreciated Saharan coinage in place of official Moroccan currency. Finally, El Hiba's policy that tribes select their own governors and that only Koranic taxes be assessed drove the great qāid-s into opposition, since both measures directly threatened their authority.[89] In order to retain the support of the tribes, a dramatic gesture became necessary. An advance on

Mangin's position at Skhour in the Rehamna district was decided upon, commanded by Mrebbi Rebbo, a brother of El Hiba.

Although aware of the advance of Mrebbi Rebbo, Mangin refrained from taking the offensive, pending the arrival of a column under Colonel Joseph that had been operating amongst the Doukalla. On August 22, Mangin received intelligence that Mrebbi Rebbo was nearby at Ouham, in a position to intercept the unsuspecting Joseph forces. He ordered an immediate attack and was able to surprise the ḥaraka of the rebels and inflict moderate losses upon it. The Moroccans were only temporarily dispersed, however, and managed to regroup their forces and attack the French camp two days later. They were repulsed after several costly assaults. On the morning of the twenty-ninth Mangin went on the offensive. Marching south from Skhour, he encountered the forces of the pretender near Ben Guerir. The Moroccans attacked in mass formation but proved no match for the cannon and machine guns of the French. After a brief but fierce encounter, the Moroccan forces broke. The battered remnants fled south toward Marrakech. While the French cavalry and partisans pursued the enemy, Mangin and the bulk of his force returned to the Oum er Rbia River and encamped at Mechra Ben Abbou.[90]

At about this time, Lyautey received assurances from the great qāid-s that they would guarantee the safety of the French hostages at Marrakech.[91] Although care still had to be taken to avoid a massacre of the prisoners, the way was open to a French offensive. Accordingly, Mangin's column advanced boldly to intercept the ten thousand-man force of El Hiba at Sidi Bou Othman, the first significant settlement along the road to Marrakech. There, on the morning of September 6, Mangin's force of five thousand, having first drawn itself into the classic square formation with the artillery on the inside, was attacked by the massed tribesmen, more than half of whom were on foot and armed only with rocks and clubs. Confident in the promises of El Hiba that French bullets would turn into water and French shells into watermelons, the tribesmen advanced directly upon the French position. They ran into murderous fire from the French artillery; machine-gun fire and rifle volleys completed the rout. After two hours of such punishment, those Moroccans left alive fled in panic and Mangin had won a great victory. The way to Marrakech lay open before him.[92]

The battle was in effect a massacre: more than two thousand Moroccans were killed outright and thousands more wounded, while Mangin suffered only four killed and twenty-three wounded.

One is reminded of the cynical observation of Commandant Fariau that, "real peaceful penetration consists of putting a thousand with rifles against a hundred fellows with pop-guns."[93] Whatever else may be said, it was a crushing defeat that completely destroyed the élan of the resistance movement and with it the credibility of El Hiba as an alternative to French rule.

Mangin followed up the victory with considerable daring. That night a flying column under Colonel Henri Simon was sent to Marrakech, arriving early the next morning to discover El Hiba already in flight to the Sous and the prisoners unharmed in the hands of the great qāid-s. From this point onward any hopes for a rising at the end of Ramadān quickly vanished. French military control had been dramatically and effectively demonstrated. Tribesmen who only a few days earlier had openly sided with El Hiba now thought twice about where their real interests lay. Although unrest continued in the Marrakech region for some weeks afterward, and the tribal leagues continued to stay in written communication with one another, the movement was robbed of all its momentum. Follow-up activity by the French concentrated on restoring security within central Morocco and in breaking up the tribal leagues. A new period in Moroccan history was beginning.

Moroccan Resistance Movements: A Preliminary Verdict

Following the defeat of El Hiba, French troops occupied Marrakech, and the protectorate regime was firmly established. Resistance continued, however, in the mountains and wastelands of the country, and it was not until 1934 that the last holdouts had been compelled to surrender. By this time nationalist agitation had begun in the cities. In the north the bands of fighters who had lain siege to Fez in May remained intact, and for several years were thereafter able to pose a threat to French control. French penetration of the Middle Atlas did not begin in earnest until 1914, and more than a decade was required before resistance was suppressed. To the south, El-Hiba continued to preach the jihād and to organize the tribes in the Sous against the great qāid-s and their French allies. He remained a significant force in the region until after World War I. Despite occasional anxious moments, however, the protectorate regime established by Lyautey was able to survive without serious challenge.

The contrasting styles of resistance of the tribes around Fez and of those in the south deserves further examination. In this way additional light may be shed upon the aims, as well as the social bases and organization, of the resistance. The movement of the tribes around Fez in May 1912 was in its essential outlines strikingly similar to the abortive siege of Fez in 1911 which had provoked French intervention. Since it was the French native-affairs officers who now for all intents and purposes constituted the makhzan in the rural areas around Fez, however, the revolt, instead of being directed against the minions of al-Glawī, was directed against the French. Deeply rooted traditions of patriotic resistance to Christian invaders no doubt also played their part in rallying support. The tribal groups that participated in the siege of Fez in May under the leadership of al-Ḥajjāmī had limited objectives, were well-organized, and adopted a quite pragmatic strategy aimed at cutting the French off from the coast and defeating them piecemeal. They took considerable pains not to alarm the notables of Fez and made clear their quarrel was only with France. Although secured by religiously sanctioned oaths and led by lesser rural religious figures, the 1912 movement in the north was not a jihād, and eschewed radical religious slogans. Quite the opposite was the case of resistance efforts in the south.

The desperate economic conditions which prevailed in the Sous, aggravated by the brutal struggle among the great qāid-s over control of the Ras el Oued Sous district and the crisis of legitimacy occasioned by the signing of the Treaty of Fez, were ideally suited to the development of a radical popular revolt. The movement of El-Hiba represented an answer to specific conditions in the Sous region. But the radical thrust of its rhetoric and the charisma which the movement acquired by virtue of its early successes made it a threat to the political order in the entire region of the Western High Atlas and the plains around Marrakech. The millenarian nature of the ideology placed in jeopardy the regime of the great qāid-s by appealing to downtrodden rural populations. The doctrine of jihād provided a social program as well as a focal point for resistance. Relatively little attention appears to have been devoted to the task of organizing a more lasting political movement by the leadership. In the end it was the very radicality of the program of El-Hiba which did the most to alienate not only the great barons of the Atlas but the merchants and ʿulamā of Marrakech as well.

The Ḥafīẓīya movement of 1907–1908 was also a movement of jihād and, as we have seen above, was not devoid of radical overtones. (The bayʿa of the ʿulamā at Fez in January 1908 is surely one of the most uncompromising and socially explosive documents of the entire period of the Moroccan crisis.) Yet the Ḥafīẓīya remained firmly under the control of the pretender and his principal allies, the great qāid-s, and as a result posed no serious threat to the established order of things. Unlike the jihād of El-Hiba, which appears to have been prompted by a particularly acute economic crisis and from the beginning eluded the control of the wealthy and the powerful, the Ḥafīẓīya movement originated as a secular insurrection aimed at overthrowing the incumbent sultan, and only later became a jihād. (The French landings at Casablanca constituted the chief precipitating factor.) The Ḥafīẓīya was able to gather widespread popular support largely because of the ideology of jihād. Its leaders, however, were always able to concentrate the struggle against the French and the supporters of the heavily compromised ʿAbd al-ʿAzīz. The defection of the great qāid-s, and the aʿyan and ʿulamā of Marrakech in 1912, was the direct result of the quite different forces behind the two movements of jihād.

The comparison of Moroccan resistance movements shows that there were two main threats against which people tended to react. The first was the onset of governmental reforms and the increasing rapaciousness of both makhzan officials and the new, more powerful, rural notables. (While these two forces were themselves antagonistic—as has been seen for example in the study of the Chaouia siba—they were perceived by the people of the countryside as posing a similarly dangerous threat to old liberties and ways of life.) The menace of French penetration and the weakness of the government in the face of this threat constituted the other axis of resistance. The ideology of jihād fused these two traditions of resistance and protest. Depending upon who controlled the movement, jihād could be made to emphasize one or the other strand. Whereas in 1907–1908 the movement was controlled by the great qāid-s and emphasized the struggle against the French, by 1912 the wealthy and the powerful in Moroccan society analysed their interests differently and saw themselves threatened by the jihād of El Hiba. Rather than risk all in a desperate alliance with El Hiba, they chose to defect at an opportune moment, thereby guaranteeing themselves a prominent place in the new order of Moroccan politics that was beginning.

9

PATTERNS OF PRECOLONIAL PROTEST AND RESISTANCE

Between 1860 and 1912 Morocco underwent a series of important social and political changes in response to European penetration. The gradual incorporation of Morocco into the emerging world economic system undermined the bases of the old system and led to the emergence of new groups of privileged individuals within the state. The old agrarian economy was transformed and with it the artisanal mode of production to which it was closely linked. During the nineteenth century the Moroccan state experienced a steady increase in the development of a centralized bureaucratic administration, and the government began increasingly to intervene in the lives of its subjects. Many of the traditional props of government, such as the jaysh system, the makhzan and the ʿulamā, were seriously weakened as a result of these changes. New groups came to the fore, representing new forces in the society, the rural notables and urban bourgeoisie. Closely tied to European political and commercial interests, yet opposed to European domination, these groups have constituted the main subject of this study. In the end, despite widespread social and economic distress and a prolonged crisis of legitimacy in the state, Morocco experienced neither a social revolution nor a unified national resistance movement. At the same time, it was during the tumultuous period which preceded the protectorate that the ground work was laid for the later emergence of a Moroccan civic and class consciousness. How is this to be explained?

My analysis has stressed the importance of two factors in explaining the disruption of the society after 1860. The first of these is the impact of the incorporation of Morocco into the world capitalist system, which slowly undermined the viability of the old society. A second is the increasing interventionism of Europe (especially France) in Moroccan affairs. Only by examining how these two aspects of European encroachment shaped the ensuing development of the crisis of the old regime can we begin to understand the complexity of Moroccan political responses.

It is difficult to disentangle the diplomatic from the economic aspects of European penetration. Both worked powerfully to shape Moroccan political responses. The importance of the diplomatic conjuncture is the most obvious of the two. It was the diplomatic stalemate between France and Great Britain during the nineteenth century that was largely responsible for preserving Moroccan independence. While the two powers retained the will and the capacity to check one another's ambitions in Morocco, the makhzan would be able to play them off against one another. The signing of the Cambon-Lansdowne agreement in 1904 brought an end to this rivalry and opened the way for a French colonial offensive. That there was not a protectorate in 1905 was due less to Moroccan resistance than to the sudden German interest in the country. Thereafter, although a final settlement between France and Germany was delayed, the Algeciras Act largely foreclosed the remaining options of the Moroccan government and rendered its fate inevitable. But Morocco did not immediately succumb.

In order to explain the continuing independence of Morocco after 1906, some account must be taken of the peculiar constellation of political forces within the Third Republic. The bitter conflict between the Quai d'Orsay and the Rue St. Dominique forms an important aspect of this question. The struggle over French policy toward Morocco between the diplomats and the warriors divided successive governments and affected the evolution of the Moroccan question at each turn of the wheel. More general French weaknesses should also be mentioned in this context. Domestic strife and factionalism seriously hampered most of the cabinets which held office from 1905 to 1912. The growing crisis in Europe occupied energies which might otherwise have been turned to Morocco and increased government unwillingness to commit large numbers of troops to a pacification effort. French blunders in Morocco caused by the absence of a consistent policy further exacerbated the situation and actually provoked much Moroccan resistance. A piecemeal French conquest resulted in a piecemeal Moroccan resistance.

European economic penetration also helped to shape the unfolding of the Moroccan crisis. Not until the latter part of the nineteenth century did Morocco become an attractive area for European investment or commercial activities. The breakdown of the traditional agricultural system and the decay of the artisanry were therefore muffled and delayed. When the crisis burst in 1900, Morocco was ill-prepared to deal with the unprecedented challenge. The commercial penetration of the West and the encroachment of the banks and financiers had important repercussions on both the national and local levels. First, European banks gained control of most of the revenue sources of the government (beginning with the customs duties and gradually expanding from there) and obtained control over the treasury through the creation of the state bank. In consequence the makhzan became a creature of the bondholders, dependent upon them for all but routine expenses. By 1910, with the signature of the last major loan agreement, any political response by Morocco was subject to immediate economic retaliation. But already by 1904 the essential features of this system were clearly established. From the outset France was aware of the political leverage inherent in economic domination and sought to manipulate its economic favors for political advantage. The direct political relevance of economic imperialism has not always been accorded the significance it merits.

A second important aspect of the corrosive effects of incorporation in the world economy upon the existing traditional structures and institutions can be observed at the local level. The development of a new bourgeoisie in the ports and of a rural notability which differed from the traditional one by the guaranteed durability of its fortunes and the solidity of its connections with European business interests typifies the changed situation at the end of the nineteenth century. A new makhzan elite with strong interests in the centralization of the government and its reform along European lines further reflects the transformation of Moroccan society. Where new groups were rising to positions of unprecedented wealth and power, others were falling on hard times. Artisans, small businessmen and craftsmen, and large numbers of poor peasants and small holders in the countryside found the new economic circumstances increasingly onerous and were reduced to desperate expedients. The crumbling of the old society in the face of European economic penetration seriously compromised the hopes that Morocco might be able to respond effectively to the European challenge. Just when they were most needed, the old structures were gravely weakened. Beyond this, the kind of widespread social and economic changes which were in motion largely shaped and molded the political movements of protest and resistance throughout Morocco. Thus local manifestations of the broader phenomenon of European economic penetration were intimately connected to Moroccan politics in the period under study.

In summary, on both the level of high finance and the local

economy European penetration seriously affected the shape of politics in Morocco. In the former case it helped restrict and limit the Moroccan ability to respond, while in the latter it was a major contributing factor to the social and economic transformation of the society. In comparison with the states of the Middle East and North Africa, the economic decline of Morocco was much more rapid, and its effects therefore were much more devastating. Possessing a smaller and much less articulated economy than that of countries like Egypt or the Ottoman empire, and compelled by the force of circumstances to be incorporated into the world economy only after Europe had achieved a crushing superiority, Morocco was naturally the more seriously affected. Monetary difficulties, unfavorable trade balances, foreign loans, and the creation of a bondholders organization, steps which took decades in most Middle Eastern countries, were traversed by Morocco in a fraction of that time. The increasing pace of change was to be an important characteristic of the Moroccan case.

An important contributing cause to the series of crises which shook Morocco between 1900 and 1912 was the structural weakness of its political system. The complex political events of these years were the result of the inabilities of the system to deal effectively with the problems presented by mounting debts, military reverses, foreign encroachment, a prolonged monetary and financial crisis, and serious social dislocations deriving from structural changes in the economy. This political weakness had several aspects. The relentless fiscal pressures of the makhzan upon the rural populations and the efforts to elaborate a new and more efficient system of rural administration and tax collection came into direct conflict with the ambitions of the rising new group of rural notables and urban landowners. The result was a series of quarrels over patronage, governmental jurisdiction, and eventually a direct challenge to the material well-being and customary privileges of a large proportion of the rural elite. The inability of the government to devise a program of reform that would be enforceable was a source of endless difficulties. More critical, perhaps, was the failure of efforts at military modernization. The traditional army, the jaysh tribes, was seriously weakened during the nineteenth century. But the changing policies of the makhzan, the intervention of the powers, and the educational insufficiencies of the regime insured that military reforms would be continually frustrated. In the end makhzan efforts to achieve more effective central control seriously weakened older political bonds and alienated much of the ruling class.

Government efforts at change constituted the principal source of discontent among the elite. Sharp awareness of the structural weaknesses of the regime encouraged the makhzan to adopt a series of reforms aimed at strengthening its stability and control over the country. The attempt to create new institutions and to expand the role and influence of the government can be examined in terms of domestic reforms aimed at the local populations. Domestic efforts at reform concentrated upon eliminating blocks to government centralization and upon generating new institutions staffed by new men. A study of the reform process in Europe and the Middle East teaches that three main obstacles were encountered by would-be centralizing regimes: a traditional army, a provincial notability, and a traditional religious class. The privileges and immunities possessed by these groups insured that they would not relinquish their positions easily. The efforts of nineteenth-century sultans greatly reduced the importance of the jaysh tribes as a military force, but the centralizing drive of the makhzan antagonized the provincial notables and incurred the opposition of the religious brotherhoods and *zawiyas,* whose interests were threatened by salafiyya-inspired reforms. The segmentation of the elite and of the religious classes alone prevented unified opposition. It should also be noted that both the provincial notables and the ʿulamā benefited in important ways from governmental reforms. The failure of military reforms increased makhzan reliance upon the rural elite, while the creation of new bureaucratic posts (notably the umanā) meant unprecedented chances for graft for ambitious young scholars. Attempts to generate a new army and a more modern clergy were much less successful.

The movements of popular protest and resistance which engulfed Morocco in the first part of this century present the historian with a broad spectrum of precolonial political movements. The changing patterns of the participation of the elite in the various movements constitute one of the most interesting aspects of this subject. The segmentation and fragmentation of the Moroccan elite into a myriad of kin groups, patron-client networks, occupational and religious associations, and other groups greatly militated against any unified action. Profound distrust of those in other groups was further magnified by the uncertainty of the ecology and the poor communications which existed within the sharifian empire. Unlike the societies of modern Europe, with their deeply entrenched privileged classes, Morocco lacked an aristocracy or a true bourgeoisie. The Moroccan elite, as a result, was vulnerable to sudden reversals of individual fortunes. Lacking a substantial institutional base, the elite was led to look after its own interests and those of its family and retainers first, before attending to the requirements of government service. For them corruption became a way of life. When the necessity of reform made itself felt, starting at the end of the nineteenth century, the contradictions which emerged in the position of most of the elite helped deprive the reforms of whatever possibilities of success they might have had. While the encroachment of the great Paris banks in 1904 posed a serious threat to the continuance of the corruption of makhzan officials and temporarily united them against the Saint-René-Taillandier reforms, the shifting bases of their concern ultimately lessened the impact of this new development. The elite's recalculation of where their true interests lay is the most important factor in explaining the shifting patterns of participation in the great events of the period. Other factors can be cited as well. Among them are the existence of a tradition of revolt in Morocco (sanctified in the concept of siba), connections to the wider world of Islam (particularly important in the case of the intelligentsia and urban elite), and differing conceptions of the relative place of Morocco in the world (which helped give the more sophisticated a good sense of the real power-differences between France and Morocco). Finally, there was the tenacious Moroccan desire for independence, which was deeply rooted in the Islamic culture of the country and fortified by many centuries of active resistance to European expansionism. All of these factors helped to further influence the participation of the makhzan and the resistance against imperialism.

A special word needs to be said about the gaps and weaknesses in the intellectual formation of the majority of the Moroccan elite. The process of intellectual change which had transformed European society before it had begun to shake the non-Western world was still in an early stage of development in Morocco by 1900. While the Middle East experienced an intellectual renaissance during the course of the nineteenth century, Morocco lagged behind. There was nothing in Morocco to correspond to the translation movements or the changes in the education of the military and civilian elites which affected the Ottoman empire, for example. Research however, has shown that, despite the backwardness of Morocco in this regard, intellectual change was surprisingly advanced in certain urban elite circles. The aʿyān of the chief cities of the realm had the most realistic view of the power of the West and of the Moroccan margin for maneuver of any segment of the elite. The profound attachment of this group to old habits and old ways of doing things, however, largely vitiated their intellectual advancement. In retrospect, of course, it was the new ideas of which they were the main carriers that were to prove most important for the future development of modern Morocco. But these developments lay far in the future.

The most significant thing about the movements of resistance and protest which emerged in Morocco in the period under study is that they were all rooted solidly in the religion of Islam. This had a number of important consequences for the way the situation developed. To begin with, as a Muslim country, Morocco possessed an elementary cohesion which was lacking, for example, in sub-Saharan African kingdoms. The primary focus of loyalty was Islam, rather than some lesser primordial grouping. Historically, Moroccan Muslims were particularly jealous of their independence, and the bonds of faith were well adapted to functioning as a kind of prenationalism. Unlike the rest of North Africa, Morocco had never been incorporated into the Ottoman empire. Instead, like Iran, Afghanistan, and a few lesser states on the fringes of the Islamic world, it had achieved a separate identity of its own. Unlike most of these states except Iran, the sharifian empire also possessed a powerful principle of legitimacy. The sultan of Morocco by virtue of his descent from the Prophet regarded himself as the legitimate head of the *umma,* or community of the faithful, and the true descendant of the classical Islamic dynasties. He headed an empire which extended in theory at least into the Central Sahara and Mauretania, and prayer was said in his name throughout this entire area. To Moroccans, the sultan was a symbol of national identity, national unity, a tradition of centralization, and the national will to exist. His religious prestige was thus capable of being transmuted into nationalist prestige as soon as social change and the growing power of the government had undermined the competing tug of heterodox local Islamic beliefs and practices.

Since the primary focus of loyalty was Islam, then it follows that religious appeals were alone capable of bridging the gap between the different segments of the Moroccan elite and between urban and rural political movements. A crucial group in the political structure of the state was the ʿulamā. As elsewhere in the Muslim world, it was the scholars of the Koran, the traditions, and the holy law who were charged with the task of maintaining the purity and integrity of the faith. The ʿulamā and the chief religious leaders of the country were the holders of the symbols of legitimacy and the guardians of the interests and independence of the Moroccan state. In this capacity they alone had the power to depose one sultan and to proclaim a successor should the incumbent prove himself unable to fulfill his mandate. Should a sultan be unable to effectively preserve the independence of *dār al-Islām* or govern unjustly (in violation of the sharīʿa), then it was their duty to intervene. In addition, sultans often consulted the ʿulamā on important issues of the moment. We have seen several examples of this.

The importance of the ʿulamā can be grasped if we consider their involvement in the principal political movements of the period from 1900 to 1912. At the time of the French incursion into the Touat oasis complex in 1899–1900, for example, it was the protesting fatwā of the ʿulamā of Fez that underlined the seriousness of the event. Subsequently, it was ʿulamā discontent with the makhzan efforts to abolish the right of sanctuary in 1902 that played an important role in the origin and early successes of the movement of Abū Ḥimāra. Thereafter, the disillusionment of the ʿulamā with the pretender set a limit to the extent of his encroachment on central Morocco. In 1904–1905, it was again the strong collective action of the ʿulamā of Fez that enabled the government to boldly challenge the proposed French reforms and set the stage for German intervention. In the great crisis of 1907—1908, the attitude of the religious leadership, rural and urban, again had a determining effect upon the cold war of the two sultans. The deposition of ʿAbd al-ʿAzīz in January 1908 by the ʿulamā of Fez was the critical event in deciding the outcome of the complex struggle between the rival claimants to the throne. In 1911, and again in 1912 at the time of the Fez mutiny, the neutrality of the ʿulamā and their unwillingness to become engaged in further struggle set a limit to the effectiveness of widespread popular movements to the north. Finally, in the case of the movement of El Hiba the endorsement of important regional religious figures assisted the movement's rise in the Sous valley, while its eventual defeat owes much to the opposition of the ʿulamā of Marrakech. Thus in every major development during the period under study we find that the attitude of the ʿulamā played an important, often determining, role upon the outcome. In a society as segmented as Morocco's and as beset with overlapping jurisdictions, it is striking that the religious elite could affect the outcome of events. Despite a vague structural position in the state (a position far less definite than in either the Ottoman empire or Iran) and their absence of corporate identity as a group, the Moroccan ʿulamā were nonetheless able to exercise considerable influence.

A final question about the nature of the political intervention of the ʿulamā must be addressed before we can move on to a consideration of the chief strands of protest and resistance. If the intervention of the ʿulamā had a decisive impact on the course of events, in whose interests did they intervene? Or, to put the question more broadly, why did they become politically involved at one moment and avoid doing so at the next? Without going into great detail, the answer runs roughly as follows. The Moroccan ʿulamā were far from being a class in any sociological sense of the term. Members of the ʿulamā were drawn chiefly from the urban merchant class, with some sponsored mobility of the brighter elements from the countryside and other urban groups. Often the same families tended regularly to produce religious scholars over several generations. But while the status was to some extent hereditary, it is important to underline that the ʿulamā were connected to the aʿyān of the cities by a broad series of common material interests, including landholding, trade, and perquisites of official standing in the society. Moreover, in important ways the ʿulamā benefited from the centralization efforts of the makhzan in the late nineteenth and early twentieth centuries. The creation of the new government bureaus required a large influx of educated functionaries, and these were drawn from the madrasa-s and the Qarawīyīn University. In other ways, of course, their interests were directly frustrated, as in the attempt to abolish tax exemptions through the institution of the tartīb and in the attack on the right of sanctuary. In the main, the responses of the ʿulamā appear to mirror and to legitimize the interests and concerns of the urban aʿyān. Contradictory and often self-defeating, their intervention serves almost as a paradigm of the weakness of the Moroccan ruling elite with whose fortunes they were in the end identified.

The main currents of protest and resistance in Morocco reflected the pervasive influence of the ʿulamā and of the Islamic principles of legitimacy in which the state was grounded. In Islamic legal theory, there were but two reasons for which a ruler might be deposed: failure to defend Islam and failure to rule according to the sharīʿa. The turmoil and confusion which preceded the establishment of the French protectorate produced not just one but several situations of contested legitimacy. The doctrine of jihād, as we have outlined it above, seemed best suited for the expression of deeply felt concern about the growing encroachment of the state on traditional exemptions and privileges and about the failure of the government to arrest French expansionist tendencies. Jihād appealed to a wide variety of groups and individuals. For some, it summoned up visions of the primitive Islamic community of Medina in the time of the Prophet and proposed a concrete program of reform through personal renewal and the institution of the regime of the sharīʿa. Non-Koranic taxes would be abolished, borrowing at interest forbidden, and unjust abuses corrected. Corrupt elites would be overthrown and the regime of justice established. This aspect of jihād had important populist overtones and was able to gain broad support in 1907–1908 (influencing the bayʿa of ʿAbd al-Ḥafīẓ at Fez and the movement of El Hiba, for example). Ultimately, however, it was the anti-Christian and staunchly anticollaborationist thrust of the doctrine of jihād which rendered it so useful to the leaders of the Ḥafīẓīya movement. Regarded as the expression of an Islamic patriotism, jihād called up memories of the heroes of the fifteenth- and sixteenth- century resistance to the Spanish and Portugese and marked a renewal of the age-old struggle against an expansionist Christian Europe. Because of the broad and substantial appeal of the doctrine of jihād, it could provide a program and an ideology for movements as different as those of ʿAbd al-Ḥafīẓ and of El Hiba. It is no wonder that the leaders of the Ḥafīẓīya in 1907–1908 chose to emphasize the patriotic struggle aspects of jihād rather than its radical populist potentialities. By the same token, they could only oppose the far more radical jihād of El Hiba because of its threat to their interests. Despite the social program implicit in the doctrine of jihād, however, it remained an essentially traditionalist movement whose prescriptions for reform represented an attempt to recapture a lost golden age rather than a progressive force for change. In the end jihād was unable to provide a workable solution to the complex problems facing the country: there was simply no place for it in the emerging modern Morocco.

Far-reaching changes were in the meantime leading to the emergence of new political forces in Moroccan society. New currents of thought deriving chiefly from the Middle East developed an important although limited clientele among the new emerging class of makhzan officials, wealthy merchants, scholars, protégés, and prominent rural notables. These new currents of thought (it would be inappropriate to call them ideologies) were strongly influenced and to some extent patterned after the reforms adopted by the Ottoman empire and Egypt during the nineteenth century. Although based on a European (particularly French) model, Ottoman reforms derived also from a tradition of efforts at renewal in the empire and were couched in quasitraditional terms. Thus they were more acceptable to tradition-conscious Moroccans than direct borrowing from Europe would have been. Moroccan connections with the Middle East were reinforced during the latter half of the nineteenth century. In the process, Ottoman reform efforts became known among the Moroccan elite, and voices began to be raised urging their adoption. Three general currents of thought can be distinguished in Morocco, each with its prescription for change: *tanzimat* (military reform and centralization), *mushawara* (consultation), and *al-ittihād al-Islām* (pan-Islam). Access to Middle Eastern books and newspapers and travel in the area appears to have been the primary means by which these ideas spread. It is perhaps well to stress that these ideas were not competing proposals for reform but overlapping tendencies. As compared to the broad popular appeal of jihād, the appeal of these ideas found little support outside of the narrow confines of the urban elite. A brief look at each will establish their differing programs and relative success.

In the first half of the nineteenth century the Ottoman empire embarked on a daring series of reforms. Known by the Turkish term *tanzimat,* they had as their object the strengthening of the state against the West through the modernization of the Turkish army, the updating and centralization of the bureaucracy, and the introduction of a comprehensive program of internal improvements (chiefly centering upon the communications facilities). The Spanish victory at Tetouan in 1860 convinced Moroccan statesmen that only through the adoption of a similar plan of reforms would their country retain its independence. Despite the importance of these reforms, their value was greatly diminished by a number of unintended consequences. Paradoxically, instead of strengthening the state against European encroachment, tanzimat-style reforms led to greater European influence upon the government. A major difficulty was that desired reforms could not be implemented without foreign capital, and this in turn led to major loan agreements and eventually to the dominance of the bondholders. But there were other drawbacks to reform. As the strength and power of the government increased, widespread disorder and unrest were generated, while simultaneously the reformers made themselves vulnerable to criticism from traditionalist elements. While reforms increased the opportunities for well-placed officials to profit from bribes and kickbacks from European contractors, increased corruption seriously lessened the chances of real substantive change. The results of the Moroccan reform program in this respect were little different from those of the Ottoman tanzimat. At a time when European expansionism constituted a certain menace, extensive reforms were doomed in advance to failure.

Many of the same makhzan officials who had supported governmental modernization were also partisans of the need for a more collegial style of rule based upon frequent consultation between the sultan and his chief subjects, both in government and out. Members of the ʿulamā and aʿyān in the major cities (especially Fez) were also strong advocates of *mushawara,* as it is called in Arabic. Informal and occasional consultation had been practiced by previous sultans. Beginning in 1904, however, as the situation of Morocco became more bleak, there were demands for a more regularly established pattern of consultations. The establishment of the *majlis al-aʿyān* (council of notables) in 1905 by ʿAbd al-ʿAzīz was directed to this end. Some supporters of consultation later seem to have intended that a constitutional monarchy be established, with a bicameral legislature and a bill of rights, patterned after the 1908 restored Turkish "Midhat" constitution. But these Young Moroccans were a minority tendency within the elite and lacked the means to realize their aims. Thus in retrospect the achievement of the advocates of consultation was the "government of national unity" which ruled the country during the First Moroccan Crisis (1904–1905). Had the more ambitious plans of the Young Moroccans been adopted, the result would undoubtedly have been disastrous.

As the nineteenth century wore on, a sense of common crisis pervaded the Islamic world. Beleaguered Muslim states outside the Ottoman empire looked increasingly to the Ottoman sultan for assistance. It became Turkish policy to support movements aimed at bringing about greater cooperation among Muslims against European encroachment. In Morocco, supporters of the pan-Islamic tendency sought to substitute Muslim advisors and military instructors for Europeans. They also favored stronger ties between Morocco and the Ottoman empire and looked with favor upon the clandestine efforts of Middle Eastern Muslims to intervene in Morocco in the immediate preprotectorate period under the auspices of *al-ittihād al-maghribī*. Many of the supporters of pan-Islam in Morocco were therefore also among the main backers of tanzimat-style reforms, that is, makhzan officials and important religious figures. By appealing to deeply rooted sentiments of Islamic solidarity and resistance to European imperialism, however, pan-Islam could appeal to a far broader audience. Traditional religious leaders as well as the advanced elements in society found in the diffuse ideology of pan-Islam a point of purchase in an otherwise disorienting world. Yet its very vagueness as an ideology lessened its effectiveness as a response to the many-layered crisis of the times. The highly segmented character of Moroccan society made a unified political response highly unlikely in any event. In the end, therefore, pan-Islam was unable to effect any serious reversal of the political situation of the country.

On March 30, 1912, after much travail and not a little sacrifice the "Morocco that was" passed into history. The forces of the new age had already succeeded in trampling down the strong points of the old society. Now under colonial domination, it would be remodeled and rearranged to suit the needs of new masters. By 1912 the Moroccan elite had accepted the hopelessness of the task of self-transformation. It had also had many of its fears of French domination assuaged, while it had begun to see the serious risks of social turmoil and continued unrest inherent in a prolongation of the struggle. Yet it was not without backward glances and ambiguous efforts to continue resistance through other channels that it eventually gave in. Already, deeply rooted processes of change were at work that would lead to a political and cultural renewal and the eventual overthrow of the colonial yoke. These changes would confirm the position of dominance of the elite of merchants, government officials, rural barons, and important religious figures in the new Morocco. In the course of its absorption into the world capitalist system, Morocco was faced with multiple crises, which intersected in numerous ways. The unparallelled situation thus produced was perceived by some as an opportunity, by others as a threat. Traditions of resistance, atavistic desires to return to a golden age, and hope for personal gain struggled within each individual. Caught between fires and unsure of its direction, Morocco stumbled into the modern age.

ABBREVIATIONS

The following abbreviations have been used for frequently cited works in the notes.

A.A.	Auswartiges Amt (German Foreign Ministry Archives)
AB	*Archives Berbères*
AF	*Bulletin du Comité de l'Afrique Française*
AM	*Archives Marocaines*
BESM	*Bulletin Economique et Sociale du Maroc*
BSGA	*Bulletin de la Société de Géographie d'Alger*
BSGO	*Bulletin de la Société de Géographie et d'Archéologie de la Province d'Oran*
CHEAM	Centre des Hautes Etudes sur l'Afrique et l'Asie moderne
EI[1]	*Encyclopedia of Islam,* First Edition
EI[2]	*Encyclopedia of Islam,* Second Edition
F.A.T.	Fonds Auguste Terrier
F.O.	Foreign Office Archives
Guerre	Archives of the Ministère de la Guerre, Section d'Outre-Mer
JMH	*Journal of Modern History*
M.A.E.	Archives of the Ministère des Affaires Etrangeres
RC	*Renseignements Coloniaux,* supplement to *Afrique Française*
RDM	*Revue des Deux Mondes*
RGM	*Revue de Géographie Marocaine*
RMM	*Revue du Monde Musulman*

NOTES

CHAPTER ONE

1. Portions of this chapter have appeared in fuller form in my article, "Morocco and the Near East: Reflections on Some Basic Differences," *Archives Européennes de Sociologie* 10 (1969): 70–94.

2. J. Martin et al., *La Géographie du Maroc* (Paris and Casablanca, 1967); J. Despois, *L'Afrique du Nord* (Paris, 1958); and J. Celerier, "L'économie montagnarde dans le Moyen Atlas," *Revue de Géographie du Maroc* (1939), pp. 57–67.

3. The results of the 1913 census may be found in *Afrique Française* (1913), p. 182. The most authoritative discussion is that of Daniel Noin, *La population rurale du Maroc,* 2 vols. (Paris, 1970), 2: 93–96. Cf. also the review of Noin by Lucette Valensi, *Annales E.S.C.,* 27 (1972): 1224–25, and the discussion in Rom Landau, *Moroccan Drama, 1900–1955* (London, 1956), pp. 24–25.

4. Jean-Louis Miège, *Le Maroc et l'Europe, 1830–1894,* 4 vols. (Paris, 1961–63), 4: 402 (hereafter cited as *Le Maroc*). According to Noin, *population rurale,* 2: 99, the urban population was 350,000.

5. Roger LeTourneau, *Fès avant le protectorat* (Casablanca, 1949), pp. 153–56, gives the population estimates for Fez. For a useful and informative brief study of Fez see the same author's *La vie quotidienne à Fez en 1900* (Paris, 1965). The English-language literature on Moroccan cities is just beginning. The reader is referred especially to Kenneth Brown's study of Salé in the nineteenth century (Manchester University Press, 1976).

6. E. Michaux-Bellaire, "Fès et les tribus berbères en 1910," *Bulletin de l'enseignement publique du Maroc (1922): 3*–10. The economic interpenetration is also attested by numerous additional sources which I hope to publish shortly in article form. Also the forthcoming study on Sefrou by Clifford Geertz et al.

7. Jacques Berque, "Qu'est-ce qu'une tribu nord africaine?" in *Evantail de l'histoire vivante. Hommage à Lucien Febvre* (Paris, 1953) 1:261–71 poses the problem of human mobility and tribal composition. The account of Moroccan tribalism given here differs considerably, it should be noted, from the standard views.

8. The literature on segmentation is quite extensive. Most of it concentrates upon sub-Saharan African tribes. Among the best known cases are those of the Tiv and the Nuer. See Laura Bohannan, "Political Aspects of Tiv Social Organization," in J. Middleton and D. Tait, eds., *Tribes Without Rulers* (London, 1958) pp. 33–66, and E. E. Evans-Pritchard, *The Nuer* (Oxford, 1940). Also, M. Sahlins, "The Segmentary Lineage: An Organization of Predatory Expansion," *American Anthropologist* 63, no. 2 (1961): 332–45, and M. G. Smith, "Segmentary Lineage Systems," *Journal of the Royal Anthropological Institute* 86 (1956): 39–80.

In the application of segmentary theory to Morocco, see Ernest Gellner, "Tribalism and Social Change in North Africa," in W. H. Lewis, ed., *French-Speaking Africa: The Search for Identity* (New York, 1965), pp. 107–18, and D. M. Hart, "Segmentary Systems and the Role of Five-fifths in Tribal Morocco," *ROMM*, 3 (1967): 35–65. For a general view, see Jeanne Favret, "La Segmentarité au Maghreb," *L'Homme, Revue française d'Anthropologie* 6 (1966): 105–11.

9. For a study of social stratification in the Gharb, see Jean Le Coz, *Le Gharb: fellahs et colons* 2 vols. (Rabat, 1964).

10. The significance of *ʿar* lay in the fact that it was a conditional curse, employed to constrain someone to grant a special request. See Edward Westermarck, *Ritual and Belief in Morocco,* 2 vols. (London, 1926), 2:518–69.

11. The most recent treatment of maraboutism and saint worship in Morocco is that of Ernest Gellner, *Saints of the Atlas* (London and Chicago, 1969). Among the extensive French literature, see Alfred Bel, *La religion musulmane en Berbérie* (Paris, 1938); Edmond Doutté, *Notes sur l'Islam maghrébin: les marabouts* (Paris, 1900); and E. Dermengham, *Le culte des saints dans l'Islam maghrébin* (Paris, 1954). Also, Westermarck, *Ritual and Belief.*

12. On the Sufi brotherhoods, see especially Georges Drague [G. Spillmann], *Esquisse d'histoire religieuse de Maroc* (Paris, 1956). For a more general view, O. Depont and X. Coppolani, *Les confréries religieuses musulmanes* (Algiers, 1897). Also, P. Odinot, "Rôle politique des confréries religieuses et des zaouias au Maroc," *BSGO* (1930): 37–71; J. Herber, "Les Hamadsha et les Dghoughiyyin," *Hesperis* 3 (1923): 217–36; R. Brunel, *Essai sur la confrérie religieuse des ʿAissaoua au Maroc* (Paris, 1926), and Vincent Crappanzano, "The Hamadsha," in N. R. Keddie, ed., *Scholars, Saints and Sufis* (Berkeley 1972), pp. 327–48.

13. Cf. for example the way in which the order founded by Shaykh Mā al-ʿAynayn functioned as a party in the Gharb and at court. Mission Scientifique du Maroc, *Rabat et sa region,* vol. 4, *Le Gharb (Les Djebala)* (Paris, 1918), p. 60. The Tijāniya tended to recruit their following from among wealthy merchants and officials. J. Abun-Nasr, *The Tijaniyya* (Oxford, 1965), p. 94.

14. On the branches of sharifs in Morocco, EI^1, s.v. "Morocco."

15. Georges Salmon, "Les Chorfa Idrisides de Fès," *AM* 3 (1904): 425–53.

16. On *ʿazabā*, see E. Michaux-Bellaire, "La maison d'Ouezzan," *RMM* 5 (1908): 23–89. Cf. also the important study of Grigori Lazarev, "Les concessions foncières au Maroc," *Annales marocaines de sociologie* (1968): 99–135.

17. For examples of the classic formulation of the division between makhzan and siba, see E. Michaux-Bellaire, "L'organisme marocain," *RMM*, 3 (1908), and Henri Terrasse, *Histoire du Maroc*, 2 vols. (Casablanca, 1950), vol. 2. The concept has been used to explain the course of Middle Eastern history by Carleton Coon, *Caravan: the Story of the Middle East* (New York, 1958), pp. 309–23. For a revisionist critique, cf. my "The Image of the Moroccan State in French Ethnological Literature: A New Look at the Origin of Lyautey's Berber Policy," in E. Gellner and C. Micaud, eds., *Arabs and Berbers: From Tribe to Nation in North Africa* (London and New York, 1973), pp. 175–99.

18. E. Doutté, "Une mission d'études au Maroc," *Renseignements Coloniaux* (1901): 171 (hereafter cited as *RC*). Also A. G. P. Martin, *Quatre siècles d'histoire marocaine* (Paris, 1923), pp. 456–58, and Eugène Aubin [Descos], *Le Maroc d'aujourd'hui* (Paris, 1903), pp. 238–41.

19. Aubin, *Le Maroc,* p. 241.

20. The makhzan is described in detail in Aubin, *Le Maroc,* pp. 172–257. See also René Maudit, "Le Makhzen marocain," *RC* (1903), pp. 293–304, and Henri Gaillard, "L'administration au Maroc: le Makhzen, étendue et limites de son pouvoir," *BSGA* (1909): 438–70.

21. Aubin, *Le Maroc,* pp. 190, 194, 207.

22. See, among other sources, E. Doutté, "Une mission d'études au Maroc," pp. 161–77, and Gaillard, "L'administration au Maroc," on the weaknesses of the rural administration.

23. On the functioning of the ḥaraka, see E. Michaux-Bellaire and G. Salmon, "Les tribus arabes de la vallée du Lekkous," *AM* 4 (1905): 141–43.

24. Mission Scientifique du Maroc, *Le Gharb* (Paris, 1918), pp. 42–46.

25. The concept of patrimonialism was developed by Max Weber, *Economy and Society,* ed. Guenther Roth and Claus Wittich, 3 vols. (New York, 1968). It is applied to the Ottoman empire by Serif Mardin in a seminal article, "Power, Civil Society and Culture in the Ottoman Empire," *Comparative Studies in Society and History* (1969): 258–81.

26. Albert Hourani, "Ottoman Reform and the Politics of Notables," in William Polk and Richard Chambers, eds., *The Beginnings of Modernization in the Middle East: The Nineteenth Century* (Chicago and London, 1968), pp. 41–68.

Chapter Two

1. This image of Morocco is enshrined, for example, in the titles of numerous books: E. Ashmead-Bartlett, *The Passing of the Shereefian Em-*

pire; W. B. Harris, *Morocco That Was;* and F. Weisgerber, *Au seuil du Maroc moderne,* to name but a few.

2. Miège, *Le Maroc.*

Until the archives of the makhzan are opened, students of nineteenth-century Morocco will remain deeply indebted to the pioneering work of Miège. It was he who first grasped the importance of European consular reports and statistics for the study of the implantation of European commercial interests in Morocco and first assessed the impact of that penetration. To him also belongs the merit of having defined many of the major problem areas, presented an abundant documentation, and suggested a number of hypotheses on the changes which took place in nineteenth-century Morocco. Despite his importance, a number of criticisms may be leveled at Miège. One is the vast scope of his work, which necessarily restricted his exploitation of certain sources. The thesis of Pierre Guillen, *L'Allemagne et le Maroc, 1870–1905* (Paris, 1967), suggests that a more detailed country-by-country approach may yield important discoveries. Perhaps more critically, because Miège lacked a framework for analyzing traditional Moroccan society, his comments upon it and the changes wrought by European penetration remain disparate and disturbingly inconclusive.

3. The importance of the war of 1859–60 has been stressed by Germain Ayache in his article "Aspects de la crise financière au Maroc après l'expédition espagnole de 1860," *Revue Historique* 220 (1958): 271–310. Also, E. Szymanski, "La guerre hispano-marocaine (1859–1860), début de l'histoire de Maroc contemporain," *Rocznik Orientalistyczny* 29 (1965): 53–65. The monetary difficulties which afflicted Morocco after the 1860 war were similar to those which resulted from the earlier unsuccessful war with France of 1844, waged in support of the Algerian leader ʿAbd al-Qādir. Contrary to the situation in that earlier war, isolation or the partial disengagement of Western interests such as had occurred after the revolutions of 1848 was no longer possible.

4. Ayache, "La crise financière," pp. 273–78.

5. Miège, *Le Maroc,* 3:97–99.

6. Ibid., pp. 99–106; 135–44.

7. Ibid., 4:113–20.

8. Ayache, "La crise financière," pp. 303–9. Also Miège, *Le Maroc,* 4:113–15.

9. Ayache, "La crise financière," pp. 297–98. Ayache was the first to give prominence to the importance of bronze in the Moroccan monetary system and to study the impact of the inflation in bronze in the nineteenth century. See also, Miège, *Le Maroc,* 3:100–101.

10. Ayache, "La crise financière," p. 304. Miège, *Le Maroc,* 3:104–5.

11. Miège, *Le Maroc,* 4:120–23.

12. E. Michaux-Bellaire, "Les impôts marocains," *AM,* 1 (1904): 56–96, explains the intricacies of the system of taxation. The term *maks* was used in a general sense to refer to all non-Koranic taxes. Cf. also Michaux-

Bellaire, "L'organisation des finances au Maroc," *AM* 11 (1908): 171–251.

13. Ayache, "La crise financière," pp. 285–91.

14. Ibid., 367–69.

15. Ibid., 370–74.

16. Guillen, *L'Allemagne et le Maroc,* pp. 440–46, 477–78, discusses the German trading offensive in Morocco after 1890.

17. On the agricultural depression of 1867–69 and its effects, see Miège, *Le Maroc,* 3:145–59.

18. Ibid., 375–467.

19. Ibid., 443–46.

20. Ibid., 449–58.

21. J.-L. Miège, "Documents inédits sur l'artisanat de Rabat et Salé au milieu de xixme siècle," *BESM* (1959): 173–74, 183; and idem, "Note sur l'artisanat marocain en 1870," *BESM* (1953). For a view of the decline of the cotton industry at Salé in the latter half of the nineteenth century, see Kenneth L. Brown, "The Social History of a Moroccan Town: Salé, 1830–1930," Ph.D. dissertation University of California at Los Angeles, pp. 195–99.

22. Miège, *Le Maroc,* 4:391–94. Cf. also his article "Origine et développement de la consommation du thé au Maroc," *BESM* (1957): 377–98.

F. Olivier, writing about the 1930s, noted that 30 percent of the ordinary family's budget was spent on tea and sugar. The one hamlet in the Meknes area which remained unaffected by the depression did not consume tea. "Mémoire sur l'évolution économique des tribus de la banlieue de Meknes depuis l'occupation française," unpublished article (1937), *CHEAM,* no. 77.

23. Miège, *Le Maroc,* 3:443–46.

24. Figures drawn from ibid., pp. 14, 461; 4:397.

25. On the capitulatory treaties of the Ottoman empire see Nasim Sousa, *The Capitulatory Regime of Turkey* (Baltimore, 1933).

26. The impact of the capitulations in Morocco is treated in Francis R. Flournoy, *British Policy Towards Morocco in the Age of Palmerston* (London and Baltimore, 1935) (see pp. 36–40 for a discussion of extraterritoriality).

27. The European population of the ports in 1850 was just 389. In 1872, it was 1,650; in 1877, 2,860; in 1886, 3,500; and in 1890, c. 6,000. Figures cited in Miège, *Le Maroc,* 2:474; 3:260; and 4:285.

28. The emergence of the European consuls as important political patrons in the Ottoman empire is discussed by Albert Hourani. See his "Ottoman Reform and the Politics of Notables," pp. 64–68.

29. Miège, 3:449–55; 4:333–47.

30. On the protégé system in Morocco, cf. L. Martin, "Le régime de la protection au Maroc," *AM*, 15:1–32; Hugo Wendel, 'The Protégé System in Morocco,' *JMH* 2(1930): 48–60; and Earl F. Cruickshank, *Morocco at the Parting of the Ways* (Philadelphia, 1935).

31. Michaux-Bellaire, "Les impôts marocains," p. 29; and Guillen, *L'Allemagne et le Maroc,* p. 503.

32. Miège, *Le Maroc,* 2:405–6; Cruickshank, *Morocco,* pp. 180–81.

33. Michaux-Bellaire and Salmon, "Les tribus arabes de la vallée du Lekkous," pp. 141–44.

34. L. Martin, "Le régime de la protection au Maroc," pp. 16–17. For a graphic description of the workings of the system of abuses, see Ion Perdicaris, *Mohamed Benani. A Story of Today* (London, 1887), a roman à clef in which the American Consul at Tangier figures as chief villain.

35. On the French incursion to put down dissident Beni Snassen tribesmen, cf. Augustin Bernard, *Les confins Algéro-Marocains* (Paris, 1911), pp. 144–47.

36. British backing for Moroccan independence was assured through the influence of their minister at Tangier from 1844 to 1886, Sir John Drummond Hay. On his life see L. A. E. Brooks, *A Memoir of Sir John Drummond Hay* (London, 1896).

37. The discussion of G. Ayache, "Le sentiment national dans le Maroc du XIXe siècle," *Revue Historique* (1969): 403–7, shows how deeply European innovations were resented and how such bodies as the sanitary commission at Tangier could work real hardships on Moroccan citizens. See also Miège, *Le Maroc,* 4:153–55.

38. Miège, *Le Maroc,* 4:155–57.

39. The Madrid Convention is discussed in ibid., 3:272–92.

40. On the Ordega period see ibid., 4: 44–81. For the attitude of Germany, Guillen, *L'Allemagne et le Maroc,* pp. 106–15.

41. The Euan Smith mission is described by a participant American, Stephen Bonsal, *Morocco As It Is* (London and New York, 1893).

42. On the battle of Isly and following events, see the account of Charles-André Julien, *Histoire de l'Algérie contemporaine,* vol. 1, *Conquête et Colonisation* (Paris, 1964), pp. 195–200. Also Bernard, *Les confins,* pp. 138–43.

43. Bernard, *Les Confins,* pp. 147–50.

44. On the revolt of Bou Amama, see Commandant Graulle, *L'insurrection de Bou Amama* (Paris, 1905); A. G. P. Martin, *Quatre siècles,* pp. 213–17, 545.

45. Ross E. Dunn, *Morocco's Crisis of Conquest: The Southwest, 1881–1912* (Madison, Wisc., 1976). See also his dissertation, "The French Colonial Offensive in Southeastern Morocco, 1881–1912: Patterns of Response" (University of Wisconsin, 1968).

46. The Mellila affair is discussed in Miège, *Le Maroc,* 4:223–24.

47. On the general crisis of Islam see, for example, Sylvia Haim, *Arab Nationalism* (Berkeley, 1964), p. 6.

48. Miège, *Le Maroc,* 3:343–72; 4:249–54. Also A. G. P. Martin, *Quatre siècles,* especially good on Moroccan relations with Touat and Mauretania.

49. Miège, *Le Maroc,* 4:173–79, discusses the question of Moroccan-Ottoman relations. During World War I, the French sought to utilize the Moroccan claim to the caliphate against the Ottoman sultan and British

parallel attempts to utilize Sharif Husayn. Cf. Pierre Lyautey, ed., *Lyautey L'Africain,* 4 vols. (Paris, 1953–57), 2:228–231; 3:70–85.

50. For a survey of Ottoman attempts to initiate diplomatic relations with Morocco during the nineteenth century, see Guillen, *L'Allemagne et le Maroc,* 181–89. He refutes Miège's acceptance of French suspicions that Germany was behind the attempt to link Istanbul and Fez.

51. On the military reforms, see Jules Erckmann, *Le Maroc moderne* (Paris, 1885) pp. 252–67; Louis Arnaud, *Au Temps des mehallas ou le Maroc de 1860 à 1912* (Casablanca, 1952), pp. 9–13; and Miège, *Le Maroc,* 3:224–34; and 4:104–9.

52. On the young Moroccans trained in Europe, cf. Jacques Caillé, "Les Marocains à l'École de Génie de Montpellier," *Hesperis,* 41 (1954): 131–45. Much work remains to be done on this important topic.

53. The most important expeditions of Mawlāy al-Ḥasan were those of 1882 and 1886 to the Sous, that of 1888 against the Ait Njild, and that of 1893 to Tafilalet. On the results of the military reforms, see Miège, *Le Maroc,* 4:104–11.

54. Guillen, *L'Allemagne et le Maroc,* pp. 497–98, mentions the German shipping concern Atlas Linie as being especially active in the contraband trade during the 1890s, operating through the ports of Tangier, Casablanca, and Essaouira. He gives the impression that German firms alone were responsible for smuggling over 100,000 rifles to the tribes during the decade. To this must be added the weapons which British, French, and Spanish firms smuggled into Morocco, or sold to the makhzan for later distribution to the tribes sub rosa. The British military instructor "Qaid" Harry Maclean was known for his enterprising spirit in this pursuit. Cf. Miège, *Le Maroc,* 4:105–6.

55. See the analysis of the rise to power of the great qāid-s as connected to their possession of military superiority, in Robert Montagne, *Les berbères et la makhzen dans le sud du Maroc* (Paris, 1930), pp. 326–64.

56. The subject of contraband, especially the numbers and kinds of arms in the possession of different tribes, is of considerable importance to the historian who aims at an understanding of the internal dynamics of rural Morocco. Yet work on this subject is just beginning, and documentation is sparse. The information in the text is derived from a series of interviews conducted during August 1967 among the tribes of the Fez and Meknes regions. See also the shrewd speculations of Miège, *Le Maroc,* 4:105–6, and Capitaine Delhomme, "Les armes dans le Sous Occidental," *Archives Berbères* (1916), 1:123–29.

57. Erckmann, *Le Maroc,* pp. 221–22.

58. The full contradiction of this policy was not visible during the lifetime of Mawlāy al-Ḥasan because he was able to keep the great qāid-s divided amongst themselves. Their great expansion came between 1894 and 1902. Cf. Montagne, *Les berbères,* pp. 334–37.

59. G. Salmon, "L'administration marocaine à Tanger," *AM,* 1:15–17; Aubin, *Le Maroc,* pp. 247–50.

60. Salmon, "L'administration marocaine," p. 15. A study of the *amīns*

of Salé has clearly sketched these characteristics. See Brown, "Social History of a Moroccan Town," pp. 315–18, 326–31.

61. Mohamed Lahbabi, *Le gouvernement marocain à l'aube du XXe siècle* (Rabat, 1958), pp. 157–58.

62. Aubin, *Le Maroc,* p. 247.

63. Ibid., p. 248. Also Lahbabi, *Le gouvernement,* pp. 159–60.

64. See G. Salmon (trans.), "Le tertib," *AM*, 2:154–58.

65. On the Qarawīyīn university during the nineteenth century, see Jacques Berque, "Ville et Université: Aperçu sur l'histoire de l'Ecole de Fès," *Revue historique de droit française et étranger* (1949), pp. 64–117. Cf. also E. Levi-Provençal, *Les Historiens des Chorfa* (Paris, 1922), for a brief survey of the traditional education system, pp. 6–16. On p. 349 Lévi-Provençal speaks of a "renaissance des lettres musulmans" during the reign of Mawlāy al-Ḥasan.

66. For a careful descriptive study of the Moroccan educational system prior to the protectorate, see E. Michaux-Bellaire, "L'enseignement indigène au Maroc," *RMM,* 15 (1911): 422–52. One of the few graduates of the madrasa dār al-makhzan who appears to have achieved later prominence was Muḥammad Ghibbās (in the French spelling, Guebbas), Minister of War (ʿAllāf al-Kabīr) under ʿAbd al-ʿAzīz.

67. On the role of the Alliance Israélite, cf. André Lecocq, "Les écoles israélites au Maroc," *Questions diplomatiques et coloniales,* 31 (1911): 682. For a more general treatment, Georges Ollivier, *L'Alliance Israélite Universelle* (Paris, 1959), and N. Leven, *Cinquante Ans d'histoire: L'Alliance Israélite Universelle (1860–1910)* 2 vols. (Paris, 1911). The AIU published a monthly and annual *Bulletins* which contain interesting materials on the Moroccan Jewish community.

68. Jamil Abun-Nasr, "The Salafiyya Movement in Morocco: The Religious Bases of the Moroccan Nationalist Movement," *St. Antony's Papers* 16 (London, 1963): 92–97, is the best introduction to the early tendencies toward the reform of Islam in Morocco prior to 1900.

69. Aḥmad ibn Khālid al-Nāṣirī al-Salāwī, *Kitāb al-istiqṣā lī akhbār duwwāl al-maghrib al-aqṣa* (Casablanca, 1956), 9:193–99 (trans. E. Fumey, *AM,* 10:358–68).

70. See, for example, the anonymous poem in "La corruption des moeurs à Tangier," (P. Paquignon trans.) *RMM,* 7 (1909): 23–38.

71. Muḥammad Bāqir al-Kattānī, *Tarjama al-Shaykh Muḥammad al-Kattānī al-Shahīd* (n.p., 1962), pp. 93–94.

72. Al-Nāṣirī, *Kitāb,* p. 106.

73. On the debate between "reformers" and "resisters" for the later part of the nineteenth century, cf. Miège, *Le Maroc,* 3:109–13, 128; 4:135–42.

74. For a general survey of the legacy of Mawlāy al-Ḥasan, which demonstrates just how fragile an equilibrium the sultan had achieved, see E. Michaux-Bellaire, "L'héritage de Moulay el Hassan," *RMM,* 9:412 ff. Some twenty years later, the same author was even more severe. He denounced the cult of Mawlāy Ḥasan that reigned in the protectorate administration among Moroccan officials: "Si l'on examine les choses de près

on est obligé de se rendre compte que ce regne devenu légendaire comme un idéal réalisé était en réalité l'apothéose de la corruption sous toutes les formes" (*AM*, 17 [1927]: 256).

Chapter Three

1. F. Weisgerber, *Au Seuil*, p. 118.

2. The most complete account of the circumstances of the death of Ḥasan I may be found in Dr. Linarès, "Après le voyage au Tafilalet," *Bulletin de l'Institut d'Hygiène du Maroc* (1933): 71–77. Also, Arnaud, *Au temps des mehallas,* pp. 75–90.

3. Martin, *Quatre siècles,* pp. 370–71.

4. Ibid. On the insurrection of the Rehamna and Mawlāy Muḥammad's abortive attempt to become sultan, see Arnaud, *Au temps de mehallas,* pp. 91–121, which includes colorful but unreliable material on the disturbances upon the accession of ʿAbd al-ʿAzīz.

5. Aubin, *Le Maroc,* 8th ed. (Paris, 1913), pp. 191–92.

6. Montagne, *Les berbères,* pp. 334–37.

7. R. Pinon, *L'empire de la Méditerranée* (Paris, 1904), pp. 155, 239.

8. E. Doutté, *En tribu* (Paris, 1914), p. 348, mentions this tendency of ʿAbd al-ʿAzīz.

9. On the influence of Wahhabi doctrine and the Salafīya movement in Morocco, see the article of J. Abun Nasr, "The Salafiyya Movement in Morocco," pp. 92–98.

10. *Al Moghreb al Aksa* (Tangier), May 26, 1900. Also Guillen, *L'Allemagne et le Maroc,* p. 317.

11. Martin, *Quatre siècles,* pp. 368–69, discusses the conquest of Touat and establishes a kind of complementarity between Touat and the Seguia el Hamra.

12. For a brief summary of French expansionist interest in Touat, see Christopher Andrew, *Théophile Delcassé and the Making of the Entente Cordiale* (London, 1968), pp. 153–57. Also, Dunn, *Morocco's Crisis of Conquest.*

13. A. G. P. Martin, *Quatre siècles,* p. 388.

14. Robert de Caix, "La Marche vers le Touat," *AF* (1900): 125–35, reviews the circumstances of the French colonial offensive in the southeast in 1899–1900.

15. Documents diplomatiques français, *l*[e], Serie, vol. 16, no. 134 (hereafter cited as DDF1).

16. Ibid. Also "Une opinion marocaine sur la conquête du Touat" (trans. G. Salmon), *AM,* 1 (1905): 416–24. The *Ḥalāl al-Bahīya* is discussed by Levi-Provençal, *Les Historiens des Chorfa,* pp. 371–72.

17. "Notre action dans le Sud-Oranais," *AF* (1900): 205–7. Also Dunn, *Morocco's Crisis of Conquest.*

18. J. de Segonzac, *Voyages au Maroc (1899*–1901) (Paris, 1903), p. 137; and DDF1, 16, no. 141.

19. This was the opinion of Aubin. Cf. *Le Maroc,* pp. 220–21.

20. The most complete account of Mā al-ʿAynayn's activities can be found in J. Caro Baroja, "Un Santon Sahariano y su familio," *Estudios Saharianos* (Madrid, 1955), especially pp. 295–326. It has been suggested that the name Mā al-ʿAynayn is a name-avoidance taboo usage (cf. the newspaper *Al Moghreb al Aksa,* November 2, 1901). Also, "Les Fadelia," *RMM,* 31 (1915–16): 160–66.

21. Al-Moutabassir, "Ma el Ainin Ech Changuity," *RMM* 1:348.

22. Baroja, "Un Santon Sahariano," pp. 318–20. France, Archives d'Outre-mer (Aix-en-Provence) Fonds Algérie. Série H. 30 H 54, Charles René-Leclerc, "L'action française au delà de l'extrême Sud," Tangier, May 30, 1907, no. 64. For the Mauretainian resistance against the French, see Commandant Gillier, *La Pénétration en Mauretanie* (Paris, 1926), pp. 101–74.

23. For a colorful description of the period of the "commis voyageurs," see W. B. Harris, *Morocco That Was* (London, 1921).

24. There is some dispute about ʿAbd al-ʿAzīz's age at the time of his accession to full rule. Weisgerber, *Au Seuil,* says twenty-two. Le Tourneau in *EI*², Arnaud, *Au temps des mehallas,* p. 75, and Saint-René-Taillandier, *Les origines du Maroc français* (Paris, 1930), p. 46, all put it at nineteen. The latter figure is probably correct.

25. A. G. P. Martin, *Quatre siècles,* p. 370, and Gabriel Veyre, *Au Maroc dans l'intimité du sultan* (Paris, 1905), pp. 152–54.

26. M.A.E., Maroc, n.s., vol. 2, Gaillard to Saint-René-Taillandier, July 25, 1902 (annex to Tangier dispatch of August 2, 1902).

27. M.A.E. Maroc. n.s., vol. 27, Dr. Zumbiehl to Guerre, May 28, 1902, "Le Sultan du Maroc. Ses idées, ses réformes, ses conseillers."

28. In addition to Harris, *Morocco That Was,* a good description of ʿAbd alʿAzīz's character can be found in M.A.E. Maroc, n.s., vol. 27, Dr. Zumbiehl to Guerre, May 28, 1902, "Le Sultan."

29. The existence of the advisory panel has not previously been noted. On it see M.A.E. Maroc. n.s., vol. 307, Cogordan interview with Gaillard, Paris, June 27, 1903. There is reason to believe that it had been in existence as early as December 1901, when the court left Marrakech for Fez.

30. Gharnīṭ had previously served as Foreign Minister under Mawlāy al-Ḥasan. Ibn Sulaymān had served in the same capacity under Bā Aḥmad and was also of Andalusian origin. Al-Munabbhī, in spite of assertions that he was of humble origin, was in fact well connected in the rural elite, being the cousin of Madanī al-Glawī. (His mother was the sister of al-Glawī's father.) Cf. E. Michaux-Bellaire, "Au palais du sultan," *RMM,* 5:657. The Tāzīs were an old makhzan family, in origin Jews converted to Islam. They enjoyed a brief ascendancy after the disgrace of al-Munabbhī, 1904–1907. On them, see "L'évolution du makhzen, la famille Tazi," *AF* (1904): 50–51.

31. F. Ponteil, *La Méditérranée et les puissances* (Paris, 1964), pp. 57–58, 81–83.

32. Saint-René-Taillandier, *Les origines,* pp. 21–23, on Maclean. See Guillen, *L'Allemagne et le Maroc,* p. 609, on Verdon.

33. On Linarès see R. Cruchet, *La conquête pacifique du Maroc* (Paris, 1930), pp. 42–54. The French internal political situation is well covered in Andrew, *Delcassé*, pp. 26–52.

34. Saint-René-Taillandier, *Les origines,* pp. 54, 101–2.

35. The first mention of the reform plans which I have found is F.O. 413/33, Nicolson to Lansdowne, March 31, 1901, no. 36 (secret). It attributes the initiative to Ibn Sulaymān, and other members of the makhzan. This would tend to make the project a more purely Moroccan one, while leaving aside the question of British influence, especially that of Maclean. The latter certainly was suspected of being the author. Cf. Arnaud, *Au temps des mehallas,* pp. 140–142; H. Cambon, *Histoire du Maroc* (Paris, 1952), pp. 104–6.

36. Guillen, *L'Allemagne et le Maroc,* pp. 598–602, discusses the diplomatic missions of 1901.

37. On the impact of the Boer War see E. Anderson, *The First Moroccan Crisis, 1904–1906* (Chicago, 1930), pp. 66–67. On Nicolson, see H. Nicolson, *Portrait of a Diplomatist* (Boston, 1930).

38. A. G. P. Martin, *Quatre siècles,* pp. 364–66, presents the text of the accord of 1901 with a brief explanation.

39. F.O. 413/33, Nicolson to Lansdowne, August 26, 1901, no. 118 mentions the creation of this council. It is uncertain exactly what its functions were, or if it ever in fact met.

40. *Al Moghreb al Aksa,* September 14, 1901.

41. F.O. 413/33, Nicolson to Lansdowne, Tangier, August 26, 1901, no. 118.

42. Aubin, *Le Maroc,* pp. 254–55.

43. For the text of the tartīb, cf. E. Michaux-Bellaire, "Les protectorats et les revenus marocains," *RMM* (1912): 86–90; G. Salmon (trans.), "Le tertib," *AM* 2:154–58. A. G. P. Martin, *Quatre siècles,* pp. 391–93, presents a translation of a sharifian letter to the *ʿamal* of Mediouna explaining the new regulations.

44. E. Michaux-Bellaire, "Les impôts marocains," pp. 81–82. The French especially feared that the inauguration of reforms under British sponsorship would seriously undermine their position in Morocco.

45. Despite the seeming impossibility that a government would ever abolish old revenue sources before new ones were assured, evidence on the abolition of the old taxes is convincing, M.A.E. Maroc. n.s., vol. 183, Saint-René-Taillandier to Direction Politique, November 9, 1902, no. 112. See also A. G. P. Martin, *Quatre siècles,* pp. 391–96.

46. On some of the repercussions of the reforms, cf. Aubin, *Le Maroc,* pp. 255–56; and A. G. P. Martin, *Quatre Siècles,* pp. 395–96.

47. F.O. 413/34, Nicolson to Lansdowne, January 31, 1902, no. 23.

48. F.O. 413/34, Nicolson to Lansdowne, March 15, 1902, no. 47.

49. A. Cobban, *A History of Modern France* (Baltimore, 1963), vol. 1, pp. 61–62.

50. See the very full discussion in D. Landes, *Bankers and Pashas* (London, 1958).

51. See the statistics in *RC* (1906): 64–75, and *AF*(1911): 57–63.

52. Weisgerber, *Au seuil,* p. 118, mentions the reserves in the treasury in 1900.

53. As nearly as can be judged from the general headings on imports in *RC* (1906): 64–75, with extrapolations from the trend revealed in Guillen, "L'implantation de Schneider, Les débuts de la Compagnie marocaine (1902–1906)," *Revue d'histoire diplomatique* (1965): 113–68.

54. On this period see Harris, *Morocco That Was.* Also Veyre, *Dans l'intimité du sultan.*

55. Guillen, *L'Allemagne et le Maroc,* pp. 602–6. An unconfirmed French report of 1902 claims that Manabbhī sent thirty small chests of money to England in October and purchased a considerable amount of land near Rabat. M.A.E. Maroc, n.s., vol. 183, Adjutant Bernaudat, extrait du rapport de October 15, 1902.

56. Guillen, *L'Allemagne et le Maroc,* p. 611.

57. On Fabarez and Veyre, see Guillen, "L'implantation de Schneider," pp. 118–20.

58. Maclean had just heard of the initial talks between Lansdowne and Cambon. The object of his mission, in addition to the loan, was to secure a joint Anglo-German guarantee of the territorial integrity of Morocco. Guillen, *L'Allemagne et le Maroc,* p. 620.

59. *RC* (1906): 64–75, presents statistics on the preceding four years of importation and exportation between Morocco and Europe.

60. Guillen, "L'implantation de Schneider," p. 122.

61. The circumstances of the loan negotiation are discussed in ibid., p. 129, and Saint-René-Taillandier, *Les origines,* pp. 96–97.

62. See above, chapter 2, for this discussion. The monetary situation in the period 1900–1912 is outlined by E. Michaux-Bellaire, "Les crises monétaires au Maroc," *RMM* (1920): 47–52.

63. A. G. P. Martin, *Précis de sociologie Nord-Africaine,* 2 vols. (Paris, 1913) 1:194–95. Also idem, *Quatre siècles,* pp. 394–95.

64. A. G. P. Martin, *Quatre siècles,* pp. 394–95. Also Pierre Guillen, "La Finance française et le Maroc de 1902 à 1904," *Bulletin de la Société d'Histoire du Maroc* (1969): 39.

65. Guillen, "La finance française," p. 39.

66. F.O. 174/267, Macleod to Lowther, October 26, 1906, no. 52, inclosure no. 1.

67. Ibid.

68. Budgett Meakin, *Life in Morocco* (London, 1905), p. 277.

69. Charles René-Leclerc, "Le commerce et l'industrie à Fez (2e partie)," *RC* (1905): 321 implicates the muhtasib and amīn al-mustafad in speculation in grain at Fez.

70. On the impact of insecurity on prices see René-Leclerc, "Le commerce et l'industrie à Fez (1re partie)," *RC* (1905): 244, 250–51.

71. A. G. P. Martin, *Quatre siècles,* pp. 396–97.

72. Harris, *Morocco That Was,* pp. 50–51.

73. E. Doutté, "ʿAbd al-ʿAzīz," in *EI*¹.

74. Harris, *Morocco That Was,* pp. 46–48, describes the elaborate court ritual.

75. On the oath, see *AF* (1902): 188.

76. M.A.E. Maroc. n.s., vol. 2, Gaillard to Saint-René-Taillandier, July 25, 1902 (annex to Tangier dispatch of August 2, 1902).

77. The ʿId al-Kabīr is the Moroccan name for the ʿId al-Qurbān, and falls on the tenth of the Muslim month of Dhū al-Hijja. At this festival in Morocco the sultan must initiate the proceedings by sacrificing a lamb before the citizens can proceed to sacrifice their own lambs. ʿAbd al-ʿAzīz's tardiness meant that much of the population of Fez stood in the sun for several hours waiting for his arrival so they could begin the feast. Aubin, *Le Maroc,* pp. 169–70.

78. Ibid., pp. 108–9. Also *AF* (1902): 362–63.

79. F.O. 413/34, White to Lansdowne, July 18, 1902, no. 103 (confidential).

80. The dispatches of Harris describe the scene well. *The Times* (London), October 24, 1902. See also *AF* (1902): 395; Pinon, *L'Empire,* pp. 153–57, for an explanation of the anger of the guardians of the shrine. For a dramatized account see Arnaud, *Au temps des Mehallas,* pp. 153–57.

81. A good portrait of the Ghiata at the turn of the century can be found in G. Delbrel, "De Fez a l'Oranie," *La Géographie* (1900: 167–82, where the 1898 makhzan decision to impose a tax of 25 pesetas per head on cattle exported to Algeria is noted. The name "Abū Ḥimāra" refers to the Moroccan army custom of parading recaptured deserters around camp mounted sitting backwards on a she-ass to receive the jeers of the soldiers. Cf. Jean Du Taillis, *Le Maroc pittoresque* (Paris, 1905), pp. 75–76. There is also a tradition in North African Islam that the Mahdī will appear from the East, riding on a donkey.

82. On the origins of the pretender, see Aubin, *Le Maroc,* pp. 116–17.

83. Pinon, *L'Empire,* p. 171.

84. On the career of the pretender, see A. Maitrot de la Motte Capron, "Le Roghi," *BSGA* (1929): 514–76, and Eduardo Maldonado, *El Rogui* (Tetuan, 1952). The career of Abū Ḥimāra is largely extraneous to our concern here, since he was active chiefly in eastern Morocco. There is ample material in French archives, however, to justify a more detailed study of his movement.

85. Maitrot de la Motte Capron, "Le Roghi," pp. 567–68.

86. Guillen's researches in the French diplomatic archives, and mine in the French military archives, including those of the Algerian-based XIX Corps, have failed to turn up a trace of official French government support. Guillen, *L'Allemagne et le Maroc,* p. 619.

87. On the support from Oran see Maitrot de la Motte Capron, "Le Roghi," p. 567; Du Taillis, *Le Maroc,* pp. 67, 70, visited the camp of the Rogui in 1904. See also the comments of Leonhard Karow, *Neun Jahre in marokkanischen Diensten* (Berlin, 1909), p. 123, reporting on private mili-

tary and financial support for the pretender from Oranais merchants and semiofficial groups, and public newspaper support for the pretender. An article by an anonymous Frenchman in the *Echo d'Oran* (December 9, 1905) mentions the earlier presence of a young Turk artillery officer, ʿArif Bey, at the camp of the pretender. He apparently stayed only a brief time before returning to Istanbul. He is likely the same pan-Islamic agent and adventurer who appeared again in Morocco in 1912. See above, chapter 7.

88. Guillen, *L'Allemagne et le Maroc,* p. 645.

89. On al-Raysūnī, see the biography by Rosita Forbes, *El Raisuni* (London, 1924).

90. Ibid., pp. 68–82. Also Arnaud, *Au temps des mehallas,* pp. 218–21, and the relevant sections in *AF* (1903–1905).

91. An opponent of an incumbent sultan becomes a pretender when he has the Friday prayer (*khutba*) said in his own name in the mosque rather than in the sultan's name; when he adopts the accoutrements of royalty, like the imperial tent and parasol; and when he appoints a rival makhzan.

92. There were four pretenders between 1900 and 1912 who posed a serious challenge to the throne. These were ʿAbd al-Ḥafīẓ (who succeeded), Mawlāy al-Kabīr, and Mawlāy Zayn (all brothers of ʿAbd al-ʿAzīz), and Mowlāy Aḥmāḍ Haybat Allāh (El-Hiba). There were at least a half-dozen other lesser pretenders during the period.

Chapter Four

1. The discussion which follows is drawn from the literature on the Moroccan Question. See the following: P. J. V. Rolo, *Entente Cordiale* (London, 1969), for an overview of the diplomacy of these years; George Monger, *The End of Isolation* (London, 1963), for British policy; Christopher Andrew, *Théophile Delcassé and the Making of the Entente Cordiale* (London, 1968), for French policy; Pierre Guillen, *L'Allemagne et le Maroc, 1870–1905* (Paris, 1967) for German policy.

2. The duality of French policy is treated by Christopher Andrew and A. S. Kanya-Forstner, "The French 'Colonial Party': Its Composition, Aims and Influence, 1885–1914," *The Historical Journal* 14 (1971). Cf. also R. de Caix, "Notre politique morocaine," *AF* (1903): 274–75; R. de Caix, "La France et le Maroc," *AF* (1903): 298–306; E. Doutté, "Les deux politiques," *AF* (1903): 306–11; and A. Gourdin, *La politique française au Maroc* (Paris, 1906), pp. 183–98.

3. Gourdin, *La politique française,* pp. 192–94, and E. Doutté, "Les deux politiques," p. 306–11. The article of Kim Munholland, "Rival Approaches to Morocco: Delcassé, Lyautey and the Algerian-Moroccan Border, 1903–1905," *French Historical Studies* (1968): 328–43, never quite grasps this point.

4. Saint-René-Taillandier, *Les origines,* pp. 122–24, and Andrew, *Delcassé.* Also Gourdin, *La politique Française,* pp. 192–94.

5. E. de Leone, *La Colonizzazione dell'Africa del Nord,* 2 vols. (Padua,

1960). Also Rolo, *Entente cordiale,* pp. 127, 130, 136–37 and Andrew, *Delcassé*, pp. 138–46.

6. T. Garcia Figueras, *La Accion Africana de Espana en Torno al 98* (Madrid, 1966) 2:52–53. Andrew, *Delcassé*, pp. 146–51, 190–94, 216–27, gives a good account of the partition plans. See especially Andrew's map, p. 224.

7. C. Andrew, "France and the Making of the Entente Cordiale," *The Historical Journal* 10 (1967): 89–105, presents the most recent discussion of the entente. In addition, see his *Delcassé*, and his "The Entente Cordiale from its Origins to 1914," in Neville Waiter, ed., *Troubled Neighbors: Anglo-French Relations in the 20th Century* (London, 1970), pp. 11–39. Also P. Guillen, "Les accords coloniaux franco-anglais de 1904 et la naissance de l'entente cordiale," *Revue d'histoire diplomatique* (1968); S. R. Williamson, Jr., *The Politics of Grand Strategy: Britain and France Prepare For War, 1904–1914* (Cambridge, Mass., 1969); and Rolo, *Entente Cordiale*.

8. The question of the origins of the 1904 loan is treated in P. Guillen, "L'implantation de Schneider," pp. 113–68. See also his *Les emprunts marocains 1902–1904* (Paris, 1971). Initially the Paris banks were reluctant to take up a loan which would be limited to French financial circles. They favored an international consortium including British, Belgian, and possibly even Spanish and German interests because of the greater security and freedom which it promised them. The internationalization of Morocco that the banks favored contrasts with the narrow nationalism of Delcassé and suggests that it was they, rather than the foreign minister, who represented the new emerging style of imperialism in the world. Guillen is certainly correct when he asserts the dominant role of diplomacy over finance in French penetration of Morocco.

9. Guillen, "L'implantation de Schneider," pp. 133–36.

10. On the Tāzī clan, cf. "L'évolution du makhzan: La famille Tazi," *AF*, (1904): 50–51.

11. Ghibbās was one of the few former students of the military missions sent to study abroad who later made good. He accompanied the Ibn Sulaymān mission to Paris in 1901. Under the protectorate he served briefly in 1915 as grand vizier. On Ghibbās, see Guillen, *L'Allemagne et le Maroc*, p. 646.

12. "L'Evolution du Makhzen," p. 50.

13. Documents diplomatiques français, 2e Série, vol. 4, no. 88 (hereafter cited as DDF2).

14. Saint-René-Taillandier, *Les origines,* pp. 211–15. See the account of Saint-Aulaire in his memoirs, *Confession d'un vieux diplomate* (Paris, 1953), pp. 91–111. Auguste de Beaupoil, Comte de Saint-Aulaire, born in 1862, entered the diplomatic service in 1892 and served in Tunisia, Chile, and Brazil before being appointed secretary of the French legation at Tangier, in which post he served from 1902 to 1909. In 1912 he was made

Délégué à la Résidence générale under Lyautey. He finished his career as ambassador at London.

15. DDF2, 4, nos. 88, 125.

16. DDF2, 4, no. 125.

17. Guillen, "L'implantation de Schneider," pp. 133–47. Also, DDF2, 4, nos. 133, 201.

18. DDF2, 4, no. 201. Df. also Saint-Aulaire, *Confession d'un vieux diplomate,* pp. 97–101.

19. DDF2, 4, no. 201.

20. The text of the loan contract can be found in *Affaires du Maroc (1901–1905),* 1, no. 170. On the bondholders' organization, P. Guillen, "La Finance française," pp. 37–42. Also, "La contrôle de la dette," *AF* (1904), p. 238, and DDF2, 4, no. 284. Henri Regnault began his North African career as a collaborator of Paul Cambon in Tunisia, served as consul general in Geneva before coming to Morocco as Délégué des porteurs de la dette marocaine. Second in command to Paul Révoil of the French delegation at Algeciras, he succeeded Saint-René-Taillandier as French Minister at Tangier, 1906–12. He negotiated the protectorate treaty in 1912.

21. On the border region see Bernard, *Les confins,* for a general survey of conditions. Lyautey presents some of his main ideas in *Vers le Maroc, Lettres du sud-oranais (1903–1906)* (Paris, 1937). Moroccan responses along the frontier are given full and insightful treatment by Ross E. Dunn, *Morocco's Crisis of Conquest.*

22. Saint-René-Taillandier, *Les origines,* also Munholland, "Rival Approaches."

23. Saint-René-Taillandier, *Les origines,* pp. 200–202.

24. Ibid., pp. 198–200.

25. The early stages of the opposition movement are treated in DDF2, 4, no. 473. Saint-René-Taillandier, *Les origines,* pp. 210–13, adds a few precious additional details. We still lack a good treatment of the links between the abortive resistance of April–May 1904 and that of October–December 1904. Yet it is clear that the two efforts should be viewed as part of a general change in the political dispositions of the makhzan.

26. On the role of al-Kattānī, see DDF2, 4, no. 473. An apologetic biography is Muḥammad Bāqir al-Kattānī, *Tarjama al-Shaykh Muḥammad al-Kattānī al-Shahīd* (n.p., 1962). On the role of the ʿulamā, see my "The Moroccan Ulama, 1860–1912: An Introduction," in N. R. Keddie, ed., *Scholars Saints and Sufis* (Berkeley, 1972), pp. 93–125.

27. M.A.E. Maroc. n.s., vol. 31, Saint-René-Taillandier to Delcassé, December 10, 1904, no. 248, Also, *AF*(1905): 40.

28. "Le fetoua des oulamà de Fès," *AM* 3:141–43. Also, "Les relations entre la France et le makhzan," *AF* (1905): 36–37.

29. *Affaires du Maroc 1901–1905,* 1, no. 210. Also Saint-René-Taillandier, *Les origines,* p. 214. DDF2, 4, no. 486.

30. DDF2, 4, no. 473.

31. DDF2, 4, no. 478. Also Guillen, *L'Allemagne et le Maroc,* p. 821,

and *The Times* (London) December 22, 1904. The Cairo visit is covered in M.A.E. Maroc. n.s., vol. 32, La Boulinière to Delcassé, February 20, 1905, Telegram no. 9.

32. The early efforts to bring about relations with the Ottoman empire are treated by Guillen, *L'Allemagne et le Maroc,* pp. 682–83.

33. See my article, "Pan-Islam and Moroccan Resistance to French Colonial Penetration, 1900–1912," *Journal of African History* 13 (1972): 97–118.

34. *The Times* (London), December 28, 1904. Other accounts, notably A. Pimienta, "La naissance de la crise," *AF* (1905): 40, deny that such an event took place. Only makhzan archives can resolve the conflict.

35. DDF2, 4, no. 483. This offer of massive bribes was declined by Saint-René, who doubted its efficacy. DDF2, 4, no. 487.

36. The threat to break relations eventually accomplished its aim but not before it occasioned a momentary strain in the personal relations of Delcassé and his minister at Tangier. See Saint-René-Taillandier's account in his memoirs, *Les origines,* pp. 213–30.

37. Guillen, *L'Allemagne et le Maroc,* pp. 813–27, outlines the transformation of German policy toward Morocco.

38. Ibid., p. 825.

39. Saint-René-Taillandier, *Les origines,* pp. 230–37.

40. Ibid., pp. 237–38. Also ʿAlāl al-Fāsī, *al-Ḥarakat al-Istiqlālīya fī al-Maghrib al-ʿArabī* (Marakech, 1948), pp. 106–7 (English translation Hazem Zaki Nuseibeh, *The Independence Movements in Arab North Africa* [Washington, D.C., 1954], p. 86).

41. DDF2, 5, no. 93. Also "La France au Maroc," *La Nouvelle Revue* (1905) n.s. 35, p. 148.

42. Saint-René-Taillandier, *Les origines,* pp. 245–46. British vice consul Macleod observed of the notables, "Many of them were of course of the most fanatical classes but on the other hand, the majority appeared to be as Moors go, moderate, intelligent, and fairly reasonable men." F.O. 174/266, Macleod to Lowther, July 4, 1905, no. 19.

43. al-Fāsī, *al-Ḥarakat al-Istiqlālīya,* pp. 106–7.

44. Miège, *Le Maroc,* 4:272–73, on the Euan Smith mission.

45. DDF2, 5, nos. 93 and 121.

46. M.A.E. Maroc, n.s., vol. 32, Saint-René to Delcassé, March 2, 1905, no. 18 bis. ʿAbdullāh Ibn Saʿīd was simultaneously governor of Salé (1892–1905). He was a member of the Kattānīya brotherhood. Cf. Kenneth Brown, "The Social History of a Moroccan Town."

47. Guillen, *L'Allemagne et le Maroc,* p. 830.

48. DDF2, 5, no. 134.

49. Ibid., nos. 130, 160, 370.

50. The German diplomatic offensive is treated by Guillen, *L'Allemagne et le Maroc,* pp. 827–37, 854–61.

51. Ibid., pp. 837–41.

52. Ibid., pp. 847–51. On Moroccan reactions to the Kaiser's visit, see

F.O. 413/37, White to Lansdowne, Tangier, March 29, 1905, Telegram no. 23. Also Saint-Aulaire, *Confession* pp. 131–40.

53. DDF2, 5, no. 473.

54. On the origins of the conference idea, see Guillen, *L'Allemagne et le Maroc,* pp. 841. As early as March 2 Ibn Saʿīd was suggesting the calling of an international conference.

55. On the background of the Algeciras conference, see A. Tardieu, *La conférence de Algeciras* (Paris, 1909). Also Saint-René-Taillandier, *Les origines,* and *AF* (1905), passim.

56. On the convocation of the tribes, see F.O. 413/38, Macleod to Lowther, Fez July 30, 1905, no. 204. On the first al-Wazzānī mission, F.O. 413/38, W. Smith to Lansdowne, August 7, 1905 (personal). The tribes were to select their own delegates, rather than have them nominated by the sultan. Invitations to send delegates were also sent to siba tribes.

57. A.O.M. Algeria. Serie 30 H/50, Prefect to Governor General, June 17, 1905, no. 3368.

58. F.O. 413/38, Lowther to Lansdowne, Fez, June 26, 1905, no. 162, gives Tattenbach's reported impressions of Moroccan strategy.

59. On the accomplishments of the conference, in addition to Tardieu, *La conférence,* see *Affaires du Maroc, 1906,* 2, which includes the full text of the Act of Algeciras. On the Banque d'Etat, see *AF* (1906): 168–69.

60. *AF* (1906): 134.

61. The Malmusi mission was suggested by Saint-René-Taillandier. See his memoirs, *Les origines,* pp. 356–60. Also *Affaires du Maroc, 1906,* 3, nos. 28, 41–44.

62. F.O. 413/49, War Office to Foreign Office, May 7, 1908, no. 37, inclosure no. 2, "Memorandum by Count Gleichen respecting the Police Force in Morocco." *Affaires du Maroc, 1906–1907,* 2, no. 93 gives a glimpse of the problems of organizing the police garrison at Tangier (also no. 185).

63. A point well made by Ayache, "Le sentiment national," pp. 407–9.

64. On the use of doctors as agents of peaceful penetration, see R. Cruchet, *La conquête pacifique,* pp. 55–66. The idea appears to have developed out of French experience dating from the service of Dr. Ferdnand Linarès at the court of Mawlāy al-Ḥasan (see ibid., pp. 42–54).

65. *AF*(1906): 292.

66. Ibid., pp. 259–60.

67. *Affaires du Maroc, 1906–1907,* 3, nos. 3–5; *AF* (1906): p. 260.

68. *Affaires du Maroc, 1906–1907,* 3, no. 48; *AF* (1906): 338, 373.

69. *Affaires du Maroc, 1906–1907,* 3, nos. 108, 186, and 207.

70. E. Doutté, "Au pays de Moulaye Hafid," *Revue de Paris* 5 (1905): 487–89, 872–73.

71. The intensity of the economic crisis of 1905–1907 can best be grasped by a careful reading of the British consular reports for these years. See Great Britain, Foreign Office, *Diplomatic and Consular Reports,* Annual Series, nos. 3697, 3892, 3893, 3914, 4146, and 4167.

72. M.A.E. Maroc. Politique Intérieure, 7, Marchand to Bourgeois, March 29, 1906. The same letter cites the revolt of Abū Ḥimāra as having undermined local security, leading to an increase in prices. Given continuing severe monetary instability, the loss of the transit trade between Tafilalet and the coast (trade which now went via Algeria) drove many merchants into bankruptcy. A survey of prices for fifty common consumer items between 1896 and 1906 by British vice consul Macleod reveals an average increase of from 300 to 400 percent. F.O. 174/267, Macleod to Lowther, October 26, 1906, no. 52, inclosure no. 1.

73. M.A.E. Maroc. n.s., vol. 186, Regnault to Bourgeois, August 22, 1906, no. 113.

74. M.A.E. Maroc. n.s., vol. 186, Marchand to Bourgeois, March 29, 1906.

75. The Charbonnier affair is covered by *Affaires du Maroc, 1906–1907,* 3, nos. 9–12, 25–27, 29, 31, and 179. Also *AF* (1906): 169, 205–6. The French government demanded reparations from the makhzan, including: (1) arrest and punishment of the guilty parties; (2) payment of an indemnity of 100,000 francs to the family of the victim; (3) resolution of certain outstanding affairs; (4) a formal apology; (5) erection of a commemorative monument at the place of the attack. After seeking to evade these demands, the makhzan was eventually forced to give in on all of them.

76. *AF*(1906): 259, 333–35, 337–38, 368–70. Also, *Affaires du Maroc, 1906–1907,* 3, nos. 82, 85, 88, 115, and 121. The situation at Tangier tended to foreshadow events elsewhere in Morocco, since all of the contradictions and strains which helped produce a crisis situation elsewhere were felt most intensely at Tangier. The joint French-Spanish naval demonstration at Tangier seems by its very ineffectiveness to have provided the prointerventionists at Paris with strong arguments for unilateral French action after the next major incident.

77. *Affaires du Maroc, 1906–1907,* 3, nos. 122, 163–66 and 201. Cf. also, *AF* (1906–1907), passim.

78. *AF* (1907): 155. *Affaires du Maroc, 1906–1907,* 3, no. 212.

79. *AF* (1906): 339.

80. On French views of the causes of the Mauchamps murder, see *Affaires du Maroc, 1906–1907,* nos. 244 and 261. Also, *AF* (1907): 129–33.

81. On the life of Dr. Mauchamps, see H. Guillemin, "Biographie du Docteur Emile Mauchamps," *Bulletin mensuel de la Société des Sciences Naturelles de Saone-et-Loire* (1907–1909), n.s. vols. 13–15, and *AF* (1907): 137–38. British Vice-Consul Lennox's views can be found in F.O. 174/253, Lennox to Madden, received March 24, 1907, private. Lennox argues against the existence of any kind of plot. The governor, Ḥājj ʿAbd al-Salām, who serves as the villain in some French accounts, is specifically exempted from any part in the origins of the riot, although he is charged by Lennox with not quickly dispersing the mob after the murder had taken place.

82. A French industrialist, Henri Popp, sought to obtain a concession for the installation of a wireless telegraph network from the makhzan in 1907.

He went so far as to have some of the equipment shipped to Morocco in anticipation of successful negotiations. The affair underwent numerous twists and turns thereafter, and makhzan letters were sent alerting its customs inspectors to the attempted import of telegraph equipment. On the affairs, see *AF* (1907): 186–87. The letters are presented by J. Allouche, "Lettre chérifiennes inédites relatives à l'assassinat du Dr. Mauchamp et à l'occupation d'Oujda en 1907," *Twenty-first International Congress of Orientalists. Proceedings* (1948), pp. 302–4.

83. Allouche, "Lettres chérifiennes."

84. *Affaires du Maroc, 1906–1907,* 3, no. 228. French demands included the following: (1) Imprisonment of the pasha of Marrakech; (2) inquest by the French consul at Essaouira to determine the guilty parties; (3) punishment of those guilty of the attacks on Charbonnier, Lassalas, de Gironcourt, and Mauchamps; (4) payment of a suitable indemnity to be decided later by the French government to the family of the victim; (5) immediate organization of the port police; (6) application of the 1901 and 1902 frontier accords; (7) immediate recall and official disavowal of Mawlāy Idrīs, makhzan agent in the Sahara; (8) cessation of aid to Mā al-ʿAynayn; (9) settlement of all other outstanding differences. The sweeping scope of the French demands makes it clear that the attack on Mauchamps was but a pretext for a far-reaching diplomatic and military operation aimed at crushing all further attempts at resistance by the makhzan. The bankruptcy of the policy of peaceful penetration stands clearly revealed.

85. *Affaires du Maroc, 1906–1907,* 3, no. 242.

86. On the growth of Casablanca, see Miège, *Le Maroc,* 4:397–98. Also J. L. Miège and E. Hughes, *Les européens à Casablanca au XIXe siècle* (Paris, 1954), and André Adam, *Histoire de Casablanca (des origines à 1914)* (Aix-en-Provence, 1968).

87. On the Chaouia in the late nineteenth and early twentieth centuries, Dr. F. Weisgerber, "Les Chaouia: Le territoire des Chaouia," *RC* (1907): 209–24. Also, the same author's *Casablanca et les Chaouia en 1900* (Casablanca, 1935), and Mission Scientifique du Maroc, *Casablanca et les Chaouia,* 2 Vols. (Paris, 1915), in the series *Villes et Tribus du Maroc*. The Mission Scientifique's publication is of fundamental importance.

88. Weisgerber, "Les Chaouia," pp. 222–23. Also, Mission Scientifique du Maroc, *Casablanca et les Chaouia,* vols. 1–2, passim. J. Ladreit de Lacharrière "L'Oeuvre française en Chaouia," *RC* (1910): 372–76.

89. M. Baudit, *Le monde des affaires en France de 1830 à nos jours* (Paris, 1952), p. 479.

90. Guillen, *L'Allemagne et le Maroc,* pp. 507–12. There is in fact a misleading precision to these figures, since the total amount of land owned by Europeans would equal the total area of the province (11,000 hectares). Until further investigation can be done, all that can be said is that European holdings were very substantial. Until the French landings, they were no doubt also largely theoretical.

91. Miège, *Le Maroc,* 4:339–43.

92. A list of protégés by nationality in 1909 can be found in de Lacharrière, "L'oeuvre française en Chaouia," p. 378. He notes, p. 374, that 15 to 20 percent of the profits could easily be realized by Europeans interested in agriculture, while for stock raising profits could reach 30 percent (p. 375), although with greater risks. Information on the operation of the protégé system in agriculture can also be found in A. de Montalembert, "La protection et les associations agricoles au Maroc," *RC* (1907): 109–15; E. Vaffier-Pollet, "L'agriculture et l'élevage au Maroc," *RC* (1906): 205–9; and Vaffier-Pollet, "Les associations agricoles au Maroc," *RC* (1906): 234–39 and 263–65.

93. H. G. Conjeaud, *Histoire militaire de la Chaouia jusqu'à 1914* (Casablanca, n.d.), p. 27. A. G. P. Martin, *Quatre Siècles,* pp. 371–73.

94. Mission Scientifique de Maroc, *Casablanca et les Chaouia,* 1:165–68.

95. A. G. P. Martin, *Quatre Siècles,* p. 372.

96. Mission Scientifique du Maroc, *Casablanca et les Chaouia,* 1:167–68; 2:207–8. On the tartīb, cf. above, chapter 3.

97. Ibid., 1:167–71; 2:207–8.

98. Ibid.

99. Roland Mousnier, *Peasant Uprisings in Seventeenth Century France, Russia and China* (New York, 1972).

100. Mission Scientifique du Maroc, *Casablanca et les Chaouia,* 2:209–10.

101. On the career of Abūʿ Azzāwī, cf. A. G. P. Martin, *Quatre Siècles,* pp. 404–5. Also Mission Scientifique du Maroc, *Casablanca et les Chaouia,* 1:186–87.

102. On the succession crisis, see Mission Scientifique du Maroc, *Casablanca et les Chaouia,* 2:78–81. Wuld al-Ḥājj Ḥamū had become qāid of the Oulad Hariz as a result of the siba, in which he had succeeded in ousting his cousin. A. G. P. Martin, *Quatre Siècles,* p. 439.

103. For a Moroccan view of the Casablanca events, ʿAbd al-Raḥmān Ibn Zaydān, *Itḥāf aʿlām al-Nās bī-Jamal Akhbār Ḥāḍirat Miknās* (Rabat, 1929), 1:419–30. The incident is treated in *Affaires du Maroc, 1906–1907,* 3, nos. 246, 250, 258, 265, and 285. Also, *AF*(1907); 187.

104. F.O. 174/253, Madden to Lowther, July 30, 1907, no. 151, and August 4, 1907, no. 163. Also, Adam *Histoire de Casablanca,* pp. 110–11.

105. E. Ashmead-Bartlett, *The Passing of the Shereefian Empire* (Edinburgh and London, 1910), pp. 22–23. Also, Adam, *Histoire de Casablanca,* p. 105–7.

106. F.O. 174/255, Madden to White, February 9, 1908, no. 42, a retrospective summary of the events of July 1907. Also, F.O. 174/253, Madden to Lowther, August 4, 1907, no. 163.

107. On the Casablanca incidents, see Ashmead-Bartlett, *Shereefian Empire;* V. G. Bourdon, *Ce que j'ai vu au Maroc. Les journées de Casablanca* (Paris, 1908); Conjeaud, *Histoire;* and André Adam, "Sur l'action du Galilée à Casablanca en août 1907," *ROMM* (1969), no. 6, pp. 9–21.

Adam, *Histoire de Casablanca* is a good recent account, although one which seriously neglects the interpenetration of urban and rural movements in the origins of the uprising. See also, *AF* (1907): 284–87 and 328–37.

108. A good study of the fighting in the Chaouia by a veteran British war correspondent can be found in Ashmead-Bartlett, *The Shereefian Empire* pp. 54–156. In addition to the monthly summaries in *Afrique Française* (1907), for a more careful study of the early part of the Chaouia campaign, with emphasis on the action of the tribes, see A. G. P. Martin, *Quatre Siècles,* pp. 436–46.

109. A. Le Chatelier, "Au Maroc: Le Politique Nécessaire," *Revue Bleue* (1908): 419. The quote continues: "It has clearly been seen in ascertaining how the relation of cause to effect has led via loan, debt, and control to popular rising against foreign intervention, to the massacre of Casablanca, to the landing [of troops] and to the battles of the Chaouia."

CHAPTER FIVE

1. Arnaud, *Au temps des mehallas,* p. 303. ʿAbd al-Ḥafīẓ died at Fez on April 4, 1937. A study of his life is urgently needed.

2. Mission Scientifique du Maroc, *Casablanca et les Chaouia,* 1:179–80; idem, *Villes et Tribus du Maroc* series.

3. A. G. P. Martin, *Quatre siècles,* pp. 379–84, 397.

4. Jamil Abun-Nasr, 'The Salafiyya Movement," pp. 97–98. The book was called *Kashf al-qinaʿ ʿan iʿtiqad tawāʾif al-ibtidaʿ* (Fez, 1327/1909). Among his other books is *Kitāb niẓam maṣṭalaḥ al-hadith li-man nasakha min al-ʿulūm* (Fez, 1327/1909).

5. Personal communication, Kenneth Brown, letter of June 19, 1970. In the *ijāza,* the shaykh addresses ʿAbd al-Ḥafīẓ in a particularly intimate fashion as "my son and the son of my beloved one" (this last a reference to Mawlāy al-Ḥasan).

6. Abun-Nasr, "The Salafiyya Movement." Also J. Berque, "Ça et là dans les débuts du reformisme religieux au Maghreb," *Etudes d'orientalisme dediés à mémoire de Levi-Provençal* (Paris, 1962), 2:480–83.

7. Middle Eastern Arabic newspapers appear to have been known in Morocco from the turn of the century, although only to a tiny minority of the educated elite. The foreign legations at Tangier, noting the potential importance of the press for explaining the position of their countries, began to finance a small number of Arabic newspapers, which were edited by Lebanese journalists. The most successful of these was the French-sponsored *al-Saʿāda,* edited by the Syrian Wadīʿ Karām. On it, see Louis Mercier, "La presse musulmane au Maroc," *RMM* 4 (1908): 622–23.

8. Lawrence Harris, *With Mulai Hafid at Fez. Behind the Scenes in Morocco* (London, 1909), pp. 88–92.

9. For appreciations of ʿAbd al-Ḥafīẓ's character, see Weisgerber, *Au Seuil,* pp. 160–61; E. Doutté, "A la côte occidentale du Maroc," *AF* (1908): 55; and Bringau, "Moulay Hafid intime," *BSGA* (1912): 25–26.

10. See above, Chapter 6, for examples.

11. A. G. P. Martin, *Quatre siècles,* p. 416. Martin is generally reliable where he has firsthand knowledge. He was a military interpreter in the Chaouia campaign, and often translates the texts of captured Arabic documents. Otherwise his treatment of the 1900 to 1912 period is largely a rehash of the monthly chronologies of *Afrique Française.*

12. Charles René-Leclerc, "Les débuts de règne de Moulay Hafid," *RC* (1908): 43.

13. Ernest Vaffier[-Pollet], "Une grande famille marocaine: les Glaoua," *France-Maroc* (1907), p. 24. Vaffier-Pollet was an employee of the Compagnie marocaine who first became acquainted with Madanī al-Glawī and eventually became a good friend when the latter withdrew to Oudjda in the later stages of the 1903 campaign against Abū Ḥimāra. From this time on al-Glawī appears to have taken care to cultivate French contacts even while working for the overthrow of ʿAbd al-ʿAzīz. On Vaffier-Pollet, see Christian Houel, *Mes aventures marocaines* (Casablanca, 1954), pp. 63–64.

14. René-Leclerc, "Les débuts," p. 43. See, for another view of al-Glawī, Marquis de Segonzac, *Au coeur de l'Atlas. Mission au Maroc, 1904–1905* (Paris, 1910), pp. 205–6.

15. René-Leclerc, "Les débuts," pp. 41–42.

16. Marthe and Edmond Gouvion, *Kitāb Aâyane al-Marhrib 'l-Akça* (Paris, 1939), p. 342. Also on the role of Corcos see Vidi [pseud.], "Ichoua Corcos," *L'Avenir Illustré* (1929), pp. 4–6, and J. Benech, *Essai d'Explication d'un Mellah* (Kaiserslauten, s.d.), pp. 256–70.

17. Holzmann's role has not been clarified entirely yet, even by Guillen. By birth an Ottoman subject, he apparently studied medicine in Germany and spoke, by his own admission, some thirteen languages. On him see Doutté, "Au pays de Moulaye Hafid," p. 866. Guillen, *L'Allemagne et le Maroc,* pp. 487–88, notes that Holzmann dealt with the Mannesmann brothers at Berlin.

18. M. A. E. Maroc. n.s., vol. 186, Regnault to Bourgeois, August 22, 1906, no. 113.

19. De Segonzac, *Au coeur de l'Atlas,* p. 213.

20. Cf. the secret correspondence between Ḥafīẓ and Mauchamps released by Jaurés. *Journal Officiel,* Chambre des Deputés. Débats Parlementaires. Séance du 28 Janvier 1908, pp. 140–41.

21. De Segonzac, *Au coeur de l'Atlas,* p. 212.

22. At about this time al-Ḥājj Tahamī al-Glawī was made a *mukhlat* of the Compagnie marocaine. ʿAbd al-Ḥafīẓ received a Gobelins tapestry from the French government as a testimony of friendship.

23. E. Doutté, "La Situation politique du Houz au 1er Janvier 1907," *RC* (1907): 241–48, surveys the rivalry of the great qāid-s. Also Montagne, *Les Berbères,* pp. 334–39.

24. A. G. P. Martin, *Quatre siècles,* pp. 418–19.

25. Ibid., pp. 425–26. On the *rimāiya,* Mission Scientifique du Maroc, *Casablanca et les Chaouia,* 1:227–30.

26. René-Leclerc, "Les débuts," p. 42.

27. M. A. E. Maroc, n.s., vol. 186, Regnault to Bourgeois, September 11, 1906, no. 155.

28. A. G. P. Martin, *Quatre siècles,* pp. 426–28. Doutté, "Situation politique," pp. 244–46.

29. A. G. P. Martin, *Quatre siècles,* p. 428.

30. Ibid., p. 435. *AF* (1907): 184.

31. M. A. E. Maroc. n.s., vol. 186, Regnault to Pichon, May 6, 1907, no. 219, and May 23, 1907, no. 230. Also, René-Leclerc, "Les débuts," p. 44; AF (1907): 228.

32. M. A. E. Maroc. n.s., vol. 186, Saint-Aulaire to Pichon, July 4, 1907, no. 330. Also, F.O. 174/253, G. Hunot to A. Madden, May 20, 1907, personal.

33. See above, Chapter 4.

34. René-Leclerc, "Les débuts," pp. 42–43, describes the setting.

35. There are several accounts of the proclamation of ʿAbd al-Ḥafīẓ at Marrakech. *Affaires du Maroc,* 3, no. 428; and René-Leclerc, "Les débuts," pp. 43. The close association of Ḥafīẓ with the popular desire for jihād is clearly brought out by René-Leclerc's account. One of the cries was "*Allāh yanaṣar Mawlāy Ḥafīẓ ʿala niyat al-jihād*" (May God protect Mawlāy Ḥafīẓ for the cause of the holy war).

36. *Affaires du Maroc,* 3, no. 428.

37. Arnaud, *Au temps des Mehallas,* p. 245.

38. The new makhzan is listed by René-Leclerc, "Les débuts," p. 43.

39. Arnaud, *Au temps des Mehallas,* p. 245.

40. The great qāid-s, for their part, found it to their advantage to have the substantial patronage resources of the makhzan at their disposal, and used them to increase the wealth of their families and allies.

41. The appointment of Tayyib al-Tāzī as minister of finances may have been calculated to win the support of the Fāsī elite.

42. *AF* (1907): 332. For a list of tribes endorsing the pretender, see René-Leclerc, "Les débuts," p. 44.

43. *Affaires du Maroc,* 3, no. 442; *AF* (1907): 332–33, 369.

44. *AF* (1907): 369.

45. Ibid., p. 332.

46. On the financial crisis of ʿAzīz, see M.A.E. Maroc. n.s., vol. 186, Regnault to Pichon, March 28, no. 127; *AF* (1907): 333.

47. *Affaires du Maroc,* 3, nos. 427, 435.

48. For the text of the fatwā, see *AF* (1908): 34–35. *Affaires du Maroc,* no. 465.

49. A. G. P. Martin, *Quatre siècles,* pp. 459–61.

50. *AF* (1907): 333.

51. *Affaires du Maroc,* 3, no. 411.

52. *AF* (1907): 409.

53. *AF* (1908): 28–29.

54. Jean-Claude Allain, "L'emprunt des bijoux de la couronne chérifienne (1907–1910)," *Revue d'histoire diplomatique* (1971): 152–69, especially pp. 153–55; *AF* (1908): 30.

55. *AF* (1907): 370; on the Regnault-Lyautey mission, see Lyautey's account, "Lettres de Rabat (1907)," *Revue des Deux Mondes* 64 (1921): 273–304.

56. *AF* (1907): 408. Among the disturbances at Marrakech was a fight between the entourage of Mā al-ʿAynayn and some ʿAlawī sharifs from Tafilalet.

57. René-Leclerc, "Au débuts," p. 44.

58. *Affaires du Maroc,* 3, no. 485, indicates that one of the factors which may have played a role in ʿAnflūs's opposition to ʿAbd al-Ḥafīẓ was his membership in the Tijāniya brotherhood. But cf. Doutté, "La situation politique du Houz," pp. 247–48.

59. M.A.E. Maroc. n.s., vol. 187, Regnault to Pichon, October 4, 1907, no. 508. The two were Abū Bakr Shantūf, a former *ʿadil* of the *umanā* at Marrakech, and Abū Ḥassana, an early Ḥafīẓ appointee. There were persistent rumors that Ḥafīẓ had negotiated loans with the German firms of Marx and Mannesmann, the former for 500,000 francs in arms, the second for five million marks, one-half in arms. Mining rights in the Atlas were said to be the security. See, in the same volume as above, the telegrams of Saint-Aulaire to Quai d'Orsay, August 7, 1907, no. 646 and September 16, 1907, no. 690.

60. A. G. P. Martin, *Quatre siècles,* pp. 455–56. British observers were convinced that the appointment of Muḥammad ibn al-Rashīd was a political choice to win the support of the sharifs at Tafilalet. More capable men were available. The general impression which these British observers received was that the use of jihād appeals by ʿAbd al-Ḥafīẓ was a deliberate effort to broaden his political base. F.O. 413/49, Lowther to Grey, January 16, 1908, no. 15, confidential.

61. *AF* (1907): 366–67.

62. A. G. P. Martin, *Quatre siècles,* pp. 451–56, including a French translation of the complete text of the fatwā. For the Arabic text, see A. G. P. Martin, *Méthode déductive d'Arabe Nord-Africaine* (Paris, 1919), pp. 367ff.

63. A. G. P. Martin, *Quatre siècles,* p. 451.

64. On the Chaouia campaign, in addition to the monthly chronology in *AF* (1907), passim, see Houel, *Mes aventures marocaines;* R. Rankin, *In Morocco with General d'Amade* (London, 1908); Ashmead-Bartlett, *The Shereefian Empire* (Edinburgh and London, 1010); and Weisgerber, *Au Seuil.*

65. *AF* (1907): 366.

66. Ibid., p. 467. *Affaires du Maroc,* 3, no. 497, lists the conditions of submission.

67. *AF* (1907): 406–8.

68. A. G. P. Martin, *Quatre siècles,* pp. 462–65.

69. The chief stakes in the struggle over the ports were the customs revenues they provided. M.A.E. Maroc. n.s., vol. 187, Regnault to Quai d'Orsay, October 29, 1907, no. 23.

70. *AF* (1907): 451.

71. Moroccan protests against the port police were motivated by the changed nature of this body, which bore little relation to that authorized by the Act of Algeciras. It was under direct French authority and was composed of a mixed force of Algerian Muslims and Moroccans commanded by French officers. It therefore constituted a disguised French occupation force and an infringement of Moroccan sovereignty. On the protests, see *AF* (1907–1908), passim. On the deliberate French policy of deception in the recruitment of the port police, see Guerre, Série D-15, Chargé d'affaires, Tanger to Pichon, January 19, 1908, no. 28.

72. A.G.P. Martin, *Quatre siècles,* pp. 466–67.

73. *AF* (1907): 444.

74. A.G.P. Martin, *Quatre siècles,* p. 469. *Affaires du Maroc,* 4, no. 9.

75. *AF* (1907): 451.

76. For the accounts of two Frenchmen in the camp of the pretender, see de Segonzac, *Au coeur de l'Atlas,* pp. 215–29, and Houel, *Mes aventures marocaines,* pp. 52–98. ʿAbd al-Ḥafīẓ was adept at utilizing the press to influence opinion in his favor. Houel operated for a time with a retainer from the pretender. His articles were influential on several occasions. At one point Ḥafīẓ even proposed a bribe to the Comité du Maroc to change its press policy toward him. M.A.E. Maroc. n.s., vol. 187, Saint-Aulaire to Pichon, December 31, 1907, no. 572.

77. *AF* (1907): 451.

78. A.G.P. Martin, *Quatre siècles,* p. 472.

79. On the Beni Snassen jihād, ibid., pp. 469–70. A convenient account of Lyautey's campaign can be found in *AF* (1908): 19–21.

80. *AF* (1908): 30. For a unique view of the political climate at Fez during this period, see A. Maitrot de la Motte Capron and Dr. Trenga, "Journal d'un correspondant de révolution," *BSGA* (1936): 14–62, 133–92. It is the translated and edited journal of Jacob Niddam, a Jew of Fez, who served as German postal agent in that city.

81. The most recent such incident occurred in 1894, soon after the advent of Mawlāy al-Ḥasan to the throne, when Fez al-Bali revolted over the reinstitution of the maks. Terrasse, *Histoire du Maroc,* 2:331. Also Aḥmad ibn Khālid al-Nāṣirī, *Kitāb al-Istiqṣa,* pp. 129–37 (trans. Fumey, *Archives Marocaines,* 10:279–84).

82. *AF* (1908): 36. F.O. 413/48, Lowther to Grey, January, 14, 1908, no. 14, gives a slightly different version.

83. The text of the bayʿa can be found in ʿAbd al-Raḥmān ibn Zaydān, *Itḥaf aʿlām al-nās bī jamāl akhbār ḥāḍirat Miknās* (Rabat, 1929), 1:448–53, especially 452–53. See also the discussion in ʿAlāl al-Fāsī, *Ḥafriyāt ʿan*

al-Ḥaraka al-dustūrīya fī al-maghrib qabla al-ḥimayā (Rabat, n.d.), pp. 20–23. For other versions of the conditions, in addition to the sources cited in n. 84 below, cf. A. Maitrot de la Motte Capron and Dr. Trenga, "Un correspondant de révolution," p. 22.

84. E. Michaux-Bellaire, "Une tentative de restauration idrissite à Fez," *RMM*, 7:393–423. According to Saint-Aulaire, one motivation of al-Kattānī's action was the fact that his subvention had recently been cut off by ʿAbd al-ʿAzīz. But this needs to be treated with caution. M.A.E. Maroc. n.s., vol. 187, Saint-Aulaire to Pichon, January 14, 1908, telegram no. 29. For a more favorable account of al-Kattānī's action, see Muḥammad Bāqir al-Kattānī, *Tarjamah Shaykh Muḥammad al-Kattānī al-Shāhid,* pp. 196–201.

85. *AF* (1908): 66.

86. A.G.P. Martin, *Quatre siècles,* p. 472.

87. On the ambivalence of the Zemmour, see A. Maitrot de la Motte Capron and Dr. Trenga, "Un correspondant de révolution," pp. 27, 43, 147–48.

88. The waverings of ʿAbd al-Karīm Wuld Abī Muḥammad Sharqī are revealed in ibid., pp. 23–24, 59, 140, 144, 165, 175–76, 182, 187–88, 191.

89. This was of course the system developed by Lyautey on the Algéro-Moroccan frontier. Weisgerber, *Au seuil,* pp. 159–67, discusses the Chaouia campaign. See also *AF* (1908): 64–65, 100–101, 134–35; Captain Paul Azan, *Souvenirs de Casablanca* (Paris, 1911). For the official account, see République française, Ministère de la Guerre, *Campagne de 1908–1909 en Chaouia. Rapport de Général d'Amade* (Paris, 1911).

90. A.G.P. Martin, *Quatre siècles,* p. 472. Also Lieutenant Colonel Huot, "La situation politique en Chaouia," *RGM* (1922): 107–24, 232–45.

91. Informant al-Ḥājj Aḥmad B., Sefrou, August 18, 1967, claimed to have gone together with other men from the Fez region (including many from the cities) to fight in the Chaouia. This wide participation has not previously been known. Also, see F.O. 174/257, Madden to Lister, March 9, 1909, no. 48.

92. A.G.P. Martin, *Quatre siècles,* p. 475, signals the importance of the d'Amade offensive.

93. Ibid., p. 481.

94. Ibid., pp. 481–83. Also Weisgerber, *Au seuil,* pp. 184–85.

95. The other sultans were Mawlāy Sulaymān (1792–1822) and Mawlāy al-Ḥasan (1873–94). See A.G.P. Martin, *Quatre siècles,* p. 484. The exact route followed by ʿAbd al-Ḥafīẓ is to be found in E. Michaux-Bellaire, "Itinéraire de Mouley Abd el Hafid de Marrakech à Fez, 1907–1908," *RMM* (1913): 270–74.

96. A.G.P. Martin, *Quatre siècles,* p. 450.

97. Ibid., pp. 479–80.

98. Ibid., p. 480. Also Anon., "Aux frontières de l'Algérie: le combat de Menabha et les opérations de la colonne Vigy," *AF* (1908): 179–83.

99. A.G.P. Martin, *Quatre siècles,* pp. 491–92. Martin mentions that the French took prisoners from as far away as the Hawz, the Sous, and Zaian. Uniformed troops of ʿAbd al-Ḥafīẓ also took part in the battle.

100. Dunn, *Morocco's Crisis of Conquest,* passim. The above account is heavily indebted to the work of Professor Dunn, including numerous personal communications.

101. A point forcefully made by A.G.P. Martin, *Quatre siècles,* pp. 479–80. One is reminded also of Doutté's prescient remark, "The *Saqīya al-Ḥamrā* is not at all [part of the] Sudan: it on the contrary has the closest ethnic, social and religious ties with all of North Africa" ("La situation politique dans le Houz," M.A.E. Maroc. n.s., vol. 187).

102. Ibid., p. 481.

103. *AF* (1908): 189.

104. Weisgerber, *Au seuil,* pp. 186–92, describes the final expedition of ʿAbd al-ʿAzīz. Also A.G.P. Martin, *Quatre siècles,* pp. 488–90.

105. A.G.P. Martin, *Quatre siècles,* pp. 493–94. As late as September 28, 1908, a French detachment led by Captain Verlet-Hanus and conducting a convoy of munitions left Casablanca for Marrakech. Its aim was to aid the city against the forces of ʿAbd al-Ḥafīẓ. Needless to say, it was too late.

106. Ibid., also *AF*(1908): 390–91.

107. Guerre, Série C-22, Mangin, "Notice sur Sidi Mohammed el Kettani cheikh de la zaouia des Kettaniyin," March 25, 1909.

108. *AF*(1908): 250–51.

109. A.G.P. Martin, *Quatre siècles,* pp. 484–85.

110. De Segonzac, *Au coeur de l'Atlas,* p. 229.

111. *AF* (1908): 250.

112. The chronology of events in *AF* (1908): 316–17, for the month of August reveals the slippage of Ḥafīẓ's control. Disaffection with his moderation of his tax increases appear to have been primarily responsible.

113. See Terrasse, *Histoire du Maroc,* 2:144–78 and Auguste Cour, *L'Etablissement des dynasties des chérifs au Maroc* (Paris, 1904), for the fifteenth-century resistance movements.

114. R. Mousnier, "The Fronde," in Robert Forster and Jack P. Greene, *Preconditions of Revolution in Early Modern Europe* (Baltimore and London, 1970), provides an excellent succinct account.

115. John R. Willis, "*Jihād fī Sabīl Allāh*—Its Doctrinal Basis in Islam and Some Aspects of Its Evolution in Nineteenth Century West Africa," *JAH* 8 (1967): 395–415.

116. A.G.P. Martin, *Quatre siècles.* chap. 11.

117. F.O. 413/48, Moulai Abd-el-Hafid to Mr. White, January 29, 1908, inclosure 2 in no. 91.

118. See the testimony of Jaurès in *Journal Officiel,* Débats Parlementaires, Chambre des Députés, Séance du 28 Janvier 1908, p. 141.

119. Compare the radicality of the movement of El Hiba in 1912, considered in Chapter 8, below.

CHAPTER SIX

1. For a brief sketch of Ben Ghabrit see Saint-Aulaire, *Confession d'un vieux diplomate,* pp. 89–90.

2. M.A.E. Maroc. n.s., vol. 194, Regnault to Quai d'Orsay, September 18, 1908, telegram no. 706, confidential. On the role of al-Munabbhi, F.O. 413/50, White to Grey, September 10, 1908, no. 232.

3. F.O. 413/50, White to Grey, September 19, 1908, no. 233.

4. The text of the note presented by the powers can be found in *RC* (1908): 260.

5. *Affaires du Maroc, 1908–1910,* 4, no. 81.

6. *AF* (1908): 391.

7. Among the French instigators was Gabriel Veyre. Maigret strongly advised Mawlāy Muḥammad not to allow himself to be led into such a project. M.A.E. Maroc. n.s., vol. 194, Maigret to Regnault, September 18, 1908, personal.

8. *AF* (1908): 416.

9. F.O. 413/50, White to Grey, August 26, 1908, no. 214.

10. Ibid., September 16, 1908, no. 232; *AF* (1908): 344.

11. F.O. 413/51, Lister to Grey, November 16, 1908, no. 288.

12. Forbes, *El Raisuni,* pp. 96–101. Also *AF* (1908): 414.

13. *Lisān al-Maghrib* was published on a press taken from the Beirut Catholic press and was financed by the German legation at Tangier. See ʿAbd al-Qādir al-Sahrāwī, "Jaridah Lisān al-Maghrib," *Al-Ahdāf,* March 6, 1965; also L. Mercier, "La presse musulmane," p. 620. The newspaper was in relation with the Turkish Committee on Union and Progress. See Christiane Souriau, "La presse maghribine, son évolution historique, sa situation en 1965, son organisation et ses problèmes actuels." Thèse complémentaire, Université d'Aix-Marseilles, 1967.

14. ʿAlāl al-Fāṣī, *Harakat al-Istiqlālīyah fī al-maghrib al-ʿArabī,* pp. 87–91.

15. The Arabic text may be found in ʿAbd al-Karīm Ghallāb, *Difaʿan ʿan al-dimuqrātīya* (Tangier, 1966). For a French translation, see Jacques Robert, *La Monarchie marocaine* (Paris, 1963), appendix 1. An English translation of the Turkish constitution of 1908 can be found in *The American Journal of International Law* (1908), part 2, supplement, pp. 367–87.

16. Ibn al-Mawāz was the author of the conditional bayʿa of 1908 (according to al-Fāsī). During the reign of ʿAbd al-ʿAzīz he was the first secretary to al-Gharīt. In 1909 he conducted a peace mission to Madrid. ʿAbd al-Ḥafīẓ al-Fāsī later became known as a leading salafīya intellectual, author of *Riyād al-Janna aw al-mudhish al-mutrib,* 2 vols (Fez, A.H. 1350). The others are lesser-known figures. Cf. ʿAlāl al-Fāsī, pp. 87–88. Also, al-Fāsī, *Ḥafriyāt ʿan al-ḥaraka al-dustūrīya.*

17. See Louis Mercier, "La presse arabe au Maroc," *RMM* (1909): 128–33. On the creation of a makhzan-sponsored paper at Fez, see also Lawrence Harris, *With Mulai Hafid at Fez,* pp. 88–92, 158–59. Harris was

asked by the sultan to help start a paper, but refused. Only then did the sultan turn to Daḥdaḥ and Vaffier-Pollet.

18. Guerre, Série C-22, Mangin to Guerre, February 4, 1909, no. 9.

19. Ibid., March 25, 1909, no. 24, Also *Affaires du Maroc, 1908–1910,* 5, no. 155.

20. Informant Mohand N'Hamusha at Bou Derbala, August 8, 1967.

21. F.O. 174/268, Macleod to Lowther, March 23, 1909, no. 18.

22. Guerre, Série C-22, Mangin to Guerre, April 3, 1909, no. 26.

23. F.O. 174/270, Macleod to Lowther, November 22, 1909, no. 39, political.

24. Abun-Nasr, "The Salafiyya Movement," pp. 97–98.

25. Paquignon, "Un livre de Moulay Abd al Hafid, *RMM* 7 (1909): 125–28. Cf. also above, Chapter 5, n. 5.

26. ʿAlāl al-Fāsī, *Ḥadīth al-mashriq fī al maghrib* (Cairo, 1956), p. 10. On al-Dukāllī, cf. Abun-Nasr, "The Salafiyya Movement," also Jacques Berque, "Ça et là," 2:480–83.

27. F.O. 413/42, Lister to Grey, March 7, 1911, no. 40. According to Abun-Nasr, "The Salafiyya Movement," p. 98, the title of the book was *Kashf al-qināʿ ʿan iʿtiqad tawāʾif al-ibtidāʿ* (Fez, 1909). Also Guerre, Série C-22, Mangin, "Notice sur Sidi Mohammed el Kettani," March 25, 1909.

28. Guerre, Série C-22, Mangin to Guerre, July 2, 1909, no. 58. Also *AF* (1909): 186–87.

29. J. Ladreit de Lacharrière, "L'Action de la France au Maroc après l'accord Franco-Allemand," *Revue Politique et Parlementaire* (1912): 61.

30. *AF* (1909): 222–23.

31. Guerre, Série C-22, Mangin to Guerre, June 4, 1909, no. 47. Also *AF* (1909): 222–23.

32. F.O. 174/268, Macleod to Grey, June 18, 1909, no. 24, political, confidential. Also *Affaires du Maroc, 1908–1910,* 5, no. 197, and *AF* (1909): 186.

33. On the later career of Abū Ḥimāra, see E. Maitrot de la Motte Capron, "Le Roghi," pp. 514–76; E. Maldonado, *El Rogui;* and Forbes, *El Raisuni.* His capture and death have been given in a number of versions. See Guerre, Série C-22, Mangin to Guerre, August 12, 1909, no. 75 and Sedira to Mangin, August 22, 1909, no. 53, for the French version; F.O. 174/270, Macleod to Lister, August 16, 1909, no. 29, political, and August 30, 1909, no. 38, political, for the British version.

34. *AF* (1909): 262–63, 296. A map of the terrain can be found in E. Vincent, "Trois semaines à Mellila," *AF* (1909): 307–11.

35. F.O. 174/270, Macleod to Lister, August 5, 1909, no. 28, political.

36. Guerre, Série C-22, Mangin to Guerre, October 3, 1909, no. 89.

37. *AF* (1909): 327–28, 355–57.

38. *Affaires du Maroc, 1908–1910,* 5, no. 107.

39. The text of the provisional Chaouia accord may be found in *Affaires du Maroc, 1908–1910,* 5, no. 150. The stages of the negotiation process are covered in nos. 112, 120, 129, 144, and 145 of the same volume.

40. The provisional accord on the frontiers is in ibid., no. 161. Cf. also nos. 133, 141, and 154.

41. Ibid., nos. 124 and 142.

42. Ibid., nos. 159, and 164, including the procès-verbaux.

43. The other Moroccan members of the embassy to Paris were Muḥammad ibn ʿAbdullāh al-Marākishī, and Amīn al-Ḥājj Ḥamid al-Muqrī. Ibid., no. 171.

44. Ibid., no. 249.

45. The French note can be found in ibid., no. 314. The Moroccan reply is in no. 323.

46. *AF* (1909): 296. On ʿAbd al-Ḥafīẓ's earlier dealings with the Mannesmann brothers, Guillen, *L'Allemagne et le Maroc,* pp. 487–88. The dissertation of Neil Lewis on German-Moroccan relations, 1905–1914 (Department of History, University of Michigan) can be expected to provide needed clarifications on the Mannesmann connection.

47. Campini arrived at Fez on November 17, 1909. On him see E. De Leone, *La Colonizzazione dell 'Africa del Nord* (Padova, 1960), 2:70, 101. Also *AF* (1909): 429–30.

48. Jean Deny, "Instructeurs militaires turcs au Maroc sous Moulay Hafidh," *Memorial Henri Basset* (Paris, 1928), 1:218–22 gives the general outlines of the episode from the reminiscences of a Turkish participant; also, Guerre, Série C-22, Mangin to Guerre, November 20, 1909, no. 99. For a more general view, see my "Pan-Islam and Moroccan Resistance."

49. Guerre, Série C-22, Mangin to Guerre, November 20, 1909, no. 99.

50. *AF* (1910): 141. Also Guerre, Série C-22, Mangin to Guerre, April 1, 1910, no. 20.

51. Deny, "Instructeurs militaires turcs," p. 224. The German estimate of these pan-Islamic tendencies is to be found in A.A. Marokko 4, Bd. 190 A7984, press clipping from the *Berliner Neueste Nachrichten* of May 19, 1911 (article by H. Walter). Also, A.A. Marokko 4, Bd. 191 A8517, Seckendorff to Bethman-Hollweg, May 29, 1911. I wish to thank Professor Neil Lewis for these last two references.

52. Deny, "Instructeurs militaires turcs," pp. 224–25.

53. *Affaires du Maroc, 1908–1910,* 5, no. 389.

54. Ibid., nos. 396, 413, 415, 423.

55. Ibid., no. 426.

56. Ibid., nos. 439, 458.

57. *AF* (1910): 349—50. Herbert Feis, *Europe, the World's Banker* (New York, 1965), pp. 410–11. The loan was purchased by the banks at 89 million francs, sold to the public at 97, and bore a face value of 107 million francs. Once again there were windfall profits for the bankers in interest and commissions.

58. See the tables of prices of fifty common consumer items for the period 1896–1909 prepared by James Macleod, British Consul at Fez. F.O. 174/267, Macleod to Gray, October 26, 1906, no. 52; and F.O. 174/283, Macleod to Grey, May 21, 1914, no. 6. (Prices in constant pounds.)

59. F.O. 174/270, Macleod to Grey, October 6, 1909, no. 73.

60. The French in fact largely took over the negotiations. Si Kaddour Ben Ghabrit was temporarily attached to the French embassy at Madrid, and important details were ventilated first at the Quai d'Orsay. Henri Marchat, "Les origines diplomatiques du 'Maroc Espagnol,' " *ROMM* no. 7, (1970): 140–46. Also, *Affaires du Maroc, 1910–1912,* nos. 16, 21 (text).

61. F.O. 174/270, Macleod to Lister, August 16, 1909, no. 30, Political. Since none of the men tortured were Fāsīs, there was no public response from the elite of the city.

62. F.O. 174/271, Macleod to Lister, letters of June 20, and July 29, 1910, nos. 34 and 37, respectively. *Affaires du Maroc,* 1908–1910, 5, no. 478.

63. *Affaires du Maroc, 1908–1910,* 5, nos. 460, 475, 478. *AF* (1910): 297.

64. This classificatory system became a bone of contention between the military and the French legation at Tangier, a part of the split between the two approaches to Morocco which persisted until 1912. Guerre, Série EM-2, de Billy to Moinier, February 7, 1911, no. 16.

65. Even had it wished to intervene, there is doubt that the makhzan could have done much to change the situation. *AF* (1910): 271–72. On French interests in the Gharb, see J. Le Coz, *Le Gharb,* 1: 357–58. Also, *Affaires du Maroc, 1908–1910,* 5, no. 339.

66. *AF* (1910): 351.

67. Killed in the ambush was a French lieutenant. *AF* (1910): 105–6.

68. Guerre, Série EM-2, Moinier to Regnault, April 25, 1910, no. 200.

69. F.O. 174/271, Macleod to Grey, January 19, 1910, no. 1, political, confidential.

70. F.O. 174/258, Madden to Lister, April 9, 1910, no. 49.

71. The new military regulations are outlined in F.O. 174/271, Macleod to Grey, November 11, 1910, no. 84 confidential. Also *Affaires du Maroc, 1910–1912,* 6, no. 17.

72. F.O. 174/271, Macleod to Grey, November 11, 1910, no. 84, confidential. Also, Guerre, Série C-22, Mangin to Guerre, November 1, 1910; no. 81.

Chapter Seven

1. F.O. 174/271, Macleod to Lister, July 25, 1910, no. 53, presents a full list of these changes. Si ʿAissa ibn ʿUmar remained vizier of complaints, Tayyib al-Muqrī was vizier of finance, Muḥammad al-Glawī was ʿAllāf, and the Ḥājjib was al-Ḥājj Aḥmad ibn Mubarak al-Shawī al-Krīsī.

2. The profitability of reform projects to well-placed ministers is a phenomenon long noted in the Middle East. On the wealth of al-Glawī see Guerre, Série C-22, Brémond to Guerre, May 1, 1910, no. 34.

3. The trend toward dividing the chief offices between the two families was first noticed by Mangin in Guerre, Série C-22, Mangin to Guerre, February 1, 1910, no. 10, wherein the hostility of the two toward France is noted. Al-Muqrī is singled out as having always been against reforms "d'allure algérien" even when he was with ʿAbd al-ʿAzīz at Rabat.

4. Guerre, Série C-22, Mangin to Guerre, January 1, 1911, no. 1, notes that the gifts presented at the ʿId al-Kabīr ceremonies in December reflected the wealth of the south. Tribal delegations from the north and the ports presented a total of 85,000 douros, against 150,000 douros presented by the tribes of the Marrakech region.

5. Guerre, Série C-22, Mangin to Guerre, October 1, 1910, no. 72.

6. Charles René-Leclerc, "L'année administrative marocaine en 1910," *AF* (1911): 96.

7. *AF* (1911): 75.

8. M.A.E. Maroc. n.s., vol. 210, de Billy to Pichon, February 15, 1911, no. 137, enclosing Gaillard to de Billy, February 8, 1911. Madanī al-Glawī, for his part, sought to improve relations with the French as a hedge against uncertainty.

9. *AF* (1911): 44, 75, 115–16.

10. F.O. 174/259, Madden to Lister, February 18, 1911, no. 34.

11. M.A.E. Maroc, n.s., vol. 64, de Billy to Cruppi, April 1, 1911, no. 271, annex.

12. M.A.E. Maroc. n.s., vol. 64, Marc to de Billy, April 24, 1911, personal. In the same letter it is reported that the activities of German firms in the Sous had greatly increased recently and that they were making extensive land purchases near Agadir.

13. Mission Scientifique du Maroc, *Rabat et sa région,* vol. 3, *Les tribus* (Paris, 1920), pp. 125–74.

14. M.A.E. Maroc. n.s., vol. 210, "Note relative à la question des Zaer," February 15, 1911.

15. Guerre, Série C-23, Mangin to Guerre, February 1, 1911, no. 14.

16. F.O. 413/54, Macleod to Lister, February 21, 1911, no. 14, confidential. Macleod speculates as to whether Mangin and his staff have any idea of how important the *manner* of reform is in a country like Morocco.

17. F.O. 413/54, Macleod to Lister, June 9, 1911, no. 43, confidential.

18. See my paper "The Tribal Factor in North African History: The Ait Ndhir and Morocco, 1900–1914," presented to the Second Annual Meeting of the Middle East Studies Association, Austin, Texas, November, 1968 (forthcoming).

19. Guerre, Série EM-2/A[1], de Billy to Branlière, March 2, 1911, no. 28.

20. *Affaires du Maroc,* 6, no. 493, especially pp. 446–47. The report also appears in *RC* (1911): 257–64. Cf. also F.O. 413/54, Macleod to Lister, February 28, 1911, no. 15.

21. *Affaires du Maroc,* 6, no. 493.

22. Ibid., p. 447.

23. F.O. 413/54, Macleod to Lister, March 13, 1911, private. Also *Affaires du Maroc* 6, no. 493, p. 448.

24. F.O. 174/271, Macleod to Grey, April 7, 1911, no. 2, political, confidential.

25. It was recognized by both the French and British consuls that the withdrawal of the Cherarda maḥalla would leave Fez cut off from the coast.

Cf. *Affaires du Maroc,* 6, no. 144. Also F.O. 431/54, McLeod to Lister, March 29, 1911, private.

26. F.O. 413/54, Lister to Grey, March 5, 1911, no. 33.

27. Ibid., Macleod to Lister, April 8, 1911, no. 3. There is some dispute over the new demands. Mangin includes abolition of the maks, evacuation by the makhzan of the two forts overlooking Fez, and the abdication of the sultan. Guerre, Série C-23, Mangin to Guerre, April 10, 1911, no. 36.

28. There is some reason to believe that Mawlāy Zayn may have been a stand-in for ʿAbd al-ʿAzīz. See F.O. 413/54, Rattigan to Grey, April 30, 1911, no. 99. On Mawlāy Zayn see Guerre, Série C-23, Mangin to Guerre, April 20, 1911, no. 38, and F.O. 174/271, Macleod to Lister, May 1, 1911, no. 26. Also, *AF* (1911): 184–85.

29. F.O. 174/271, Macleod to Lister, May 1, 1911, no. 26, enclosing a letter from Aḥmad Mikwār. Also, *AF* (1911): 184–85.

30. *Affaires du Maroc,* 6, no. 252.

31. *Affaires du Maroc,* 6, no. 493.

32. The letters were published in *The Times* (London) May 8 and 9, 1911.

33. The correspondence of the pretender is preserved most completely in the German correspondence. A.A. A 1. Marokko 7. no. 1/5, Seckendorff to Bethmann-Hollweg, May 14, 1911, encloses two letters. Cf. also his letters of May 29, 1911, no. 175, and June 2, 1911, no. 183. For the British relations with Mawlāy Zayn see F.O. 413/54, Lister to Grey, May 14, 1911, no. 116, confidential.

34. F.O. 413/54, White to Grey, June 14, 1911, no. 159.

35. Ibid.

36. Guerre, Série C-23, Mangin to Guerre, May 24, 1911, no. 44.

37. F.O. 174/271, Macleod to Grey, April 7, 1911, no. 2, political, confidential.

38. *Affaires du Maroc,* 6, no. 493.

39. Ibid.

40. On the size of the rebel groups, see Guerre, Série C-23, Mangin to Guerre, May 2, 1911, no. 41. On the practice of tribesmen relaying one another on military duty, cf. F.O. 174/271, Macleod to Grey, April 7, 1911, no. 2, political, confidential.

41. The head of the Moroccan garrison, Ben Jilāli, passed 1,200 rifles to the rebels after the battle of March 7, Guerre, Série C-23, Brémond to Guerre, "Note au sujet de la dernière insurrection," July 24, 1911, no. 464.

42. *Affaires du Maroc,* 6, no. 493. The story of the relief of Fez is related in its entirety by Paul Azan, *L'Expédition de Fez* (Paris, 1924).

43. *Affaires du Maroc,* 6, no. 25.

44. Ibid., no. 43.

45. Ibid., no. 61.

46. Ibid., no. 67.

47. Ibid., no. 69, annex.

48. Ibid., no. 105.

49. Ibid., no. 106. The following quote is also from this source.

50. Ibid., no. 48.

51. Mawlāy Ḥafīẓ first learned of the projected Zaer expedition in the *Dépêche Marocaine*. M.A.E. Maroc. n.s., vol. 210, de Billy to Pichon, February 22, 1911, no. 72, telegram. Also the letter of February 6, 1911, no. 107, where the sultan expresses his fears of the consequences of the expedition.

52. *Affaires du Maroc,* 6, no. 102.

53. Ibid., no. 116.

54. The de Monis government is discussed in Jacques Chastenet, *Histoire de la Troisième République* (Paris, 1955), 4:77–78. For the estimation of a participant, Joseph Caillaux, *Mes Mémoires* (Paris, 1943), 2:43–49.

55. F.O. 413/54, Lister to Grey, March 5, 1911, no. 34, confidential.

56. *AF* (1911): 75.

57. *Affaires du Maroc,* 6, no. 69, annex.

58. Maurice LeGlay, who was with the Cherarda maḥalla notes the surprising arrival of Ben Ghabrit. See his *Chronique marocaine* (Paris, 1933), pp. 75–76.

59. *Affaires du Maroc,* 6, no. 172.

60. J. Caillaux, *Mémoires,* pp. 64–67, and A. Messimy, *Mes Souvenirs* (Paris, 1937), pp. 55–56, report the circumstances of the decision. For a fuller discussion see Andrew and Kanya-Forstner, "The French 'Colonial Party,' " pp. 122–25.

61. *Affaires du Maroc,* 6, no. 185.

62. Ibid., no. 252.

63. M.A.E. Maroc. n.s., vol. 223, de Billy to Cruppi, May 8, 1911, no. 307.

64. *Affaires du Maroc,* 6, no. 280.

65. Guerre. Série C-23, Mangin to Guerre, April 30, 1911, no. 40.

66. *Affaires du Maroc,* 6, no. 314.

67. Macleod reports that until the last minute the people of Fez believed that they were being rescued by al-ʿAmrānī's maḥalla. Two hours before the French arrived, criers went around saying "the maḥalla of our lord is entering, decorate your shops!" A large crowd went out to greet the delivering forces and were devastated to discover that it was the French. F.O. 413/54, Lister to Grey, June 1, 1911, citing a Macleod despatch.

68. Houel, *Mes aventures marocaines,* pp. 219–20.

69. *Affaires du Maroc,* 6, no. 341.

70. In fact, the attack on El Ksar was a manufactured affair. F.O. 413/54, Lister to Grey, June 10, 1911, no. 152. On the Spanish government's diplomatic campaign, see Henry Marchat, "Les origines diplomatiques du 'Maroc Espagnol' (1880–1912)," *ROMM,* no. 7 (1970): 101–70, especially p. 155.

71. The Moroccan government protested against what it called "Spanish aggression," *Affaires du Maroc,* 6, no. 396. On the French response, *Affaires du Maroc,* 6, no. 364.

72. Marchat, "Les origines diplomatiques," pp. 155–70.

73. *Affaires du Maroc,* 6, no. 399.

74. For a comprehensive view of the Agadir crisis, see I. M. Barlow, *The Agadir Crisis* (Chapel Hill, N.C., 1940).

75. For the text of the Franco-German accord of November 4, 1911, see *Affaires du Maroc,* 6, no. 644.

76. There is an additional question which can be posed: Why was it thought necessary to sign a formal protectorate treaty? Why could there not have been a gradual transition to a de facto protectorate similar to the methods which the British pursued in Egypt? The November 4, 1911, Franco-German accord would appear to have removed the last roadblock in the way of such a development by removing German objections to French predominance in Morocco. According to Macleod, even Lyautey professed himself mystified by the insistence on a written document. F.O. 174/270, Macleod to Lister, July 16, 1912, personal, confidential.

77. *AF* (1911): 206–11, "La délivérance de Fez et les opérations de pacification." Also Azan, *L'Expédition de Fez,* pp. 99–168.

78. F.O. 174/271, Macleod to Lister, July 10, 1911, no. 61, on wireless installation at Fez.

79. Azan, *L'Expédition de Fez,* pp. 169–82, and 257–76, gives the details on the construction of these two forts, and the purposes they were built for.

80. *AF* (1911): 208–11, on the operations in eastern Morocco.

81. Azan, *L'Expédition de Fez,* pp. 102–4.

82. Ibid., pp. 104–6.

83. Weisgerber, *Au seuil,* pp. 261–62. The same criticism was made by ʿAbd al-Ḥafīẓ in an interview with Hubert Jacques in *Le Matin,* May 3, 1912, following the April 17 mutiny at Fez.

84. Azan, *L'Expédition de Fez,* pp. 105–6.

85. ʿAbd al-Ḥafīẓ's complaints are fully aired in Guerre, Série E-2, Mercier to de Billy, January 12, 1912 (number lacking). The interviews which the sultan accorded Hubert Jacques in April and May, 1912, contain a clear view of his attitude; see *Le Matin,* April 8, 1912, and May 3, 1912. The sultan's good faith may be called into question in certain of his statements, but their import is clear.

86. Guerre, Série C-24, de Lamothe, May 1, 1912, no. 705R.

87. F.O. 174/270, Macleod to Lister, April 9, 1912, no. 24, discusses the quality of the native-affairs officers and military instructors.

88. F.O. 174/271, Macleod to White, July 17, 1911, private.

89. On Mangin's attitude cf. Guerre, Série C-22, Mangin to Guerre, January 1, 1910 [1911], no. 1. Gaillard's view is in *Affaires du Maroc,* 6, no. 493.

90. F.O. 413/55, Lennox to Madden, June 24, 1911, no. 178, enclosure no. 2. Also Madden to White, June 24, 1911, no. 116, on the dangers of a jihād as a result of the firing of all of the Glawa family.

91. F.O. 413/55, Lister to Grey, October 22, 1911, no. 329, for the British role in the rehabilitation of al-Ḥājj Tahamī.

92. F.O. 371/1162, White to Grey, June 17, 1911, no. 163.

93. Guerre, Série C-24, Brémond to Guerre, February 1, 1912, no. 30. Also *AF* (1912): 112–13.

94. F.O. 413/55, Lister to Grey, October 22, 1911, no. 329; and Lister to Grey, November 12, 1911, no. 337.

95. F.O. 174/270, Macleod to Lister, February 15, 1912, no. 9. Guerre, Série E-2, Moinier to Guerre, December 30, 1911, no. 19.

96. F.O. 413/56, White to Grey, March 9, 1912, no. 49.

97. F.O. 174/270, Macleod to Lister, February 15, 1912, no. 9.

98. Guerre, Série C-24, de Lamothe, May 1, 1912, no. 705R. Also Simon to Moinier, April 25, 1912. F.O. 174/270, Macleod to White, March 16, 1912, no. 17, reports the sultan's anger at the French military for collecting the tartīb at Meknes.

Chapter Eight

1. The following have been found especially suggestive: Y. Porath, "The Peasant Revolt of 1858–1861 in Kisrawan," *Asian and African Studies Annual* 2 (1966): 77–157; P. Shinar, "ʿAbd al-Qadir and ʿAbd al-Krīm: Religious Influences on Their Thought and Action," *Asian and African Studies* 1 (1965): 139–74; B. Slama, *L'Insurrection de 1864* (Tunis, 1967); and A. Vinogradov, "The 1920 Revolt in Iraq: the Role of Tribes in National Politics," *IJMES* (1972).

2. Guerre, Série C-24, "Rapport sur les événements de Fez," May 1, 1912, no. 705R.

3. The circumstances of the signing of the treaty are discussed in F.O. 174/270, Macleod to Grey, March 29, 1912, no. 5, political, confidential.

4. F.O. 174/270, Macleod to Grey, April 6, 1912, no. 7, political, confidential. For comparison of the two treaties, see *AF* (1912): 131–32. The other alternative plans are to be found in M.A.E. Maroc. n.s., vol. 219.

5. F.O. 174/270, Macleod to White, March 7, 1912, no. 14, confidential.

6. For a detailed criticism of the protectorate treaty, see F.O. 174/270, Macleod to Grey, March 29, 1912, no. 5, political, confidential.

7. F. Weisgerber, *Au seuil,* pp. 272–73.

8. F.O. 174/270, Macleod to Grey, April 29, 1912, no. 9, political, confidential. Also, Weisgerber, *Au seuil,* pp. 271–72.

9. Weisgerber, *Au seuil,* pp. 278–79.

10. The general problem as it affected the colonies is discussed in "Dans l'Armée d'Afrique," *AF* (1911): 376–80.

11. The most recent and authoritative discussion is by Charles-Robert Ageron, *Les Algériens musulmans et la France,* 2 vols. (Paris, 1968) 2:1056–78.

12. There is a good discussion of the "force noire" concept in *AF* (1912): 125–30. Also R. Payn, "Les contingents auxiliares et les goums en A. O. F.," *RC* (1911): 285–90, and C. Mangin's memoirs, *Regards sur la France d'Afrique* (Paris, 1924).

13. For a brief history of the goums, see General Spillmann, "Les goums

mixtes marocains," *Revue historique de l'Armée* (1952): 137–53. See also H. Simon, "La naissance et la jeunesse des goums mixtes marocains," *Revue Nord-Sud* (1934), and more generally, A. Cour, *EI*[1] s.v. "Qawm."

14. On the plan to recruit a makhzan force at Marrakech, see Guerre, Série E-2, E. Mangin, "Note sur la formation de troupes chèrifiennes à Marrakech," August 21, 1911.

15. For a general discussion of the sharifian army, see "L'organisation de l'armée chérifienne," *AF* (1912): 142–43. Also Colonel Frisch, "Au Maroc avant le Protectorat. L'organisation des troupes," *Le Temps,* March 5, 1912.

16. Guerre, Série C-24, de Lamothe, "Rapport sur les événements de Fez du 17, 18, et 19 Avril 1912," May 1, 1912, no. 705R.

17. F.O. 174/270, Macleod to Grey, April 29, 1912, no. 9, political, confidential.

18. Ibid., Macleod to White, March 22, 1912, no. 20, confidential.

19. The text of the letter is contained in ibid., Macleod to Grey, April 29, 1912, no. 9, political. confidential, inclosure no. 2.

20. The Fez mutiny is discussed in ibid., Macleod to Grey, April 29, 1912, no. 9, political, confidential. See also *AF* (1912): 172–78; Weisgerber, *Au seuil,* pp. 281–99; and Hubert Jacques, *Les journées sanglantes de Fez 17–18–19 Avril 1912* (Paris, 1913). Only two of the six tabors remained loyal.

21. F.O. 174/270, Macleod to Grey, April 29, 1912, no. 9, political, confidential; Guerre, Série C-24, de Lamothe, "Rapport sur les événements de Fez," May 1, 1912, no. 705R, and H. Simon to Moinier, April 25, 1912.

22. A. A. Al Marokko no. 4-204, Proebster to Seckendorff, June 6, 1912, no. 156.

23. Raymond Poincaré, *Au service de la France,* vol. 1, *Le lendemain d'Agadir 1912* (Paris, 1926), p. 99.

24. See for example, M.A.E. Maroc. n.s., vol. 222, Regnault to Poincaré, May 9, 1912, private. The eighteen months which Regnault spent in Paris from the fall of 1910 until the spring of 1912 in preparing the Moroccan education of the different ministers who succeeded one another at the Quai d'Orsay during that period could better have been spent, critics averred, in completing his own. "L'Affaire morocaine," *Les Débats,* May 1, 1912.

25. Ibid., pp. 99–100.

26. Poincaré, *Au service,* pp. 98–99.

27. Saint-Aulaire, *Confession d'un vieux diplomate,* pp. 238–41.

28. Weisgerber, *Au seuil,* pp. 296, 300–301.

29. F.O. 174/270, Macleod to Grey, April 29, 1912, no. 9, political, confidential.

30. Ibid., Macleod to Lister, May 23, 1912, no. 40, mentions a total of 120 people executed as of that date, in the repression which followed the riots.

31. Ibid., May 9, 1912, no. 32.

32. Ibid., May 18, 1912, no. 39. Also the intelligence reports for May in Guerre, Série B-4.

33. Guerre, Série B-4, Bulletin de Renseignements, May 15, 1912, no. 52 and ff. Informant, Mohand N'Hamusha, interview of August 8, 1967, at Bou Derbala.

34. On the attitude of ʿAbd al-Hafiz, see his interviews with Hubert Jacques, *Le Matin* (Paris), May 3 and 24, 1912, and the excerpts in *AF* (1912): 181–82. Also F.O. 174/270, Macleod to Lister, May 11, 1912, no. 35, and Pierre Lyautey, "L'abdication de Moulay Hafid," *RDM* (1953): 609–18.

35. Guerre, Série C-24, Simon to Moinier, April 25, 1912.

36. In addition to the intelligence reports in Guerre, Série B-4, cf. "Deux agitateurs marocains, le Roghi et al Hajjami," *AF* (1914): 210–14.

37. F.O. 174/270, Macleod to Lister, May 18, 1912, no. 39, and Macleod to Lister, May 24, 1912, no. 41. Information on alliance mechanisms is derived from an interview, Mohand N'Hamusha, Bou Derbala, August 8, 1967.

38. F.O. 174/270, Macleod to Lister, May 25, 1912, no. 42, describes the entry of Lyautey into Fez.

39. Poincaré, *Au service,* p. 102. When the dispatch which contained this phrase was published by a Parisian daily, a minor political crisis resulted.

40. F.O. 174/270, Macleod to Lister, May 26, 1912, no. 44. Cf. also Weisgerber, *Au seuil,* pp. 300–306. For a retrospective view of the siege, see F.O. 174/272, Macleod to Grey, August 6, 1912, no. 11, political. confidential.

41. A French translation of the battle plan, together with a narrative of the events, can be found in *AF* (1912): 215–18. Cf. also P. Lyautey, *Lyautey l'Africain,* 1:22–24.

42. Guerre, Série A²6, Moinier, "Opérations autour de Sefrou," August 1, 1912.

43. F.O. 174/270, Macleod to Lister, June 18, 1912, private. Also Macleod to Lister, June 21, 1912, no. 67, and Macleod to Lister, July 4, 1912, no. 79.

44. Guerre, Serie A²6, Lyautey to War Ministry, June 22, 1912, no. 115BM¹. The text may also be found in P. Lyautey, *Lyautey l'Africain,* 1:20.

45. The Lyautey program of June 1912 may be found in *AF* (1912): 218–19. Also, F.A.T. MSS 5955/3, "Le Protectorat Marocain: Un an de Protectorat," Rabat, June 12, 1913, pp. 426–430.

46. French occupation troops in western Morocco totalled 32,050 Frenchmen and 5,651 native auxiliaries; those in eastern Morocco numbered 11,266 Frenchmen and 560 native auxiliaries. Figures cited by Raymond Poincaré, *Journal Officiel,* Chambre des Députés, 1er Séance, 1 Juillet 1912, p. 1854.

47. On changes in French policy toward Fez, see Macleod's reports for

the period, especially F.O. 174/270, Macleod to Lister, May 29, 1912, no. 48, confidential; June 21, 1912, no. 51; June 29, 1912, no. 76, confidential; and July 20, 1912, personal, confidential.

48. Ibid., July 20, 1912, personal.

49. F.O. 174/272, Macleod to Kennard, August 31, 1912, private. The timing and symbolism of this act was exquisite. ʿAbd al-Hāyy al-Kattānī was later to achieve notoriety as one of the key figures in the deposition of Muḥammad V in 1953.

50. M.A.E. Maroc. n.s., vol. 224, Lyautey to Poincaré, July 6, 1912, no. 46.

51. The majlis had been in the planning stages since the occupation of Fez in May 1911. Consul Gaillard had been its principal exponent. It was resurrected after the arrival of Lyautey and formally presented to the aʿyān of Fez on July 24, 1912. F.A.T. MSS 5953/4, "Medjless El Medina," July 24, 1912. Also, F.A.T. MSS 5955/8, "Ville de Fez. Medjles el Baladi ou Conseil Municipal," 1913, and F.O. 174/272, Macleod to Kennard, September 12, 1912, no. 101. On the elections, F.A.T. MSS 5955/2, Anon. to Lyautey, September 18, 1912, no. 94.

52. The early difficulties of French forces in the area are discussed in our "The Image of the Moroccan State in French Ethnological Literature: New Light on the Origins of Lyautey's Berber Policy," in Ernest Gellner and Charles Micaud, eds., *Arabs and Berbers. Ethnicity and Nation-Building in North Africa* (London and New York, 1972), 175–199.

53. *AF* (1912): 352–53. Also, M.A.E. Maroc, Affaires Politiques. Rapports politiques du Protectorat, May 1912–June 1914.

54. F.O. 371/1408, Madden to Lister, May 30, 1912, no. 89.

55. F.O. 174/270, Macleod to Lister, June 16, 1912, private, confidential.

56. *La Vigie Marocaine* (Casablanca), June 14 and 15, 1912.

57. Both Weisgerber and Verlet-Hanus have left published records of their participation in the mission. For the former, Weisgerber, *Au seuil,* 322–48, and for the latter, Henri Simon, *Un officier d'Afrique; le Commandant Verlet-Hanus* (Paris, 1930). Also Guerre, Série A²-6, "Rapport sur les événements de Marrakech (Aout-Septembre 1912)," October 1, 1912.

58. C. Mangin, *Regards sur la France d'Afrique,* and *AF* (1912): 347–56.

59. Saint-Aulaire, *Confession,* pp. 246–63, and *AF* (1912): 347–56. Cf. the abdication of Mawlāy Muḥammad ibn ʿArafa in 1953. Joseph Luccioni, "L'eloignement de Sidi Mohammed ben Arafa du trône des Alaouites en Septembre 1955," *ROMM* (1970): 101–12.

60. *AF* (1912): 354–56.

61. F.O. 836/1, contains correspondence relating to the political situation at Marrakech in 1912.

62. F.O. 174/270, Macleod to Lister, June 6, 1912, no. 60, confidential.

63. F.O. 413/57, Kennard to Grey, August 11, 1912, no. 214. Mawlāy ʿAbd al-Ḥafīẓ's four-year-old son, Mawlāy Idrīs, was also mentioned as a possible candidate.

64. Saint-Aulaire, *Confession,* pp. 251–63.

65. F.O. 371/1409, Verdon to Lister, letters of July 21 and 24, 1912, private. Verdon was the sultan's British physician.

66. The preliminary terms of the abdication were worked out during the preceding winter by notes of November 8, 1911, and December 19, 1911, from the French government and by subsequent negotiations. See M.A.E. Maroc. n.s., vol. 221, Regnault to ʿAbd al-Ḥafīẓ, May 18, 1912. Debate over the terms continued between the French government and Ḥafīẓ even after his abdication. See also F.O. 413/57, Kennard to Lister, August 16, 1912, no. 218, and F.O. 174/272, Macleod to Kennard, October 24, 1912, confidential.

67. A.G.P. Martin, *Quatre siècles,* p. 576, notes the breaking of the seal and parasol. Also, *AF* (1912): 347–49, and Pierre Lyautey, "L'abdication de Moulay Hafid," *RDM* (1953): 609–18.

68. M.A.E. Maroc. n.s., vol. 64, French Legation to Quai d'Orsay, April 1, 1911, no. 271, annex. For a brief biography of El Hiba see Robert de Segonzac, "El Hiba fils de Ma El Ainin," *RC* (1917); 62–69, 90–94. Also "El Hiba et les Allemands," *AF* (1918): 28, where his full name is given.

69. M.A.E. Maroc. n.s., vol. 64, Consul, Mogador to de Billy, April 24, 1911, private.

70. M.A.E. Maroc. n.s., vol. 224, Marc to Lyautey, May 28, 1912, no. 1. Based on the information of an informer in Tiznit. Also *La Vigie Marocaine* (Casablanca) September 5, 1912, and J. Ladreit de Lacharrière, "Grandeur et décadence de Mohammed el Hibba, sultan bleu," *BSGA* (1912): 473–86, the latter a highly partisan account.

71. M.A.E. Maroc n.s., vol. 226, Lyautey to Quai d'Orsay, August 30, 1912, no. 457 B.M.[1], enclosing Hof to Lyautey, August 23, 1912.

72. ʿAbbās ibn Ibrāhīm al-Marākishī, *al-iʿlām bī man ḥall marakish wā aghmāt min al-Aʿlām.* 5 vols. (Fez, 1936) 2:290–91.

73. The preceding discussion is based primarily upon ibid., 2:291–96. The most useful treatment of the doctrine of jihād is John R. Willis, "*Jihād fī Sabīl Allāh*—Its Doctrinal Basis in Islam and some Aspects of Its Evolution in Nineteenth Century West Africa," *JAH* 8, no. 3 (1967): 395–415.

74. For a partial list of the sons of Mā al-ʿAynayn, see R. de Segonzac, "El Hiba," p. 64; J. Caro Boroja, "Un Santon Sahariano" p. 313.

75. M.A.E. Maroc. n.s. vol. 226, Lyautey to Quai d'Orsay, August 30, 1912, no. 457 B.M.[1], enclosing Hof to Lyautey, August 23, 1912.

76. Ibid.

77. F.O. 371/1408, Lennox to Lister, June 5, 1912, no. 11. The same dispatch mentions that the royal parasol which El Hiba used had been made for him in Marrakech the preceding winter.

78. Ladreit de Lacharrière, "Grandeur et décadence," p. 484. *La Vigie Marocaine* (Casablanca), August 23, 1912.

79. Cf. F.O. 836/1, political situation, Marrakech 1912. (Entire file devoted to Marrakech situation.)

80. On the Rehamna situation, see ibid. The central importance of the

Rehamna tribe to the political edifice of the south is indicated by Commandant Verlet-Hanus. Guerre, Série A^{2}6, Verlet-Hanus to Lyautey, October 1, 1912, "Rapport sur les événements de Marrakech (Août-Septembre 1912)."

81. *AF* (1912): 358.

82. al-Marākishī, *al-Iʿlām,* 2:294–95. *AF* (1912): 349–50.

83. Guerre, Série A^{2}6, Verlet-Hanus to Lyautey, October 1, 1912, "Rapport sur les événements de Marrakech (Aout-Septembre 1912)."

84. Guerre, Série E-2, Lyautey to Foreign Ministry, September 4, 1912, no. 483 B.M.; Guerre, Série A^{2}6, Lyautey to Foreign Ministry, November 14, 1912, no. 717 B.M.; and Guerre, Série E.M.-2, Lyautey to Regional Commanders, August 31, 1912, no. 1069 B.M.^{2}

85. Guerre, Série E-2, "Note pour M. Persil au sujet de la situation du Maroc occidental," August 24, 1912, no. 4405.

86. On pan-Islamic intervention, see my "Pan-Islam and Moroccan Resistance," pp. 97–118, from which the information in this paragraph is derived.

87. F.O. 413/57, Kennard to Hunter, August 13, 1912, urgent and confidential.

88. *AF* (1912): 354–56, 361. Also, *Le Temps,* September 12, 1912. For more on the Spanish role, see my "Pan-Islam and Moroccan Resistance."

89. *La Vigie Marocaine,* September 5, 1912, and Guerre, Série A^{2}6, Verlet-Hanus, "Rapport sur les événements de Marrakech," October 1, 1912.

90. *AF* (1912): 359–60. Also al-Marrākishī, *al-Iʿlām,* 2:298.

91. *AF* (1912): 360, and P. Lyautey, *Lyautey l'Africain,* 2:33–35.

92. Guerre, Série A^{2}6, Mangin, "Rapport sur les opérations de la colonne du sud du 5 au 7 Septembre 1912," September 13, 1912; C. Mangin, *Regards sur la France d'Afrique,* pp. 134–49; *AF* (1912): 356–60, 394, 397, and Lyautey, *Lyautey l'Africain,* 1:52–65.

93. Cited by Saint-Aulaire, *Confessions,* p. 123.

GLOSSARY

ʿalim (pl. ʿulamā) A member of the learned classes, specifically a member of the formally constituted corps of religious scholars.

amīn (pl. umanā) Agent, authorized representative, superintendent.

amīn al-mustafad Administrator of makhzan properties, including those which were confiscated by the makhzan and those of persons dying intestate and without heirs. The *amin al-mustafad* was charged with collecting the revenues on makhzan properties, and the maks or gate tax.

ʿar Literally, "shame." In Morocco a religiously sanctioned conditional curse in which some form of sacrifice is an important element.

ʿaskar Army. In Morocco the Western-trained elite infantry corps formed under Sultan Mawlāy al-Ḥasan.

aʿyān People of distinction, notables, leading personalities. Especially the urban elite.

baraka Blessing, grace. In Morocco popularly attributed to certain individuals by virtue or talent.

bayʿa Document recognizing submission to a new sultan, signed by the ʿulamā of the major cities in Morocco.

bilād al-makhzan "Land of government," or that portion of the Moroccan empire which accepted government appointed qāid-s, paid taxes, and sent delegations to the sultan. Distinguished from bilād al-siba.

bilād al-sība "The land of dissidence," or that portion of the Moroccan empire which refused to accept government appointed qāid-s or to pay taxes. Tribes which were in sība could and did maintain a variety of relations with the central government, however.

dirḥām Moroccan basic monetary unit. The dirham was silver, originally at the weight of 50.2 grains of wheat. The weight was changed several times during the nineteenth and early twentieth centuries. Originally there was a gold coin, the dinar, but it ceased to be current at the end of the eighteenth century.

dīya Blood money, paid by the kinsmen of a homicide to the kinsmen of the slain according to tribal customary law and negotiation, generally arranged by a marabout.

fatwā Formal legal opinion issued by a mufti.

ḥafiẓiya The name given to the conspiracy of the great qāid-s of the south of Morocco and the notables of the northern cities, on behalf of Mawlāy ʿAbd al-Ḥafīẓ.

ḥajj Title of respect given a man who makes the pilgrimage to Mecca.

ḥājib Title of royal chamberlain, court functionary in charge of royal household and reception of visitors.

ḥammām Public bath generally supported by *hubus,* or pious foundations, and closely connected to the requirements of ritual purity.

ḥaraka Movement. In Morocco (1) a military expedition of government or irregular forces; (2) local security forces, supplied by local notables and called out by the local qāid.

ḥubus Pious foundation; also known in the Middle East as *waqf.* Established by private endowment for religious ends.

ʿid al-Fitr In Moroccan Arabic *ʿId al-Saghir,* the "lesser feast"; celebrated on the first of Shuwwāl the end of Ramaḍān, the month of fasting. The feast of the breaking of the fast.

ʿId al-Kabīr In the Middle East *ʿId al-Qurbān,* celebrated the tenth of the month of Dhū al-Hijja by the sacrifice of a lamb, one to a household. In Morocco the sultan initiated proceedings, according to custom, by making the first sacrifice.

jaysh In the Moroccan dialect known as *gish* (Fr. *guich*), the army. In Morocco refers to those Arab tribes accorded tax and other privileges in return for providing the sultans with troops. The makhzan was largely staffed by jaysh families, as state service was derived from military service.

jihād Strenuous effort, Holy War. In strict, classical Muslim doctrine jihad could only be proclaimed by the amir.

khalifa Deputy, assistant, successor. In Morocco (1) a provincial viceroy, (2) an assistant to a government official.

mahdī In popular Islamic doctrine, the mahdi is he who is to come, he who will fill the earth with justice as it is now filled with corruption. A Muslim millenarian leader.

maḥalla Government military expedition.

majlis Council.

majlis al-aʿyān Council of notables, the name given to the 1905 assemblage of notables called by ʿAbd al-ʿAzīz to hear the French reform proposals. See also *mushawara.*

maks In general, non-Koranic taxes or extraordinary levies, especially market dues or gate tax.

makhzan Storehouse, treasury, or by extension, in Morocco, the government or administration.

maliki rite The first and one of the most rigorous of the four principal legal *madhab*-s of *fiqh* (Islamic law). The legal rite observed in Morocco and most of the rest of Northwest Africa.

mithqāl (1) Unit of weight, (2) unit of currency based on the weight of gold. In the reign of Mawlāy al-Ḥasan one mithqal was equal to ten dirham.

muhandis Engineer, technician.

muhtasib Market provost; official charged with surveying and regulating the market in the city.

mujāhidūn Fighters in the holy war, combatants for the faith, patriots.

mukhlaṭ Native agricultural agent, afforded European diplomatic protection in return for assisting a European merchant in his dealings in the countryside.

muqaddam Supervisor, overseer, chief, administrator.

murābiṭ French "marabout"; a popularly acclaimed saint, living or dead, recognized as possessing baraka.

mushāwara Consultation, deliberation. In Morocco, the practice of the sultan seeking the advice of prominent men on particular questions of importance.

ṇāiba (pl. nuwayib) Tax paid by nonmilitary tribes to support contingents of military tribes instead of direct military service.

qāid (1) Chief, governor of a tribe, a city; (2) a military rank—*qāid al-mia.*

qasba Citadel, fortress.

qawm Tribe, kinfolk. For the French, "goum," native auxiliary troops, chiefly cavalry, first raised in Algeria. The system was further developed in the Chaouia after 1908 and eventually spread to the rest of Morocco.

shaykh Chief, old man, head (of a tribe), title of learned scholars in the traditional religious sciences.

shaykh al-rabiʿ Chief of the spring, or of the new grass; emergency system of urban government, sanctioned by ʿar, in which one or more individuals were selected to maintain order in the city with the assistance of the chief notables until security and regular government could be restored.

sība Dissidence, turmoil, upset. The opposite of *niẓam,* order.

silhām A hooded overgarment, generally of wool; in Morocco also known as *burnūs.*

simsar Native commercial agent, afforded European diplomatic protection in return for assisting a European merchant.

ṭālib (pl. ṭullāb) Student or scholar in a *madrasa.*

ṭarīqa (pl. ṭuruq) Literally, "way." A formalized mystical way or religious brotherhood with a distinctive liturgy (*wird*) and mystical genealogy. In Morocco *ṭuruq* were often heterodox in their practices.

tartīb In Morocco a special tax, created by articles 12 and 13 of the Madrid convention of 1881, on the basis of fixed percentages of agricultural income and applicable to all inhabitants, with no exemptions. A revised version was promulgated in 1901, with higher rates.

tobjia (Turkish) artilleryman.

ʿulamā (sing. ʿalim) Cf. above, ʿalim.

umanā (sing. amīn) Cf. above, amīn.

umma The Muslim community, *dār al-Islām,* sometimes used by modern writers to refer to the nation.

ʿushr Tithe, tenth part. A Koranic tax on the tenth part of agricultural produce.

wahhābiya A puritanical Islamic sect founded by Muhammad ibn ʿAbd al-Wahhab (d. 1792) in eighteenth-century Arabia and spread by the Ibn Saʿud family.

wuqīya A Moroccan monetary unit, based on bronze.

ẓahir In Morocco a decree, edict, or ordinance issued under the seal of the sultan.

zakāh Almsgiving, alms, charity. In Morocco a Koranic tax on agricultural animals; in theory, around 2.5 percent.

zawīya (1) A ṭarīqa. (2) The local lodge of a ṭarīqa, generally a tomb of a Muslim saint, often with a small mosque and teaching facilities attached to it.

zeṭṭata A Moroccan institution, based on ʿar, for the peaceful passing of caravans from the territory of one tribe to that of another, for the payment of a sum.

SELECTED BIBLIOGRAPHY

The present study is based primarily upon unpublished documents on Morocco in diplomatic and military archives in France, Great Britain, and the German Federal Republic. It also draws heavily upon the vast bibliography of published European materials on Morocco, as well as upon published Arabic materials. As the archives of the Moroccan government remain difficult of access to scholarly researchers, the story must be told largely from what can be gleaned from the copious European documentation. While this is an enterprise not without grave risks (about which more below), the potential benefits in increased knowledge and understanding about this vital period in Moroccan history appeared substantial. The interpretation of Moroccan politics that has been presented in the preceding pages must be regarded therefore as only a provisional version. The definitive history of the period will be written by a new generation of western-trained Moroccan historians when the archives of the makhzan are finally made available to researchers.

At the present time the political correspondence of the diplomatic representatives of Great Britain, Germany, and France constitute the most important body of source material for the period from 1900 to 1912. The view of Moroccan politics which emerges from this correspondence is especially detailed on Moroccan diplomatic relations with the powers, the political infighting at court among the viziers and principal interest groups, and the responses of the makhzan to the major problems confronting it. Most important among these sources are the archives of the French Ministère des Affaires Etrangères, Paris, first opened to researchers under special authorization in January 1969. French diplomatic and political involvement in Morocco during the period was considerable, and thus French documentation on internal Moroccan politics is the most complete of the great powers. On the whole, however, the view presented in these documents is highly partisan, and they must therefore be supplemented with the archives of the British Foreign Office. In addition to the political correspondence of the British minister at Tangier, the British consular records (containing the regular reports of British consular agents in the major Moroccan cities), afford a glimpse of local and provincial politics which constitutes an essential antidote to the generally court-oriented and official view of the Tangier legations. The political archives of the German Auswartiges Amt are also of importance on makhzan politics, although rather partisan in tone. They were not extensively utilized. Finally, the correspondence of the French military mission in Morocco (1873–1912) and of the various French expeditionary forces in Morocco is helpful in dealing with the military aspect of Moroccan internal politics during the period. Conserved at the Service Historique de l'Armée, Section d'Afrique, the French military archives are also important for the military side of the dispute between the Quai d'Orsay and the Ministère de l'Armée over French policy toward Morocco.

Other unpublished documents utilized in the preparation of this study include the archives of the former Gouvernement Général de l'Algérie, and various collections of private manuscripts located in the libraries and archives of Paris and London. These are listed fully in the bibliography. For the most part they merely add details to the diplomatic record.

The European sources taken together can tell us much about the conduct of politics in Morocco during the period of the Moroccan Question. But a large gap will remain in our understanding of the period as long as the archives of the makhzan remain inaccessible.* The absence of Arabic documentary sources is a serious handicap, which no amount of new European evidence will be able to overcome. Lacking indigenous written sources, the historian of Moroccan politics is unable to penetrate very deeply into an analysis of the ideas, membership, and functioning of the various political groupings discussed in the European sources. The intellectual history of the period, in particular, suffers greatly from this difficulty. Oral history, where it is still possible, can help fill out the Moroccan side of the story, but can never make up for the current absence of written Arabic sources. A further disability of relying upon European documentary sources is that they all reflect in varying degrees the European sense of superiority, not to say chauvinism, of the period in which they were written. Moroccan attempts to deal with the imperialist threat are systematically discounted, the right of intervention to safeguard European interests is never questioned, and the intense nationalist passions aroused in the European participants in the struggle for Morocco prevent them at times from arriving at balanced judgments about Moroccan affairs. In the end, the European sources manifest a confusion and lack of comprehension of Moroccan politics which does much to explain the many European political blunders in dealing with Morocco during the period. From our present postcolonial vantage point many of these Europeans' errors appear elementary. Yet how few were able to correctly perceive the nature of the political changes then taking place in Morocco beneath the storm-tossed surface of apparent anarchy and fanaticism!

*On the current status of the makhzan archives, see G. Ayache, "La question des archives historiques marocaines," *Hesperis-Tamuda* 2 (1961): 3111–26, and idem, "L'utilization et l'apport des archives historiques marocaines," *Hesperis-Tamuda* 7 (1966).

There is no comprehensive general bibliography that covers the period of Moroccan history with which this study is concerned. The following selected and annotated bibliography represents only those works which were most helpful in the writing of this study, not a complete listing. A full bibliography of the sources consulted would be tediously long and repetitive. A start on a bibliography of Morocco in the late nineteenth and early twentieth centuries can be found in the following works: Lieutenant Colonel Robert Playfair and Dr. Robert Brown, *A Bibliography of Morocco from the Earliest Times to the End of 1891* (London, 1892); Jean-Louis Miège, *Le Maroc et l'Europe,* vol. 1, *Sources-Bibliographie* (Paris, 1960); anon., *Bibliographie militaire des ouvrages français ou traduits en français, et des articles des principales revues françaises relatives à l'Algérie, Tunisie, Maroc de 1830 à 1926* (Paris, 1930); and P. de Cenival, C. Funck-Brentano, and M. Bousser, *Bibliographie marocaine (1923–1933)* (Paris, n.d.). The last, although it begins after the establishment of the protectorate, contains references which deal with the period under study. The reader is also referred to the bibliographies that appeared periodically in *Hesperis* and that continue where de Cenival et al. leave off. The most complete bibliography of German works on Morocco to appear to date can be found in P. Guillen, *L'Allemagne et le Maroc, 1871–1905* (Paris, 1967). On Arabic historical materials, the reader is referred to ʿAbd al-Salām Ibn Sūdah's excellent two-volume *Dalīl mu'arrikh al-maghrib al-aqṣā* (Casablanca, 1965).

Manuscript Sources

1. Private Papers

France

Larras MSS. Archives. Ministère de la Guerre. Section d'Afrique, Paris. The papers of General Larras, who served with the French military mission in Morocco from 1898 to 1905. He was responsible for preparing many of the maps of Morocco later utilized during the first stages of pacification. The papers relate principally to the period of his service in Morocco.

Mangin MSS. Archives Nationales, Paris. The papers and reports of General Charles Mangin, the hero of the battle of Sidi Bou Outhman and deliverer of Marrakech. In its essentials, it duplicates the holdings of the Ministère de la Guerre, Section d'Afrique, although there are additional papers. Only a portion deals with Mangin's Moroccan career.

Pellé MSS. Institut de France, Paris. The papers of General Maurice Pellé, who served as Lyautey's chef de cabinet militaire particulière, 1912–13. Little of interest concerning Morocco.

Terrier MSS. Institut de France, Paris. The papers of Auguste Terrier, secretary general of the Comité de l'Afrique Française and the Comité du Maroc, and later director of the Office Cherifien du Maroc. Much important material on the acquisition of Morocco, including military reports and descriptions of the various scientific missions to Morocco sponsored by the Comité du Maroc.

Centre des Hautes Etudes sur l'Afrique et l'Asie moderne, Paris. CHEAM houses a private collection of monographs and *fin de stage* studies done by would-be colonial administrators for the former French colonies. The following were utilized:

"Ouezzane et les Taibiyine-Thamiyine" (no. 29).

"Les confréries religieuses du Maroc" (no. 28 bis). (Both of the above are by Georges Spillmann, evidently early drafts of his book, *Esquisse d'histoire religieuse du Maroc,* on which see below).

"Les Forces Suppletives Marocaines," G. Spillmann (no. 407).

"Etude sur les guichs marocains," Delmas-Fort (no. 1409).

"L'Unification maghzen dans les Abda: le caid Si Aissa ben Aomar, 1842–1924," Fresneau (no. 1930). Important, although derivative.

"L'Evolution d'un grand commandement marocain: Le caid Mtougui et le protectorat," Fuchs (no. 2137). Very good study of a little-known figure.

"Aspects de la transhumance dans la Grande Atlas Mtougghi," Robine (no. 2774).

Great Britain

Satow Papers. Public Record Office, London. PRO 30/33. Includes the correspondence of Sir Ernest Satow from his mission to Morocco in 1893 and his correspondence with Sir James Macleod, H. M. Consul at Fez, 1893–1916. Of subsidiary interest only.

Nicolson Papers. Public Record Office, London. F.O. 800/336–381. Miscellaneous papers of Sir Arthur Nicolson, H. M. Minister at Tangier from 1894–1904. Of little interest.

Lansdowne Papers. Public Record Office, London. F.O. 800/115–146. The papers of the Marquess of Lansdowne. Contains some items of interest on Morocco.

2. Official Papers

France

Archives de l'Alliance Israélite Universelle, Paris. Valuable chiefly for the annual reports of the official inspectors sent to survey the works of the Alliance in Morocco.

Archives de l'Ancien Gouvernement Général de l'Algérie, Aix-en-Provence. Série H. Affaires Musulmans et Sahariennes. Little of value on central Morocco. Of great importance for French penetration into eastern Morocco.

Archives du Ministère des Affaires Etrangères, Paris. Maroc, n.s., 1893–1916. In January 1969 this archival collection was officially released to researchers. It forms the essential basis of the diplomatic history of the Moroccan question and is of major importance for the light which it sheds on Moroccan internal developments. The general outlines of the picture of French penetration of Morocco which can be derived from the published French diplomatic documents (the *livres jaunes*) remain unchanged, however.

I. Politique Etrangère. Relations Internationales.
  1. Dossier Général
  2. Negociations secretes relatives au Maroc
  3. Relations avec la France
  4. Relations avec l'Allemagne
  5. Relations avec l'Espagne
    A. Dossier Géneral
    B. Affaires du Rif
    C. Negociations Franco-Espagnole
    D. Statut de Tanger
    E. Zone Espagnole
  6. Conférence d'Algeciras
    A. Préliminaires
    B. Conférence
    C. Documentation imprimée
  7. Police des Ports
  8. Contrabande des Armes
II. Affaires Politiques
  1. Politique générale
  2. Etablissement du Protectorat Dossier Reservé
  3. Territoires Est et Sud Régions frontières
  4. Rif
  5. Rapports mensuels du Résident Général
  6. Bulletins politique du protectorat
III. Défense Nationale. Mission Militaire Française
VI. Organisation administrative du Protectorat
  1. Dossier Général
  2. Suppression des capitulations
  3. Régime Judiciaire
  4. Régime Foncier
V. Finances
  1. Dossier Général
  2. Banque d'État

3. Budget des oeuvres françaises
4. Documentation
VI. Commerce
1. Dossier Général
2. Relations avec la France
3. Relations avec la Grande Bretagne
4. Douanes
VII. Industrie. Travaux publiques.
1. Mines
2. Chemins de fer
IX. Questions culturelles et religieuses
1. Enseignement publique
2. Ecoles
3. Expositions
4. Intérêts religieux français au Maroc
X. Questions sanitaires.

Archives du Ministère de la Guerre, Section d'Afrique et d'Outre-Mer, Paris. The archives of the Section d'Afrique were especially useful in providing detailed studies of the resistance among the tribes in Morocco. There are also important insights into Moroccan politics, the military-diplomatic rivalry, and the formation of policy.

Maroc
Série RSD Cabinet militaire
Affaires Indigènes
Série C (24 cartons). The records of the French military mission in Morocco (1877–1912). Important.
Série D (31 cartons). Military and political action of France in Morocco from 1907–11. The records of French expeditionary forces in the Chaouia.
Série E (30 cartons). Organization of the protectorate, the Great War, the occupation of "le Maroc utile," and the Rif War. Not open after 1919.
Archives des Régions
Fez (208 cartons)
Marrakech (46 cartons, two series)
Série E.M. (15 cartons)
Série A^1 Organization (8 cartons)
Série A^2 Operations (5 cartons)
Série R.P. (27 cartons)

Archives du Ministère de la Marine, Service historique, Paris. The archives of the Ministry of Marine contain interesting observations on the origins of the Chaouia rising of 1907 and the political temper of the port cities along Morocco's Atlantic coast.

Série BB[2] Correspondence, Fleet Movements, Morocco

Série BB[3] Correspondence, Fleet Movements, Morocco

Série BB[4] Correspondence, Fleet Movements, Morocco

Archives Nationales, Paris. Very little of interest on Morocco

Série F[80] Algeria

Great Britain

Foreign Office Political Correspondence, London. The archives of the Foreign Office relating to Morocco are very important for the study of Moroccan internal developments during the period prior to 1914. Great Britain was blessed with a great number of diplomatic agents who were especially good observers and reporters. The Foreign Office archives are quite full and the consular correspondence provides a unique view of life in the major cities of the empire.

F.O. 174 Consular correspondence

F.O. 831 Reports on the insurrection in Southern Morocco (1912)

F.O. 836 Political situation, Marrakech, 1912

F.O. 413 Confidential print series

F.O. 371 General correspondence, political

Federal Republic of Germany

The archives of the German Foreign Ministry have been divided between the Federal Republic of Germany (conserved at Bonn) and the Democratic Republic of Germany (conserved at Potsdam). Still other important archival materials were lost during the world wars. We were able to consult only the archives at Bonn. On the whole, they proved disappointing on internal Moroccan politics but much richer on German diplomatic policy concerning Morocco.

Abteilung 1A Marokko (1879–1920)

PRINTED SOURCES

1. Official Publications

Bulletin Officiel du Protectorat de la République Française au Maroc, Rabat, 1912–1913.

Documents diplomatiques français, 1871–1914. 41 vols. Paris, 1929–1960. Série I, 1871–1901. Série 2, 1901–1914.

Documents diplomatiques. Affaires du Maroc. 1901–1912. 6 vols. Paris, 1905–1912.

Documents diplomatiques. Affaires du Maroc. Protocoles et comptes rendus de la Conférence d'Algeciras. Paris, 1906.

Journal Officiel de la République Française.

2. Works in Arabic

Dāwud, Muḥammad. *Mukhtaṣar Tārīkh Tiṭawān*. 2 vols. Tetouan, 1955.

———. *Tārīkh Tiṭawān*. 15 vols. Tetouan, 1955–66. The history of the city of Tetouan from its foundations to the War of 1860, drawing on published and unpublished Arabic materials and published European sources, by the present director of the royal Archives in Rabat.

al-Fāsī, ʿAlāl. *Ḥadīth al-mashriq fī al-maghrib*. Cairo, 1956.

———. *al-Harakat al-Istiqlālīya fī al-maghrib al-ʿArabī*. Marrakesh, 1956. English translation by H. Z. Nuseibeh. *The Independence Movements of Arab North Africa*. Washington, American Council of Learned Societies, 1954. An indispensable Moroccan nationalist view of the history of Moroccan resistance to France. Notably biased but quite useful.

———. *Ḥafrīyāt ʿan al-ḥaraka al-dustūrīya fī al-maghrib qabla al-ḥimāya*. Rabat, 1970. A brief rethinking of some of the significant developments of the 1904–1908 period in Moroccan reformism.

al-Fāsī, ʿAbd al-Ḥafīẓ. *Riyād al-janna aw al-mudhish al-mutrib*. 2 vols. Fez, A. H. 1350.

Ghallāb, ʿAbd al-Karīm. *Difāʿan ʿan al-dīmuqrāṭīya*. Tangier, 1966. Includes the Arabic text of the draft constitution of 1908.

Gharīṭ, Muḥammad. *Fawāṣil al-jamān fī arbā wazarā wa kuttāb al-zamān*. Fez: Mutbuʿah al-Jadīda, 1347/1928.

Ibn Sūdah, ʿAbd al-Salām ibn ʿAbd al-Qādir. *Dalīl mu'arrikh al-maghrib al-aqṣā*. 2 vols. Casablanca, 1965. Essential bibliographical guide to the Arabic sources on Moroccan history.

Ibn Zīdan, ʿAbd al-Rahmām. *al-durar al-fākhira bi maāthir al-mulūk al-ʿalawīyīn bi-fās al-ẓāhira*. Rabat: mutbu'ah al-iqtiṣādīya, 1356/1937.

———. *Itḥāf aʿlām al-nās bī jamāl akhbār hāḍirat miknās*. 5 vols. Rabat, 1929. Very important. Includes many official documents.

Kattānī, Muḥammad Bāqir. *Tarjamah al-Shaykh Muḥammad al-Kattānī al-shahīd*. N.p., 1962. Based on family sources and the files of the Tangier newspaper *al-Saʿada,* this is a justificatory biography of Shaykh Kattanī.

Manūnī, Muḥammad. "Maẓāhir yaqthah al-maghrib al-ḥadīth fī al-maydān al-taʿlīmī," *Baḥth al-ʿilmī* (1387 A.H./1966), pp. 1–48.

al-Marrākishī, ʿAbbās ibn Ibrahīm. *al-Aʿlām bi-man ḥall marrākish wa aghmāt min al-a'lām*. 5 vols. Fez, 1938.

al-Nāṣirī, Muḥammad Makkī. "Wadaʿa mashrūʿa al-dustūr al-maghrib mundhu khamsīn ʿamman," *Al-Shaʿb* (Tangier), Shuwwāl 1376, p. 4. The Arabic text of the draft constitution first published in *Lisān al-maghrib* in 1908.

al-Nāṣirī, Aḥmad ibn Khālid. *Kitāb al-istiqṣā fī akhbar al-maghrib al-aqṣā*. 9 vols. Casablanca, Dār al-Kuttāb, 1956. French translation by E. Fumey. In *Archives marocaines* 9 (for vols. 7–9 of Arabic edition).

Sahrāwī, ʿAbd al-Qādir. "Jarīdah Lisān al-maghrib," *al-Ahdaf,* March 6, 1965. Important article on the 1908 Tangier newspaper *Lisān al-maghrib* which connects it with pan-Islamic attempts to influence Morocco.

al-Zayyānī, Abū al-Qasim ibn Aḥmad. *al-Turjamān al-muʿarib ʿan duwal al-mashriq wa al-maghrib.* French translation by Octave V. Houdas. *Le Maroc de 1631 à 1812.* Amsterdam, Philo Press, 1969. Reprint.

3. Memoirs and Correspondence

d'Amade, Albert. *Campagne de 1908–1909 en Chaouia. Rapport.* Paris, 1911.

Arnaud, Dr. Louis. *Au temps des mehallas ou le Maroc de 1860 à 1912.* Casablanca, Editions Atlantides, 1952. The memoirs of al-Hajj Salem el Abdi (Fr.) as told to Dr. Arnaud. A professional makhzan soldier's view of his life, which includes a great many important events. Colorful.

Brooks, L. A. E. *A Memoir of Sir John Drummond Hay.* London, 1896.

Caillaux, Joseph. *Mes mémoires* (Paris, 1943).

Forbes, Rosita. *El Raisuni.* London, 1924. Very good.

Gouraud, General. *Au Maroc, 1922–1914. Souvenirs d'un africain.* Paris, Plon, 1949. Good on military-civilian relations during the transition period, 1911–12.

Harris, Walter B. *Morocco That Was.* Edinburgh and London, W. Blackwood and Sons, 1921. Amusing and colorful description of the old Morocco by the correspondent for *The Times* of London. As Harris tells one-tenth of what he knows, the book must nevertheless be rated a vast disappointment.

Houel, Christian. *Mes aventures marocaines.* Casablanca, 1954. Houel first came to Morocco in 1907 and was the founder of *La Vigie Marocaine.* Very frank, if not always reliable.

Karow, Leonard. *Neun Jahre in Marokkanischen Diensten.* Berlin, 1909. Naval officer who served in the Moroccan service and commanded the vessel *Sidi al-Turki.*

Kühlmann, Richard von. *Erinnerungen.* Heidelberg, 1948. Secretary of the German legation at Tangier, 1904–5.

Lamartinière, H. de. *Souvenirs du Maroc.* Paris, 1932. Served in the French legation at Tangier, 1887–91, 1901–2. One of the proponents of a more forward policy. His memoirs are on the whole disappointing.

Lyautey, Louis-Hubert-Gonzalve. "Du rôle social de l'officier." *Revue des Deux Mondes,* March 15, 1891.

———. *Dans le sud de Madagascar. Pénétration militaire. Situation politique et économique (1900–1902).* Paris, Lavauzelle, 1903.

———. *Lettres du Tonkin et de Madagascar (1894–1899).* Paris, A. Colin, 1920.

———. "Lettres de Rabat (1907)." *Revue des Deux Mondes,* July 15, 1921.

Lyautey, Louis-Hubert-Gonzalve. *Paroles d'action: Madagascar, Sud-Oranais, Oran, Maroc (1900–1926).* Paris, A. Colin, 1927.

———. *Lettres du Sud de Madagascar* (*1900–1902*). Paris, A. Colin, 1935.

———*Vers le Maroc. Lettres du Sud-Oranais* (*1903–1906*). Paris, A. Colin, 1937.

Lyautey, Pierre, ed. *Lyautey l'Africain, textes et lettres.* 4 vols. Paris, Plon, 1953–58. An important collection, very badly edited. To be used with caution.

———. *Les plus belles lettres de Lyautey.* Paris, Calmann-Levy, 1962.

Mangin, General Charles. *Regards sur la France d'Afrique.* Paris, Plon, 1924.

———. *Souvenirs d'Afrique. Lettres et carnets de route.* Paris, Denoel et Steele, 1936. More useful than the preceding, especially on the Marrakech campaign.

Nicolson, Harold. *Portrait of a Diplomatist.* Boston, 1930.

Poincaré, Raymond. *Au service de la France: Neuf ans de souvenirs.* vol. 1, *Le lendemain d'Agadir.* Paris, 1926.

Rosen, Friedrich. *Aus einem diplomatischen Wanderleben.* Vol. 1, *Auswartiges Amt. Marokko. 1901–1910.* Berlin, 1931.

Saint-Aulaire, Comte de. *Confession d'un vieux diplomate.* Paris, Flammarion, 1953. Witty and informative on the author's role.

Simon, Henri. *Un officier d'Afrique: le Commandant Verlet-Hanus.* Paris, J. Peyronnet, 1930. A very important collection of letters of a leading French native-affairs expert, badly edited.

Saint-René-Taillandier, G. *Les origines du Maroc français.* Paris, 1930. Very important.

Weisgerber, Dr. Felix. *Au seuil du Maroc moderne.* Rabat, La Porte, 1947.

4. Secondary Works

Abun-Nasr, Jamil. "The Salafiyya Movement in Morocco: The Religious Bases of the Moroccan Nationalist Movement." *St. Antony's Papers* 16, London, Oxford University Press, 1963. Important on reformist Islam.

———. *The Tijaniyya.* London, Oxford University Press, 1966.

Adam, André. *Histoire de Casablanca (des origines à 1914).* Aix-en-Provence, Publications des Annales de la Faculté des Lettres. N.s., no. 66, 1968.

———. "Sur l'action du Galilée à Casablanca en août 1907." *Revue de l'Occident Musulman et de la Méditerranée,* no. 6 (1969): 9–22.

Aflalo, M. *The Truth About Morocco.* London, 1904. Opposes the 1904 Anglo-French entente.

Ageron, Charles-Robert. *Les Algériens musulmans et la France.* 2 vols. Paris, Presses Universitaires de France, 1968. An authoritative treatment of the period 1871–1919.

———. "La politique berbère du protectorat marocain de 1913 à 1934." *Revue d'Histoire moderne et Contemporaine* 18 (1971): 50–90.

Allain, Jean-Claude. "L'emprunt des bijoux de la couronne chérifienne (1907–1910)." *Revue d'Histoire Diplomatique* 85 (1971): 152–69.

Anderson, Eugene. *The First Moroccan Crisis, 1904–1906*. Chicago, 1930.

Andrew, Christopher. "The Entente Cordiale from Its Origins to the First World War." In Neville Waiter, ed., *Troubled Neighbors: Anglo-French Relations in the 20th Century*. London, Weidenfeld, 1970.

———. "France and the Making of the Entente Cordiale." *The Historical Journal* 10 (1967).

———. *Theophile Delcassé and the Making of the Entente Cordiale*. London, St. Martin's Press, 1968. Indispensable for the politics of Delcassé.

———, and A. S. Kanya-Forstner. "The French Colonial Party: Its Composition, Aims and Influences, 1885–1914." *The Historical Journal* 17 (1971), pp. 99–128. An important and trailblazing study.

Anon. "El Hiba et les Allemands," *Afrique Française* (1918): 24.

———. "L'évolution du makhzen, la famille Tazi." *Afrique Française* (1904).

———. "Les relations entre la France et le makhzen." *Afrique Française* (1905).

———. "Le fetoua des 'oulama des Fes.' " *Archives Marocaines* 1:56–96.

———. "La France au Maroc." *La Nouvelle Revue,* n.s. 35 (1905): 148–57. Very important for the activities of al-Kattānī and the elite nationalists at Fez by a man who evidently was well informed.

———. "Le panislamisme et la France." *Le Temps* (Paris) November 2, 1912. On *al-ittihād al-maghribi* and the abortive 1912 general rising.

———. *La renaissance du Maroc. Dix ans du protectorat, 1912–1922*. Rabat, 1923. An officially sponsored survey of the achievements of the protectorate.

———. "Echos marocain." *Renseignements Coloniaux* (1908): 130–32. A good discussion of the ʿAzīz-Ḥafīẓ quarrel.

———. "Les Fadelia." *Revue du Monde musulman* 31 (1915–16): 135–220.

Antonius, George. *The Arab Awakening*. London, 1938.

Ashmead-Bartlett, E. *The Passing of the Shereefian Empire*. Edinburgh and London, 1910. A veteran war correspondent reports on the Chaouia campaign of the French. Important views of resistance.

Aubin, Eugene [Descos]. *Le Maroc d'aujord'hui*. 8th ed. Paris, A. Colin, 1913.

Ayache, Albert. *Le Maroc: Bilan d'une Colonisation*. Paris, Editions Sociales, 1956.

Ayache, Germain. "Aspects de la crise financière au Maroc après l'expédition espagnole de 1860." *Revue Historique* 220 (1958): 271–310.

Ayache, Germain. "Le sentiment nationale dans le Maroc du XIXe siècle." *Revue Historique* (1969): 393–410.

Azan, Paul. *L'expédition de Fez.* Paris, A. Colin, 1924. Treats military operations of the 1911 French expeditionary force. Important.

———. *Franchet d'Esperey.* Paris, Flammarion, 1949.

———. *Souvenirs de Casablanca.* Paris: Hachette, 1911.

Babin, Gustave. *Au Maroc. Par les camps et par les villes.* Paris, 1912.

Baghdadi, R. el. *Le pacha et soldat Si Mohammed el Baghdadi.* Paris, 1936.

Bartels, Alfred. *Fighting the French in Morocco.* London, 1932. The author was involved in organizing resistance in the Rif during World War I.

Begue, Leon. *Le secret d'une conquête. Au Maroc avec Lyautey.* Paris, J. Taillandier, 1929.

Benabdullah, Abdelaziz. *Les grands courants de la civilisation du maghreb.* Casablanca, 1958. Contains a detailed summary of the proposed 1908 draft constitution.

Benech, Jose. *Essai d'explication d'un mellah.* Kaiserslauten, s.d. Valuable study of the Marrakech mellah, with some important observations on Joshua Corcos, banker of al-Glawi.

Benghabrit, Kaddour. "S. E. El Hadj Mohammed el Mokri." *France-Maroc* (May 1918): 141–43.

Bernard, Augustin. *Les confins Algéro-Marocains.* Paris, Larose, 1911. A good summary treatment of the southeastern frontier and Oudjda.

Berque, Jacques. *Etudes d'histoire rurale maghrebine.* Tangier and Fez, Editions Internationales, 1938.

———. "Ville et université, aperçu sur l'histoire de l'école de Fès." *Revue historique du droit français et étranger* (1949).

———. *Structures sociales du Haut-Atlas.* Paris, 1955.

———. "Quelques problèmes de l'Islam maghrebin." *Archives de Sociologie des Religions* 3 (1957): 3–20.

———. "Medinas, villeneuves et bidonvilles." *Les Cahiers de Tunisie* (1958).

———. "Ça et là dans les débuts du réformisme religieux au Maghreb." *Etudes d'orientalisme dediées à la mémoire de Levi-Provençal.* 2 vols. Paris: G. P. Maisonneuve et Larose, 1962, 2:471–94.

Berriau, Col. "Méthodes modernes de Conquête." *France-Maroc* (April 1917): 4–9.

———. "L'officier de renseignements au Maroc." *Renseignements Coloniaux* (1918): 85–93.

Bonnet, Pierre. *La Banque d'Etat du Maroc et le problème marocain.* Paris, 1913.

Bonsal, Stephen. *Morocco As It Is.* London and New York, 1893. By an American who accompanied the Euan Smith mission to Fez, 1893.

Bowie, Leland. "The Impact of the Protégé System in Morocco, 1880–1912." *Ohio University Papers in International Studies. Africa Series,* no. 11 (1970): 1–16.

Boyer, Pierre. "Contribution à l'étude de la politique religieuse des Turcs dans la régence d'Alger." *Revue de l'Occident Musulman et de la Méditerranée*, 1 (1966): 11–50.

Brignon, Jean, et al. *Histoire du Maroc.* Paris, Hatier, 1967. The most recent Moroccan textbook, which incorporates a great many of the latest advances in the literature. Strangely orthodox French treatment of 1900–1912.

Bringau. "Moulay Hafid Intime." *Bulletin de la Société de Géographie d'Alger* (1912): 18–49. By the court photographer. A defense of the sultan against attacks on his character.

Brives, A. *Voyages au Maroc 1901–1907.* Algiers, A. Jourdan, 1909.

Brown, Kenneth L. "The Social History of a Moroccan Town: Salé: 1830–1930." Ph.D. dissertation, University of California at Los Angeles, 1969.

Brown, L. C. "The Sudanese Mahdiyya." In Robert I. Rotberg, ed., *Rebellion in Black Africa.* London and New York, Oxford University Press, 1971.

Burke, Edmund. "Moroccan Resistance, Pan-Islam and German War Strategy, 1914–1918." *Francia* 3 (Munich) (1976).

———. "Morocco and the Middle East: Reflections on Some Basic Differences." *Archives Européennes de Sociologie* 10 (1969): 70–94.

———. "Pan-Islam and Moroccan Resistance to French Colonial Penetration, 1900–1912." *Journal of African History* 13, no. 1 (1972): 97–118.

———. "The Image of the Moroccan State in French Ethnological Literature: New Light on the Origins of Lyautey's Berber Policy." In Charles Micaud and Ernest Gellner, eds., *Arabs and Berbers: Ethnicity and Nation-Building in North Africa.* New York, D.C. Heath, and London, Duckworth, 1972.

———. "The Political Role of the Moroccan Ulama, 1860–1912." In N. R. Keddie, ed., *Scholars, Saints, and Sufis.* Berkeley, 1972.

Cagne, Jacques. "Les origines du mouvement Jeune Marocain." *Bulletin de la Société d'histoire du Maroc,* no. 1 (1968): 8–17. The firstfruits of an important French doctorate currently in preparation.

Caillaux, Joseph. *Agadir.* Paris, A. Michel, 1918. Post-hoc justifications.

Caillé, Jacques. "Les Marocains à l'École de Génie de Montpellier." *Hesperis* 41 (1954): 131–45. On the experiment in educating Moroccan officer candidates in France.

Caix, Robert de [de Saint-Aymour]. "La France et le Maroc," *Afrique Française* (1903).

———. "Notre politique marocaine." *Afrique Française* (1903). Long-time editor of the *Bulletin de la Comité d'Afrique Française,* member of the Comité, and ardent supporter of Delcassé's policy. He later became head of the Comité de l'Asie Française and editor-in-chief of its *Bulletin.*

Cambon, Henry. *Histoire du Maroc.* Paris, 1952.

Campoamor, J. M. *La actitud de España ante la cuestion de Marruecos (1900–1904).* Madrid, 1951.

Caro Baroja, Julio. *Estudios Saharianos.* Madrid, 1955.

Castries, Lt. Col. de. "Aux jardins de Bou Jeloud (mai/juin 1912)." *France-Maroc* (1920): 130–34. The abdication of ʿAbd al-Ḥafiẓ recalled.

Chailley, Joseph. "Comment organiser notre Protectorat au Maroc." *Revue Politique et Parlementaire* (1912): 233–55.

Chalmin, Pierre. "Lex bureaux arabes de leur creation à la chute du Second Empire." *Actes du 79e Congrès national des Sociétés Savantes.* Paris, Imprimerie Nationale, 1955.

Chouraqui, André. *L'Alliance Israélite universelle et la renaissance juive contemporain.* Paris, 1965.

Cobban, Alfred. *A History of Modern France.* 3 vols. Baltimore, Penguin Books, 1963.

Cochin, Denys. *Affaires Marocaines, Discours prononcés à la chambre des députés 1907–1911.* Paris, Plon, 1912.

Confer, Vincent. "The Depot in Aix and Archival Sources for France Outre-Mer." *French Historical Studies* 6 (1969): 120–26.

Coon, Carleton. *Caravan, The Story of the Middle East.* New York, 1958.

Cornet, Charles. *A la conquête du Maroc sud avec la colonne Mangin, 1912–1913.* Paris, 1914. Very important account of the relief of Marrakech and the subsequent pacification of the Marrakech region by a participant.

Cour, August. *L'établissement des dynasties des Chérifs au Maroc.* Paris, 1904.

Crabitès, Pierre. *Ismail, the Maligned Khedive.* New York, 1933.

Cruchet, R. *La conquête pacifique du Maroc.* Paris, 1930. The French doctor's role in the conquest of Morocco from Linarès is surveyed.

Cruickshank, Earl F. *Morocco At the Parting of the Ways.* Philadelphia, 1935.

Cunningham Graham, R. B. *Moghreb el Akca, A Journey in Morocco.* London, 1898. Interesting traveler's account of the Sous valley at the turn of the century.

Decroux, Paul. "Le souverain du Maroc, legislateur." *Revue de l'Occident Musulman et de la Méditerranée,* no. 3 (1967): 31–64.

Delbrel, Gabriel. "De Fez à l'Oranie." *La Géographie* (1900): 167–82.

Deleone, Enrico. *La Colonizzazione dell'Africa del Nord.* 2 vols. Padua, Editione Cedam, 1960.

Deny, Jean. "Instructeurs militaires turcs au Maroc sous Moulay Hafidh."

Memorial Henri Basset. Paris, 1928. Based on an article in the Turkish press by a former member of the military mission.

Depont, Octave, and Xavier Coppolani. *Les Confréries religieuses musulmanes*. Algiers, 1897.

Desiré-Vuillemin, G. -M. "Cheikh Ma el Ainin et le Maroc ou l'échec d'un moderne almoravide." *Revue d'histoire des colonies* 45 (1958): 29–52.

Desparment, J. "La résistance à l'occident." *Afrique Française* (1933): 265–69.

Déthan, Georges. "Le rapprochement franco-italien après la chute de Crispi jusqu'aux accords Visconti Venosta sur le Maroc et la Tripolitanie (1896–1904) d'après les archives du Quai d'Orsay," *Revue d'Histoire Diplomatique* 70 (1956).

Doutté, Edmond. "Abd al-Aziz." *Encyclopedia of Islam*. First edition.

———. *L'Islam Algérien en l'an 1900*. Algiers, Giralt, 1900.

———. *Notes sur l'Islam Maghrebin. Les Marabouts*. Paris, E. Leroux, 1900.

———. "Une mission d'études au Maroc." *Renseignements Coloniaux* (1901): 161–77. One of the most knowledgeable Frenchmen about the Marrakech region, Doutté made a number of expeditions for the Comité du Maroc and had some impact on the formation of French native policies, notably in the early period. A very acute observer, his articles are always worth reading.

———."Les deux politiques." *Afrique Française* (1903): 306–11.

———. "Les Marocains et la société marocaine." *Revue Générale des Sciences pures et appliqués* (1903): 190–208, 258–74, 314–27, 372–87.

———. "Au pays de Moulaye Hafid." *Revue de Paris* 5 (1905).

———. *Marrakech*. Paris, Comité de l'Afrique Française, 1905.

———. "Les causes de la chute d'un sultan." *Renseignements Coloniaux*. Nos. 7–12 (1909). Six lectures on the fall of ʿAbd al-ʿAziz. Disappointing.

———. *En tribu*. Paris, P. Geuthner, 1914.

Drague, Georges [Général Georges Spillmann]. *Esquisse d'histoire religieuse du Maroc*. Paris, 1951. The role of the *ṭuruq* in Moroccan history. Important.

Dunn, Ross. E. "The French Colonial Offensive in Southeastern Morocco, 1881–1912: Patterns of Response." Ph.D. dissertation. University of Wisconsin, 1968. An original and important contribution to our understanding of the response of the tribes in the *confins* region to French penetration.

———. "The Trade of Tafilalet: Commercial Change in Southeast Morocco on the Eve of the Protectorate." *African Historical Studies* 4 2(1971): 271–304.

———. *Morocco's Crisis of Conquest: The Southwest, 1881–1912*.

Madison, Wisconsin: University of Wisconsin Press, 1977.

Edwards, E. W. "The Franco-German Agreement on Morocco of 1909." *English Historical Review* 78 (1963): 483–513.

Erckmann, Jules. *Le Maroc moderne.* Paris, 1885. By a former member of the French military mission in Morocco.

Fallot, Ernest. "La solution française de la conquête du Maroc." Paris, 1904. Thèse de droit.

Feis, Herbert. *Europe: The World's Banker.* New York, Norton, 1965.

Flory, Maurice. "Le concept de révolution au Maroc." *Revue de l'Occident Musulman et de la Méditerranée,* no. 5 (1968): 145–52.

Flournoy, Francis. *British Policy Towards Morocco in the Age of Palmerston.* London and Baltimore, 1935.

Forbes, Rosita. *El Raisuni.* London, 1924. A very good account of the life of al-Raysūnī as he told it to Miss Forbes.

Forster, Robert, and Jack P. Greene, eds. *Preconditions of Revolution in Early Modern Europe.* Baltimore and London: Johns Hopkins University Press, 1970.

Frisch, Colonel. "Au Maroc avant le Protectorat. L'Organisation des Troupes." *Le Temps* (March 5, 1912).

Fumey, Eugene. *Choix de correspondances marocaines.* 2 vols. Paris, 1903. Fifty official letters of the makhzan, with translations.

Gaillard, Henri. "L'administration au Maroc. Le makhzen, étendue et limites de son pouvoir." *Bulletin de la Société de Géographie d'Alger* (1909): 433–70. Important.

———. "L'insurrection des tribus de la région de Fez." *Renseignements Coloniaux* (1911): 257–69. Reprinted from the *Livres Jaunes,* vol. 6.

Ganiage, Jean. *L'expansion coloniale de la France sous la Troisième République, 1871–1919.* Paris, Payot, 1968.

Garcia Figueras, Tomas. *La Accion Africana de España en Torno al 98.* 2 vols. Madrid, Instituto des Estudios Africanas, 1966.

Geertz, Clifford. "The Integrative Revolution: Primordial Sentiments, and Civil Politics in the New States." In C. Geertz, ed., *Old Societies and New States.* New York: The Free Press, 1963.

Gellner, Ernest. "Saints of the Atlas." In J. Pitt-Rivers, ed., *Mediterranean Countrymen.* Paris and The Hague, 1963.

———. *Saints of the Atlas.* London, Weidenfeld and Nicolson, 1969; Chicago, University of Chicago Press, 1969.

Gentil, Louis. *Dans le bled es siba. Explorations au Maroc.* Paris, P. Masson, 1906.

Gibb, H. A. R. *Studies in the Civilization of Islam.* Boston, Beacon Press, 1962.

Gillier, Commandant. *La pénétration en Maurétanie*. Paris, P. Geuthner, 1926.

Goldschmidt, Arthur. "The Egyptian Nationalist Party, 1882–1914." In P. M. Holt, ed., *Political and Social Change in Modern Egypt*. London, 1967, pp. 308–33.

Gottmann, Jean. "Bugeaud, Gallieni, Lyautey, The Development of French Colonial Warfare." In E. M. Earle, ed., *Makers of Modern Strategy*. Princeton, Princeton University Press, 1943.

Gourdin, André. *La politique française au Maroc*. Paris, 1906.

Gouvion, Edmond and Marthe. *Kitāb Aâyane al-Marhrib 'l-Akça*. Paris, Larose, 1939. A kind of *Who's Who* on the Moroccan nobility, including government officials from the grade of qaid on up. To be used with caution, as the details on family history appear not to have been systematically cross-checked. Nonetheless, highly useful.

Grasset, Capitaine. *A travers la Chaouia*. Paris, Hachette, 1911.

Grove, Lady. *Seventy-one Days Camping in Morocco*. London, 1902. Including a visit to the fief of al-Glawi.

Guiard, Marcel. "Avec Lyautey (mai 1912)." *Revue de Paris* (September, 1932): 141–71.

Guillaume, Général A. *Les berbères marocains et la pacification de l'Atlas central*. Paris, Julliard, 1946.

Guillen, Pierre. "Les accords coloniaux franco-anglais de 1904 et la naissance de l'entente cordiale." *Revue d'Histoire Diplomatique* 82 (1968).

———. *Les emprunts marocains 1902–1904*. Paris, Editions Richelieu, 1970.

———. "Les milieux d'affaires français et le Maroc." *Revue Historique* 229 (1963): 397–422.

———. "L'implantation de Schneider, les débuts de la Compagnie marocaine (1902–1906)." *Revue d'Histoire Diplomatique* (1965): 113–68.

———. "Les sources européennes sur le Maroc fin XIXe-début XXe siècle." *Hesperis-Tamuda* 1 (1966).

———. *L'Allemagne et le Maroc, 1870–1905*. Paris, Presses Universitaires de France, 1967. A very important thesis on the origins of the Moroccan Question from the German point of view. Much interesting material on internal Moroccan developments.

———. "La résistance du Maroc à l'emprise française au lendemain des accords franco-anglais d'avril 1904." *Actes du IIe congrès international d'études nord-africaines*. Special number of *Revue de l'Occident Musulman et de la Méditerranée* (1970): 115–22. Suggestive.

Haim, Sylvia. *Arab Nationalism*. Berkeley, University of California Press, 1962.

El-Hajoui, Mohammed Omar. *Histoire diplomatique du Maroc, 1900–1912*. Paris, G. P. Maisonneuve, 1937.

Halstead, John P. *Rebirth of a Nation. The Origins of Moroccan Nationalism, 1912–1944*. Cambridge, Mass., Harvard University Press, 1967. The most recent study of the evolution of Moroccan nationalism.

———. "A Comparative Historical Study of Colonial Nationalism in Egypt and Morocco." *African Historical Studies* 3, 1 (1969): 85–100.

Harris, Lawrence. *With Mulai Hafid at Fez. Behind the Scenes in Morocco*. London, Smith, Elder and Company, 1909. A British journalist entrusted for a time with starting a makhzan newspaper at Fez, 1908.

Harris, Walter Burton. *The Land of an African Sultan*. London, Samson, Low, Marston, Searle and Rivington, 1889.

———. "The Nomadic Berbers of Central Morocco." *Geographic Journal* (1897).

Hart, David M. "Segmentary Systems and the Role of 'Five-fifths' in Tribal Morocco." *Revue de l'Occident Musulman et de la Méditerranée*, no. 3 (1967): 65–96.

Hess, Jean. *La question du Maroc. Ce qu'on dit, ce qu'on écrit, ce qui est vrai. Mon Livre Jaune*. Paris, 1903. A view from the French opposition.

Hobsbawm, E. J. *The Age of Revolution, 1789–1848*. New York, Mentor, 1964.

Hoffmann, Bernard. *The Structure of Traditional Moroccan Rural Society*. Paris and The Hague, Mouton, 1967. An attempt at a synthesis of the literature on Moroccan society, done with a knowledge of only one-third of the literature. Less than a complete success.

Holt, Peter M. *The Mahdist State in the Sudan, 1881–1898*. London, Oxford University Press, 1958.

Hourani, Albert. *Arabic Thought in the Liberal Age, 1798–1939*. London, Oxford University Press, 1962.

Huot, Lt. Colonel. "La situation politique en Chaouia (août-decembre 1907)." *Bulletin de la Société de Géographie du Maroc* (1922): 107–24.

Jacques, Hubert. *Les journées sanglantes de Fez*. Paris, 1913. A sensationalist account by a newspaper reporter.

Julien, Charles-André. *L'Afrique du Nord en marche. Nationalismes musulmanes et souveraineté française*. Paris, 1952.

———. *Histoire de l'Algérie contemporaine*. Vol. 1, *Conquête et Colonisation*. Paris, Presses Universitaires de France, 1964.

Justinard, Col. L. *Un grand chef berbère: le caid Goundafi*. Casablanca, 1951. By one of France's foremost experts on the Sous valley.

Keddie, Nikki R. "Iranian Politics 1900–1905: Background to Revolution." *Middle Eastern Studies* 5 (1969): 3–31, 151–67.

——— *Islamic Responses to Imperialism: Jamal ad-Din al-Afghani.* Berkeley, University of California Press, 1969.

———. "Pan-Islam as Proto-Nationalism." *Journal of Modern History* (1969): 17–28.

Kedourie, Elie. *Afghani and Abduh.* London, 1966.

Kerr, Robert. *Morocco After Twenty-Five Years.* London, 1912.

Khorat, Pierre. *En colonne au Maroc.* Paris, Peronnet, 1913. Anti-Lyautey. First appeared in *Revue des Deux Mondes* as a series of articles under the pseudonym "Khorat," for Captain Ibos.

Ladreit de Lacharrière, J. "L'action de la France au Maroc après l'accord franco-allemand." *Revue Politique et Parlementaire* (1912).

———. "Grandeur et décadence de Mohammed el-Hibba, sultan bleu." *Bulletin de la Société de Géographie d'Alger* (1912): 473–86.

Lahbabi, Mohamed. *Le gouvernement marocain à l'aube du XXe siècle.* Rabat, 1958.

Lamartinière, H. M. P. de. *Essai de bibliographie marocaine, 1844–1886.* Paris, Drapeyron, 1886.

———, and Nicholas Lacroix. *Documents pour servir à l'étude du nord-ouest africain.* Algiers, Gouvernement Général, 1894. 5 vols. First major study of the Algéro-Moroccan frontier, sponsored by government sources and based chiefly on French native-affairs officers' reports.

Landau, Rom. *Moroccan Drama, 1900–1955.* London, Robert Hale, 1956. The first work in English on the Moroccan nationalist movement by a sympathizer.

Landes, David. *Bankers and Pashas.* London, 1958. A very important work on the operations of financiers and speculators in Egypt in the 1860s and 1870s.

Langer, William L. *European Alliances and Alignments, 1871–1890.* New York, 1931. Second edition, 1964.

———. *The Diplomacy of Imperialism, 1890–1902.* New York, 1950.

Larras, N. "La population du Maroc." *La Géographie* (1906): 337–48. An early estimate.

Lazarev, Grigori. "Les concessions foncières au Maroc." *Annales marocaines de Sociologie* (1968): 99–135. Important on the institution of *ʿazīb.*

Leared, Arthur. *A Visit to the Court of Morocco.* London, 1879.

Le Chatelier, Alfred. "Au Maroc: la politique nécessaire." *Revue Bleue* (1908).

———. "Politique musulman. Lettre à un conseiller d'état." *Revue du Monde musulman* (1910).

———. "Le Maroc, politique d'hier, politique de demain." *Action*

Nationale (May, 1912): 225–38. A highly significant figure in the scholarly penetration of Morocco, Le Chatelier fought for a policy of tribes against the makhzan policy of Delcassé. He founded the Mission scientifique du Maroc, *Archives Marocaines,* and the *Revue du Monde musulman.* On him, see R. Messal, *La Genèse de notre victoire au Maroc.* Paris, 1931.

Lecocq, André. "Les écoles israélites au Maroc." *Questions diplomatiques et coloniales* 31 (1911): 681–83.

Le Coz, J. "Les tribus guichs au Maroc. Essai de géographie agraire." *Revue de Géographie marocaine* (1965): 1–50. The *thèse complementaire* of one of the foremost French geographers of Morocco. It reveals a great deal about the transformations which the guich system went through and the principles of its operation.

Le Glay, Maurice. "Les chefs de la résistance berbère: Sidi Raho." *France-Maroc* (1918).

———. *Chronique marocaine.* Paris, Berger-Levrault, 1933. The year 1911, reported by an important member of the French military mission, chiefly on the siege of Fez and the Bremond column. Le Glay is convinced that French intervention was deliberately provoked by Gaillard.

Lemoine, Paul. *Mission dans le Maroc occidental (automne 1904). Rapport au Comité du Maroc.* Paris, Comité du Maroc, 1905. Also to be found in *Renseignements Coloniaux* (1905): 65–92; 141–55; 157–82. It was Lemoine who first seriously proposed that France make an alliance with the great chiefs of the Western High Atlas, the germ from which grew the native policy later followed in the Marrakech region.

Lesne, Marcel. "Lex Zemmours. Essai d'histoire tribale." *Revue de l'Occident Musulman et de la Méditerranée,* no. 2 (1966): 111–54; no. 3 (1967): 97–132; no. 4 (1967): 31–80. A seminal study of an important Berber tribe.

Le Tourneau, Roger. *Fez avant le protectorat.* Casablanca, 1949.

———. *Evolution politique de l'Afrique du nord musulmane, 1920–1961.* Paris, 1961.

———. "Abd al-Aziz." *Encyclopedia of Islam.* Second edition.

———. *La vie quotidienne à Fès en 1900.* Paris, 1965. An excellent summary and up-dating of the author's massive *Fez Avant le Protectorat.*

———. "Le Maroc sous le règne de Sidi Mohammed ben Abdallah (1757–1790)." *Revue de l'Occident Musulman et de la Méditerranée,* no. 1 (1966): 113–34.

———. "L'Algérie et les chorfa d'Ouezzane à la fin du XIXe siècle." *Actes du IIe congrès international d'études nord-africaine.* Special number of *Revue de l'occident Musulman et de la Méditerranée* (1970): 153–62.

Levi-Provençal, Evariste. *Les historiens des Chorfa: essai sur la littérature historique et biographique au Maroc du XVIe au XIXe siècle.* Paris, 1922. Still one of the most impressive books on Morocco.

Lewis, Bernard. *The Emergence of Modern Turkey.* London, 1961.

Luccioni, Joseph. "L'éloignement de Sidi Mohammed ben Arafa du trône des Alaouites en Septembre 1955." *Revue de l'Occident musulman et de la Méditerranée,* no. 8 (1970): 101–12. Interesting to compare with the abdication of ʿAbd al-Ḥafīẓ.

Lyautey, Pierre. "L'Abdication de Moulay Hafid." *Revue des Deux Mondes* (1953): 609–18. An official account.

Maitrot de la Motte Capron, A. "Le Roghi." *Bulletin de la Société de Géographie d'Alger* (1929): 514–76. An important article on Abu Himāra.

———. "Un correspondant de révolution, le journal de Jacob Niddan." *Bulletin de la Société de Géographie d'Alger* (1936). The journal of a Jewish postal agent at Fez in 1908–1910; gives a unique view of the Hafīẓīya revolution at Fez.

Maldonado, Eduardo. *El Rogui.* Tetuan, 1952. An important book on a difficult subject, but one which still leaves many questions unanswered.

Marchat, Henry. "L'affaire marocaine en 1911." *Revue d'Histoire Diplomatique* 77 (July–September 1963): 194–235.

Marsden, Arthur. *British Diplomacy and Tunis 1875–1902.* New York, Africana Publishing Corp., 1971.

Marsh, R. M. "The Venality of Provincial Office in China and in Comparative Perspective." *Journal of Comparative Studies in Society and History* 4 (1962): 454–66. A trailblazing study, very suggestive for the Middle East.

Martin, A. G. P. *Quatre siècles d'histoire marocaine.* Paris, Felix Alcan, 1923. One of the most important books on the subject of Moroccan responses to French penetration, especially good on the frontier and the oases. The period after 1908 tends to be a rewriting of the "Chronique marocaine" section in *Afrique Française,* and therefore less valuable. But the earlier parts rely extensively on Arabic documentary material, most of which is reproduced in French translation in its entirety. Martin was, however, a maverick (see the preface) with strong prejudices and must be used carefully.

———. *Le Maroc et l'Europe.* Paris, E. Leroux, 1928.

Martin, J.; J. Jover; J. le Coz; G. Maurer; D. Noin, et al. *Géographie du Maroc.* Paris, Hatier, 1967; Casablanca, Inprimerie Nationale, 1967.

Martin, Louis. "Le régime de la protection au Maroc." *Archives Marocaines* 15: 1–32.

Mas-Laterie, Colonel de. "La politique des grands qaids au Maroc." *Revue Militaire Française* (September 1, 1930): 359–94. An important article by a prominent French native-affairs officer.

Maudit, René. "Le makhzen marocain." *Renseignements Coloniaux* (1903): 293–304. One of the most important explanations of the makhzan.

Maura, Gabriel. *La question du Maroc au point de vue espagnole.* Paris, A. Challamel, 1911.

Mauran, Dr. *Le Maroc d'aujourdhui et de demain. Rabat. Etudes sociales.* Paris, H. Paulin, 1909. Dr. Mauran was one of the médecins des Affaires Etrangères sent to Morocco in 1905, like Mauchamps. His observations on the bourgeoisie of Rabat-Salé are often quite acute.

———. *La société marocaine.* Paris, 1912.

Meakin, Budgett. *The Moorish Empire.* London, S. Sonnenschein, 1899. The editor of the *Times of Morocco* and one of the best informed Europeans about Morocco by virtue of his long residence there (twenty-five years) and acute powers of observation. His books are among the best descriptions of life in Morocco around the turn of the century.

———. *The Land of the Moors.* London, S. Sonnenschein, 1901.

———. *Life in Morocco.* London, 1905.

Mercier, Louis. "La presse musulmane au Maroc." *Revue du Monde musulman* 4 (1908).

Messal, Raymond. *La genèse de notre victoire marocaine: Un précurseur, Alfred Le Chatelier, 1855–1929.* Paris, Dunoel, 1931. A very important source on scholarly studies of Morocco, which considerably enlightens the role of Le Chatelier. The author is, however, very uncritical of his subject and suppresses damaging evidence. A good biography of this important figure is still needed.

Michaux-Bellaire, Edouard. "Les impôts marocains." *Archives Marocaines* 1:56–96. The author is one of the foremost French scholars, with a profound knowledge and experience of central Morocco, especially north of Casablanca. He was head of the Mission scientifique, 1908–30.

———. "La maison d'Ouezzan." *Revue du Monde musulman* 5 (1908). Very important.

———. "Au palais du sultan." *Revue du Monde musulman* 5 (1908): 657–58.

———. "Une tentative de restauration idrissite à Fez." *Revue du Monde musulman* 7 (1908): 393–423. Highly partisan.

———. "L'héritage de Moulay el Hassan." *Revue du Monde musulman* 9 (1909): 412–20.

———. "Système d'impôts le mieux approprié, leur rentrée régulière."

Bulletin de la Société de Géographie d'Alger (1909): 401–37. The best treatment of the makhzan tax system.

———. "L'organisme marocaine." *Revue du Monde musulman* 9 (1909): 1–33.

———. "L'enseignement indigène au Maroc." *Revue du Monde musulman,* 15 (1911): 422–52.

———. "Les protectorats et les revenus marocains." *Revue du Monde musulman* (1912).

———. "Les crises monétaires au Maroc." *Revue du Monde musulman,* (1920): 47–52.

———. "Le Touat et les chorfa d'Ouezzan." In *Memorial Henri Basset.* Paris, 1928, 2:139–51.

Miège, Jean-Louis. "Note sur l'artisanat marocain en 1870." *Bulletin Economique et Sociale du Maroc,* no. 59 (1953).

———. "Les missions protestantes au Maroc (1875–1905)." *Hesperis* 43 (1955): 153–92.

———. "Origine et développement de la consommation du thé au Maroc." *Bulletin Economique et Sociale du Maroc* (1957): 377–398.

———. "Documents inédits sur l'artisanat de Rabat et Salé au milieu de XIXe siecle." *Bulletin Economique et Sociale du Maroc,* no. 82 (1959).

———. *Le Maroc et l'Europe, 1830–1894.* 4 vols. Paris, Presses Universitaires de France, 1961–63.

———. *Documents d'histoire économique et sociale marocaine au XIXe siècle.* Paris, 1969.

Millet, René. *La conquête du Maroc.* Paris, Perrin et Cie., 1913.

Monger, George. *The End of Isolation: British Foreign Policy 1900–1907.* London, Thomas Nelson and Sons, 1963.

Montagne, Robert. "La formation du pouvoir des caids de Tagontaft." *Memorial Henri Basset,* Paris, 1929.

———. *Les Berbères et le Makhzen dans le Sud du Maroc.* Paris, 1930.

Monteil, Vincent. "Les bureaux arabes au Maghreb, 1833–1961." *Esprit* (November 1961): 575–606. The beginnings of a reconsideration of the role of the native-affairs officer in North Africa. Important.

Moore, Frederick. *The Passing of Morocco.* Boston, 1908.

Morel, E. D. *Morocco in Diplomacy.* London, Smith, Elder and Company, 1912. By an opponent of the Entente Cordiale.

al-Moutabassir. "Ma el Ainin Ech Changuity." *Revue du Monde musulman* 1 (1908). Although violently anti-Mā al-ʿAynayn, an important article.

Munholland, Kim. "The Emergency of the Colonial Military in France, 1880–1905." Ph.D. dissertation. Princeton University, 1964.

———. "Rival Approaches to Morocco: Delcassé, Lyautey, and the

Algerian-Moroccan Border, 1903–1905." *French Historical Studies* (1968): 328–43.

Nataf, Felix. *Le crédit et la banque au Maroc.* Paris, 1929.

Nehlil. *Lettres chérifiennes, Première partie: textes.* Paris, 1915. Arabic administrative correspondence, chiefly nineteenth and twentieth centuries.

Noel, P. "Les rapports de la France et du Maroc." Paris, 1905. Thèse de droit.

Oberle, M., and H. P. J. Renaud. "La Pénétration pacifique par le médicin au maroc depuis 1900." *Archives de médicine et de pharmacie militaire* 77 (1927).

Odinot, Paul. "Role politique des confréries religieuses et des zaouias au Maroc." *Bulletin de la société de géographie et d'archéologie d'Oran* (1930): 37–51.

Ollivier, Georges. *L'Alliance Israélite Universelle.* Paris, 1959.

Paquignon. "Un livre de Moulay Abd al Hafid." *Revue du Monde musulman* (1909).

Parsons, F. V. "L'Allemagne et le Maroc de 1810 à 1905: A Review Article." *English Historical Review* 84 (1969).

———. "The Morocco Question in 1884: An Early Crisis." *English Historical Review* 77 (1962).

———. "The Northwest African Company and the British Government, 1875–1895." *Historical Journal* 1 (1958).

———. "The Proposed Madrid Conference on Morocco 1887–1888.'" *Historical Journal* 8 (1963).

Payn, R. "Les contingents auxiliares et les goums en A.O.F." *Renseignements Coloniaux* (1911): 285–90.

Perdicaris, Ian. *Mohamed Benani: A Story of Today.* London, 1887. A roman à clef set in Tangier.

Péretié, A. "Les medrasas de Fes." *Archives Marocaines* 18 (1912): 257–372. A fundamental contribution on Moroccan education.

Peyreigne, Charles. *Les influences européennes au Maroc avant la conference d'Algeciras.* Toulouse, 1908.

Pinon, René. *L'Empire de la Méditerranée.* Paris, 1904. Important treatment of the frontier question and the rise of Bou Hamara.

Playfair, R. L., and R. Brown. *A Bibliography of Morocco from the Earliest Times to the End of 1891.* London, Royal Geographical Society Supplementary Papers 3, 1893.

Ponteil, Felix. *La Méditérranée et les puissances.* Paris, Payot, 1963.

Ranger, T. O. "Connexions Between 'Primary Resistance' Movements and Modern Mass Nationalism in East and Central Africa." *Journal of African History* 9 (1968): 437–53; 631–41.

———. "African Reaction to the Imposition of Colonial Rule in East and Central Africa." In Gann, L. H., and P. Duignan, eds., *Colonialism in Africa, 1870–1960*. Vol. I. Cambridge, 1969.

Rankin, Reginald. *In Morocco with General d'Amade*. London, 1908. A journalist's account of the later stages of the Chaouia war, 1908.

Raymond, André. "Tunisiens et Maghrebins au Caire de dixhuitième siècle." *Cahiers de Tunisie* (1959): 335–71. Very suggestive for Moroccan relations with Egypt.

René-Leclerc, Charles. "Les débuts de règne de Moulay Hafid." *Renseignements Coloniaux* (1908). The author was the chief correspondent for the Comité du Maroc in Tangier, where he directed the bureau from 1907. The "Chroniques Marocaines," in *Afrique Française* each month, are his work. He was a very shrewd observer of the Moroccan scene.

Renouvin, Pierre. "Finance et politique: à propos de l'entente cordiale franco-anglaise." In *Eventail de l'Histoire vivante. Hommage à Lucien Febvre*. Paris, 1954. 1:357–65.

———. *Histoire des Relations internationales*. Vol. 6, *Le XIXe Siecle 2° partie: de 1871 à 1914*. Paris, Presses Universitaires de France, 1955.

Rober-Reynaud. "A Fez il y a dix ans." *Afrique Française* (1922): 132–36.

———. *En marge de la livre jaune: le Maroc*. Paris, 1923. By a newspaper correspondent with long experience in Morocco.

Rolo, R. J. V. *Entente Cordiale. The Origins and Negotiations of the Anglo-French Agreements of 8 April 1904*. New York: St. Martins Press, 1969.

Rouard de Card, E. *Les Traités entre la France et le Maroc*. Paris, 1898. The fundamental collection of diplomatic documents on French relations with Morocco.

———. *Documents diplomatiques pour servir à l'étude de la question marocaine*. Paris, A. Pedone, 1911.

———. *Traités et accords concernant le protectorat de la France au Maroc*. Paris, A. Pedone, 1914.

Sainte-Chapelle, A. M. G. *La conquête du Maroc (Mai 1911–Mars 1912)*. Paris, 1913.

Salmon, Georges. "L'Administration marocaine à Tanger." *Archives Marocaines* 1:1–37. An article which shows in detail how the Tangier administration functioned, with especially interesting details on the transformation of the Tangier customs administration under the impact of the West.

———. "Une opinion marocaine sur la conquête du Touat." *Archives Marocaines* 1:416–24.

———. "Le Tertib." *Archives Marocaines* 2: 154–58.

Salmon, Georges. "Le droit d'asile des canons." *Archives Marocaines* 3:144–153.

Segonzac, J. de. *Voyages au Maroc (1899–1901)*. Paris, 1903. One of the few French explorers to travel throughout the Middle Atlas prior to the protectorate. (Charles de Foucauld was another.)

Segonzac, R. de. "El Hiba fils de Ma el Ainin." *Renseignements Coloniaux*. Supplement to *Afrique française* (1917): 62–69, 90–94.

Selous, Gerald. *Appointment to Fez*. London, Richards, 1956. A rather poor account of a stay at Fez as assistant to Consul Macleod from 1911.

Servier, André. *Le Péril d'Avenir. Le Nationalisme musulman en Egypte, en Tunisie, en Algérie*. Constantine, Imprimerie E. Boet, 1913. How Pan-Islam threatens the French position in North Africa.

Shinar, Pessah. "ʿAbd al-Qādir and ʿAbd al-Krīm: Religious Influences on their Thought and Action." *Asian and African Studies* 1 (Jerusalem) (1965): 139–74. Excellent.

Simon, Henri. "La naissance et la jeunesse des goums mixtes marocains." *Revue Nord-Sud* (1934). The best article on the origins of the goums.

Souriau, Christiane. "La presse maghrebine, son évolution historique, sa situation en 1965, son organisation et ses problèmes actuelles." Thèse complémentaire, Université d'Aix-Marseilles, Aix-en-Provence, 1967.

Sousa, Nasim. *The Capitulatory Regime of Turkey*. Baltimore, Johns Hopkins University Press, 1933.

Spillmann, General Georges. "Les goums mixtes marocains." *Revue historique de l'Armée* (1952): 137–52.

———. *Du Protectorat à l'indépendénce: Maroc, 1912–1955*. Paris, 1967. A history of the protectorate by a prominent French native-affairs authority.

Staley, E. "Mannesmann Mining Interests and the Franco-German Conflict over Morocco." *Journal of Political Economy* 40 (1932): 52–72.

Steiner, Zara S. *The Foreign Office and Foreign Policy, 1898–1914*. Cambridge, The University Press, 1969.

Stoddard, Philip Hendrick. "The Ottoman Government and the Arabs, 1911 to 1918: A Preliminary Study of the Teskilat-i Mahsusa." Ph.D. dissertation, Princeton University 1963.

Stokes, Eric. "Traditional Resistance Movements and Afro-Asian Nationalism: The Context of the 1857 Mutiny Rebellion in India." *Past and Present* (1970): 100–118. An attempt to broaden the scope of the argument of Ranger on East African resistance.

Stuart, Graham. *French Foreign Policy from Fashoda to Serajevo (1898–1914)*. New York, 1921.

———. *The International City of Tangier*. New York, 1931. An important book on Tangier, utilizing U.S. legation archives.

Szymanski, Edward. "La guerre hispano-marocaine (1859–60), début de l'histoire du Maroc contemporaine." *Rocznik Orientalistyczny* 29 (1965): 53–65.

———. "Lex tribus de 'Guich' et le makhzen sous le regne de Sidi Mohammed ben Abd Allah." *Actes du IIe congrès international d'études nord-africaines*. Special number of *Revue de l'Occident musulman et de la Méditerranée* (1970): 195–202.

Taillis, Jean du. *Le Maroc pittoresque*. Paris, 1905. An Algerian journalist who visited the camp of Bou Hamara in 1904 and left an interesting account.

Tardieu, André. "Cinq ans de politique marocaine." *Revue politique et parlementaire* (November 1908): 225–54.

———. *La politique marocaine de la France*. Paris, 1909.

———. *La conférence d'Algeciras*. Paris, 1909.

Taylor, A. J. P. "British policy in Morocco 1886–1902." *English Historical Review* 66 (1951): 342–73.

———. *The Struggle for Mastery in Europe, 1848–1918*. Oxford, Oxford University Press, 1954.

Terrasse, Henri. *Histoire du Maroc*. 2 vols. Casablanca, Editions Atlantides, 1952. The standard history.

Terrier, Auguste. "La crise marocaine." *Questions diplomatiques et coloniales* (1905): 1–12. An important article, which underlines the role of al-Kattānī in 1904–1905 and the rejection of the French reforms.

Townsend, Mary E. *The Rise and Fall of Germany's Colonial Empire, 1884–1918*. New York, Howard Fertig, 1966. Reprint of original Macmillan, 1930, edition.

Trotter, Philip D. *Our Mission to the Court of Morocco in 1880 under Sir John Drummond Hay*. Edinburgh, 1881.

Trout, Frank E. *Morocco's Saharan Frontiers*. Geneva, Librairie Droz, 1969.

Vaffier-Pollet. "Une grande famille marocaine: les Glaoua." *France-Maroc* (December 1917). By a long-time friend of Madanī al-Glawī and former employee of the Compagnie marocaine.

Veyre, Gabriel. *Au Maroc. Dans l'intimité du Sultan*. Paris, 1905. By an agent of Gautsch and Company who was a photographer in the court of ʿAbd al-ʿAzīz.

Vidi [pseud.]. "Ichoua Corcos." *L'Avenir Illustre* (1929).

Voinot, Louis. "Les conséquences de la lutte du makhzan et du Roghi, 1903–1905." *Bulletin de la société de géographie d'Oran* 55 (1934).

———. *Sur les traces glorieuses des pacificateurs du Maroc*. Paris, Charles-Lavauzelle et Cie, 1939.

Voinot, Louis. *Pélérinages judéo-musulmans au Maroc*. Paris, 1948.

Weisgerber, Dr. Felix. "L'insurrection d'el Hiba." *Afrique Française* (1930) 593–600.

Wendel, Hugo. "The Protégé System in Morocco." *Journal of Modern History* 2 (1930): 48–60.

Wertheim, W. F. *Indonesian Society in Transition*. The Hague, W. van Hoeve Ltd., 1964.

Westermarck, Edward. *Ritual and Belief in Morocco*. 2 vols. London, Macmillan, 1926.

Williamson, Samuel R., Jr. *The Politics of Grand Strategy: Britain and France Prepare for War, 1904–1914*. Cambridge, Mass.: Harvard University Press, 1969.

Willis, John Ralph. "*Jihād fī sabīl Allāh*—Its Doctrinal Basis in Islam and Some Aspects of Its Evolution in Nineteenth Century West Africa." *Journal of African History* 8 (1967): 395–415.

INDEX

ʿAbbās, Mawlāy, 102
Abda, 9
ʿAbd al-ʿAzīz, Sultan Mawlāy (d. 1943), 19, 90, 92–93, 122, 132, 197, 217, 221, 258 n. 28; ʿAbd al-Ḥafīẓ and, 102–9, 111–15, 117–18, 120; abdicates, 121; and crisis of 1904–5, 74, 77–88; early life and regency, 19, 39, 41, 42, 47–48; personal qualities, 58–60; and reforms, 54–56, 59–61, 89
ʿAbd al-Ḥafīẓ, Sultan Mawlāy (d. 1937), ʿAbd al-ʿAzīz and, 102–9, 111–15, 117–18, 120–21; abdicates, 198–99; early life and personal qualities, 99, 101–2; Fāsī elite and, 115–17, 121–22, 129–30, 133–35, 146–47; foreign policy of, 128–29, 140–42, 145–46, 165; France and, 112–13, 128–29, 138–39, 142–45, 148–49, 164–66, 181–82, 188–89, 197–98; great *qāid*-s and, 102–10, 120–21, 136, 150, 154–55, 176–78; Islamic modernism of, 101, 134–35; 1911 rebellion and, 156–63, 167–71, 173–74; 1912 rebellion and, 185–86
ʿAbd al-Mālik, Mawlāy, 85
ʿAbd al-Qādir, Amīr, 201
Abode of Islam. See *dār al-Islam*
Abū ʿAzzāwī, 95–96, 104, 106, 112, 117, 125
Abū Ḥassana, 249 n. 59
Abū Ḥimāra, 62–68, 71, 102, 136–37, 139, 146, 190, 243 n. 72
Abu ʿImāmah, 29, 83
Abū Zayd, Abū Bakr b., 96
Administration: fiscal, 34–36, 50–53; rural, 14–15, 34, 36, 43, 51, 94–95, 150–51, 154–55, 214. See also *Makhzan; Tartīb;* Taxation; *Umanā*
Agadir, 145, 172, 199, 257 n. 12
Aglou, 200
Agricultural Agent. *See* Protégé
Agriculture, 5, 8–9, 22–23, 90–91, 93–94. See also *Azīb;* Famines; *Tartīb*
Ain Sefra, 29
ʿAissa b. ʿUmar al-Abdī, 9, 136, 196, 256 n. 1; and Ḥafīẓīya, 102, 105, 107–8, 110, 121
Ait Atta, 7
Ait Idrassen, 8
Ait Iznassen, 28, 113
Ait Ndhir, 8, 46, 60, 114, 134, 136–37, 154, 157, 159–60, 174, 178, 190
Ait Njild, 46, 134, 157–58, 190
Ait Ouarain, 64, 162, 190
Ait Saddin, 162, 190
Ait Seghrouchen of Immouzer, 190
Ait Waryaghar, 7
Ait Yafelman, 7
Ait Yusi, 46, 174, 190
Alexandria, 19
Algeciras: Act of, 87–89, 103, 109, 123, 128–31, 140, 143–44, 156, 165, 166, 211; Conference of, 85–87
Algeria, 15, 20, 44, 62, 86, 102, 149, 183, 201
Algéro-Moroccan frontier, 28–30, 44–47, 75–77; accords of 1901, 50, 143; accords of 1902, 72; accords of 1909, 138–39
ʿAlīya Sattātīya, 99, 106
Allāh, Faraj, 131
Alliance Israélite Universelle, 36–37, 151. *See also* Jews
Almoravids, 199
Amade, General d', 117–18, 173, 187
Amhawsh, Mawlāy ʿAlī, 119
Amīn al-Khirs, 35
Amīn al-Mustafad, 35
ʿAmrānī, Muḥammad, 159–60, 169, 171, 197
Anflūs, Aḥmad al-, 109–10, 112, 120